Lecture Notes in Computer Science 6138

Commenced Publication in 1973
Founding and Former Series Editors:
Gerhard Goos, Juris Hartmanis, and Jan van Leeuwen

Editorial Board

David Hutchison
 Lancaster University, UK
Takeo Kanade
 Carnegie Mellon University, Pittsburgh, PA, USA
Josef Kittler
 University of Surrey, Guildford, UK
Jon M. Kleinberg
 Cornell University, Ithaca, NY, USA
Alfred Kobsa
 University of California, Irvine, CA, USA
Friedemann Mattern
 ETH Zurich, Switzerland
John C. Mitchell
 Stanford University, CA, USA
Moni Naor
 Weizmann Institute of Science, Rehovot, Israel
Oscar Nierstrasz
 University of Bern, Switzerland
C. Pandu Rangan
 Indian Institute of Technology, Madras, India
Bernhard Steffen
 TU Dortmund University, Germany
Madhu Sudan
 Microsoft Research, Cambridge, MA, USA
Demetri Terzopoulos
 University of California, Los Angeles, CA, USA
Doug Tygar
 University of California, Berkeley, CA, USA
Gerhard Weikum
 Max-Planck Institute of Computer Science, Saarbruecken, Germany

Thomas Kühne   Bran Selic
Marie-Pierre Gervais   François Terrier (Eds.)

Modelling Foundations and Applications

6th European Conference, ECMFA 2010
Paris, France, June 15-18, 2010
Proceedings

Volume Editors

Thomas Kühne
Victoria University
Wellington, New Zealand
E-mail: thomas.kuehne@ecs.vuw.ac.nz

Bran Selic
Malina Software Corp.
Nepean, Ontario, Canada
E-mail: selic@acm.org

Marie-Pierre Gervais
Laboratoire d'Informatique de Paris 6
Paris, France
E-mail: marie-pierre.gervais@lip6.fr

François Terrier
CEA LIST, LISE
Gif-sur-Yvette, France
E-mail: francois.terrier@cea.fr

Library of Congress Control Number: 2010928265

CR Subject Classification (1998): D.2, F.3, D.3, C.2, H.4, K.6

LNCS Sublibrary: SL 2 – Programming and Software Engineering

ISSN	0302-9743
ISBN-10	3-642-13594-3 Springer Berlin Heidelberg New York
ISBN-13	978-3-642-13594-1 Springer Berlin Heidelberg New York

This work is subject to copyright. All rights are reserved, whether the whole or part of the material is concerned, specifically the rights of translation, reprinting, re-use of illustrations, recitation, broadcasting, reproduction on microfilms or in any other way, and storage in data banks. Duplication of this publication or parts thereof is permitted only under the provisions of the German Copyright Law of September 9, 1965, in its current version, and permission for use must always be obtained from Springer. Violations are liable to prosecution under the German Copyright Law.

springer.com

© Springer-Verlag Berlin Heidelberg 2010
Printed in Germany

Typesetting: Camera-ready by author, data conversion by Scientific Publishing Services, Chennai, India
Printed on acid-free paper   06/3180

Preface

The 2010 European Conference on Modelling Foundations and Applications (ECMFA 2010) was dedicated to assessing the state of the art and the state of the practice in model-based engineering. It was the sixth edition in the series of conferences previously known under the title "European Conference on Model-Driven Architecture – Foundations and Applications (ECMDA-FA)." The name change reflects the de facto broadening of the conference scope beyond the MDA® initiative of the Object Management Group® to cover all major advances related to model-based engineering approaches.

These proceedings, like the ones from previous editions in the conference series, will undoubtedly serve as a reference to all who follow model-based engineering theory and practice. The included papers document the steady evolution of model-based development methods into a mature discipline, with well-established standards, industrial-strength tools, and emerging theoretical foundations. They also serve to illustrate that model-based approaches are capable of significant productivity and quality improvements relative to more traditional development methods.

This year, the Programme Committee received 73 submissions of which 15 foundations papers and 9 applications papers were accepted. Despite the "European" connotation in the title of the conference, the authors of the submitted papers represent 28 different countries from four continents. The significant number of applications papers was particularly encouraging, providing evidence of the increasing rate of adoption on model-based approaches in industry. With the latter comes an even greater need and responsibility to establish a sound theoretical underpinning, which is what the foundations papers in the proceedings aim to provide. The progress in this direction is both tangible and significant, each year bringing an expanded understanding of the key abstractions and ideas behind core topics such as metamodelling, model transformations, code generation, and modelling language design.

We are most grateful to our 68 Programme Committee members for providing their expertise in the form of detailed reviews and dedicated discussions. Their constructive feedback to the authors and indispensable contribution to the selection of the papers is most appreciated. We also owe special gratitude to the members of the ECMFA Conference Steering Committee, who supported us in many ways. In particular, we are thankful for the tremendous help offered by the previous year's Programme Chair, Richard Paige. Finally, we would like to thank all authors who submitted papers to ECMFA 2010, our keynote speakers—Colin Atkinson and Diarmuid Corcoran—and the sponsors of ECMFA 2010.

June 2010

Thomas Kühne
Bran Selic

Conference Organization

Programme Chairs

Thomas Kühne — Victoria University, Wellington, New Zealand
Bran Selic — Malina Software Corp., Nepean, Ontario, Canada

Programme Committee

Jan Aagedal
Uwe Assman
Terry Bailey
Mariano Belaunde
Reda Bendraou
Xavier Blanc
Behzad Bordbar
Marc Born
Phil Brooke
Jordi Cabot
Tony Clark
Arnaud Cuccuru
Zhen Ru Dai
Miguel De Miguel
Birgit Demuth
Phillippe Desfray
Juergen Dingel
Gregor Engels
Anne Etien
Luís Ferreira Pires
Mathias Fritsche
Marie-Pierre Gervais
Sébastien Gérard
Alan Hartman
Reiko Heckel
Andreas Hoffmann
Gabor Karsai
Olaf Kath
Steven Kelly
Joerg Kienzle
Vinay Kulkarni

Ivan Kurtev
Ralf Laemmel
Tiziana Margaria
Erhan Mengusoglu
Dragan Milicev
Parastoo Mohagheghi
Juan Carlos Molina
Nanjagud Narendra
Tor Neple
Ileana Ober
Richard Paige
Christoph Pohl
Arend Rensink
Laurent Rioux
Tom Ritter
Julia Rubin
Bernhard Rumpe
Andrey Sadovykh
Houari Sahraoui
Ina Schieferdecker
Doug Schmidt
Andy Schürr
Bikram Sengupta
Alin Stefanescu
Friedrich Steimann
Gabriele Taentzer
Francois Terrier
Juha-Pekka Tolvanen
Tim Trew
Andreas Ulrich
Markus Voelter

Regis Vogel
Jules White
Steffen Zschaler

Pieter van Gorp
Marten van Sinderen
Michael von der Beeck

External Reviewers

Adolf Abdallah
Adwoa Donyina
Alix Mougenot
Andrej Bachmann
Anthony Anjorin
Arnaud Cuccuru
Brahmananda Sapkota
Brian Dougherty
Bruno Dufour
Camlon Asuncion
Christian Gerth
Christian Wende
Claas Wilke
Cristina Gómez
Dan Chiorean
Dimitrios Kolovos
Elodie Legros
Emilio Salazar
Florian Heidenreich
Florian Noyrit
Gerd Wierse
Hans Groenniger
Hervé Leblanc
Holger Rendel
Jan-Christopher Bals
Jendrik Johannes
Juan Pedro Silva

Klaas van den Berg
Laure Gonnord
Louis Rose
Luiz Olavo Bonino da Silva Santos
Maarten de Mol
Marcos Almeida
Mariano Belaunde
Marouane Kessentini
Martin Faunes
Martin Schindler
Martin Wieber
Michael Spijkerman
Muhammad Naeem
Nicholas Matragkas
Osmar Marchi dos Santos
Phil Greenwood
Rodrigo Machado
Sebastian Richly
Selim Ciraci
Steven VÃlkel
Sven Patzina
Tamim Khan
Thorsten Arendt
Tim Gülke
Vadim Zaytsev
Vincent Aranega
Zhen Ru Dai

Table of Contents

Orthographic Software Modelling: A Novel Approach to View-Based
Software Engineering (Invited Talk) 1
   Colin Atkinson

The Good, the Bad and the Ugly: Experiences with Model Driven
Development in Large Scale Projects at Ericsson (Invited Talk) 2
   Diarmuid Corcoran

Comparing Approaches to Implement Feature Model Composition 3
   Mathieu Acher, Philippe Collet, Philippe Lahire, and Robert France

A UML 2.0 Profile to Model Block Cipher Algorithms 20
   *Tomás Balderas-Contreras, Gustavo Rodriguez-Gomez, and
   René Cumplido*

Towards Model Driven Tool Interoperability: Bridging Eclipse and
Microsoft Modeling Tools 32
   *Hugo Brunelière, Jordi Cabot, Cauê Clasen, Frédéric Jouault, and
   Jean Bézivin*

Aspect-Oriented Business Process Modeling with AO4BPMN 48
   Anis Charfi, Heiko Müller, and Mira Mezini

A Reflective Approach to Model-Driven Web Engineering 62
   *Darren Clowes, Dimitris Kolovos, Chris Holmes, Louis Rose,
   Richard Paige, Julian Johnson, Ray Dawson, and Steve Probets*

Requirements Analysis and Modeling with Problem Frames and
SysML: A Case Study 74
   Pietro Colombo, Ferhat Khendek, and Luigi Lavazza

Generative Technologies for Model Animation in the TOPCASED
Platform 90
   *Xavier Crégut, Benoit Combemale, Marc Pantel,
   Raphaël Faudoux, and Jonatas Pavei*

Model-Driven Engineering of Machine Executable Code 104
   *Michael Eichberg, Martin Monperrus, Sven Kloppenburg, and
   Mira Mezini*

eSPEM – A SPEM Extension for Enactable Behavior Modeling 116
   *Ralf Ellner, Samir Al-Hilank, Johannes Drexler, Martin Jung,
   Detlef Kips, and Michael Philippsen*

Adding Abstraction and Reuse to a Network Modelling Tool Using the
Reuseware Composition Framework 132
  Jendrik Johannes and Miguel A. Fernández

Model-Based Development of Automotive Electronic Climate Control
Software 144
  Rupesh Kakade, Mohan Murugesan, Bhupal Perugu, and
  Mohanan Nair

Example-Based Sequence Diagrams to Colored Petri Nets
Transformation Using Heuristic Search 156
  Marouane Kessentini, Arbi Bouchoucha, Houari Sahraoui, and
  Mounir Boukadoum

Model Search: Formalizing and Automating Constraint Solving in
MDE Platforms... 173
  Mathias Kleiner, Marcos Didonet Del Fabro, and Patrick Albert

MoPCoM Methodology: Focus on Models of Computation............. 189
  Ali Koudri, Joël Champeau, Jean-Christophe Le Lann, and
  Vincent Leilde

Dynamic Computation of Change Operations in Version Management
of Business Process Models...................................... 201
  Jochen Malte Küster, Christian Gerth, and Gregor Engels

Detecting Inconsistencies in Multi-View Models With Variability........ 217
  Roberto Erick Lopez-Herrejon and Alexander Egyed

A Model-Based Method for Evaluating Embedded System Performance
by Abstraction of Execution Traces 233
  Kouichi Ono, Manabu Toyota, Ryo Kawahara, Yoshifumi Sakamoto,
  Takeo Nakada, and Naoaki Fukuoka

Concordance: A Framework for Managing Model Integrity 245
  Louis M. Rose, Dimitrios S. Kolovos, Nicholas Drivalos,
  James R. Williams, Richard F. Paige, Fiona A.C. Polack, and
  Kiran J. Fernandes

An Integrated Facet-Based Library for Arbitrary Software
Components... 261
  Matthias Schmidt, Jan Polowinski, Jendrik Johannes, and
  Miguel A. Fernández

Precise Specification of Design Pattern Structure and Behaviour 277
  Ashley Sterritt, Siobhán Clarke, and Vinny Cahill

Coping with Variability in Model-Based Systems Engineering: An
Experience in Green Energy 293
    Salvador Trujillo, Jose Miguel Garate,
    Roberto Erick Lopez-Herrejon, Xabier Mendialdua,
    Albert Rosado, Alexander Egyed, Charles W. Krueger, and
    Josune de Sosa

On the Combination of Domain Specific Modeling Languages 305
    Antonio Vallecillo

Joint Language and Domain Engineering 321
    Tobias Walter, Fernando Silva Parreiras, Steffen Staab, and
    Jürgen Ebert

An Automated Approach to Transform Use Cases into Activity
Diagrams 337
    Tao Yue, Lionel C. Briand, and Yvan Labiche

Author Index 355

Orthographic Software Modelling: A Novel Approach to View-Based Software Engineering

Colin Atkinson

Software Engineering Group,
University of Mannheim,
68161 Mannheim, Germany
atkinson@informatik.uni-mannheim.de

The need to support multiple views of complex software architectures, each capturing a different aspect of the system under development, has been recognized for a long time. Even the very first object-oriented analysis/design methods such as the Booch method and OMT supported a number of different diagram types (e.g. structural, behavioral, operational) and subsequent methods such as Fusion, Kruchten's 4+1 views and the Rational Unified Process (RUP) have added many more views over time. Today's leading modeling languages such as the UML and SysML, are also oriented towards supporting different views (i.e. diagram types) each able to portray a different facets of a system's architecture. More recently, so called enterprise architecture frameworks such as the Zachman Framework, TOGAF and RM-ODP have become popular. These add a whole set of new non-functional views to the views typically emphasized in traditional software engineering environments.

As the number and variety of views has grown, so has the problem of managing and working with them. Most view-based architecture visualization approaches today lack a coherent metaphor for organizing the different views and navigating around them. They usually organize the different diagrams or reports that collectively describe a system's architecture in a simple tree structure and one "concern" invariably overwhelms the others. For example, in approaches focused on architecture description languages (ADL) the composition hierarchy dominates the way in which the architecture is conceptualized and visualized. On the other hand, in model-driven approaches, the different levels of abstraction (platform-dependence/independence) tend to dominate the way in which architectures are conceptualized.

Most view-oriented architecture visualization environments also have a major problem keeping the different views synchronized and consistent with one another, and often require significant human effort to do so. This is often due to inadequacies in the underlying metamodel or method, which necessitate the use of additional synchronization specifications and tools to keep views consistent.

In this talk we introduce a new paradigm for view definition, organization and access that transcends (i.e. is generic to) the specific views and concerns in specific methods. An environment that supports the paradigm can therefore be adapted to support most view-based architecture visualization methods, including those supporting non-functional as well as functional views. In this talk we introduce this paradigm, known as Orthographic Software Modeling (OSM), and describe its three key ingredients, (1) on demand view generation, (2) dimension-based navigation and (3) an inherently view-based method.

The Good, the Bad and the Ugly: Experiences with Model Driven Development in Large Scale Projects at Ericsson

Diarmuid Corcoran

This talk will deal with the practical experiences of large-scale deployment of Model Driven Engineering practises within parts of the Ericsson development organisation. We try to present a balanced argument in favour of why Model Driven Development is a powerful concept in large-scale engineering projects, but also cover many of its nasty aspects and attempt to reason upon the nature of these failings. We then finish up with a look at the future of Model Driven Development as we see it and present a taste of our vision of the future.

First of all we need to set the context: Ericsson is the world's largest supplier of telecom infrastructure with 40% of all GSM and 50% of all 3G call passing through Ericsson equipment. Underneath its telecom face Ericsson is very much a software company. In fact about 80% of our development costs are software related. The systems we develop, both HW and SW are complex in the extreme. In fact we would argue that the SW systems we develop are among the most complex interacting software agents developed by humans. And this challenge continues as we approach LTE systems that promise up to 1G/s data rate to an end device. To meet these challenges we need software techniques, tools and know how that are the cutting in their class. One software technique we have found extremely powerful in our quest to tackle complexity and succeed in delivering high systems within time and budget is Model Driven Development.

The kind of complexity we need to tackle in a large-scale engineering project (including both HW and SW) is two fold. The first is complexity relating to the number of people involved in the project, which in turn affects information flow and information dependencies. Having very clear semantic definitions about what things mean and reducing information redundancy and in a perfect world having a single, repository based, source of information drastically simplifies this collaboration problem. Model Based Development helps here through its principles of abstraction, formalization of concepts and a single repository based information model. We have implemented a concept of Model Driven System Engineering (MBSE), which we feels helps to tackle both the people dependency and problem domain complexity issues. We will discuss this technique and balance its merits against its problems.

We also use Model Driven techniques to specify parts of our system implementation. From these implementation or design models we generate compete code for substantial parts of our system. This technique has proven enormously powerful and beneficial but doesn't come for free and has it own set of issues. We will look at this technique and discuss the pros and cons.

From our experiences above we have a very clear view where we would like to take our concept of Model Driven Development. We talk about this vision and the issues along our journey, which have convinced us that this is the right approach.

Comparing Approaches to Implement Feature Model Composition

Mathieu Acher[1], Philippe Collet[1], Philippe Lahire[1], and Robert France[2]

[1] I3S Laboratory (CNRS UMR 6070)
University of Nice Sophia Antipolis, France
{acher,collet,lahire}@i3s.unice.fr
[2] Computer Science Department,
Colorado State University, USA
france@cs.colostate.edu

Abstract. The use of Feature Models (FMs) to define the valid combinations of features in Software Product Lines (SPL) is becoming commonplace. To enhance the scalability of FMs, support for composing FMs describing different SPL aspects is needed. Some composition operators, with interesting property preservation capabilities, have already been defined but a comprehensive and efficient implementation is still to be proposed. In this paper, we systematically compare strengths and weaknesses of different implementation approaches. The study provides some evidence that using generic model composition frameworks are not helping much in the realization, whereas a specific solution is finally necessary and clearly stands out by its qualities.

1 Introduction

The concept of Software Product Line (SPL) [1] is based upon an appealing idea: instead of considering applications individually, the co-development of a family of related programs is planned from the beginning. The family's common features are collected in reusable assets that can be later adapted to derive and fit the requirements of an individual product. In domain and application engineering, *feature models* [2,3,4] are widely used to describe a family (e.g., an SPL) in terms of common and variable features. A feature model represents a set of valid combination of features, each one corresponding to an actual product of a family.

Current feature modeling techniques often do not scale up to SPLs with a large number of features and a high degree of variability [5,6]. In these situations, the techniques produce large feature models that are too complex to be easily understood by engineers or analyzed by reasoning tools. Applying separation of concerns principles and providing support for modularising and composing feature models can improve scalability. Yet a study of the literature about SPL engineering demonstrates that providing automated support for composing feature models still remains an open challenge [7,8,5,9,10]. In previous work [11], we designed a set of *composition* operators for feature models and defined semantic properties that must be preserved during composition.

There are several ways to implement the composition operators. On the one hand, previous work in the feature modeling community can be revisited to implement the composition operators. On the other hand, Model-Based Engineering (MBE) and Aspect-Oriented Modeling (AOM) communities have developed a set of model composition techniques and tools. Therefore, there is an interest in determining how these techniques perform with feature model composition and which techniques are the most suitable. The intended audience of this paper are *i)* SPL researchers working on feature modeling techniques or developers of feature modeling tools ; *ii)* researchers involved in the AOM community or more generally dealing with model transformation.

The remainder of this paper is organized as follows. In Section 2, we give an overview of feature models, motivate the need to support a set of composition operators and present their semantic properties. We then discuss the properties we expect in a good implementation of the composition operators (Section 3) so that we can set up an experimental comparison to systematically evaluate and compare the considered implementation techniques (Section 4). Results are reported and interpreted while most suitable approaches are determined and discussed (Section 5).

2 Background and Motivation

2.1 Feature Models

A Feature Model (FM) is a representation of a family, e.g., a family of medical images, in terms of features [4,3]. Let us consider FM_{ep3} depicted in the right part of Figure 1: A medical image has two *mandatory* features, Modality and Format, which implies that each valid configuration of a medical image should include these two features. There are two alternatives for Modality acquisition: SPEC and PET features form an *Xor*-group (i.e., at least and at most one feature must be selected). An *optional* feature is Anonymized, which states whether all patients metadata of the medical image are included or not. Finally, a medical image Header supports either the format DICOM or Nifti or both of them: DICOM and Nifti form an *Or*-group. A FM thus describes the set of valid feature combinations. Every member of a family is represented by a unique combination of features. In the remainder of the paper, *a combination of selected features is called a configuration of a FM and is represented as a set of features*. In Figure 1, a valid configuration of FM_{ep3} is {MedicalImage, Modality, SPEC, Format, Anonymized, Header, DICOM}.

2.2 Composition Operators

In realistic SPL development, large and monolithic FMs must be built, evolved and analyzed. These tasks are cumbersome, error-prone and costly owing to the large amount of features to be considered by (different) stakeholders [5]. To manage complexity, FMs can be separated and *composed*, with then the crucial need to ensure that relevant properties are preserved during composition. In

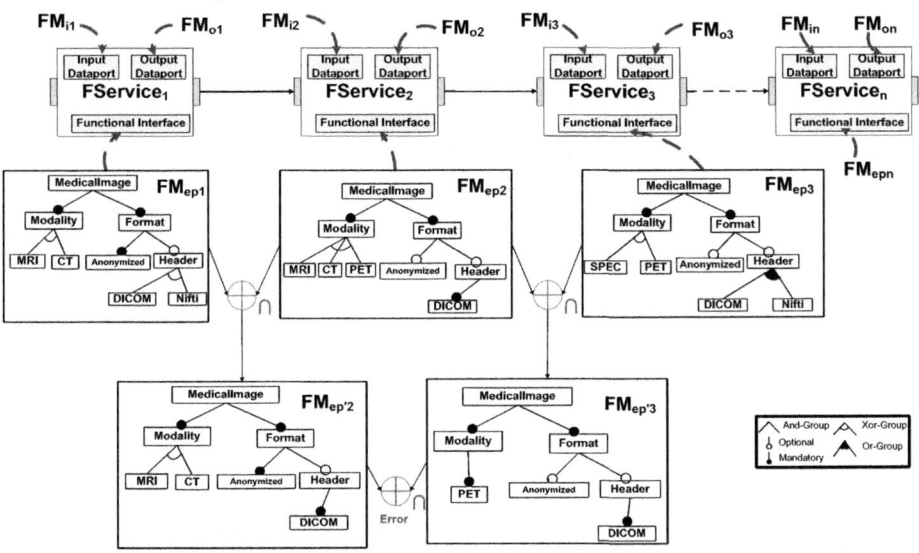

Fig. 1. Chaining Merge of Feature Models

prior work [11], we promote the use of multiple FMs, each one focusing on a well-identified concern and we define a set of composition operators for FMs. Two main composition operators, *insert* and *merge*, were proposed. For each operator, the semantics is given in terms of the expressed configurations and implementation feasibility is demonstrated. Here, we focus on the *merge* operator and detail the preserved properties when two FMs are merged.

Merge Operator Semantics. When two FMs share several features and are different viewpoints of a concern, the goal of the merge operator is to merge the overlapping parts of the two FMs to obtain an integrated model of the system. Two modes are defined for the merge operator. The *intersection* mode is the most restrictive option: the merged FM, $FM_{ep'2}$, expresses the common valid configurations of FM_{ep1} and FM_{ep2}. The *union* mode is the most conservative option: the merged FM, can express either valid configuration of first input FM or second input FM. The variability information associated to features in the merged FM is different according to the merge mode and the properties that one want to preserve. The properties of the merged FM is formalized with respect to the sets of configurations of input FMs. Let f be a FM and $[\![f]\!]$ denotes its set of configurations. The relationship between a merged FM *Result* in intersection mode and two input FMs *Base* and *Aspect* can be expressed as follows:

$$[\![Base]\!] \bigcap [\![Aspect]\!] = [\![Result]\!] \qquad (M_1)$$

The merge operator in the intersection mode is noted: $Base \oplus_\cap Aspect = Result$. In the intersection mode, a valid configuration of the merged FM, *Result*, is valid in *Base* and in *Aspect* at the same time. In Figure 1, the DICOM feature is always part of any valid configuration of FM_{ep2} whereas the Nifti feature cannot be part of any valid configuration of FM_{ep2}. As a result, DICOM feature is a mandatory feature of the merged FM $FM_{ep'2}$ while the Nifti feature is not part of the merged FM $FM_{ep'2}$. The reader can check that the following relations hold: $[\![FM_{ep1}]\!] \cap [\![FM_{ep2}]\!] = [\![FM_{ep'2}]\!]$ and $[\![FM_{ep2}]\!] \cap [\![FM_{ep3}]\!] = [\![FM_{ep'3}]\!]$.

In the union mode, we want to obtain a merged FM that represents the set of configurations of *Base* and *Aspect*. The union of two FMs, Base and Aspect, is a new FM where each configuration that is valid *either* in Base *or* Aspect, is also valid:

$$[\![Base]\!] \bigcup [\![Aspect]\!] \subseteq [\![Result]\!] \qquad (M_2)$$

A more restrictive property in union mode, called *strict union*, is defined as follows:

$$[\![Base]\!] \bigcup [\![Aspect]\!] = [\![Result]\!] \qquad (M_3)$$

2.3 Motivating Scenario

In the grid-based medical imaging community, scientists compose a wide variety of parameterized image services to create processing pipelines, and the lack of variability management mechanisms causes major issues in provisioning and composing such services [12, 13].

We illustrate here how the merge operator can be used. Figure 1 shows three services $FService_1$, $FService_2$ and $FService_3$ connected in sequence. The connection between services implies that some of their entities are dependent in some way. For instance, we consider that the functional interfaces of $FService_i$ which is connected to $FService_{i+1}$ has to be compatible for $i \in 1...n$. In particular, the medical image associated to $FService_i$ must be compatible with the one of $FService_{i+1}$. This implies to check that *i)* FM_{ep1} and FM_{ep2} are consistent and also that *ii)* FM_{ep2} and FM_{ep3} are consistent. It is necessary to check if, e.g., the set of configurations of FM_{ep1} is equal or included in the set of configurations of FM_{ep2} (and vice versa). In this case, the use of the merge operator occurs: The technique is to compute the merge in intersection mode of two FMs. If the merged FM should not represent an empty set of configurations, then there should be at least one configuration that is valid in the former *and* latter FM. The consistency checking can thus be achieved: In the example, such an FM exists when merging FM_{ep1} and FM_{ep2} (see $FM_{ep'2}$) and also when merging FM_{ep2} and FM_{ep3} (see $FM_{ep'3}$). Nevertheless, there is no solution when merging $FM_{ep'2}$ and $FM_{ep'3}$. It implies that $FService_1$, $FService_2$ and $FService_3$ are not compatible.

2.4 Related Work

In the literature, several papers suggest the design and implementation of a merge operator, as in [7], in which separate FMs are used to model decisions taken by different stakeholders and the need to compose and merge FMs is identified. In [8],

Hartmann and Trew dealt with multiple product lines and identified several compositional issues, especially the significance of the merging activity. Recently, Hartmann et al. propose a Supplier Independent Feature Model (SIFM) which contains the "super-set of the features from all the FMs of suppliers" [14], corresponding to property (M_2) in union mode. The creation of the SIFM relies on the work described in [10] and further considered in Section 4.1. Reiser and Weber propose to use multi-level feature trees consisting of a tree of FMs in which the parent model serves as a reference FM for its children [5]. Their purpose is mostly to cope with large diagrams and large-scale organizations, rather than different concerns. They thus do not provide operators to merge FMs. A few approaches use multiple FMs during the SPL development (e.g., see [15]). Such contributions do not consider FMs that are sharing some features, whereas this can happen when FMs interact, when multiple perspectives or views on a FM needs to be managed or when SPLs are composed with SPLs.

In [16], an algorithm is designed to automatically determine the kind of relations between two FMs in terms of sets of configuration. In [17], the case of *synchronizing* existing configurations of a FM that have evolved over time (e.g., some features are added) is considered and can be seen as a merge. However the properties preserved by the synchronization are not formalized and the authors consider FMs with attributes and cardinality. The composition operators previously defined are restricted to basic [18] FMs and do not consider such FM formalism.

Other relevant works [3, 19, 11, 9, 10, 18] are discussed and compared in the rest of the paper.

3 Comparison Framework

In this section, we describe the properties we expect in a good implementation (see Section 3.2) of the merge operators and outline how we evaluate different implementation approaches.

3.1 An Illustrative Approach

We use the following implementation of the merge operator, inspired from [3] and [19], to discuss the properties considered to evaluate approaches. The overall idea is that intersection or (strict) union can be realized by maintaining *separate* input FMs and inter-relating them with constraints. In intersection mode, the merged FM consists of a root feature R which joins *Base* and *Aspect* FMs, the roots of *Base* and *Aspect* being child mandatory features of R. Then, features are renamed so that they are disjoint in *Aspect* and *Base* (e.g., priming them in *Aspect*). Finally, constraints are added: P requires P' and P' requires P for each feature P (P' is the renaming of P in *Aspect*).

The merge in intersection mode between *Base* FM of Figure 2a and *Aspect* FM of Figure 2b computes the *Separate* FM shown in Figure 2d. The resulting FM respects the property (M_1) given in Section 2.2 assuming that the primed features A', B', C' and the root feature R are removed in each set of features

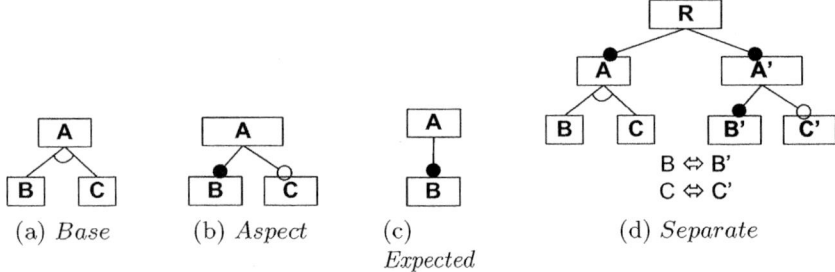

Fig. 2. Merging FMs in intersection mode

belonging to ⟦*Separate*⟧. Based on this assumption, *Separate* FM represents exactly the set of configurations of *Expected* FM (see Figure 2c). It is straightforward to check the following equality:

$$\{u \in [\![Separate]\!] \mid u \setminus \{A', B', C', R\}\} = \{\{A, B\}\} = [\![Base]\!] \bigcap [\![Aspect]\!] = [\![Expected]\!]$$

3.2 Properties of a Good Implementation

Quality of the Result. A good implementation of the merge operators should possess Semantics Properties defined in Section 2.2. This is truly the case in our illustration, even if additional effort is required to remove primed features from the set of configurations of the resulting FM. Although the semantics properties are correctly preserved in the resulting FM, the implementation is deficient from several perspectives. In [3, 19], the authors precisely recognize that "the resulting FM should probably be simplified for readability." As this *readability* criterion is too general, we define specific factors that affect success in reading and understanding FMs: Hierarchy Respect, Number of Features and FM Errors.

Hierarchy Respect requires that the resulting FM preserves the hierarchy used in the input models. The essence of FMs have often been defined as feature hierarchy and variability [20]. The hierarchy indeed helps to organize features with increasing detail [20] and loosing the initial hierarchy of input FMs affects the understandability of the model and complicates selections and deselections of features. In Figure 2d, the resulting FM clearly illustrates these issues, with a root feature different from the root features of *Base* and *Aspect*, a new sub-tree and some additional constraints making it confusing.

An interesting property of the merge operator is its ability to reduce the set of features to be considered (i.e., merging two features with the same name into one feature). For example, $FM_{ep'2}$ has only 8 features while input FMs FM_{ep1} and FM_{ep2} have 9 features each in Figure 1. In the illustrative approach, there is no such benefit: The entire set of features of input FMs is included in the resulting FM (see Figure 2d). This becomes worse when merge calls are chained (e.g., when FM_{ep1}, FM_{ep2} and FM_{ep3} are merged, see Figure 1) since the number of features increases and large FMs are produced. We draw the conclusion that a good implementation of the merge operators should produce a composed FM that contains the minimum Number of Features needed to express the desired set of configurations.

With some final observations on Figure 2d one can note that features C and C' are not included in any configuration. Trinidad et al. identify *dead features* and *full-mandatory features* as FM errors [21]. A dead feature is a non-instantiable feature, i.e., a feature that despite being defined in a FM, it appears in no product in the SPL. C and C' are dead features. A child feature in a non-mandatory relationship is a full-mandatory feature if it has to be instantiated whenever its parent feature is, i.e., it is neither an optional nor an alternative feature. C is a full-mandatory feature since it belongs to an *Xor*-group but appears in every configuration. The presence of dead or full-mandatory features introduces incorrect relationships between features and should be avoided [21].

Error Handling. In intersection mode, if the condition $[\![Base]\!] \cap [\![Aspect]\!] = \emptyset$ holds, the FM *Result* then defines no configuration at all and is considered as an unsatisfiable or *void* FM [22, 21]. When two input FMs cannot be merged (see $FM_{ep'2}$ and $FM_{ep'3}$, in Figure 1), we consider that there is an error to be *detected* by the merge operator. Error Detection can be done during the merge computation or *a priori*. In the illustrative approach, there is no *a priori* detection. The only way to detect an error is to determine whether the resulting FM of Figure 2d is void or not.

If an error is detected, providing the causes why the two input FMs cannot be merged can assist users to diagnose and repair variability contradictions. The source of error can be a feature or a variability information associated to a feature. For instance, the observation that the (mandatory) feature PET of $FM_{ep'3}$ is not included in $FM_{ep'2}$ can be a conceivable Explanation. In our example, locating the source of errors *during* the computation of the resulting FM is not possible. Automated error-analysis techniques presented in [4, 21, 23] can be applied *once* the FM of Figure 2d is computed but the primed features may disturb the understandability of the diagnosis.

Assumption on Input FMs. The interest here is to determine the degrees of difficulties arising from the handling of several kinds of input FMs (FMs with Constraints, Different Sets of features or Hierarchy mismatch) by an implementation of the merge operator.

Basic FMs support Constraints between features such as *implies* or *excludes*. Constraints crosscut the hierarchy of features (the feature tree) and can be arbitrary propositional formulas [4]. In previous work [11], we intentionally do not consider constraints. Nevertheless handling constraints in FMs can be useful. The presence of constraints alters the set of valid combinations of features but does not change the semantics of the merge operator that still remains to preserve properties (see Section 2.2) in terms of sets of configurations represented by input FMs.

Given the open nature of software architecture or domains, the assumption that FMs to be merged have the same granularity may no longer be valid. The merge operator should be able to deal with input FMs defined on Different Sets of features. Input FMs can also have different hierarchies, e.g., the depth of a feature B in the *Base* FM can be equal to 2 whereas the depth of a feature B in the *Aspect* FM can be equal to 4. Supporting Hierarchy mismatch between input FMs is an interesting quality of a merge operator implementation. As for our illustrative approach, it supports hierarchy mismatch, since there is no assumption made about the hierarchy of input FMs, as well as different set of features or constraints.

Aspects of the Implementation. Finally, additional properties are defined to evaluate some qualities of the implementation. The Ease of Implementation attempts to capture how much effort is required to implement the approach, looking at how built-in mechanisms of considered tools help in the implementation. In the illustration, the implementation is trivial. The Testing Effort property concerns evidences of the respect of the semantics properties, e.g., tests or proof that the implementation is sound, or additional effort to get more confidence in the implementation. Finally, there is need to evaluate the Computational Complexity since the number of calls to the merge operator can be dramatically important (e.g., when a large number n of services are connected in the motivating scenario). In the illustrative approach, the computation of the result FM is solved in linear time [3].

3.3 Comparison Set Up

In order to compare the other approaches according to the defined properties, we set up a comparison protocol described in Figure 3.

The first step is to generate two FMs, *aspect* and *base*. Then merge operator provided by a given approach (see ①) is used to compute the merged FM (R_1 corresponds to the merged FM computed by $Approach_1$, R_2 corresponds to the merged FM computed by $Approach_2$, etc.). The generation process of FMs is manually or randomly performed ②. The way FMs are generated depends on the assumptions made on input FMs by an approach. For example, if an approach is known to *not* support hierarchical mismatch of input FMs, then only input FMs with the same hierarchy are generated. The generation process controls the

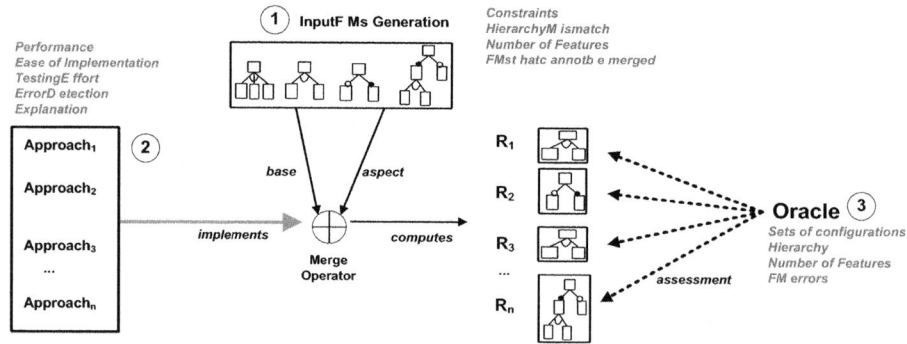

Fig. 3. Comparison Protocol

number of features of input FMs and may propose input FMs that cannot be merged to evaluate the ability of the approach to detect errors. Pre-conditions of the merge operator can be tuned to determine how approaches deal with several kinds of input FMs. In addition, once the merge operator has computed a FM, an oracle (see ③) states whether the result is correct, i.e., in terms of sets of configuration, hierarchy respect, FM errors, etc. For most of the properties, the oracle can be automated and post-conditions of the merge operator be evaluated. The algorithm presented in [16] allows us to reason on the relationship between input FMs and the output FM in terms of sets of configurations. We make use of the tree edit distance metric [24], a common similarity measure for rooted ordered trees, to evaluate the hierarchy respect of the output FMs.

4 Systematic Comparison

Our selection of approaches for establishing the comparison covers a large spectrum of paradigm and technology. We do not claim to cover all possible solutions but we choose, for each paradigm, at least one possible technique, i.e., AGG and Kermeta for model transformation, Kompose for model composition and an FM-specific solution. For each candidate approach, we report our experience and experimental results considering the set of criteria and the comparison protocol previously described.

4.1 Catalogue Rules

We first consider the work of Segura et al. [10] who propose a catalogue of visual rules to merge FMs using AGG technology [25].

In AGG, a transformation rule is composed mainly of a source graph or Left-Hand Side (LHS) and a target graph or Right-Hand Side (RHS). For each merge rule of the catalogue, LHS consists of two input FM patterns (pre-conditions) and an output FM pattern representing the merging result (post-conditions). In Figure 4a, two rule samples are given. LHS patterns are searched iteratively into the FMs to be merged. Let us show how the catalogue rules apply for the merge in *union* mode with *Base* the FM of Figure 4b and *Aspect* the FM of Figure 4c. The expected merged FM is *Base* FM. The reader can check that the property (M_2) defined in Section 2.2 holds. Rule 1 applies for Anonymized features such that Anonymized is optional in the merged FM. Rule 2 applies for Header features such that the Header feature is optional in the merged FM.

The implementation turned out to be time-consuming and error-prone. The catalogue rules should be modified and maintained according to properties expected in union or intersection mode. The number of rules to specify in the union mode is around 30. Validating the catalogue of rules such that the semantics properties are preserved for any input FMs is still missing. A brute force testing strategy, which consists in generating randomized input FMs and then ensuring each output FM as correct, is not sufficient to cover all cases. Interestingly, AGG implements the mechanism of critical pair analysis which can be used to check consistency of catalogue rules. However, there is no proof about

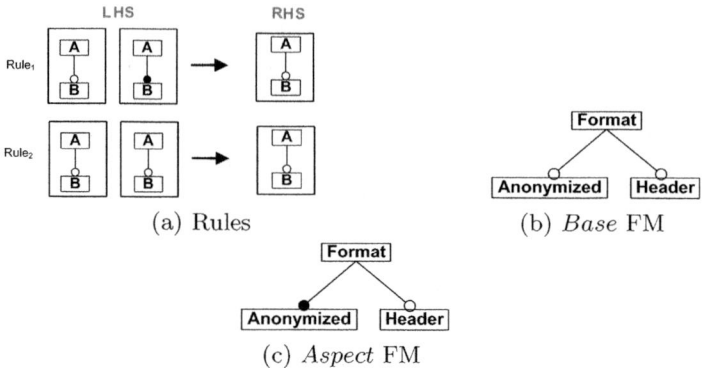

Fig. 4. Rules to merge in union mode

the *completeness* of the rules. Studying theorem provers and model checkers, as done in [26] *for* refactoring rules (the starting point of [10]), is still to be done and requires intensive research.

The semantics properties currently implemented are limited to the merge in union mode (see property (M_2) in Section 2.2). The intersection mode remains particularly challenging to be implemented. Considering the merge in intersection mode of *Base* (see Figure 5a) and *Aspect* (see Figure 5b), it is hard to specify, in the general case, a rule and an associated pattern that deduce the removal of the feature B. Indeed, the expressiveness of AGG is limited to non recursive-patterns (thus prohibiting traversal of multi-level parent-child relationships) and does not support multi-objects. Handling constraints largely disturbs the strategy based on graph patterns since the presence of constraints may lead to the removal of a feature which may be located elsewhere in the FM.

The elements not mentioned in any of the patterns remain unchanged by default [10]. Then, considering the number of features in the merged FM, there is a risk to unnecessarily adding features and FM errors. Moreover, additional rules are needed to deal with different sets of features of input FMs. As the approach is based on graphs, the hierarchy of the resulting FM is well restored assuming that "The parental relationship between features is equal in all the FMs. That is, a feature must have the same parent feature in all the models in which it appears." [10]. It seems hardly conceivable to deal with hierarchy mismatch. Finally, the approach can detect that two input FMs cannot be merged in intersection mode *during* the iterative application of rules but not *a priori*. Interestingly, negative application conditions (NAC) can provide explanations and precisely locate the source of errors.

4.2 Compositional Approach

The second approach considers the use of Kompose [27, 28] which implements a generic structural composition operator that can be specialized to a particular

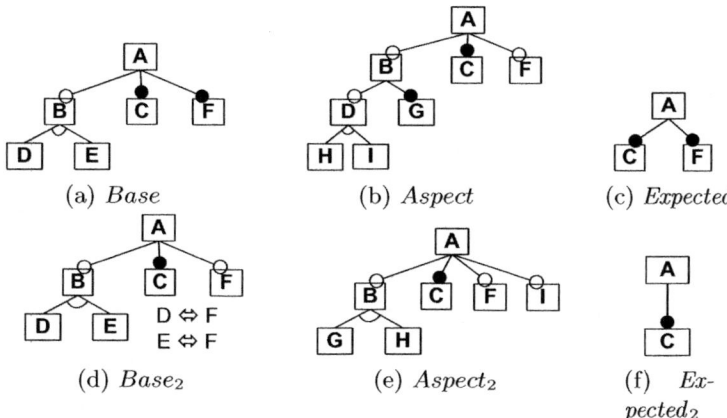

Fig. 5. Non-trivial example of merging FMs in intersection mode

modeling language. We implement the merging rules and strategy proposed in [11] using as much as possible the composition facilities of Kompose.

In Kompose, the composition mechanism is structured in two major phases: (1) The **Matching** phase identifies model elements that describe the same concepts in the input models to be composed; (2) The **Merging** phase where matched elements are merged to create new elements in the resulting model.

Each element type has a *signature* that determines the uniqueness of elements, i.e, two elements with equivalent signatures are merged. A signature is a set of syntactic properties associated with an element type. To achieve our goal we first define the signature of type *Feature* as the name of the feature. The hardest issue is to specify the various types *Operator* (i.e., Xor-, Or-, And-) associated to features. Such operators are likely to be in conflict : two features having the same name may be associated to different operators. The decision to merge them or not and the nature of the resulting operator depends on the intended semantics properties (e.g., as defined in [11] the merging of an *Or*-group with an *Or*-Group gives an *Or*-Group in union mode).

In Figure 5, the merge operator in intersection mode is applied on *Base* (Figure 5a) and *Aspect* (Figure 5b). *Result* (Figure 5c) is the expected FM according to the semantics of the merge operator defined in Section 2.2. The merge operator provided by Kompose has a behaviour which interferes with it. It is obvious that feature A of *Base* and A of *Aspect* must be merged and produces feature A of *Result* (this is exactly what Kompose does automatically). But Kompose applies recursively the same strategy to feature B and this is not what is expected according to *Result*. This shows that a compositional approach only structured in two-stages (matching and merging) is too restrictive for implementing an FM-specific merge operator. In particular, the recursive detection of matching elements is not sufficient since we need a more global vision to decide whether elements should be merged or not. To address this issue we could use the post-directives mechanism provided by Kompose. This would allow automatically removing feature B but this solution is practically hard to implement since it is specific to each composition.

As Kompose implies local reasoning, handling constraints is not conceivable as well (see the removal of feature F in Figure 5f). Moreover due to its recursive merging strategy, Kompose does not handle hierarchy mismatch. Consequently input FMs must be already aligned. Finally, the current approach cannot determine *a priori* when two FMs cannot be merged. Thanks to the case-based reasoning during the matching process, source of errors can be located and accurate explanations can be provided.

4.3 Transformational Approach

Due to the limits previously observed with AGG or Kompose, we decide to leverage the expressiveness of the model manipulation language used to implement the merge operator. We rely on Kermeta [29] an executable, imperative and object-oriented (meta-)modeling language which is designed to define both structures and behaviors of EMOF and Ecore (meta-)models.

We apply the same strategy as with Kompose but without strictly following the compositional approach which consists in match and merging phases. We gain some benefits, notably a better coverage of semantics properties. Now that global and more complex reasoning is possible, some features are not necessary added and less FM errors are generated.

Although the implementation is not obliged to apply a recursive reasoning and to strictly follow the hierarchy during traversal of input FMs, there is still an issue when dealing with different hierarchies. Finally, difficulties arise in constructing a merged FM that preserves properties with the presence of constraints.

4.4 Boolean Logic Based Composition

Enumerating all valid configurations of an FM is usually infeasible. Fortunately, the set of configurations represented by a FM can be compactly described by a propositional formula defined over a set of Boolean variables, where each variable corresponds to a feature. The intersection of two sets of configurations represented by two FMs, *Base*, and *Aspect*, is computed as follows. First, *Base* (resp. *Aspect*) FMs are encoded into a propositional formula ϕ_{base} (resp. ϕ_{aspect}) as defined in [4]. Then, the following formula is computed:

$$\phi_{Result} = (\phi_{base} \wedge not(\mathcal{F}_{aspect} \setminus \mathcal{F}_{base})) \wedge (\phi_{aspect} \wedge not(\mathcal{F}_{base} \setminus \mathcal{F}_{aspect}))$$

with $\mathcal{F}_{base}$ (resp. $\mathcal{F}_{aspect}$) the set of features of *Base* (resp. *Aspect*) FM. $\mathcal{F}_{aspect} \setminus \mathcal{F}_{base}$ denotes the complement (or difference) of $\mathcal{F}_{aspect}$ with respect to $\mathcal{F}_{base}$. If we consider *Base* FM of Figure 5a and *Aspect* FM of Figure 5b, then $\mathcal{F}_{aspect} \setminus \mathcal{F}_{base} = \{G, H, I\}$

not is a function that, given a non-empty set of features, returns the Boolean conjunction of all negated variables corresponding to features:

$$not(\{f_1, f_2, ..., f_n\}) = \bigwedge_{i=1..n} \neg f_i$$

Computing the strict union of two sets of configurations represented by two FMs, *Base*, and *Aspect*, follows the same principles and we obtain:

$$\phi_{Result} = (\phi_{base} \wedge not(\mathcal{F}_{aspect} \setminus \mathcal{F}_{base})) \vee (\phi_{aspect} \wedge not(\mathcal{F}_{base} \setminus \mathcal{F}_{aspect}))$$

Interestingly, ϕ_{Result} can be simplified. If $\phi_{Result} \wedge f$ is unsatisfiable, the feature F is dead and can be removed. Similarly, the feature F can be identified as a full mandatory feature if $\phi_{Result} \wedge \neg f$ is unsatisfiable. Moreover, the current approach can detect *a priori* that two FMs cannot be merged in intersection mode: In this case, ϕ_{Result} is unsatisfiable. Such operations on ϕ_{Result} can be realized using SAT solvers or BDD representation. The semantics properties are by construction respected. The technique does not introduce FM errors or does not increase unnecessarily the number of features. Constraints in FMs can be expressed using the full expressiveness of Boolean logic and different sets of features can be manipulated. At the moment, ϕ_{Result} is solely a compact representation of the sets of configurations of the expected FM. The hierarchy of the FM and the structuring information (e.g., parent-child relations between features) are still to be constructed. Czarnecki et al. propose an algorithm to construct a FM from Boolean formula [18]. More precisely, the algorithm constructs a tree with additional nodes for feature groups that can be translated into a basic FM. We first experiment their work on a set of input FMs sharing a same set of features and a same hierarchy. The simplifications of the formula ϕ_{Result} described above have been applied and then fed to the algorithm. Importantly, the algorithm indicates all parent-child relationships (mandatory features) and all possible optional sub-features such that the hierarchy of the merged FM corresponds to hierarchies of input FMs. *And*-group, *Or*-group and *Xor*-group can be efficiently restored in the resulting FM when it was necessary.

The limitations come when different hierarchies of input FMs or different sets of features are proposed to the merge operator. Although the resulting FM is correct in terms of sets of configuration, determining the most suitable hierarchy for the resulting FM requires the intervention of the user since it can be the hierarchy of the *Base* FM, the hierarchy of the *Aspect* FM, or a combination of the two hierarchies. It comes even more challenging when several features are to be removed in intersection mode. As a result, there is need to impose a given FM hierarchy to the resulting FM and the current technique should be adapted.

5 Results and Concluding Remarks

5.1 Results

Figure 6 summarizes our results. ++ is the highest score (i.e., the criteria is fully fulfilled by the approach) whereas −− is the lowest score (i.e., a non acceptable

	Separate App.	Catalog Rules	Composition	Transform.	Boolean Logic
Related Work	[3, 19]	[10, 9]	[11]	[11]	[18]
Technology	-	AGG	Kompose	Kermeta	SAT/BDD
Quality of the Result					
Semantics Properties	+	=	=	+	++
Hierarchy Respect	--	++	++	++	+
Number of Features	--	-	-	=	++
FM errors	--	-	-	=	++
Aspects of the Implementation					
Ease of Implementation	++	--	-	=	+
Computational Complexity	++	-	-	=	+
Testing Effort	++	-	-	-	++
Assumption on Input FMs					
Different Sets	++	+	+	+	++
Hierarchy mismatch	+	--	--	-	++
Constraints	++	-	-	=	++
Error Handling					
Error Detection	+	+	+	+	++
Explanation	-	+	+	+	-

Fig. 6. Comparison of approaches

solution). We can observe that only FM-specific solutions fully implement semantics properties. Current MBE or AOM solutions have issues related to the intersection or the strict union modes, especially when constraints are present. Strategies to avoid the adding of unnecessary features in the merged FM were difficult to implement. The confidence in modeling solutions appears to be too low (e.g., there is no proof that the set of rules in AGG is comprehensive such that semantics properties are preserved in all cases) and intensive testing effort is required. This is not the case with FM-specific solution which preserves, by construction, the sets of configurations.

Open Issues. Scalability. The manageable size (i.e., number of features) of input FMs is still to be determined. Using Boolean logic, preliminary experiments indicate that on typical propositional formula the algorithm presented in [18] scales up to 300 variables, e.g., the number of features commonly shared by input FMs should not exceed 300 features. Other approaches have scalability issues (100 features in each input FMs is the limit).

Explanation. When two inputs FMs cannot be merged, ϕ_{Result} is unsatisfiable and no FM can be synthesized from ϕ_{Result}. It is only possible to reason at the Boolean logic level (e.g., by computing a small unsatisfiable subset of the formula's clauses) and thus hard to provide the source of errors at the FM level. Rule-based approaches (AGG, Kompose) have better results. They provide precise explanations (e.g., NAC in AGG) when features' relations lead to FMs merging failure. Nevertheless, there is no evidence that the rules are sufficient to cover all merging failures.

Hierarchy mismatch. FM-specific solutions are more efficient to deal with different hierarchies of input FMs (no assumption is made about hierarchies) but the current proposals are not fully satisfying (see Section 4.4).

Revisiting Model-based Solutions. The study provides some evidence that MBE or AOM solutions considered in this paper are not suitable for implementing the merge of FMs. Below we give some possible reasons.

In AOM, many existing approaches to match and merge focus on *structural* similarities between models and on their *syntactical properties*. Most of these approaches treat models as graphical artifacts while (largely) ignoring their semantics. This treatment provides generalizable tools that can be applied to many different modeling notations. Our first intuition was to resolve every syntactical conflict and to reason recursively on the hierarchy of FMs – a classical approach in model composition. However, complex reasoning that takes into account the semantics of FMs is required to compute the combination of two or more FM elements into new FM elements. The experimentation of MBE techniques gives an insight to the characterization of FMs composition. A merging strategy mainly based on syntactical properties (as applied with AGG, Kompose and Kermeta) is likely to fail so that we can now consider that FMs composition is *not* purely structural. On the contrary, semantical transformations or semantics preserving model composition are needed to preserve the semantics properties of model. An open question in this area is how to achieve semantics preservation, both formally and practically. For instance, recent work on behavioural models has concentrated on establishing semantic relationships between models (e.g., see [30]). Merging FMs can be seen as a non-trivial case of semantics preserving model composition. Currently, model composition techniques are not necessary dedicated to support semantics preserving model composition: This is another way to interpret the difficulties of the modeling techniques considered in this paper. Nevertheless, the selection of approaches in the present study does not pretend to be comprehensive regarding MBE or AOM solutions. Other solutions based on different paradigms or technologies (e.g., QVT) are still conceivable and may successfully implement a merge operator. For instance, graph transformation tools with advanced transformation language constructs or supporting many-to-one transformations [31] may help to better cover semantics properties.

5.2 Future Work

The implementation of a merge operator for FMs is an interesting challenge for MBE and AOM techniques. Other modeling approaches and technologies can be considered and may emerge to outperform the solutions considered in this paper. Nevertheless, the use of Boolean logic turns out to fulfill most of the criteria expected from a merge operator. As future work, we plan to accurately determine for which amount of features the logic-based approach scales and to fully support different hierarchies of input FMs. The use of CSP solvers can also be considered in addition to SAT and BDD techniques.

A longer term perspective is to consider the implementation of *diff* and *refactoring* [9,16] operations for FMs. These operators are commonly used in MBE for various kinds of models, but the specificity and the semantics properties of FMs should be taken into account. The efficiency of modeling techniques can be evaluated for diff and refactoring of FMs as similarly done for the merge operator. Another research direction is to consider other formalisms of FM including cardinality-based FMs and feature attributes. In this case, the sole use of Boolean logic is not sufficient to represent the semantics of FMs: MBE and AOM techniques may provide interesting support and built-in mechanisms to deal with such extended formalisms.

Acknowledgments. We thank Sergio Segura and Steven She for sharing with us their implementation related to work described resp. in [10] and [18].

References

1. Pohl, K., Böckle, G., van der Linden, F.J.: Software Product Line Engineering: Foundations, Principles and Techniques. Springer, Heidelberg (2005)
2. Kang, K., Cohen, S., Hess, J., Novak, W., Peterson, S.: Feature-Oriented Domain Analysis (FODA). Technical Report CMU/SEI-90-TR-21, SEI (November 1990)
3. Schobbens, P.Y., Heymans, P., Trigaux, J.C., Bontemps, Y.: Generic semantics of feature diagrams. Comput. Netw. 51(2), 456–479 (2007)
4. Batory, D.S.: Feature models, grammars, and propositional formulas. In: Obbink, H., Pohl, K. (eds.) SPLC 2005. LNCS, vol. 3714, pp. 7–20. Springer, Heidelberg (2005)
5. Reiser, M.O., Weber, M.: Multi-level feature trees: A pragmatic approach to managing highly complex product families. Requir. Eng. 12(2), 57–75 (2007)
6. Tun, T.T., Heymans, P.: Concerns and their separation in feature diagram languages - an informal survey. In: Proceedings of the Workshop on Scalable Modelling Techniques for Software Product Lines (SCALE@SPLC 2009), pp. 107–110 (2009)
7. Czarnecki, K., Helsen, S., Eisenecker, U.: Staged Configuration through Specialization and Multilevel Configuration of Feature Models. Software Process: Improvement and Practice 10(2), 143–169 (2005)
8. Hartmann, H., Trew, T.: Using feature diagrams with context variability to model multiple product lines for software supply chains. In: SPLC 2008, pp. 12–21. IEEE, Los Alamitos (2008)
9. Alves, V., Gheyi, R., Massoni, T., Kulesza, U., Borba, P., Lucena, C.: Refactoring product lines. In: GPCE 2006, pp. 201–210. ACM, New York (2006)
10. Segura, S., Benavides, D., Ruiz-Cortés, A., Trinidad, P.: Automated merging of feature models using graph transformations. In: Lämmel, R., Visser, J., Saraiva, J. (eds.) Generative and Transformational Techniques in Software Engineering II. LNCS, vol. 5235, pp. 489–505. Springer, Heidelberg (2008)
11. Acher, M., Collet, P., Lahire, P., France, R.: Composing Feature Models. In: Gašević, D. (ed.) SLE 2009. LNCS, vol. 5969, pp. 62–81. Springer, Heidelberg (2010)
12. Acher, M., Collet, P., Lahire, P., Montagnat, J.: Imaging Services on the Grid as a Product Line: Requirements and Architecture. In: Service-Oriented Architectures and Software Product Lines (SOAPL 2008), at SPLC 2008, IEEE, Los Alamitos (2008)

13. Acher, M., Collet, P., Lahire, P., France, R.: Managing Variability in Workflow with Feature Model Composition Operators. In: 9th International Conference on Software Composition (SC 2010), June 2010. LNCS. Springer, Heidelberg (2010)
14. Hartmann, H., Trew, T., Matsinger, A.: Supplier independent feature modelling. In: SPLC 2009, pp. 191–200. IEEE Computer Society, Los Alamitos (2009)
15. Tun, T.T., Boucher, Q., Classen, A., Hubaux, A., Heymans, P.: Relating requirements and feature configurations: A systematic approach. In: SPLC 2009, pp. 201–210. IEEE Computer Society, Los Alamitos (2009)
16. Thüm, T., Batory, D., Kästner, C.: Reasoning about edits to feature models. In: ICSE 2009, pp. 254–264. IEEE, Los Alamitos (2009)
17. Kim, C.H.P., Czarnecki, K.: Synchronizing cardinality-based feature models and their specializations. In: Hartman, A., Kreische, D. (eds.) ECMDA-FA 2005. LNCS, vol. 3748, pp. 331–348. Springer, Heidelberg (2005)
18. Czarnecki, K., Wasowski, A.: Feature diagrams and logics: There and back again. In: SPLC 2007, pp. 23–34 (2007)
19. Heymans, P., Schobbens, P.Y., Trigaux, J.C., Bontemps, Y., Matulevicius, R., Classen, A.: Evaluating formal properties of feature diagram languages. Software, IET 2(3), 281–302 (2008)
20. Czarnecki, K., Kim, C.H.P., Kalleberg, K.T.: Feature models are views on ontologies. In: SPLC 2006, pp. 41–51. IEEE, Los Alamitos (2006)
21. Trinidad, P., Benavides, D., Durán, A., Ruiz-Cortés, A., Toro, M.: Automated error analysis for the agilization of feature modeling. J. Syst. Softw. 81(6), 883–896 (2008)
22. Batory, D., Benavides, D., Ruiz-Cortés, A.: Automated analysis of feature models: Challenges ahead. Communications of the ACM (December 2006)
23. White, J., Schmidt, D.C., Benavides, D., Trinidad, P., Ruiz-Cortés, A.: Automated diagnosis of product-line configuration errors in feature models. In: SPLC 2008, pp. 225–234. IEEE, Los Alamitos (2008)
24. Bille, P.: A survey on tree edit distance and related problems. Theor. Comput. Sci. 337(1-3), 217–239 (2005)
25. Taentzer, G.: AGG: A graph transformation environment for modeling and validation of software. In: Pfaltz, J.L., Nagl, M., Böhlen, B. (eds.) AGTIVE 2003. LNCS, vol. 3062, pp. 446–453. Springer, Heidelberg (2004)
26. Gheyi, R., Massoni, T., Borba, P.: A theory for feature models in alloy. In: Proceedings of First Alloy Workshop, pp. 71–80 (2006)
27. Reddy, Y.R., Ghosh, S., France, R.B., Straw, G., Bieman, J.M., McEachen, N., Song, E., Georg, G.: Directives for composing aspect-oriented design class models. In: Rashid, A., Aksit, M. (eds.) Transactions on Aspect-Oriented Software Development I. LNCS, vol. 3880, pp. 75–105. Springer, Heidelberg (2006)
28. Fleurey, F., Baudry, B., France, R.B., Ghosh, S.: A generic approach for automatic model composition. In: Giese, H. (ed.) MODELS 2008. LNCS, vol. 5002, pp. 7–15. Springer, Heidelberg (2008)
29. Muller, P.A., Fleurey, F., Jézéquel, J.M.: Weaving executability into object-oriented meta-languages. In: Briand, L.C., Williams, C. (eds.) MoDELS 2005. LNCS, vol. 3713, pp. 264–278. Springer, Heidelberg (2005)
30. Nejati, S., Sabetzadeh, M., Chechik, M., Easterbrook, S., Zave, P.: Matching and merging of statecharts specifications. In: ICSE 2007, pp. 54–64. IEEE, Los Alamitos (2007)
31. Mens, T., Gorp, P.V., Varró, D., Karsai, G.: Applying a model transformation taxonomy to graph transformation technology, March 2006. Electronic Notes in Theoretical Computer Science, vol. 152, pp. 143–159 (2006)

A UML 2.0 Profile to Model Block Cipher Algorithms

Tomás Balderas-Contreras, Gustavo Rodriguez-Gomez, and René Cumplido

National Institute of Astrophysics, Optics and Electronics
Computer Science Department
Luis Enrique Erro 1, 72840 Santa María Tonantzintla, Puebla, Mexico
{balderas,grodrig,rcumplido}@inaoep.mx
http://ccc.inaoep.mx

Abstract. Current mobile digital communication systems must implement rigorous operations to guarantee high levels of confidentiality and integrity during transmission of critical information. To achieve higher performance, the security algorithms are usually implemented as dedicated hardware functional units attached to the main processing units of the embedded communication system. To save hardware resources, the designer usually performs a number of manipulations in the cipher algorithm lying at the core of the confidentiality and integrity operations to implement a simplified version of it that is suitable to be efficiently used in an embedded environment. This paper describes an extension to UML 2.0 to model the structure of contemporary block cipher algorithms, with the ultimate goal of synthesizing representations in a hardware description language from these models according to a model-driven development principle. This automated process should alleviate design complexity and increase the productivity of the developer during experimentation with different design alternatives.

Keywords: Block cipher algorithm, UML 2.0 profile.

1 Introduction

A computer-based system is a combination of hardware and software that implements a set of algorithms to automate the solution to a number of problems. Computer design technology transforms the designers ideas and objectives into a number of representations describing software modules and hardware components that can be tested and manufactured [11]. The design process is not straightforward; the developers always deal with the problem of alleviating the complexity of their designs to develop high-quality products within rigid time constraints. This problem arose as a consequence of the steady evolution of technology and the constant demand for new functionality.

Computer-based systems are not becoming easier to design as time goes by; on the contrary, the advancement of development and manufacturing technologies, and the need to meet new usage demand encourage the development of devices incorporating more and more functionality. There are a number of functionality aspects that have demanded attention from hardware/software engineers during the last years: communication, security, power management, multimedia processing, and fault tolerance.

When designing the digital hardware of a computer-based system the developers must deal with the challenge of making a trade-off between a number of design requirements, that can not be optimized all at the same time, while implementing the desired functionality. The digital hardware system must usually achieve a *high level of performance*, its operation should be *efficient in terms of power consumption*, and, when a large number of hardware resources is not available, its *circuitry must be small* and reutilize a component iteratively until operation completion. It is not possible to stop the evolution of technology or to prevent computer-based systems from implementing more and more functionality over time and becoming more complex. Hardware and software engineers are condemned to face the challenge of designing products that implement lots of functionality, while meeting difficult constraints, in shorter periods of time. In this document we focus our attention on the process of developing the digital hardware sub-system of a whole computer-based system.

1.1 Productivity Gap

In spite of having more resources to design with, design complexity imposes serious limits to the ability of hardware designers to develop high quality products that fully meet their requirements in a short period of time; that is, to their productivity. The productivity gap is the challenge that arises when the number of available transistors grows faster than the ability to meaningfully design with them [11]. Flynn, et al. [6] illustrates the considerable separation between the exponential increase in the number of transistors per chip along the last 28 years and the increase in design productivity along the same period of time.

1.2 Abstraction Levels

An effective way to alleviate design complexity and to reduce the productivity gap during the design of digital hardware systems is to raise the level of abstraction at which developers carry out their activities. The goal is to design correct systems faster by making it easier to check for, identify, and correct errors.

The raise in the level of abstraction has been done many times in the past for both software and hardware development. The first solid-state computers were built using *discrete transistors and other electronic components*, consumed several kilowatts of power, and became more complex to design as advanced architectural techniques to increase performance arose. Medium-Scale Integration (MSI) and Large-Scale Integration (LSI) integrated circuits that encapsulated whole computer modules within single dies allowed to design digital hardware systems as a set of *schematics* specifying the interconnection of a number of integrated circuits. Later, the behavior of a circuit started to be defined in terms of a *flow of signals (data transference) between hardware registers and the logical operations performed on those signals* using hardware description languages like VHDL and Verilog. This representation was transformed into a description of the electronic components that made up the system and the interconnections between them (*netlist*), which could be implemented in a Very Large Scale Integration (VLSI) silicon platform like an Application-Specific Integrated Circuit (ASIC) or a Field Programmable Gate Array (FPGA). The current *Electronic System Level* (ESL) design trend proposes the use of high level languages, derived from languages like C and Java for instance, to describe the functionality of a digital hardware system and tools to automate the implementation process [2]; thus achieving a higher degree of comprehension and reutilization of the functional descriptions.

1.3 ESL and UML

At the ESL there are lots of similarities between the process of *describing the functionality of digital hardware systems* and the process of *developing software*. A research effort is needed to determine if we can take advantage of the recent advances in software engineering, like the *Model-Driven Engineering* (MDE) paradigm [7], to raise the level of abstraction even further, increase productivity, alleviate design complexity, exploit reuse of existing designs, and automate the production of representations of digital hardware systems at lower levels of abstraction.

Riccobene, et al. [10] propose a UML 2.0 profile containing the constructs of the SystemC language to allow the designer to build diagrams instead of writing code. Björklund, et al. [3] describe the use of an intermediate representation called SMDL to transform general-purpose state machine diagrams to VHDL. While these two proposals synthesize hardware description language code from UML, they do not customize UML to an application domain to allow the developer to describe a system in terms of the concepts he/she knows instead of the concepts of the implementation language or hardware platform.

This paper describes an extension to UML 2.0 [8] that includes abstractions to model the structure of block cipher algorithms with the purpose of them being implemented in hardware. The profile should allow the designer to modify the structure of the algorithm, without altering its operation, to design a hardware implementation that meets the required trade-offs between performance and resource consumption. For instance, an area-efficient hardware implementation of a block cipher algorithm for 3G cellular communications that reuses a basic function block iteratively until completion is able to encrypt information at a rate of 164.45 Mbps. [4], whereas a high-performance implementation of the same algorithm that requires 8.05 times more hardware resources (slices in a Virtex-E FPGA) has a performance of 5.32 Gbps [5]. This profile will be a crucial component of a model-based design flow that will transform a high level description in UML to a lower level VHDL representation that could be implemented in either an ASIC or a FPGA platform.

This document is organized as follows: section 2 documents the proposed profile to model block cipher algorithms, section 3 illustrates the application of the profile in a practical case of study, and section 4 concludes.

2 The Block Cipher Profile

Current versions of UML include a formal definition of the language's constructs and abstract syntax that is called meta-model (a model of a model). The meta-model contains a set of meta-classes that define the UML modeling elements, and describes the relationships between meta-classes that indicate how the modeling elements are assembled together by the user to build the UML models of a system. A *profile* is an extension mechanism for UML, a kind of dialect that customizes the language for particular platforms or application domains. Profiles are made up of *stereotypes* that extend particular meta-classes; *tagged values* that define additional attributes for the stereotype; and *restrictions* that specify rules, pre- and post-conditions for the extended modeling elements.

2.1 Block Ciphers

A *block cipher* is an algorithm that unvaryingly transforms a fixed-length group of bits, called plaintext block, into a different group of bits, called ciphertext block, under the control of a symmetrical secret key. The algorithm carries out

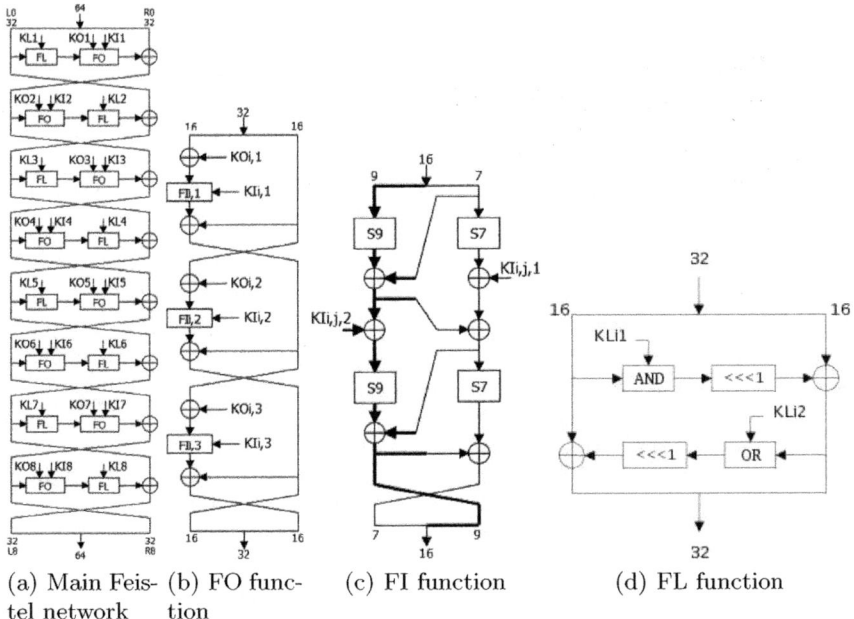

(a) Main Feistel network (b) FO function (c) FI function (d) FL function

Fig. 1. The components and full structure of the KASUMI block cipher (from [1])

the inverse process when it receives both the ciphertext block and the secret key as inputs.

Most block ciphers employ simple operations like bitwise logical operations (and, or, xor), shifts and rotations, n-bit substitution functions (referred to as S-Boxes), arithmetic operations, and permutations in an iterative manner until completion. The structure of these algorithms is usually shown as an iterative Feistel network, an structure whose iterations are called rounds and perform an internal round function.

As an example consider the KASUMI block cipher, illustrated in the block diagrams in Figure 1, used nowadays to implement security functions, like confidentiality and integrity, in modern 3G cellular communication networks [1]. Each of the eight rounds of KASUMI's Feistel network carries out a pair of operations called FL and FO, where FO is, in turn, a Feistel network with three rounds, each performing a function called FI that is made up of two seven-bit input S-Boxes (S7) and two nine-bit input S-Boxes (S9). The informal block diagram notation frequently used to describe this kind of algorithms does not represent either a digital circuit schematic or an UML diagram.

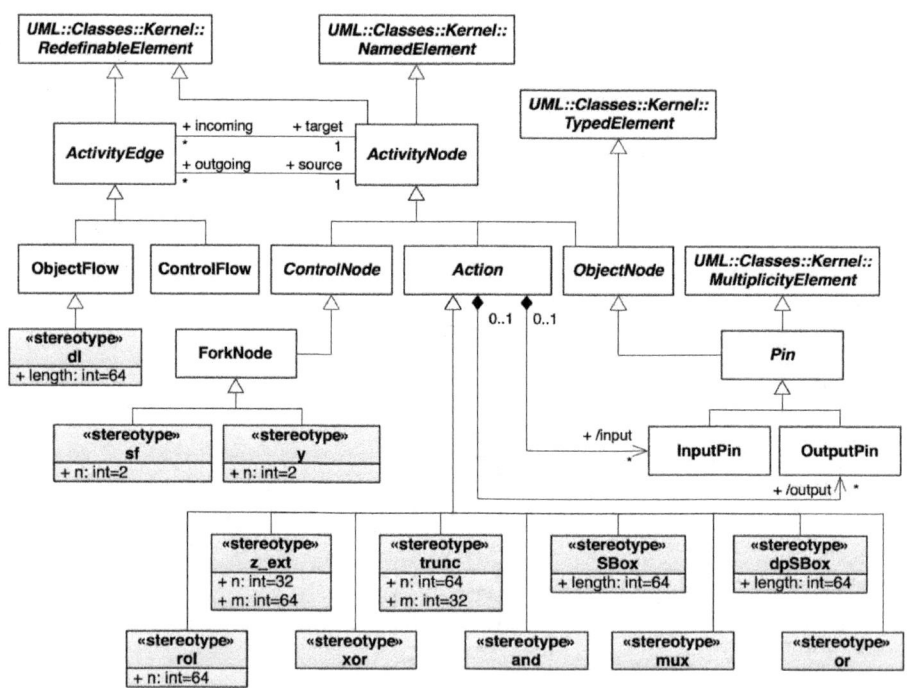

Fig. 2. Fragment of the UML 2.0 meta-model for Activity Diagrams extended with the stereotypes that make up the Block Cipher Profile

2.2 Defining the Block Cipher Profile

The UML Activity Diagram is used to describe procedural logic, business processes, and work flows. This diagram is conceptually similar to a flowchart, but differs from it in its ability to describe parallel behavior and model both control and data flows; these two distinctions make this kind of diagram the most adequate one to model the data flows and the operations required to fulfill the block cipher algorithms in a correct manner.

The Activity Diagram's modeling elements include: actions representing behavior execution, input/output pins working as parameters for the actions, edges indicating the flow of either data or control, decision elements to choose one out of several paths, fork nodes to initiate parallel paths, asynchronous signaling mechanisms, and constructions to elaborate a hierarchy of sub-activity diagrams. Our profile's stereotypes extend the meta-classes of the existing modeling elements to derive specialized modeling constructs representing the operations required by block ciphers.

Figure 2 illustrates the hierarchy of meta-classes from which we derive our profile's stereotypes, which are indicated by the shaded class boxes. A stereotype is a meta-class labeled with the keyword «stereotype»that is derived from an existing meta-class with the intention of extending its behavior and defining a new modeling element. The stereotype's attributes shown in Figure 2 are called tagged values and define properties for the new modeling construct that are additional to the ones it inherits from its parent meta-class.

Our profile is encapsulated within a package that extends the package UML::Activities::IntermediateActivities and uses the package UML::Actions::-

Table 1. Definition of the z_ext stereotype in the Block Cipher Profile

Name:	z_ext.
Generalizations:	Action.
Description:	An action that zero-extends the incoming bit-block.
Attributes:	n. An integer attribute indicating the length in bits of the incoming bit-block. Its default value is 32.
	m. An integer attribute indicating the length in bits of the outgoing bit-block. Its default value is 64.
Associations:	*input*: **InputPin**. A pin connected to the action that holds input bit-blocks to be consumed by the action.
	output: **OutputPin**. A pin connected to the action that holds output bit-blocks produced by the action.
Constraints:	$n \leq m$.
	There must be exactly two pins connected to this action; one of them must be an instance of the **InputPin** meta-class, whereas the other must be an instance of the **OutputPin** meta-class.
	The input pin must be attached to an edge that is an instance of the **dl** meta-class.
	The output pin must be attached to an edge that is an instance of the **dl** meta-class.
	The length of the bit-block in the incoming edge attached to the input pin must be equal to the n attribute.
	The length of the bit-block in the outgoing edge attached to the output pin must be equal to the m attribute.
Semantics:	Instances of **z_ext** are actions in a Block Cipher Diagram that receive an n-bit block as input and produces a m-bit block as output, with $n \leq m$. The output block's n least significant bits are set to the input block, and its $(m-n)$ most significant bits are all set to zero.

Table 2. Definition of the **dl** stereotype in the Block Cipher Profile

Name:	dl.
Generalization:	ObjectFlow.
Description:	An edge that models the flow of bit-blocks between nodes.
Attributes:	*length*. An integer attribute indicating the length, in bits, of the block flowing along the edge.
Associations:	*source*: **ActivityNode**. The node the edge departs from.
	target: **ActivityNode**. The node the edge arrives to.
Constraints:	$1 \leq length \leq 128$.
	The edge must be attached to an instance of either the **Pin** meta-class or the **Action** meta-class or the **ForkNode** meta-class. See Figure 2.
	If the edge is attached to two pins then one of those pins must be an instance of the **InputPin** meta-class, the other must be an instance of the **OutputPin** meta-class.
Semantics:	Instances of **dl** (data line) are special edges intended to model transferences of bit-blocks between nodes in a Block Cipher Diagram. Data lines transfer bit-blocks whose length is greater than zero but less than or equal to 128 bits. When a **dl** instance's length attribute is set to 1 then the edge transfers a signal.

Table 3. Definition of the **sf** stereotype in the Block Cipher Profile

Name:	sf.
Generalization:	ForkNode.
Description:	Splits an incoming bit-block into n bit-blocks of different lengths.
Attributes:	n. An integer attribute indicating the number of bit blocks outgoing the fork node.
Associations:	*incoming*: **ActivityEdge**. Edge that has the fork node as target.
	outgoing: **ActivityEdge**. Edges that have the fork node as source.
Constraints:	There must be exactly n outgoing edges, where n is the fork node's attribute.
	The incoming edge and all of the outgoing edges must be instances of the **dl** meta-class.
	The sum of the *length* attributes of each of the outgoing edges must be equal to the *length* attribute of the incoming edge.
Semantics:	Instances of **sf** (split fork) are special fork nodes that partition the bit-block in the incoming edge into n bit-blocks, and issue each of these bit-blocks through an independent outgoing edge. All of the outgoing edges are concurrent. The length of the incoming bit-block is indicated by the *length* attribute of the incoming edge. Similarly, the length of each of the outgoing bit-blocks is indicated by the *length* attribute of the corresponding outgoing edge. The sum of the *length* attributes for the outgoing edges must be equal to the length of the incoming edge.

BasicActions in the Superstructure of UML [8]. IntermediateActivities was chosen because it defines all the necessary meta-classes to base the new modeling elements on and is not polluted with other complex meta-classes. The profile derives several stereotypes from the **Action** meta-class to model the bitwise operations that are common to the block ciphers, as well as the S-Box components; it also derives a stereotype from the meta-class **ObjectFlow** to model edges transmitting bit-blocks; and it also derives a stereotype from the meta-class **ForkNode** to either distribute a bit-block along two or more different paths, or to partition a n-bit block into several bit-blocks of different lengths. An UML Activity Diagram built using this profile is called a Block Cipher Diagram.

Tables 1, 2, and 3 describe three stereotypes included in the Block Cipher Profile. Due to space limitations, it is not possible to describe all of the stereotypes that make up the profile in this document.

3 Applying the Block Cipher Profile

The hardware implementation of the KASUMI block cipher in its full structure is prohibitive for some embedded applications because it requires lots of hardware components. In cases like this the designers usually manipulate the structure of the algorithm to obtain a representation that uses a minimal number of components. After a fixed number of successive iterations over this small set of components, by feeding back the result of the current iteration to the input of the design, the algorithm completes its task. Figure 3 illustrates the final result of a simplification process that is described in detail by Balderas, et al. in [4].

The simplified design combines two instances of the FI function into a single module that accepts two 16-bit inputs; see Figure 3(a). The four S-boxes internal to this dual-input FI function can be implemented either as combinational blocks that perform boolean functions over their inputs to generate their outputs, or as memories that store the correct value for each of the possible inputs. This dual-input FI function block is used by the simplified version of the FO function twice per round; see Figure 3(b). Therefore, the simplified KASUMI structure in Figure 3(c) requires two times eight equals sixteen iterations, as well as 16 clock cycles, to cipher a 64-bit block and has a throughput of 164.45 Mbps in a Virtex-E FPGA.

The profile is able to model the simplified structure of the KASUMI algorithm, as shown in the diagrams in Figure 4. The diagrams' modeling elements are labeled with a keyword containing the name of the stereotype they are instances of.

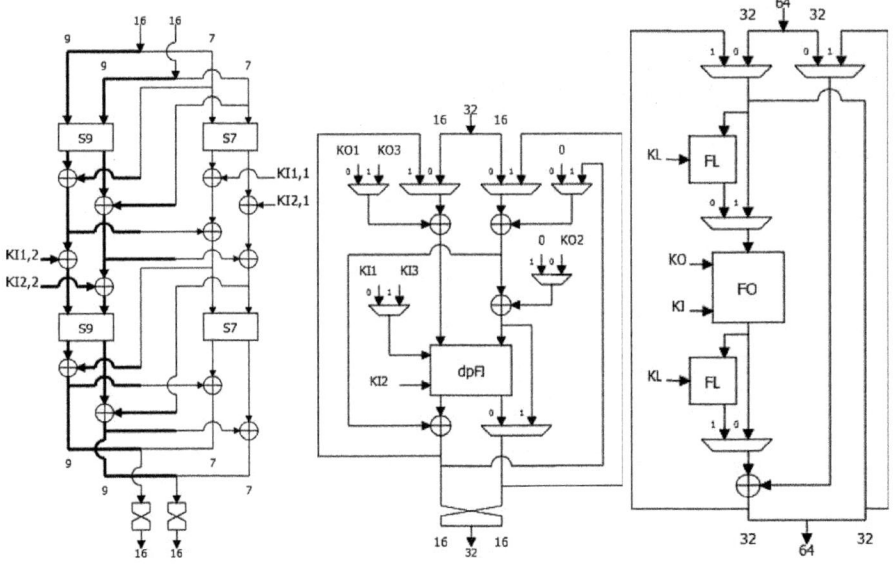

(a) Dual-input FI function   (b) Simplified FO function   (c) Simplified KASUMI structure

Fig. 3. The simplified structure of the KASUMI block cipher (from [4])

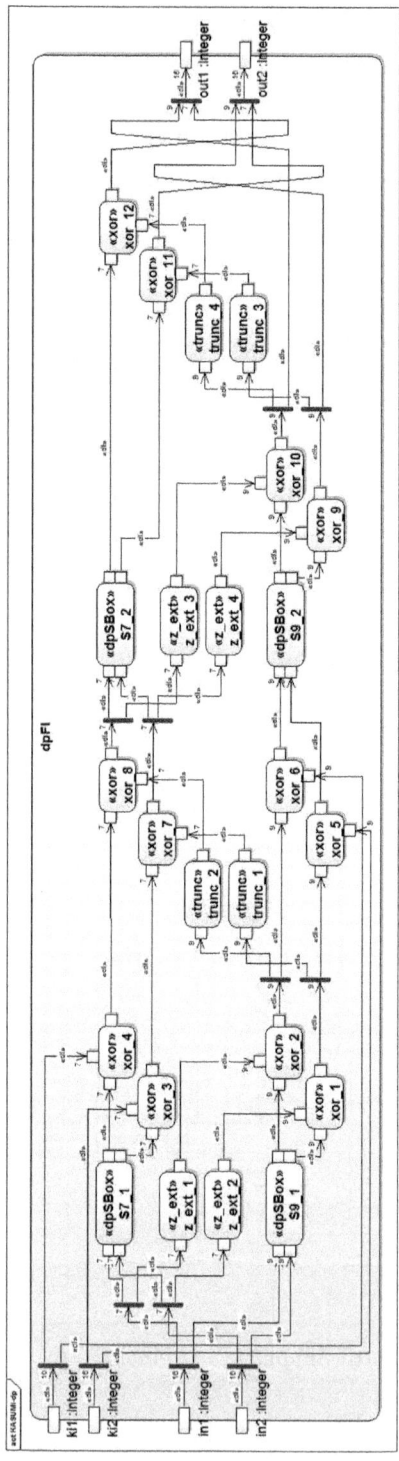

Fig. 4. Block Cipher Diagram for the simplified KASUMI structure

(a) Dual-input FI function

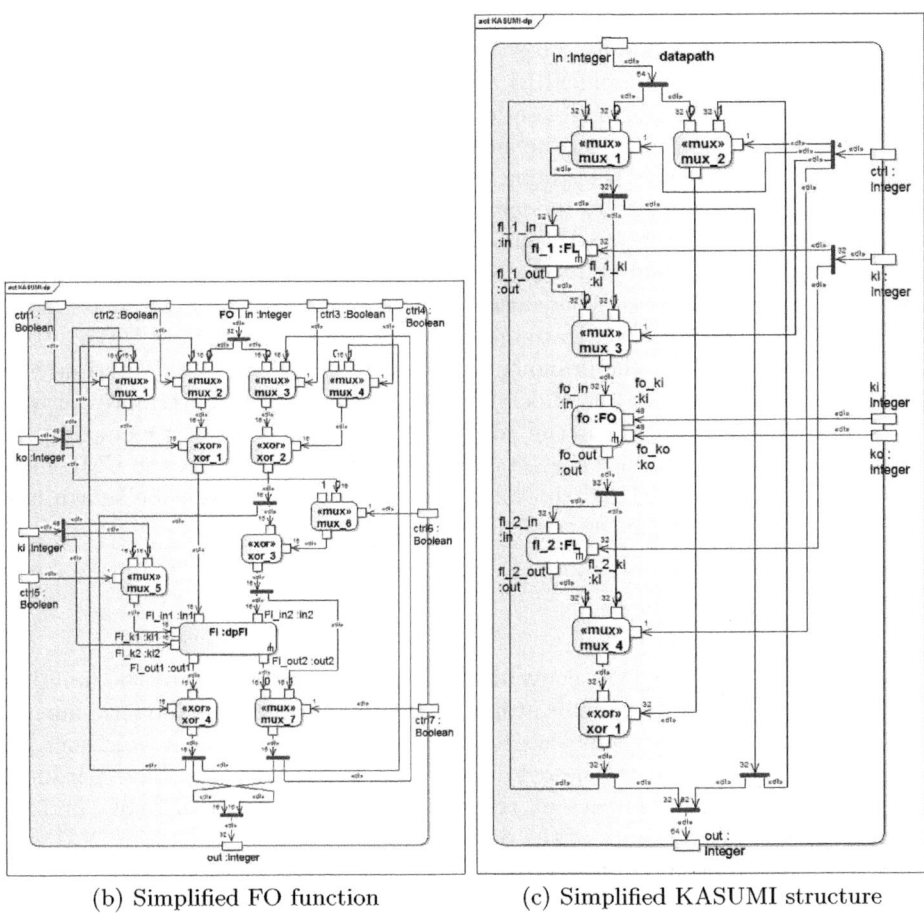

(b) Simplified FO function   (c) Simplified KASUMI structure

Fig. 4. *(continued)*

For example, all of the edges in the diagrams are labeled with the keyword «dl»to indicate that they are instances of the **dl** stereotype and, therefore, model the flow of bit-blocks. The profile is suitable to allow the designer to explore multiple design alternatives in a shorter period of time. The main idea is that the developer builds an initial model of the structure of the block cipher according to his/her architectural strategies, automatically synthesizes VHDL code from it, tests this code using a number of standard test benches, and computes the parameters of interest (performance, power consumption or area) to validate the design. If something goes wrong, or if the designer conceives a different architecture for the block cipher, it is always possible to directly manipulate the UML model to correct errors or to reorganize the architecture of the model, and then perform the test cycle again. The expectation is that handling domain-specific UML modeling elements and having a complete view of the design will be more productive than sketching the design and then writing the corresponding code in an implementation language like VHDL [9].

The models for the simplified FI and FO components, and for the simplified main Feistel structure, are self-contained and enclosed within an activity modeling element so that each can be subsequently reused by another model. This is the case of the activity containing the dual-input FI function, see Figure 4(a), which is used by the activity modeling the simplified FO function, as shown in Figure 4(b). The dual-input FI sub-activity within the simplified FO activity, denoted by the rake symbol (⋔), receives parameters and returns values through its input and output pins. The control signals expected by the activities in the models can be generated by state machine modeling constructs in UML 2.0.

It is important that the designer assigns correct values to the attributes of the modeling elements in the Block Cipher Diagrams. These attributes provide important information about the configuration of the modeling elements to a code synthesizer to produce correct VHDL code. Depending on the UML modeling tool, the attributes and the values assigned to them might be shown next to each modeling element, as tagged values, or not.

4 Conclusions

This paper has discussed the convenience of being able to describe the functionality of digital hardware systems at higher levels of abstraction and let a number of transformation tools to synthesize an specific implementation from such descriptions, according to the model-driven engineering principle. This paradigm should have a positive impact on the alleviation of design complexity and the increase of the productivity of the developer.

The Block Cipher Profile described in this document is the first step towards the implementation of a design flow that will allow us to specify the structure and behavior of a digital communications system by means of UML 2.0 models, and derive a hardware implementation from the diagrams. One of the principles behind this design flow is the definition of domain-specific modeling languages that provide constructs and abstractions that are closer to the application domain than to the implementation technologies. Due to the extension capabilities of UML 2.0, as well as its graphical nature, we chose this modeling language as the base language for our domain-specific languages.

References

1. 3rd Generation Partnership Program: Universal Mobile Telecommunications System (UMTS), Specification of the 3GPP confidentiality and integrity algorithms, Document 2: Kasumi specification (3GPP TS 35.202 version 7.0.0 Release 7) (2007)
2. Bailey, B., Martin, G., Piziali, A.: ESL Design and Verification. In: A Prescription for Electronic System-Level Methodology, Morgan Kaufmann, San Francisco (2007)
3. Björklund, D., Lilius, J.: From UML Behavioral Descriptions to Efficient Synthesizable VHDL. In: 20th IEEE Norchip Conference. IEEE, Copenhagen (2002)

4. Balderas-Contreras, T., Cumplido, R.: An Efficient FPGA Architecture for Block Ciphering in Third Generation Cellular Network. In: Technical Conference of The International Embedded Solutions Event, Santa Clara, California (2004)
5. Balderas-Contreras, T., Cumplido, R.: High Performance Encryption Cores for 3G Networks. In: 42nd Annual ACM IEEE Design Automation Conference, pp. 240–243. ACM, New York (2005)
6. Flynn, M.J., Hung, P.: Microprocessor Design Issues: Thoughts on the Road Ahead. IEEE Micro 25(3), 16–31 (2005)
7. Kent, S.: Model Driven Engineering. In: Butler, M., Petre, L., Sere, K. (eds.) IFM 2002. LNCS, vol. 2335, pp. 286–298. Springer, Heidelberg (2002)
8. Object Management Group: OMG Unified Modeling Language (OMG UML) Superstructure V2.1.2. OMG Document Number: formal/2007-11-02 (2007)
9. Picek, R., Strahonja, V.: Model Driven Development - Future or Failure of Software Development? In: Conference on Information and Intelligent Systems, Croatia (2007)
10. Riccobene, E., Scandura, P., Rosti, A., Bocchio, S.: A UML 2.0 Profile for SystemC. Technical report, ST Microelectronics (2005)
11. Semiconductor Industry Association: International Technology Roadmap for Semiconductors. Design Chapter (2007)

Towards Model Driven Tool Interoperability: Bridging Eclipse and Microsoft Modeling Tools

Hugo Brunelière, Jordi Cabot, Cauê Clasen, Frédéric Jouault, and Jean Bézivin

AtlanMod (INRIA - École des Mines de Nantes) – France
{hugo.bruneliere,jordi.cabot,caue.avila_clasen}@inria.fr,
{frederic.jouault,jean.bezivin}@inria.fr

Abstract. Successful application of model-driven engineering approaches requires interchanging a lot of relevant data among the tool ecosystem employed by an engineering team (e.g., requirements elicitation tools, several kinds of modeling tools, reverse engineering tools, development platforms and so on). Unfortunately, this is not a trivial task. Poor tool interoperability makes data interchange a challenge even among tools with a similar scope. This paper presents a model-based solution to overcome such interoperability issues. With our approach, the internal schema/s (i.e., metamodel/s) of each tool are explicited and used as basis for solving syntactic and semantic differences between the tools. Once the corresponding metamodels are aligned, model-to-model transformations are (semi)automatically derived and executed to perform the actual data interchange. We illustrate our approach by bridging the Eclipse and Microsoft (DSL Tools and SQL Server Modeling) modeling tools.

1 Introduction

Development of a software system involves the collaboration of many developers with different roles (managers, analysts, designers, programmers,...) employing various tools (from project management tools, as Microsoft Project, to tools for requirements elicitation, as DOORS or even Excel, modeling tools as EMF and Microsoft DSL Tools, and development IDEs among many others).

Clearly, a key aspect for this collaboration is proper interoperability in the tool ecosystem. Interoperability is the ability of two (or several) tools to exchange information and thus to use the exchanged information [11][22]. Interoperability is required in several scenarios: forward engineering, reverse and round-trip engineering, tool and language evolution (to address backward compatibility with previous versions) and, for instance, collaborative development, where several subteams may work on separate views of the system using different tools (e.g., modeling tools) that must be later merged.

Unfortunately, interoperability is also a challenging problem that requires addressing both syntactic and semantic issues since each tool may use a different syntactic format to store its information but, more importantly, use its own internal schema to represent and manipulate such information, most likely different from the one expected by other tools. Therefore, trying a manual solution is error-prone and very time-consuming, and it is hardly reusable even when using a similar set of tools. Instead of ad-hoc solutions, a generic set of bridges between the tools should be provided. Each bridge should ensure data-level interoperability (i.e., metadata/data interchange) and operational-level interoperability (i.e., behavior interchange) for two or more tools, independently of the specific project/context in which the tools are used.

In this sense, we propose a model-driven solution for tool interoperability. In general, model-driven interoperability approaches work by first making explicit the internal schema (i.e., metamodel) of each tool. Metamodels are then aligned by matching the related concepts. Finally, model-to-model transformations exploit this matching information to export data (i.e., models from our point of view) created with the first tool to data conforming to the second tool's internal schema. In this paper, we focus on a more general scenario in which tools that need to interoperate are able to manipulate data conforming to different metadata specifications. In this situation, data interoperability needs to interchange not only the data but also the metadata between the tools so that the target tool can correctly interpret the imported information. Therefore, in this case, alignment is not done at the metamodel level but at the metametamodel level. Note that tools that support arbitrary metadata specification necessarily represent metadata using a specific format, or structure, and cannot have fully hard-coded metadata. This format is what we refer to as the metametamodel of the tool, whether it is called a metametamodel in the tool terminology or not, and whether it is explicit in the tool or not. Also note that, in contrast to other approaches, changes on the internal schema/s used by one of the tools do not require updating the bridge.

We believe this more generic approach is required to deal with the complexity of current model-driven engineering (MDE) approaches. As an example, consider the Eclipse Modeling Framework (EMF [3]). When modeling a system with EMF, designers can use several domain-specific languages, each one represented by its corresponding metamodel, to specify different views of the system. When exporting this specification to another tool we need to export both the models and the metamodels the designers have used. We will use this scenario to illustrate our interoperability approach. In particular, we will provide a set of bridges between the Eclipse (EMF) and Microsoft (SQL Server modeling [5] and DSL Tools [4]) modeling technologies. The bridges will allow to automatically open and manipulate in Microsoft tools any model and metamodel defined in EMF and vice-versa.

As we will see, our model-based solution offers several advantages: it is generic (it can be applied to any metamodel and model independent of the domain), reusable (all tools using the same underlying framework/platform, e.g., all tools based on EMF, can reuse the bridges) and extensible (it can be easily adapted to cover new environments and formats since it addresses separately the syntactic and semantic issues). Besides, our approach is easier to integrate with current trends towards the use of modeling in many aspects of the development process.

The rest of the paper is structured as follows. Next section characterizes the problem context for our method and comments the current state of the art in this field. Section 3 introduces the Eclipse-Modeling example. Then, Section 4 presents our approach for data-level interoperability and applies it to create the Eclipse-DSL Tools bridge. Section 5 repeats the process for the Eclipse-SQL Server Modeling bridge highlighting how both bridges are built following the same generic architecture. Operational-level interoperability is commented in Section 6. Finally, we explain the tool support in Section 7 and the conclusions and further work in Section 8.

2 Problem Definition

The interoperability problem has been widely addressed in the literature (see [23,19] for existing surveys) but it is still far from being solved. For instance, the OMG has recently created the *Architecture Ecosystem Special Interest Group* to discuss this same problem.

Previous approaches tried to handle this problem by connecting the tools' APIs (e.g., [20]) or interfaces (e.g., [7]). Approaches of this kind, operating at the API-level, may notably make use of the facade pattern. However, this low-level view of tools was too limited to achieve real data interoperability. With the advent of MDE, new proposals have realized about the benefits of looking at the interoperability problem at a higher abstraction level [10] and now follow a model-based approach in which interoperability is specified at the (meta)model level: the internal metamodels of both tools are explicited and aligned and this information is used to drive the interchange of information between them.

Nevertheless, most of these approaches (including our previous experiments in this area) focus on an ad hoc solutions for two concrete tools [16,9,18,21,15,24]. The exceptions are [17] that proposes some generic patterns that facilitate a (manual) metamodel alignment based on the use of ontologies (under the assumption that integration of ontology-annotated metamodels is easier) and [8] and [6] that focus on the interoperability of modeling tools through the use of a *bus* that provides several predefined data interchange and conversion services.

Moreover, all these approaches assume that tools have a fixed metamodel (e.g., UML modeling tools only accept models conforming to the UML metamodel). This is not the case anymore. With the rise of MDE, more and more development tasks involve manipulating models conforming to different metamodels and created using generic tools able to handle several metamodels at the same time. Typical examples are the Eclipse and Microsoft modeling tools. As part of the definition of the working environment, the designer can define the metamodel to work with and then create models conforming to that metamodel. Therefore, data interchange for these tools involves bridging both the models and the metamodels at the same time.

In this sense, our approach provides a more general solution to the tool interoperability problem by allowing data interchange between tools with variable metamodels. Once the bridge has been built, metamodels and models can be automatically interchanged between the tools. Adding new metamodels does not require extending the bridge. Besides, as we will see our approch is fully model-driven and separates in different steps the processing of the syntactic and semantic aspects of the bridge. Instead many existing approaches mix both transformations which impairs the reusability of the bridge. In addition to this, many of the interoperability scenarios cited above could be expressed as a specific instance of our approach (where the variable metamodels would be just the specific metamodel of the tool) and benefit from (parts of) it.

3 Motivating Example

As a concrete example of the problem previously detailed in Section 2, we consider in this paper bridging the *Eclipse Modeling Framework* (EMF) [3] with two different Microsoft modeling environments: *Microsoft DSL Tools* [4] and *Microsoft SQL Server Modeling* [5]. This is actually a quite common interoperability scenario: these three modeling environments overlap in many aspects, in terms of both concepts and capabilities, and are becoming increasingly popular. Therefore, it is likely that many projects need to import/export metamodels (i.e., metadata) and corresponding models (i.e., raw data) from one environment to the other. This can occur for instance when the base platform has to be changed and the related legacy (meta)models must be reused. A collaborative work, in which both environments are being used at the same time and some specified models need to be merged accordingly, is another potential situation where such interoperability is required.

More pragmatically, the goal of our bridges is to allow metamodels and models built or generated in EMF to be manipulated in both Microsoft modeling environments and vice-versa. We provide here short descriptions of these three different environments.

The *Eclipse Modeling Framework* [3] is the well-known reference modeling infrastructure when developing under and for the Eclipse platform. It provides an explicit metametamodel, named *Ecore*, as well as the corresponding standard runtime, serialization and code generation features for the designed metamodels and models to be exploited. See, for instance, the *PetriNet* metamodel along with a sample model conforming to that metamodel created using EMF (cf. Fig. 1). All the Eclipse modeling tools are based on EMF such as model-to-model (M2M) transformation tools (e.g., ATL [14] used to implement the bridges), model-to-text (M2T) transformation tools, graphical or textual model editors, etc.

The *Microsoft DSL Tools* [4] are part of the Visual Studio SDK dedicated to the customization of the Visual Studio platform (largely based on the .NET framework) for specific needs or domains. DSL Tools aim more particularly at providing facilities for building graphical Domain-Specific Languages (DSLs) and corresponding editors, i.e., modeling tools. Contrary to EMF, this environment is based on an implicit metametamodel which is somehow internally hard-coded by APIs and corresponding serialization XML Schema. It also comes with code generation capabilities from the designed models.

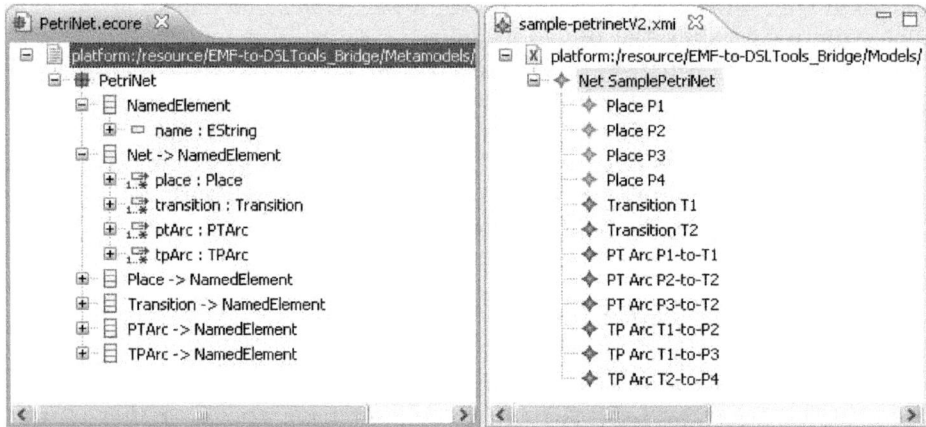

Fig. 1. Simple PetriNet metamodel in Ecore and corresponding sample model (EMF)

Microsoft SQL Server Modeling (SSM) [5], formerly "Oslo", is the latest modeling environment developed by Microsoft and targets the building of data-driven tools. This environment is based on the 'M" modeling language whose *MSchema* part is a declarative language to design domain models (or metamodels). The other parts of this language allow defining corresponding textual concrete syntaxes for DSLs as well as concrete data models (models). SSM also features a customizable tool, named "Quadrant", allowing to interact between the available models and the actual data (i.e., the databases).

In the remainder of this paper, we will focus on the possible bridges between EMF and these two Microsoft environments. Bridging the Eclipse and Microsoft worlds opens the door to import/export into/from Microsoft all (meta)models specified with any modeling tool built on top of EMF: interoperability is thus possible between many different tools at the same time. We will see the results of porting our PetriNet metamodel and sample model as an example of the application of our method.

4 Approach Presentation

This section introduces our model-driven approach for tool interoperability. First, we present the high-level architecture of the method. Then, we clarify and describe in detail each individual step, showing how to apply the method to build the bridge between *Eclipse Modeling Framework* and *Microsoft DSL Tools*.

4.1 Overview

Fig. 2 depicts a bridge to manipulate within Tool B data (i.e., models) created with Tool A, or vice-versa. Both considered tools are built upon variable metamodel environments. Therefore, each of these environments defines a metametamodel: metametamodel A used by Tool A, and metametamodel B used by Tool B.

With each tool, a given metamodel (e.g., MM_X on the figure) may be expressed in terms of the metametamodel of that particular environment. Then, models (e.g., $M1$) may be expressed in terms of MM_X. The objective of the bridge is therefore twofold:

1. At metamodel-level, the bridge must enable the transformation of any metamodel conforming to metametamodel A into an equivalent metamodel conforming to metametamodel B, and vice versa. For instance, if MM_X is initially expressed in terms of metametamodel A, then the bridge must automatically create the version of MM_X that conforms to metametamodel B.
2. At model-level, the bridge must enable the transformation of any model defined with Tool A into an equivalent model defined with Tool B, and vice versa. The metamodel of the original model and that of its derived equivalent are themselves equivalent.

The bridge is bidirectional and allows the interchange of models and metamodels in both directions. However, the implementation of the bridge itself must take place inside one of the two environments (in Fig. 2, this bridge is implemented using the environment A)[1]. The main selection criteria is that the selected environment must provide a transformation technology to perform the required adaptations. However, the capabilities of the bridge are independent from the chosen implementation environment.

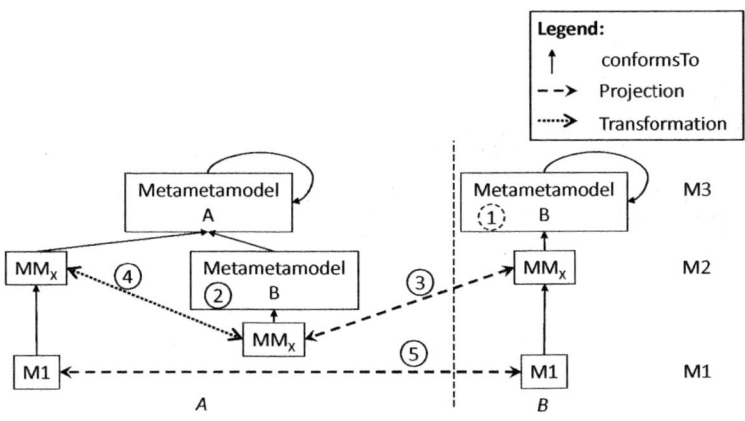

Fig. 2. General bridging approach (overview)

As seen in Fig. 2, there are four main steps (plus an optional one) involved in the process of creating such a bridge. Each step is represented as a circled number. These steps are:

---

[1] We could also use a third environment as a pivot but presenting the approach in that way adds unnecessary complexity.

① **(Optional) Metametamodel discovery.** All variable-metamodel tools necessarily have a metametamodel, in terms of which metamodels are defined. However, this metametamodel may not be explicitly available. In such a case, it is necessary to *discover* that metametamodel from the tool API, its storage schema, etc. For instance, metamodels defined with the tool can be analyzed in order to identify the set of concepts and relationships used to express them. These constitute the metametamodel of the tool. When the metametamodel is readily available (e.g., as is the case for EMF and SSM), this step can be skipped.

② **Transcription.** This step consists in expressing metametamodel B in terms of metametamodel A (in environment A). This has first to be done manually. However, as a metametamodel conforms to itself, the approach may be bootstrapped and this may be re-generated using the bridge once established.

③ **Syntactic translation.** At this step, the syntactic differences between Tool A and Tool B are solved by transcribing the elements of B within the same technical space of A, i.e., by switching from environment B to A in order to use the same kind of concrete syntax. As seen in Fig. 2, the metamodel in Tool B is re-expressed as an instance of the metametamodel B rewritten within Tool A. Therefore, this is a purely syntactic re-expression we call *projection*, since the structure of elements of B has not changed.

④ **Semantic alignment.** At this step, we cannot yet import models of Tool B in Tool A (and vice-versa) since we cannot have more modeling levels in A, according to the OMG metamodeling architecture. Therefore, we need first to express the metamodel of Tool B as a native metamodel in environment A, which conforms to the corresponding metametamodel of A. This implies a semantic adaptation between the metametamodels of A and B, which is actually realized by *transformations*. These transformations allow to import/export any metamodel between A and B. This step may be realized with the assistance of matching tools or not.

⑤ **Data interchange.** Once this is done, the previous (semantic alignment) information is used as well to generate the *transformations* that actually imports models from B to A and vice-versa. Note that complementary *projections* similar to those of the *Syntactic Translation* step are also required to allow exchanging models between A and B. This bridge is generic: even if Tool B changes its metamodel, there is no need to modify the bridge since the mappings will automatically support importing B models (with the new metamodel) into Tool A.

The important characteristics behind the proposed approach are its genericity, extensibility and reusability:

- **Genericity** because it can be applied on any metamodel and model, independently of the selected environment and considered domain or field of application;
- **Extensibility** because the built transformations and projections can be directly extended in order to target other environments or any software in

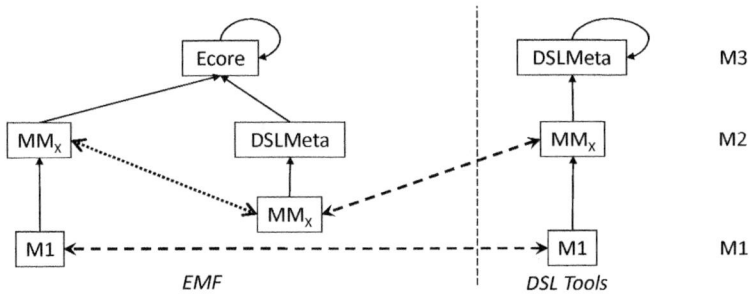

Fig. 3. EMF-DSL Tools conceptual bridge (overview)

general, specially given the separation of the syntactic and semantic alignment steps.
- **Reusability** because 1 - these transformations, projections (or at least parts of them) and metamodels can be directly reused as they are for other purposes and 2 - the bridge can be reused by all tools based on the same metametamodel.

Fig. 3 shows the application of this method to our motivating EMF-DSL Tools interoperability example. In this case, the environment A is EMF and the environment B is DSL Tools. EMF has been chosen as the implementation environment because of the several evolved transformation technologies available, such as ATL [14] for model-to-model transformation. Fig. 3 also shows that EMF has an explicit metametamodel named *Ecore* while DSL Tools has an implicit one we arbitrarly name *DSLMeta*. As an example, consider a PetriNet modeling tool in EMF (Tool A) and its equivalent in DSL Tools (Tool B). Each of these two tools is based on an explicit PetriNet metamodel, which conforms to its corresponding metametamodel. The goal is to be able to automatically exchange PetriNet models between the PetriNet EMF modeling tool and the similar DSL Tools one.

In the next subsections, we provide more details on the step-by-step application of our MDE approach to this concrete example. As we will see, for some steps, it is useful to split them into substeps that improve the modularity of our approach and reduce the complexity of each single step. This depends on the syntactic and semantic distance between the tools to be bridged and it is optional since it is always possible to built the bridge in just the five steps described above.

4.2 Metametamodel Discovery

In our scenario, this optional step is required as the metametamodel of DSL Tools is not explicitly specified. There are currently no fully automated solutions for discovering it. Thus, this has to be performed manually by using the metamodel examples we can find, but also the available documentation and APIs.

4.3 Transcription

In our case, this step requires defining metametamodel *DSLMeta* as a metamodel which conforms to metametamodel *Ecore* in EMF, as shown on Fig. 3. This is a manual step but usually a simple one since many metametamodels share the same basic conceptual elements.

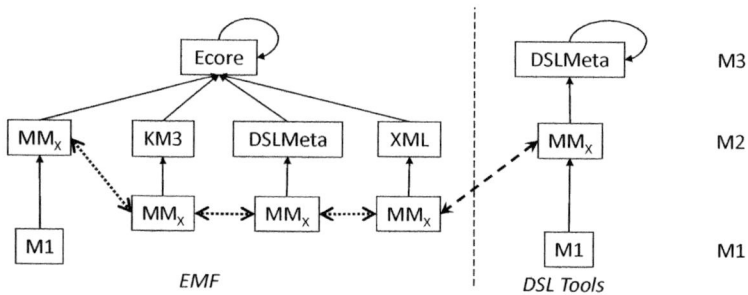

Fig. 4. EMF-DSL Tools metamodel-level bridge (overview)

4.4 Syntactic Translation

Then, we need to be able to express our PetriNet metamodel from DSL Tools as a model conforming to this newly defined *DSLMeta* metamodel in EMF. As shown in Fig. 4 (right), this has been implemented using an intermediate substep to simplify the process. Because the serialization format used by the DSL Tools is XML, we can first automatically *inject* the content of the XML document storing the PetriNet metamodel (in DSL Tools) into a model which conforms to a standard structural *XML* metamodel (note that the inverse operation is of course also possible). At this point, our DSL metamodel is already expressed as a EMF model but conforming to the XML metamodel. Therefore, the second step is to define the model transformation that generates the corresponding version of the model that conforms to the DSLMeta metametamodel in EMF created in the previous step. Using XML as a pivot metamodel simplifies the projection of the PetriNet metamodel in EMF.

4.5 Semantic Alignment

The previously projected PetriNet metamodel can be considered as the precise representation of the initial PetriNet metamodel in DSL Tools. However, this metamodel is not yet conforming to Ecore, i.e., it is not a real metamodel from an EMF point of view (in fact, for EMF, this metamodel is regarded as a simple terminal model, an instance of the DSL Tools EMF metamodel) and cannot be used by metamodeling tools using EMF. The objective of this step is to be able to get a native PetriNet metamodel in *Ecore* from this model and vice-versa, as shown in Fig. 4 (left).

Again, this step uses an intermediate representation to reduce the semantic gap. First, this *DSLMeta* PetriNet metamodel is transformed into a model which conforms to the *KM3* metamodel. Aligning DSL Tools and KM3 is easier than directly aligning DSL Tools and EMF. Furthermore, we already have existing KM3-Ecore converters that take the KM3 model and re-expresses it as a native Ecore metamodel, and vice versa.

At the end of this step, we have a metamodel-level bridge that may now be automatically reused to any metamodel specified in DSL Tools in EMF and the other way round.

4.6 Data Interchange

Now that we have our PetriNet metamodel available in both the EMF and DSL Tools environments, we want the two associated PetriNet modeling tools to be able to interoperate exchanging PetriNet models. Fig. 5 presents how this has been concretely realized.

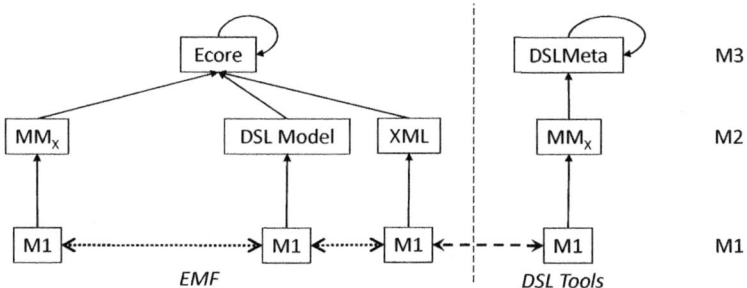

Fig. 5. EMF-DSL Tools model-level bridge (overview)

Similarily to the metamodel-level bridge (i.e., because the serialization format used by the DSL Tools is XML at both levels), the PetriNet sample models in DSL Tools are converted as first *XML* and then *DSLModel* models in EMF and vice-versa. The *DSLModel* metamodel is introduced in order to decouple concrete syntax (i.e., *XML*), and metamodel-independant abstract syntax. This metamodel represents the graph structure used in DSL Tools independently of any metamodel. This corresponds to the *projection* phase between the two different environments.

The *transformation* phase itself is separated into two distinct parts, which makes it fully generic (i.e., independent from the used metamodel). First, the transformation itself is (semi)automatically generated from the alignment information used in the previous step. Then, the transformation is added to the overall transformation chain for effectively building the output terminal model from the source one. Only parts of the transformation that are metamodel-dependant are automatically generated. Metamodel-independant parts are written by a developer once for each bridge. They are then reused for every metamodel to which the bridge is applied. Generated and manually written transformation parts are typically composed by chaining them.

This way, we can apply the generated PetriNet-DSLModel mapping transformations in order to finalize the bridge and interchange PetriNet models (coming from either EMF or DSL Tools).

In this section, our generic MDE approach for tool interoperability has been introduced and directly used on our first motivating example. The next section demonstrates the genericity and applicability of our solution by considering a second example: bridging EMF and SQL Server Modeling.

5 Bridging Eclipse and SQL Server Modeling

The generic interoperability method presented in the previous section (cf. Section 4) can be applied to make interoperate many different platforms and their corresponding tools. As a second example, we briefly describe in this section how we can use our method to build an *EMF-SQL Server Modeling* bridge. To do so, we follow again the same steps we considered for the creation of the *EMF-DSL Tools* bridge.

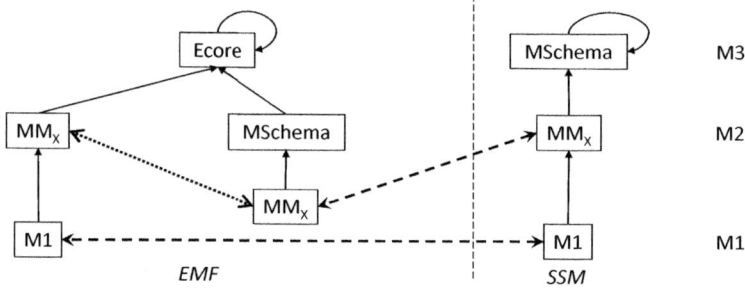

Fig. 6. EMF-SSM theoretical bridge (overview)

Fig. 6 presents the abstract view of this bridge in this specific case. We consider here *MSchema*, i.e., the part of the "M" language dedicated to metamodeling (cf. Section 3), as the SSM metametamodel. As the situation is roughly equivalent to the *EMF-DSL Tools* bridge one, as shown from Fig. 3, we do not provide more insights on this overall view.

Fig. 7 gives more concrete details on the metamodel-level bridge. Again, the architecture is roughly the same as in the *EMF-DSL Tools* bridge: *KM3* is used as a pivot metamodel which allows directly reusing the available Ecore-KM3 converters, while the actual mapping between the two metametamodels is realized by the *KM3-to-MSchema* transformation. The only difference is that, for this bridge, we are not using XML for metamodel/model serialization since the format used by SSM is not XML-based but text-based. The use of the *XML* metamodel as an intermediate step is thus not required: a textual modeling tool

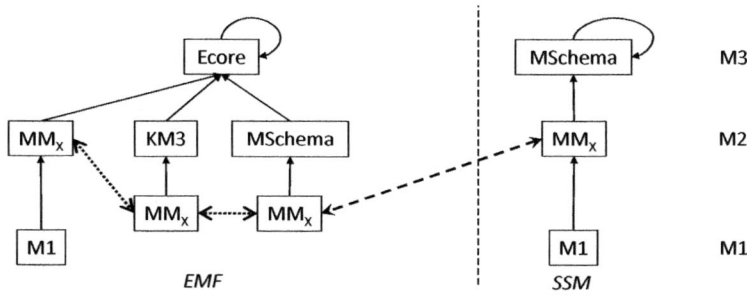

Fig. 7. EMF-SSM metamodel-level bridge (overview)

can be directly applied to switch between a textual file and the corresponding metamodel/model, and vice versa. For this purpose, we use the TCS [13] (Textual Concrete Syntax) tool.

6 Operational-Level Interoperability

So far, we have focused on the data-interoperability problem. The bridges presented in the previous section enable sharing models among the tools, including the interchange of transformation models, i.e., models that define model transformations between source and target (meta)models. However, the simple exchange of a transformation model is a necessary but not sufficient condition to achieve operational-level interoperability. The additional requirement is that the target tool includes a transformation engine able to process the information contained in the transformation model and execute the corresponding transformation.

In our scenario, operational-level interoperability between Eclipse and Microsoft modeling tools requires creating a new version of the ATL virtual machine (component in charge of executing model-to-model transformations defined using the well-known ATL transformation language [14]) adapted to the Microsoft modeling tools.

The ATL virtual machine is currently written in Java and only accepts (meta) models defined using EMF, KMF [12] or MDR as modeling frameworks. Therefore, porting the ATL virtual machine implies two different steps:

1. Migrating ATL VM to the .NET platform to facilitate its execution from within the Microsoft tools. It would be possible to directly call the Java ATL VM from .NET but this solution loses in efficiency and elegance, requiring the use of both Java and .NET Framework virtual machines (and exchanging data between them) at the same time.
2. Integrating support for the SSM and DSL Tools frameworks.

The first step has been already completed. Regarding the second step, the virtual machine has been built from the beginning in a layered structure (see Fig. 8) to facilitate its portability. The model adaptation layer decouples the virtual machine's core from the modeling framework used to define the (meta)models. This

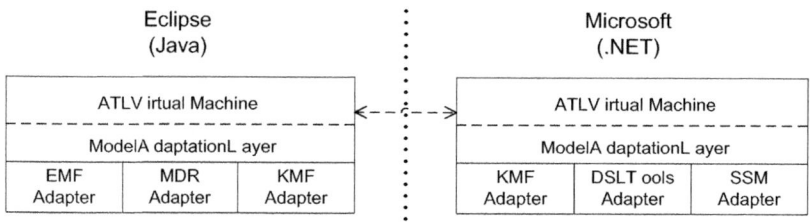

Fig. 8. ATL VM structure (overview)

allows the virtual machine to run on top of new modeling frameworks providing that an adapter for the framework is available. Therefore, adding support for SSM and DSL Tools only requires to create the corresponding adaptors.

7 Tool Support

Several of the bridges described in the previous sections have been actually implemented (see Fig. 9) and are available from [2]. As can be seen in the figure, in some cases, bridges concern both the metamodel and model levels, or just one of these two categories. We are working on completing the full set of bridges.

However, we would like to remark that, in fact, it is not necessary to implement all bridges to achieve full interoperability between each pair of tools. Existing bridges can be used, by transitivity, to connect two tools with no direct bridge between them. For instance, even if the corresponding bridge is not implemented, we can interchange metamodels and models between DSL Tools and SSM using EMF as a pivot tool. This is similar to using a metamodel as a pivot between two other metamodels. However, in this case, we use it for bridges, not single transformations.

As an example of the use of the bridges, Fig. 10 shows the result of automatically generating, for the DSL Tools, the *metamodel* and sample *model* from our *PetriNet* EMF example (Fig. 1).

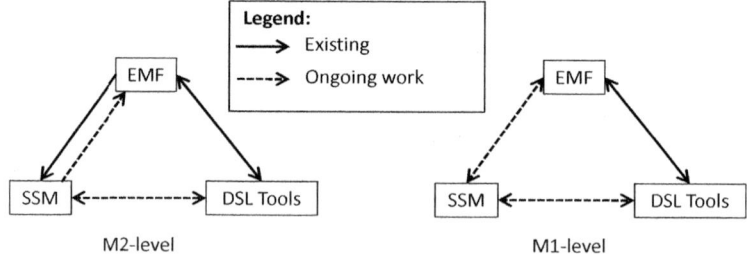

Fig. 9. Existing bridges (overview)

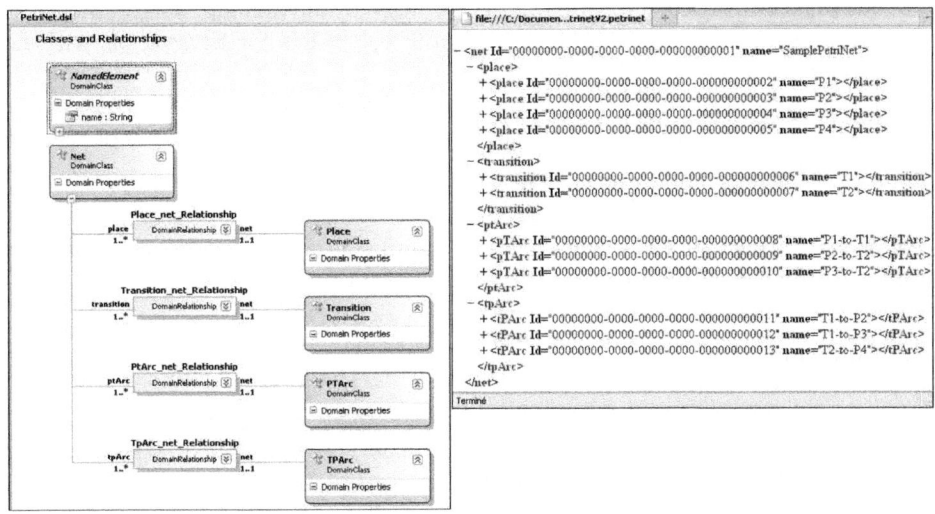

Fig. 10. PetriNet metamodel and sample model in DSL Tools format

Note that this same *PetriNet* metamodel is also available in SSM format. However, the SSM equivalent sample model (in "M") has not been produced since the direct bridge has not been yet implemented at the model-level. But, as commented before, it could be obtained by transtivity of the other bridges.

As part of our tool support, we have also released a first version of the ATL Virtual Machine for .NET [1] that allows direct execution of model transformations within the .NET environment.

8 Conclusions and Future Work

We have presented our approach for tool interoperability, focusing on the most general scenario: interoperability among tools able to handle data (i.e., models) conforming to different metadata (i.e., metamodels). Our method follows a model-driven approach in which the (meta)metamodels of the tools are explicited, aligned and used to (semi)automatically generate the model-to-model transformations that effectively bridge the tools.

Our model-driven view of the problem facilitates the reusability, genericity and extensibility of the bridges in order to cope with the increasing complexity of tool ecosystems. This model-driven view is also especially useful under the current model-driven engineering paradigm where most of the tools already use (meta)models as first-class entities.

There are several directions in which we plan to continue this work. First, we plan to improve our proof of concept by completing the implementation of all bridges between Eclipse and Microsoft modeling tools (including a bridge between the two Microsoft tools themselves) and extending them with full support for operational-level interoperability as well. Second, we would like to improve the automation of the interoperability process by advancing, for instance, in the automatic discovery of metamodels from tool APIs for those tools with no explicit metamodel. Finally, we plan to study different "instantiations" of our generic architecture to see how it can be optimized depending on the specific pair of technical spaces (e.g., XML, grammar-based, modeling-based) of the two tools to bridge.

Acknowledgments. The present work has been supported by the IST-FP6 MODELPLEX and the ITEA2 OPEES European projects.

References

1. AmmA.NET, http://www.emn.fr/z-info/atlanmod/index.php/AmmADotNet
2. Eclipse-Microsoft Bridges Implementations, http://docatlanmod.emn.fr/Eclipse-Microsoft_Bridges/Implementations/
3. Eclipse Modeling Framework (EMF), http://www.eclipse.org/modeling/emf/
4. Microsoft Domain-Specific Language (DSL) Tools, http://msdn.microsoft.com/fr-fr/library/bb126235.aspx
5. Microsoft SQL Server Modeling Technologies, http://msdn.microsoft.com/en-us/data/default.aspx
6. Open tool Integration Framework, http://www.escherinstitute.org/Plone/frameworks/otif
7. Bao, Y., Horowitz, E.: A new approach to software tool interoperability. In: SAC 1996: Proc. of the 1996 ACM Symposium on Applied Computing, pp. 500–509. ACM, New York (1996)
8. Blanc, X., Gervais, M.-P., Sriplakich, P.: Model bus: Towards the interoperability of modelling tools. In: Aßmann, U., Aksit, M., Rensink, A. (eds.) MDAFA 2003. LNCS, vol. 3599, pp. 17–32. Springer, Heidelberg (2004)
9. Didonet Del Fabro, M., Bézivin, J., Valduriez, P.: Model-driven tool interoperability: An application in bug tracking. In: Meersman, R., Tari, Z. (eds.) OTM 2006. LNCS, vol. 4275, pp. 863–881. Springer, Heidelberg (2006)
10. Elvester, B., Hahn, A., Berre, A.-J., Neple, T.: Towards an interoperability framework for model-driven development of software systems. In: Proc. of the 1st Int. Conf. on Interoperability of Enterprise Software and Applications, San Diego United States, pp. 409–420. Springer, Heidelberg (2005)
11. Geraci, A.: IEEE Standard Computer Dictionary: Compilation of IEEE Standard Computer Glossaries. The Institute of Electrical and Electronics Engineers Inc. (1991)
12. Jouault, F., Bézivin, J., Barbero, M.: Towards an advanced model-driven engineering toolbox. ISSE 5(1), 5–12 (2009)
13. Jouault, F., Bézivin, J., Kurtev, I.: TCS: a DSL for the Specification of Textual Concrete Syntaxes in Model Engineering. In: GPCE 2006: Proc. of the 5th Int. Conf. on Generative programming and Component Engineering, pp. 249–254 (2006)
14. Jouault, F., Kurtev, I.: Transforming Models with ATL. In: Bruel, J.-M. (ed.) MoDELS 2005. LNCS, vol. 3844, pp. 128–138. Springer, Heidelberg (2006)
15. Kern, H., Kuhne, S.: Model interchange between aris and eclipse emf. In: 7th OOPSLA Workshop on Domain-Specific Modeling at OOPSLA 2007 (2007)

16. Kern, H., Kuhne, S.: Integration of microsoft visio and eclipse modeling framework using m3-level-based bridges. In: Proc. of the 2nd ECMDA Workshop on Model-Driven Tool and Process Integration (2009)
17. Kramler, G., Kappel, G., Reiter, T., Kapsammer, E., Retschitzegger, W., Schwinger, W.: Towards a semantic infrastructure supporting model-based tool integration. In: GaMMa 2006: Proc. of the 2006 Int. Workshop on Global integrated model management, pp. 43–46. ACM, New York (2006)
18. Moalla, N., Chettaoui, H., Ouzrout, Y., Noel, F., Bouras, A.: Model-Driven Architecture to enhance interoperability between product applications. In: Int. Conf. on Product Lifecycle Management (PLM 2008), Séoul Corée, République de (July 2009)
19. Ossher, H., Harrison, W.H., Tarr, P.L.: Software engineering tools and environments: a roadmap. In: ICSE - Future of SE Track, pp. 261–277 (2000)
20. Sim, S.E.: Next generation data interchange: Tool-to-tool application program interfaces. In: WCRE 2000: Proc. of the 7th Working Conf. on Reverse Engineering (WCRE 2000), Washington, DC, USA, p. 278. IEEE Computer Society, Los Alamitos (2000)
21. Sun, Y., Demirezen, Z., Jouault, F., Tairas, R., Gray, J.: A model engineering approach to tool interoperability. In: Gašević, D., Lämmel, R., Van Wyk, E. (eds.) SLE 2008. LNCS, vol. 5452, pp. 178–187. Springer, Heidelberg (2009)
22. Thomas, I., Nejmeh, B.A.: Definitions of tool integration for environments. IEEE Softw. 9(2), 29–35 (1992)
23. Wicks, M.N., Dewar, R.G.: Controversy corner: A new research agenda for tool integration. J. Syst. Softw. 80(9), 1569–1585 (2007)
24. Zhang, T., Jouault, F., Bézivin, J., Li, X.: An mde-based method for bridging different design notations. ISSE 4(3), 203–213 (2008)

Aspect-Oriented Business Process Modeling with AO4BPMN

Anis Charfi[1], Heiko Müller[1], and Mira Mezini[2]

[1] SAP Research CEC Darmstadt
Darmstadt, Germany
{first.lastname}@sap.com
[2] Software Technology Group
Darmstadt University of Technology, Germany
lastname@st.informatik.tu-darmstadt.de

Abstract. Many crosscutting concerns in business processes need to be addressed already at the business process modeling level such as compliance, auditing, billing, and separation of duties. However, existing business process modeling languages including OMG's Business Process Modeling Notation (BPMN) lack appropriate means for expressing such concerns in a modular way. In this paper, we motivate the need for aspect-oriented concepts in business process modeling languages and propose an aspect-oriented extension to BPMN called AO4BPMN. We also present a graphical editor supporting that extension.

Keywords: Aspects, BPMN, Business Process Modeling, Aspect-Oriented Modeling.

1 Introduction

Several concerns in business process management are highly relevant from a business perspective such as compliance, auditing, business monitoring, accounting, billing, authorization, privacy, and separation of duties. These concerns need to be addressed already at the business process modeling level and not only at the process implementation and execution levels. However, existing modeling languages including the OMG's Business Process Modeling Notation (BPMN) [15] do not provide appropriate means for modeling such concerns in a modular way. When modeling crosscutting concerns using state of the art languages such as BPMN the following two problems are observed.

First, the model elements that address a certain crosscutting concern such as compliance or billing are scattered across various process models, i.e., they are not localized in a separate well-encapsulated model. This poses several problems of understandability and maintainability as a compliance expert for instance cannot easily see and understand how compliance - as an example - is being addressed across the different business processes of a given organization. Instead he has to understand the whole business process models and figure out which modeling elements are related to compliance and which are not. The same applies when that expert wants to change something related to the crosscutting concern as this requires fully understanding whole process models, finding the activities addressing that concern, and changing them appropriately.

Second, the business process models get tangled as they contain modeling constructs (e.g, activities and events) related to the core busines process and also modeling constructs that address other concerns such as monitoring and billing. These constructs are mixed so that there is no separation of concerns. As a result the business process models become very complex and monolithic, which hampers understandability, maintainability, and reuse.

To address the problems of crosscutting concern modularity in workflow languages, we introduced in [5,3] aspect-oriented workflow languages. These languages provide concepts that are geared toward the modularization of crosscutting concerns such as aspect, pointcut, and advice. Although these concepts have their origins in Aspect-Oriented Programming [11], their incarnation in the context of workflow languages has important differences compared to their incarnation in programming languages as explained in [3]. In [4,6], we presented the design and implementation of the AO4BPEL language, which is an aspect-oriented extension to BPEL, as proof-of-concept for aspect-oriented workflow languages. In that work, we focused on crosscutting concerns at the process execution level. In the current paper, we shift our focus from executable process languages to higher-level business process modeling languages and observe at that level similiar modularity problems. To tackle these problems we propose aspect-orineted business process modeling and present AO4BPMN, which is an aspect-oriented extension to BPMN supporting the modularization of crosscutting concerns. We also present a graphical editor for AO4BPMN.

The remainder of this paper is structured as follows. Section 2 gives some background on BPMN, AOP, and aspect-oriented workflow languages. Section 3 motivates through examples the need for means to modularize crosscutting concerns in business process models and BPMN in particular. Section 4 introduces AO4BPMN, illustrates its use through examples, and shows the AO4BPMN editor. Section 5 discusses related work and Section 6 concludes the paper.

2 Background

In this section we give some background knowledge on the Business Process Modeling Notation, aspect-oriented programming, and aspect-oriented workflow languages.

2.1 Business Process Modeling Notation

The Business Process Modeling Notation (BPMN) [16] is the standard of the Object Management Group (OMG) for the graphical representation of business process models. It aims at providing a business process notation that is readily understandable by business users. This work is based on the latest stable version BPMN1.2.

The graphical objects and relationships of BPMN are categorized in four groups: flow objects, connecting objects, swimlanes, and artifacts. The flow objects (i.e., activities, events, and gateways) define the process behavior. With the connecting objects (i.e., sequence flow, message flow, and association) the modeler can specify the order of the tasks and the interactions between the participants. The swimlanes (i.e., Pools and Lanes) represent participants in a process. The artifacts (i.e., Data object, Group, and Annotation) are the graphical elements for modeling process data and provide supplementary information. Artifacts are the basis of BPMN extensibility as they allow to introduce new language elements.

2.2 Aspect-Oriented Programming

Aspect-Oriented Programming (AOP)[11] is a programming paradigm, which introduces a new unit of modularity called aspect for modularizing crosscutting concerns. There are three key concepts in AOP: *join points*, *pointcuts* and *advice*. Join points are well-defined points in the execution of a program (e.g., method calls). Pointcuts are means to select a set of join points (e.g., select related method execution points). An advice is a piece of crosscutting functionality, which is associated with a pointcut. It can be executed *before*, *after*, or *around* the join points selected by the respective pointcut. The around advice allow to integrate the execution of the intercepted join point. Furthermore, the advice can access the join point context. An aspect consists mainly of pointcuts and advice but it may also define its own fields and methods.

2.3 Aspect-Oriented Workflow Languages

In [5,3], we introduced aspect-oriented concepts to workflow languages to address the problems of crosscutting concern modularity in these languages and called the resulting languages aspect-oriented workflow languages. These languages enable a concern-based decomposition of process specifications and process models. Consequently, the process modeling constructs that belong to some concern are specified in one module: The business process logic is encapsulated in a *process module* whereas crosscutting concerns are encapsulated in *aspect modules* [5] according to the principle of separation of concerns. In [5,3], we defined the concepts of aspect-oriented workflow languages in a generic way independently of any specific workflow language. In [4,6], we presented the design and implementation of AO4BPEL, which is an aspect-oriented workflow language for web service composition.

3 Motivation

To illustrate the issues of crosscutting concerns modularity in business process modeling, we consider in this section a simplified version of the business processes of a tour operator, which sells flights and vacation packages. The tour operator works with specific airlines and hotel chains. It sells the flights offered by its partner airlines but its main business consists in creating vacation packages through the combination of the flight and accommodation offers of the partner airlines and hotel chains.

Fig. 1 shows the flight search and vacation search business processes of the tour operator. These processes start when a customer request message is received. For simplification purposes, we assume that the flight search process interacts with two airline partners (TA and BA) and flight offers are created via the sub-process activity *make flight offers*, which also calculates the price. The vacation search process interacts with a partner airline and a partner hotel chain to find flights and hotels. The sub-process activity *make package offers* in that process combines the results of the flight search and hotel search activities and calculates the price. Both processes end by sending a message to the customer with data about the available offers.

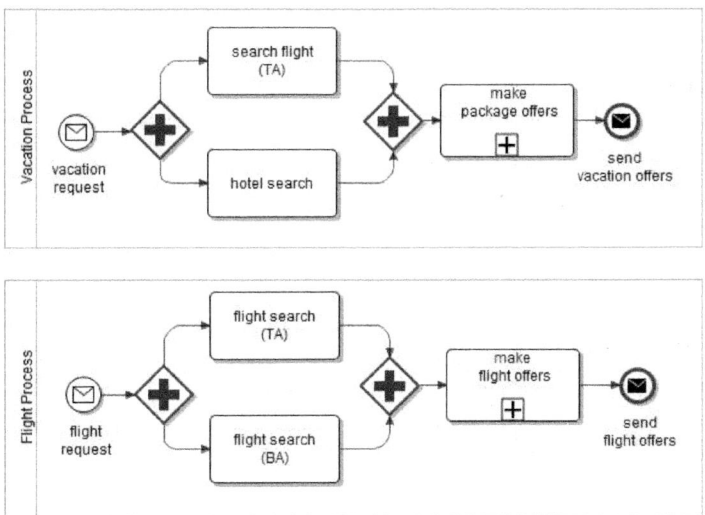

Fig. 1. Processes of a tour operator in BPMN

Next, we focus on two crosscutting concerns in the tour operator context: compliance and monitoring (also called business activity monitoring). To ensure that the customer requests and the creation of offers are compliant with the internal regulations of the tour operator compliance check activities have to be added to both processes. This happens respectively after receiving the customer requests and after creating the offers as shown in Fig. 2. For monitoring the execution time of certain process activities we extend the flight search process and the package search process with activities for respectively starting and stoping a timer before and after each monitored activity as shown in Fig. 3.

Both compliance and business activity monitoring are crosscutting concerns and one sees already the problems of scattering and tangling discussed above. In

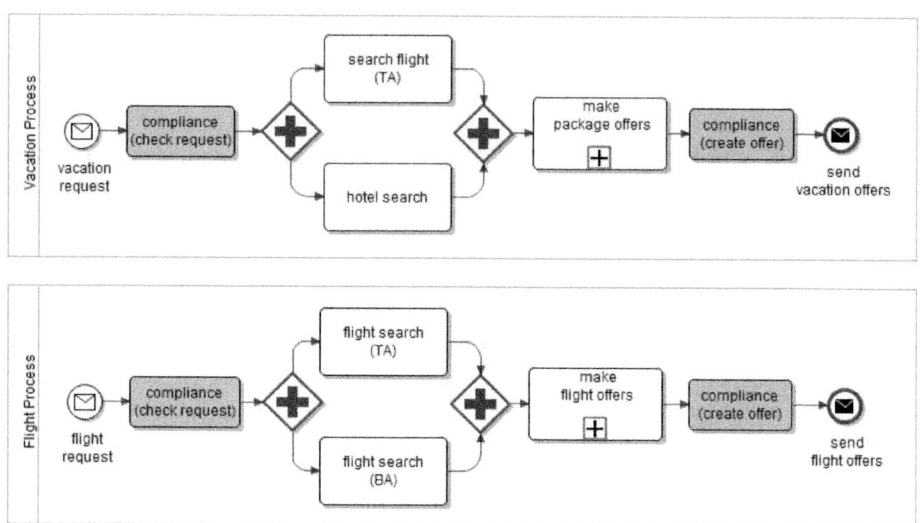

Fig. 2. Compliance cheks in the search processes

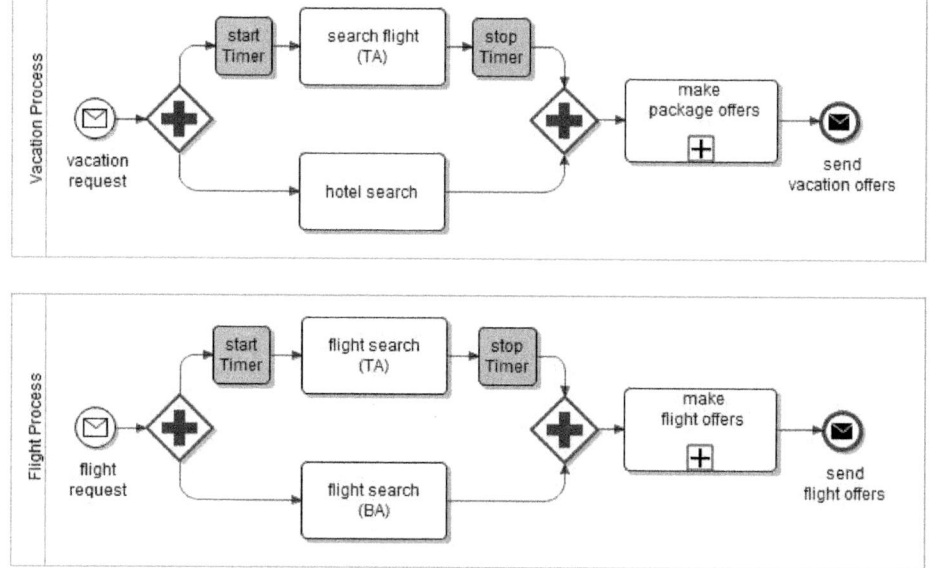

Fig. 3. Monitoring activity execution time

fact, modeling constructs related to compliance for instance are scattered over the two business processes. There is no module that encapsulates all process modeling elements related to this concern, which makes understanding how compliance is been addressed at the tour operator and changing that when needed a quite difficult task. One also observes the problem of tangling as both processes address not only the core process logic but they contain modeling elements addressing other concerns such as compliance and monitoring. This increases the complexity of the business process models and hampers understandability, maintainability, and reuse. These problems are due to the lack of appropriate concepts in business process modeling languages - including BPMN- for modularizing crosscutting concerns.

4 AO4BPMN

In this section we first give an overview of AO4BPMN and then discuss the composition of aspect and proces models. After that we present some examples for illustration and show a graphical editor for AO4BPMN.

4.1 Overview

AO4BPMN is an aspect-oriented extension to BPMN that allows the modularization of crosscutting concerns in business process models such as compliance, accounting, billing, monitoring, authorization, separation of duties, etc.

AO4BPMN was designed according to BPMN extensibility guidelines. BPMN supports extension based on artifacts. These are modeling concepts that allow modelers to add new langugage elements to satisfy a certain need such as the requirements of some vertical domain. BPMN pre-defines three types of artifacts: data objects, text annotations, and groups. These artifacts can be linked to existing flow objects (i.e, activities, events, or gateways) through associations. In our case, we use artifacts to define the aspect-oriented constructs of AO4BPMN.

Next, we introduce the AO4BPMN language concepts in a more detail starting first at the meta-model level and then we present two concrete syntaxes: a) a light-weight one, which uses existing artifacts and BPMN elements to represent the aspect-oriented constructs and b) a heavy-weight one, which proposes new graphical representations for the aspect-oriented constructs. The light-weight syntax allows using AO4BPMN with standard BPMN editors. An editor for the heavy-weight syntax will be presented at the end of this section.

Join Points and Pointcuts. Join points are points in the business process model where modeling elements implementing a crosscutting concern can be integrated. In AO4BPMN, flow objects are the supported join points, e.g., activities and events. There is no special language construct in AO4BPMN to model join points.

A pointcut is a construct that allows the selection of related join points. According to the BPMN extensibility mechanism, we define pointcuts as a new artifact, which optionally has a query attribute. In the light-weight visual syntax of AO4BPMN, pointcuts are represented as data objects that have an associated annotation with the text *Pointcut*. The queries are stored in the document property of the data object. In the heavy-weight syntax, a pointcut is represented by an oval.

The pointcut language is the language used to define pointcuts. We considered three alternative pointcut languages for AO4BPMN.

- **Explicit Pointcut to Join Points Associations.** The first alternative consists in using a simple visual pointcut language by connecting the pointcut to the join point activities via BPMN associations. The problem with this approach is scalability and also the fact that the processes and aspects should be displayed in the same view in order to connect them.
- **A Query-based Pointcut Language.** A quite powerful alternative consists in using a textual query language as pointcut language. For that purpose, one could use existing model query languages such as OCL [13] and QVT [14], which allow to select model elements like activities or events based on their types, their attributes, their associations to data objects, their connections via sequence flow to other join points, etc. The problem with this approach is that BPMN users generally do not have knowledge of model query languages. To address that problem one may define a simple query language where a) activities are selected by specifying their names in addition to the names of their lanes/pools and processes and b) pointcuts are composed with the OR operator to build more complex pointcuts.
- **Annotating the Join Points.** The third alternative consists in adding BPMN text annotations to the join points and defining the pointcut as a simple annotation-based query. As an example, one could add an annotation with the text *monitoring* to all activities for which the execution time should be measured. Then, the pointcut will simply select all activities that have an associated text annotation with the value *monitoring*. Although this alternative would relax the *obliviousness* property [9] of AOP it seems appropriate for BPMN users.

Advice. An advice is a BPMN sub-process that implements some crosscutting logic and may include the special activity *proceed*. In the light-weight syntax it is represented like a standard subprocess but it has an attached text annotation with the text *Advice*. A further optional annotation is used to indicate the advice type. In the heavy-weight syntax it is represented as a rectangle with two parts. The upper part contains the advice name and optionally the type whereas the lower part contains the subprocess activities.

The semantics of the advice is to replace the join points selected by a subprocess that contains the join point activity or event in addition to activities implementing the crosscutting concern. If the join point activity is source or target of sequence or message flows, the sub-process activity becomes the source or target of those flows. The advice is self-contained, which means that no sequence or message flows are allowed between the advice and the other activities of the business process except the join point.

In the advice, a special activity named *Proceed* can be used to integrate the join point in the middle of the advice and to indicate the order of the advice activity with respect to join points. The use a *proceed* inside the advice avoids the need for indicating the advice type (i.e., before, after, or around). It is even possible to define other execution orders according to the different workflow control patterns [21] supported by BPMN. In case the *Proceed* activity is not used the advice type has to be specified.

Aspects. Aspects are elements that modularize the modeling of a certain crosscutting concern. They consist of one or more pointcuts and associated advices. In addition, they may define their own state with data objects. In the lightweight visual syntax aspects are represented by means of a BPMN pool that has an associated text annotation with the text *Aspect*. In the heavy-weight visual syntax aspects are represented as pools that have rounded corners.

4.2 Composition of Aspects and Processes

As the workflow aspect models are separated from the process models an appropriate composition mechanism is needed. In [3], two approaches were proposed for the composition of aspects and workflow processes in aspect-oriented workflow languages: an aspect-aware engine as weaver and weaving through process transformation. As BPMN is a modeling notation only (i.e., not directly executable by an engine) the first composition approach is not applicable in this context. Only the process transformation is feasible for weaving AO4BPMN aspects with BPMN process models.

In the process transformation approch approach a model weaver composes the process and aspects models into new process models. Such as weaver can be implemented using model-to-model transformation techniques. For instance, one could realize such composition mechanism using a two-phase transformation: in the first phase pointcut matching is performed, i.e., the selected join points are discovered (by evaluating the query) and annotated; in the second phase the advice activity is inserted in the processes at the selected join points and according to the advice semantics. The process transformation has also to update the sequence and message flow that starts from or targets the join points as defined by the advice semantics, resolve the data collection constructs by adding associations, and replace special constructs such as the proceed activity by the join points.

This composition approach results in standard BPMN models that can be viewed and manipulated by existing tools. Moreover, with this approach, one may have various versions of the business process at different levels of abstraction (e.g., one would have the base process, which is appropriate for business users, in addition to the base process plus auditing, which is appropriate for auditing experts, base process plus compliance, which is appropriate for compliance experts, etc.). This is quite helpful for understanding the processes and also supports multiple-views with varying abstraction levels for different user groups of BPMN processes.

4.3 Examples

We show two examples illustrating the use of AO4BPMN to model the crosscutting concerns discussed in Section 3. Fig. 4 shows the compliance and monitoring aspects using the light-weight visual syntax of AO4BPMN. The advice of the compliance aspects adds compliance checking activities to the flight search and vacation search processes. The monitoring aspect integrates the monitored activities in the middle of two activities respectively for starting and stopping a timer.

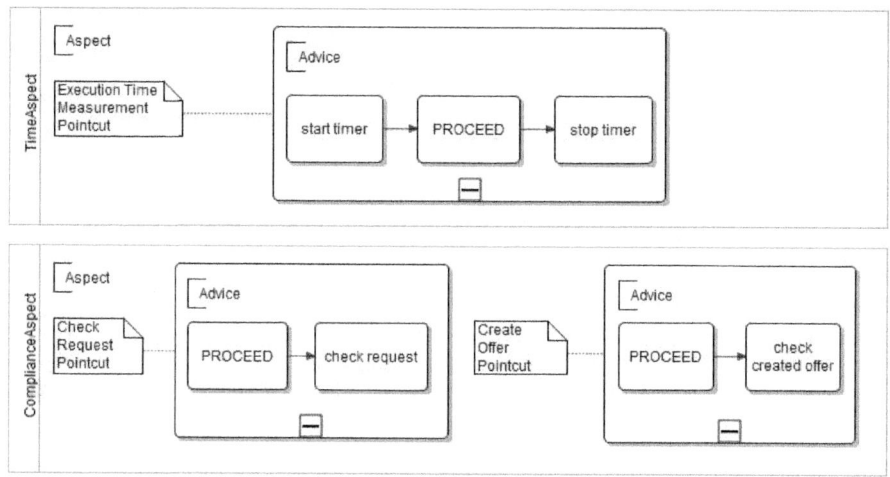

Fig. 4. Aspects in light-weight AO4BPMN visual syntax

Fig. 5 shows the same aspects as the ones shown in Fig.4, but this time using the heavy-weight visual syntax. For this syntax we have implemented an AO4BPMN editor using Eclipse GMF [8].

One observes that when compliance and monitoring concerns are modularized in aspect models the respective logic is no longer scattered across the two business process models. One can easily understand these concerns and how they are addressed in the different business processes of the tour operator through looking only at the respective aspects. Further, the process models are no longer tangled as they address only the core business logic of the process. As a result, understanding and maintaining them becomes easier .

After modulazing the crosscutting concerns compliance and monitoring the respective aspects have to be composed with the business process models. Fig. 6 shows the resulting processes after composing the aspects shown in Fig. 4 with the processes shown in Fig 1.

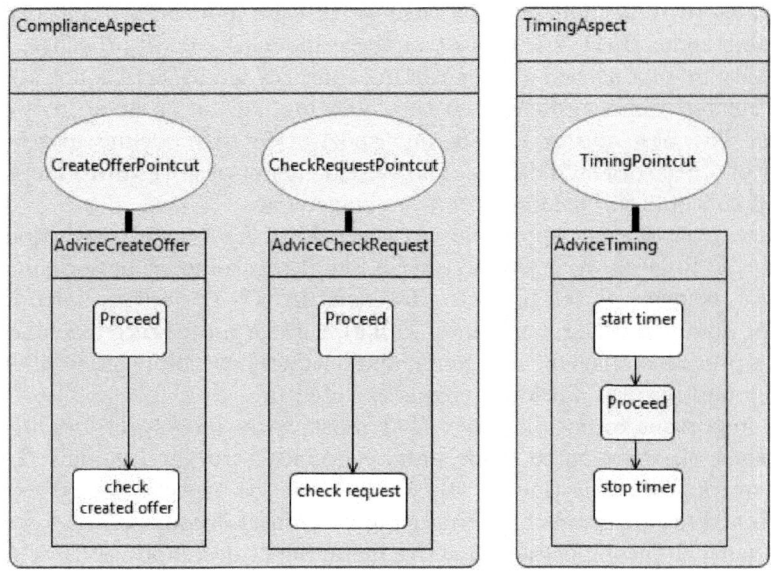

Fig. 5. Aspects in the heavy-weight AO4BPMN visual syntax

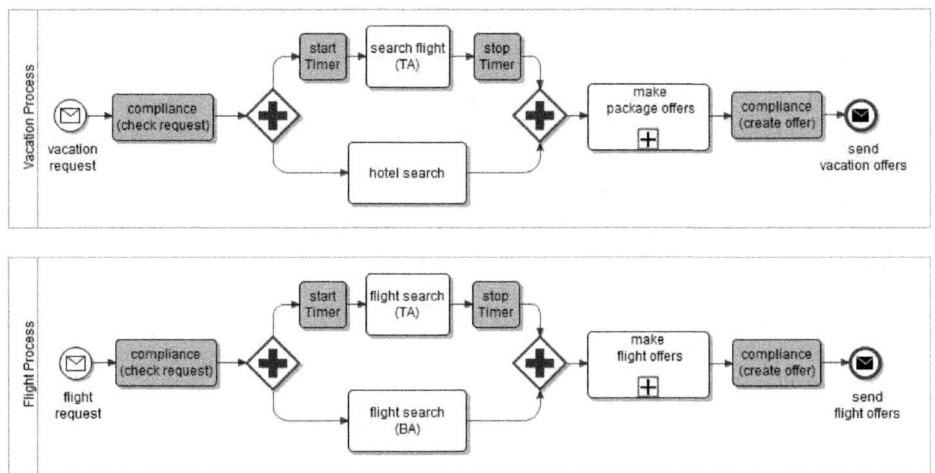

Fig. 6. The resulting processes after composition

5 Related Work

Several works intend to bridge the gap between business process models and the IT level, following the MDA paradigm. E.g., the transformation framework for IBM WebSphere Business Modeler outlined in [12] aims at rapid development of model transformations in combination with quality assurance techniques that enable to refine and refactor business process models towards correct and executable code. However, in most of these model-driven approaches, tackling complexity by modularizing cross-cutting concerns via aspects is not addressed.

The related works presented in the following can be grouped in two major clusters. The first cluster focuses on aspect-oriented modeling mostly in the context of object-oriented design. The second cluster of works introduces aspect-oriented concepts to business process management.

A survey on existing approaches in the field of Aspect-Oriented Modeling is given in [7]. Related work [23,22] can be found regarding aspect-oriented states machines, respectively UML state diagrams. In [17] the author introduces aspects for domain specific languages (DSLs), e.g. for finite state machines in the business process management domain, and outlines how composition filters could be integrated into the workflow engine architecture.

It is important to note however that most works on Aspect-Oriented Modeling target object-oriented models and especially structural models. The most related work to ours is that of [1], which proposes aspect-oriented extensions to UML activity diagrams by introducing horizontal decomposition (as opposed to the vertical decomposition i.e., the hierarchical decomposition). That work defines a UML profile specifying three types of activity nodes where horizontal decomposition can happen: interface nodes, activity nodes and subtraction nodes. Addition nodes are activity nodes that are added to an activity diagram during horizontal composition whereas subtraction nodes are deleted from an activity diagram during that step. An interface node represents a join point at which an advice (i.e., a horizontally decomposed activity diagram) can be integrated into another activity diagram.

In [20], a proposal for combining business process management and Aspect-Oriented Programming is presented. That work proposes weaving a generalized process with participant process aspects. The latter are activities, which can be included in a business process in order to customize it for execution by some resource. That approach is based on the programming language Java and the respective aspect-oriented extension AspectJ [10], i.e., that work does not introduce any aspect-oriented concepts to the BPM or workflow level as aspects are used only at the workflow implementation level, unlike our proposal, which introduces aspect-oriented concepts to BPMN.

In [19], the authors discuss business protocol compliance issues and introduce an aspect-oriented approach to ensure the correct course of collaborative interaction by weaving in services that inserts an individual signature, adds a timestamp, and verifies the order of previous evidences. The proposed interaction enhancement solution however, apart from being bound to the compliance topic, focuses on weaving aspects into BPEL and further deployment artifacts.

In contrast to this, business process modeling is in the focus of the work in [2]. The authors of that short paper propose an Aspect-Oriented Process Modeling Language (AOPML), exemplarily instantiated using the BPMN notation. The authors describe the meta-model of AOPML that is intended to be applicable in combination with any language for modeling processes. With these concepts the modeler can specify crosscutting relationships and joinpoints - however, compared to AO4BPMN, with limited expressiveness; e.g. regarding the advice language, as AOPML does not allow the definition of flexible execution orders (in AO4BPMN enabled by the PROCEED concept), and, additionally, regarding the support for modularization of the process logic that belongs to a certain crosscutting concern and its state, as AOPML does not support the definition of aspects. Furthermore, the authors do not address the topic of enabling the execution of the resulting process models, nor do they provide tool support.

With regard to these issues [18] depicts a more complete solution of aspect-oriented business process modeling in the context of service-oriented architectures (SOAs), named AOBPMN. The author provides both a model transformation targeting BPEL and an aspect-including BPEL engine, the latter being based on AO4BPEL. On the business process modeling level, aspects are integrated by extending the BPMN meta-model with three new notations, called aspect dot, aspect flow, and aspect wrapper. Though the author's AOBPMN is not based on the more commonly used STP BPMN meta-model, these concepts partly correspond to the BPMN extension proposed in this work; e.g. the aspect wrapper is similarly represented as a specialization of a pool. Aspect flows, however, enabling explicit pointcut to join point associations, are not used in AO4BPMN for the reasons given in section 4.

Besides these, and our work on aspectual workflow graphs [3], we are not aware of any other work on aspect-oriented modeling in the business process management and workflow management context. Aspectual workflow graphs define the basic concepts of aspect-oriented workflow languages in a simple way using workflow graphs. The AO4BPMN proposal can be considered as a second step toward aspect-oriented business process modeling. This activity comes in the context of our research on aspect-oriented workflow languages. In [5,3], we defined in the basic concepts of this new class of workflow languages in a generic way. In [4,6], we presented the design and implementation of a specific aspect-oriented workflow language for Web Service composition and namely AO4BPEL, which can be considered as a proof-of-concept.

6 Conclusion

In this paper, we motivated the need for appropriate support for crosscutting concerns in business process modeling languages and introduced an aspect-oriented extension to BPMN called AO4BPMN and which allows the modularization of such concerns. We explained the language concepts and illustrated the use of that extension through examples and presented two concrete syntaxes: a heavy-weight one supported by a special editor and a light-weight one that works with standard BPMN editors. In our future work we will investigate the composition of aspects and process and develop a model weaver for composing AO4BPMN aspects with BPMN process models. Furthermore, we will combine AO4BPMN and AO4BPEL into a wholistic approach to crosscutting concerns in business process management, which spans process modeling and process execution.

Acknowledgments

This work is partly supported by the Project PREMIUM-Services financed by the German Ministry of Education and Research (BMBF). Daniel Bausch has implemented a first version of the AO4BPMN editor in the context of a student project.

References

1. Barros, J.-P., Gomes, L.: Activities as Behaviour Aspects. In: Workshop on Aspect-oriented Modelling (held with UML 2002) (2002)
2. Cappelli, C., Leite, J.C.S.P., Batista, T., Silva, L.: An aspect-oriented approach to business process modeling. In: EA 2009: Proceedings of the 15th workshop on Early aspects, pp. 7–12. ACM, New York (2009)
3. Charfi, A.: Aspect-Oriented Workflow Languages: AO4BPEL and Applications. PhD thesis, Darmstadt University of Technology, Darmstadt, Germany (2007), http://elib.tu-darmstadt.de/diss/000852/
4. Charfi, A., Mezini, M.: Aspect-Oriented Web Service Composition with AO4BPEL. In: Zhang, L.-J., Jeckle, M. (eds.) ECOWS 2004. LNCS, vol. 3250, pp. 168–182. Springer, Heidelberg (2004)
5. Charfi, A., Mezini, M.: Aspect-Oriented Workflow Languages. In: Meersman, R., Tari, Z. (eds.) OTM 2006. LNCS, vol. 4275, pp. 183–200. Springer, Heidelberg (2006)
6. Charfi, A., Mezini, M.: AO4BPEL: An Aspect-Oriented Extension to BPEL. World Wide Web Journal: Recent Advances on Web Services, special issue (March 2007)
7. Chitchyan, R., Rashid, A., Sawyer, P., Garcia, A., Alarcon, M.P., Bakker, J., Tekinerdogan, B., Clarke, S., Jackson, A.: Report synthesizing state-of-the-art in aspect-oriented requirements engineering, architectures and design. Technical report, Lancaster University, AOSD-Europe Deliverable D11, AOSD-Europe-ULANC-9 (May 2005)
8. Eclipse Project. Eclipse Graphical Modelling Framework, http://www.eclipse.org/gmf/
9. Filman, R.E., Friedman, D.P.: Aspect-Oriented Programming is Quantification and Obliviousness. In: Proc. of the Workshop on Advanced Separation of Concerns in conjunction with OOPSLA, October 2000, pp. 21–35 (2000)
10. Kiczales, G., Hilsdale, E., Hugunin, J., Kersten, M., Palm, J., Griswold, W.G.: An Overview of AspectJ. In: Knudsen, J.L. (ed.) ECOOP 2001. LNCS, vol. 2072, pp. 327–353. Springer, Heidelberg (2001)
11. Kiczales, G., Lamping, J., Mendhekar, A., Maeda, C., Lopes, C., Loingtier, J.-M., Irwin, J.: Aspect-oriented programming. In: Aksit, M., Matsuoka, S. (eds.) ECOOP 1997. LNCS, vol. 1241, pp. 220–242. Springer, Heidelberg (1997)
12. Koehler, J., Gschwind, T., Küster, J., Pautasso, C., Ryndina, K., Vanhatalo, J., Völzer, H.: Combining quality assurance and model transformations in business-driven development, pp. 1–16 (2008)
13. Object Management Group. Object Constraint Language 2.0 Final Adopted Specification (October 2003), http://www.omg.org/cgi-bin/doc?ptc/2003-10-14
14. Object Management Group. Meta Object Facility (MOF) 2.0 Query/View/Transformation Specification (November 2005), http://www.omg.org/docs/ptc/05-11-01.pdf

15. Object Management Group. Business Process Modeling Notation (BPMN) 1.0, Final Adopted Specification (February 2006), http://www.bpmn.org/
16. Object Management Group. Business Process Modeling Notation (BPMN) 1.2 (January 2009), http://www.omg.org/spec/BPMN/1.2
17. Schmidmeier, A.: Aspect oriented dsls for business process implementation. In: DSAL 2007: Proceedings of the 2nd workshop on Domain specific aspect languages, p. 5. ACM, New York (2007)
18. Shankardass, A.: The dynamic adaptation of an aspect oriented business process in a service oriented architecture platform. Master's thesis, Athabasca University, Canada (September 2009)
19. Svirskas, A., Courbis, C., Molva, R., Bedzinskas, J.: Compliance proofs for collaborative interactions using aspect-oriented approach. In: Mda4Soa 2007, Modeling, Design, and Analysis for Service-oriented Architecture Workshop, in conjunction with 4th IEEE International Conference on Services Computing, Salt Lake City, USA, July 9-13 (2007)
20. Thompson, S., Odgers, B.: Aspect-Oriented Process Engineering. In: Proc. of the Workshop on Object-Oriented Technology in conjunction with ECOOP (June 1999)
21. van der Aalst, W.M.P., ter Hofstede, A.H.M., iepuszewski, B., Barros, A.P.: Workflow Patterns. Distributed and Parallel Databases 14(1), 5–51 (2003)
22. Whittle, J., Moreira, A., Araújo, J., Jayaraman, P.K., Elkhodary, A.M., Rabbi, R.: An expressive aspect composition language for uml state diagrams. In: MoDELS, pp. 514–528 (2007)
23. Zhang, G., Hölzl, M.M., Knapp, A.: Enhancing uml state machines with aspects. In: Engels, G., Opdyke, B., Schmidt, D.C., Weil, F. (eds.) MODELS 2007. LNCS, vol. 4735, pp. 529–543. Springer, Heidelberg (2007)

A Reflective Approach to Model-Driven Web Engineering

Darren Clowes[1,2], Dimitris Kolovos[3], Chris Holmes[2], Louis Rose[3], Richard Paige[3], Julian Johnson[2], Ray Dawson[1], and Steve Probets[4]

[1] Department of Computer Science, Loughborough University, Leicestershire, UK
[2] BAE Systems, SEIC, Loughborough University, Leicestershire, UK
[3] Department of Computer Science, The University of York, Heslington, York, UK
[4] Department of Information Science, Loughborough University, Leicestershire, UK

Abstract. A reflective approach to model-driven web engineering is presented, which aims to overcome several of the shortcomings of existing generative approaches. The approach uses the Epsilon platform and Apache Tomcat to render dynamic HTML content using Epsilon Generation Language templates. This enables EMF-based models to be used as data sources without the need to pre-generate any HTML or dynamic script, or duplicate the contents into a database. The paper reports on our experimental results in using this approach for dynamically querying and visualising a very large military standard.

1 Introduction

Increasingly, the design of complex engineered products and systems is becoming more reliant on computer-supported models capturing structured information. By contrast, most military standards in use are still disseminated as text-based documents. In our experience, this is also the case in other domains requiring complex detailed standards such as automotive and aeronautical industries. These standards can be over thousands of pages in volume, which can make locating and composing information in them challenging and laborious. Within the development of military hardware, engineers are typically required to produce documents based on a subset of the standards implemented by their product. Product testing will require the engineers to promptly locate information in the standard and validate that their product conforms to it. Interoperability is also crucial in military applications where engineers must validate that their implementation does not impede or conflict with other products. To address these issues, we have found it useful to extract semantic models represented in a structured format which is then amenable to automated querying and processing. In our experience this approach can greatly enhance both the accuracy and speed of locating and composing information from different parts of a standard. We have also found that in order to make models useful for engineers, it is essential to construct a suitable and familiar user interface for querying and navigating them.

In our previous work [2] we used text parsing to extract structured Eclipse Modelling Framework(EMF) based models from text-based military standards. This paper presents our work on using a combination of web and Model-Driven Engineering (MDE) technologies (in particular the Epsilon Generation Language (EGL) and Apache Tomcat) to enable dynamic querying and visualising of these models over the web. The rest of the paper is organized as follows. In section 2 we provide an overview of the domain of military standards with an emphasis on Tactical Data Links – which is the main focus of our work. Then, in section 3 we outline the motivation for querying and visualizing models over the web. In section 4 we perform a review of existing generative MDE approaches for implementing web-based applications and highlight their advantages and shortcomings. Driven by the findings of this review, in section 5 we propose a novel reflective approach for building web-based applications directly atop EMF-based models. Then, in section 6 we evaluate this approach both from a development effort and a performance perspective and assess its suitability for building real-world applications. In section 7 we conclude and provide directions for proposed future work.

2 Background

In this section we provide an overview of the military standards on which our work focuses (Tactical Data Links) and outline our previous work on extracting EMF-based models from text-based standards documents.

2.1 An Introduction to Tactical Data Links (TDLs)

The TDL provides one of the backbone technologies underpinning the defence communitys goal of network enabled capability by providing the information and infrastructure to afford users with an integrated picture of the battlefield. It also supports tasking orders and responses. A number of TDLs are in service with coalition forces, and are implemented on a variety of assets, such as aircraft, ships, land vehicles, and command stations.

The Link 16 TDL is described by the Military Standard MIL-STD-6016C [1] in the form of narrative combined with many tables and relatively few figures. At the lowest level of granularity there is a Data Dictionary identifying the set of types defined for use on the link. These types are identified by a unique key the Data Field Identifier (DFI) and Data Use Identifier (DUI) pair, referred to as the DFI/DUI. The set of messages that may be transmitted over the link are defined in the form of a Message Catalogue. Messages are functionally-orientated and contain a number of words (J-Words), each of which contains a number of fields, the type of which is defined by reference to the relevant item in the Data Dictionary (the DFI/DUI). Hence, Link 16 messages are tree-structured and must conform to certain well formed constraints, e.g. all bits in each J-Word must be associated to a DFI/DUI (i.e. all fields must have a defined type); such constraints have been captured in our models and are described elsewhere [2].

There is a small number of different types of word, and certain elements of the payload are mandated by the word type.

The description of Link 16 provided by MIL-STD-6016C [1] is known to feature a number of shortcomings affecting its usability [3]. The following are of particular relevance to the research reported in this paper:

- Document-based, no apparent underpinning model
- Largely narrative
- Open to (mis)interpretation
- Not checkable by machine
- Duplication of material invites inconsistency
- Poor document navigation due to limited use of hyperlinking
- Comprises many interdependent sections and appendices
- Size, greater than 7300 pages

The description of the Data Dictionary and Message Catalogue components comprises approximately 4000 pages of structured text, the vast majority of which does not feature hyperlinking; bookmarks are only provided in the PDF version of the standard but at a relatively coarse level of granularity. As a result, locating information within this document is a particularly challenging and tedious task for engineers.

2.2 Modelling TDLs

An analysis of the Link 16 TDL standard [1] led us to the conclusion that the domain can be effectively captured by a hierarchically layered set of metamodels, the lower two layers of which comprise the Data Dictionary and Message Catalogue; we refer to this hierarchy of models colloquially as the *semantic models*. An excerpt of the Message Catalogue can be observed in Fig. 1. Modelling commenced in mid 2005 using Xactium's XMF Mosaic tool. Full scale development and support of the XMF tool ended in 2008. As such, in early 2009 we began migrating some model components into EMF, and the Epsilon framework [4] as part of a risk reduction exercise investigating candidate successor tools for XMF. EMF provides automated metamodel generation from an XML schema, and as

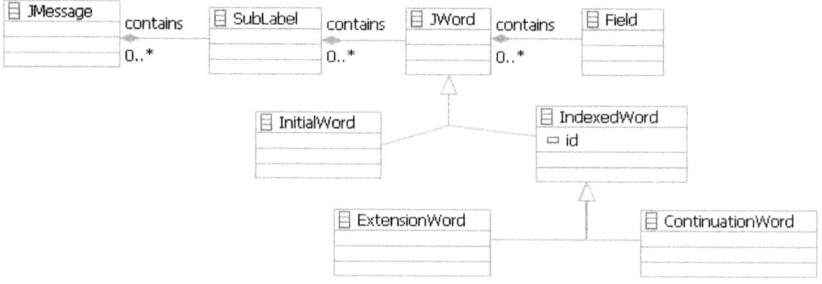

Fig. 1. Message Catalogue Excerpt

much of our source data is available in XML, generated via bespoke parsers we have written for the project, migration of the Data Dictionary and Message Catalogue proved to be feasible. The Epsilon Transformation Language (ETL) was used to transform the XML data, conforming to the automatically-generated metamodels, to conform to our derived *semantic models*.

3 Motivation

Migrating the standard to a model-based form provides an opportunity to address many of the shortcomings identified against the current document-based view. However, for a model-based representation of the standard to be accepted by TDL practitioners, we must be able to provide access to the data in these models in a format similar to that of the original document, but based on a sound foundation, validated against the relevant well formed constraints and with enhanced capabilities for document navigability. Analysis in 2007 investigated the navigation methods available to engineers and the benefits that could be gained from a model based approach [5].

Engineers use the standard in every stage of a product's lifecycle. Some key activities include using the standard to investigate and confirm message implementations, developing regulatory documents based on subsets of the standard, and reviewing interpretations and interoperability with other products. Therefore, the information in the standard needs to be visualised with usable and familiar interfaces. The engineers are typically used to navigating the information in the traditional document view of the PDF. The document also contains much explanatory prose which cannot be modelled, but which nevertheless is essential for the users' understanding. Methods to quickly traverse the Message Catalogue and Data Dictionary with the ability to move between cross-references will also potentially improve an engineer's efficiency in using the standard.

Hence, it is necessary for the underpinning *semantic models* to be rendered in a text-based but cross-linked manner. Developing visualisations of the modelled data in HTML has been deemed as a preferred solution given the current stage of development of the TDL modelling research. Using HTML also means that deployment to TDL engineers can be easily achieved through the current facilities available to them, i.e. the web browser of their desktop machines. Developing a desktop-based application has the disadvantages of requiring installation and security validation for each project/engineer that wishes to use this functionality. Also, as the models are still evolving, new development can simply extend the web application rather than requiring newer versions of the desktop-based application to be installed.

This motivation to render the model data and the desire to utilise HTML as the deployment technology has led to the need to investigate the different options for creating web applications based on our EMF models of the TDL Link 16.

4 Related Work: Model-Driven Web Engineering

The last decade has seen a growth in the adoption of Model-Driven Web Engineering (MDWE). MDWE aims to apply MDE principles to web application development. MDE advocates the use of models and model transformations as first-class artefacts in all phases of software development, and promotes the abstraction of models to be platform independent, with subsequent transformations to generate platform specific models for deployment. Many MDE methods and tools also enable the automated generation of application code from these models. MDE has the potential to greatly reduce development and maintenance costs, while increasing the quality of the software produced. There are many model driven web engineering methods, some prominent examples include, OO-H [6], UML-based Web Engineering (UWE) [7], WebML [8], and WEI [9].

Nearly all methods can be considered to consist of three platform independent models. These can be generalised to be a *concept* model, a *navigation* model and a *presentation* model. Methods of transformations to platform-specific models vary from the use of graph transformations like MIDAS [10] to template-based like WebML [8]. Predominantly, QVT and ATL are used by these approaches for the transformation between models. In addition, constraints are generally written using OCL. Several solutions make use of their own languages or language extensions. For example WebML utilises its own extensions of UML, OO-H uses Navigation Access Diagrams, WEI defines a custom toolset (GlueWeb), which is, an incomplete subset of OCL combined with QVT [9].

All model-driven web engineering approaches currently take a generative approach to producing the final web application by generating platform-specific code from the respective platform-independent models. For dynamic application, this includes the production of a data store either through generating a relational database based on the models, or through transformations to the Ecore XMI and utilising the data through XML. Some approaches do make use of the EMF models through generating the Java model code and model editor classes. The presentation coding is generated by all approaches whether the output is PHP, JSP or static HTML. In our view, generative approaches demonstrate several disadvantages. Any change to the metamodels requires the regeneration and redeployment of the code. Also, data is duplicated and this leaves open the potential for synchronisation issues. Moreover, as the amount of data in the models grows, regenerating the entire contents of the database every time a model changes can be particularly time-consuming. In addition, there can be an impedance mismatch between the object-oriented metamodels and relational storage solutions. As our *semantic models* are evolving, they are increasingly making use of more complex object-oriented features, such as multiple inheritance, therefore the corresponding changes in the relational view and the necessary mappings are becoming more challenging. However, the level of abstraction used, means that transformations are still performed at the Ecore model level and knowledge of the relational database structure is no longer a problem. There is still the execution overhead of transformations as the data grows.

5 A Reflective Approach to MDWE

To overcome the shortcomings of existing generative approaches to web development, and particularly data duplication and re-generation, we decided to investigate the feasibility of an alternative, reflective approach in which we could use the EMF-based models themselves – instead of duplicating their contents in a database – as the data source from which we would build the web application. Moreover, we decided to investigate the possibility of using the Epsilon Generation Language (EGL) to express the templates that would generate dynamic HTML content from the underlying EMF model.

5.1 Technical Infrastructure

In this section we outline the technical details of our approach. We first introduce EGL and its underpinning Epsilon platform and then discuss integrating EGL with a Java-based Web Server (Apache Tomcat) that allows us to implement reflective web-applications using EMF-based models as data sources, and EGL templates for querying and producing dynamic HTML content from them.

Epsilon and EGL. Epsilon is a component of the Eclipse Modelling GMT project that provides tools and domain-specific languages for Model-Driven Engineering. Epsilon comprises a number of integrated model management languages, based upon a common infrastructure, for performing tasks such as model transformation, comparison, merging, in-place transformation, inter/intra-model consistency checking, and model to text transformation. All languages in Epsilon build on the Epsilon Object Language (EOL), an OCL-based imperative model navigation and modification language, and can be used to manage models expressed in different technologies such as EMF, MDR and XML.

Epsilon Object Language (EOL). EOL – the core language of Epsilon – combines the procedural style of scripting languages such as Javascript with the declarative style of OCL for querying and filtering collections. EOL is a mature language that boasts a wide range of features [11] such as support for managing multiple models of arbitrary modelling technologies in the context of the same program, tight integration with Java enabling developers to instantiate Java objects and call their methods from EOL, support for defining operations in the context of existing types, reuse facilities for defining and importing libraries of operations, support for user-interactions and support for transactional management of models (where the underlying modelling technologies provides such capabilities).

Epsilon Generation Language (EGL). EGL is a template-based language that targets model-to-text transformation [12]. EGL adopts a syntax that closely resembles server-side scripting languages such as JSP and PHP. An EGL template consists of two types of regions. Dynamic regions (enclosed within [% %]) contain executable statements and expressions, while static regions contain plain text that is output verbatim. For example, consider the simple EGL template in Fig. 2.

```
[%for (i : Integer in Sequence{1..3}){%]
Number [%=i%]
[%}%]
```

Fig. 2. Example EGL template

EGL is a preprocessed language; EGL templates are transformed to EOL programs (in a similar manner to the way JSP pages are transformed to Java servlets) which are then executed in order to produce the output. By building on top of EOL, EGL inherits the rich set of features that EOL provides and which were outlined above. In addition, EGL provides a range of task-specific features such as support for dynamic template instantiation and invocation, and support for mixing manually written code with generated code through a target-language independent content preservation mechanism.

While EGL was originally developed to support code generation, its modular design makes it possible to use it to produce text in non-file output streams as well. In principle any model-to-text transformation language with similar characteristics such as XPand, MOFScript or the OMG M2T could have been used instead.

Tomcat. As discussed before, the aim of this work was to implement a solution that would allow engineers to explore EMF models through standard web browsers. To achieve this, we have implemented an integration between Apache Tomcat and EGL, which allows developers to use EGL templates as server-side pages for rendering EMF models over HTML. This section discusses the rationale and architecture of this approach as well as some of the interesting implementation challenges encountered.

Rationale. Tomcat is an industrial strength, Java-based web server with built-in support for the JSP server-side scripting language. Therefore, our first option was to use JSP in order to produce dynamic HTML pages from our EMF models. Since EMF is a Java-based library, this capability was available out-of-the-box. However, there was a major disadvantage to this. If we were to use JSP for this purpose, we would need to either generate Java code from our Ecore metamodel or navigate our models using the cumbersome reflective syntax of EMF. By contrast, integrating Tomcat with EGL would allow us to use the concise, closure-based syntax provided by EGL[12] to query models, without needing to generate and deploy code for the respective Ecore metamodels in Java.

Architecture. Although Tomcat comes with built-in support for JSP, like the majority of web servers, it also provides a flexible model for integrating additional server-side languages. This is achieved through the URL mapping mechanism which allows developers to map request URLs to custom servlets. In the case of EGL, we implemented an EGL servlet which is responsible for serving calls to EGL pages and mapped it to requests which end with .egl as shown in Fig. 3.

```
<servlet>
  <servlet-name>egl</servlet-name>
  <servlet-class>org.eclipse.epsilon.egl.servlet.EglServlet
  </servlet-class>
</servlet>
<servlet-mapping>
  <servlet-name>egl</servlet-name>
  <url-pattern>*.egl</url-pattern>
</servlet-mapping>
```

Fig. 3. Tomcat EGL Servlet mapping

Once the EGL servlet is invoked as a result of a client (browser) request, it is responsible for locating the respective EGL template for each request, executing it and returning the produced text to the client. Similar to JSP pages, EGL templates can access several built-in variables such as the *request* variable which allows a template to retrieve information related to the particular request (e.g. parameters), the *session* variable which allows templates to query and set session-wide properties (e.g. for authentication), and the *response, config* and *application* variables. These variables are inherited directly by the Java servlet specification[13]. To interact with EMF models, each EGL template is provided with a shared instance of the *ModelManager* class which provides operations for loading, storing and disposing of EMF models [14].

5.2 Technical Solution

Using the Tomcat/EGL integration, three different templates were developed in an alpha test application. These templates covered three distinct areas of the Link 16 TDL modelling work. The areas covered were the Data Dictionary, Message Catalogue and the prose document. The prose document template re-generated a rendering of a subset of the standard in the same view style as the PDF format. This template was designed to test scalability as it utilised over 900,000 instances of classes.

The Data Dictionary and Message Catalogue were intended to allow users to traverse the hierarchical structures and follow any cross-references between them. Navigation was provided by using hyperlinks and specifying new parameters using the HTML GET method. By providing parameters, this enables the template to restrict the data and traverse the hierarchy. An example of this is shown in Fig. 4. This example returns all child instances conforming to a specific type (InitialWord, ContinuationWord or ExtensionWord), as defined by the passed parameter (`wordType`). The EOL select operation returns a set where all instances conform to the type and the instances id matches the additional parameter (`wordID`) that is supplied. The excerpt also corresponds to the metamodel excerpt seen in Fig. 1.

```
var wordType := request.getParameter('jword1');
if(wordType = 'I')
{x := y.contains.select(t|t.isTypeOf(InitialWord)).first();}
else if (wordType = 'C')
{x := y.contains.select(t|t.isTypeOf(ContinuationWord) and
                       t.id = wordID.asInteger()).first();}
else if (wordType = 'E')
{x := y.contains.select(t|t.isTypeOf(ExtensionWord) and
                       t.id = wordID.asInteger()).first();}
```

Fig. 4. Excerpt of selecting element defined by passed parameters

Having determined the set or instance to display, a custom print operation is called to render the data. The custom print operations (e.g. x.print();), produce the HTML code for displaying the instance attributes to the screen. In Fig. 5, a short excerpt is given for rendering the top level class JMessage of the Message Catalogue. This results in a HTML table displaying the data associated to a JMessage.

```
operation JMessage print() {%]
<table>
 <tr><td>Name:</td><td>[%=self.name%]</td></tr>
 <tr><td>Family:</td><td>[%=self.family%]</td></tr>
 <tr><td>ID:</td><td>[%=self.id%]</td></tr>
 ...
```

Fig. 5. Excerpt of a custom print operation

It is envisaged that engineers should be able to utilise the modelled data to produce required regulatory material according to subsets of the standard. To achieve this, the solution is required to be able to create and/or edit the data. Fig. 6 demonstrates the ability to select and edit the data of a JMessage.

```
var editme := c.contains.select(x|x.id = msgID and x.family =
                              msgFamily).first();
if(editme.size() == 1){
  editme.name = msgName;
  editme.family = msgFamily;
  editme.message = msgID;
  myCatalogue.store();
}
```

Fig. 6. Example of editing a message

6 Evaluation

The development process is evaluated with respect to its value to model-driven web engineering, before considering in more detail the performance of our approach.

6.1 Development Process

Our approach has demonstrated that reflective model-driven web engineering is possible. It improves on generative approaches by reducing the amount of duplicated data and therefore reducing the risks and problems associated with synchronisation. By using the Epsilon platform, a range of model management functions can be developed using the common syntax provided by EOL, which allows developers to reuse code across the different Epsilon languages. Reuse of code is not possible in most generative approaches, as their model management functions utilise differing languages with no common syntax. EOL is also beneficial over OCL as it combines the procedural style of scripting languages such as Javascript with the declarative style of OCL for querying and filtering collections. Although EOL is a new language, the syntax is similar to Javascript. In addition, engineers with no modelling experience are not required to learn multiple languages for model management functions such as, transformation languages like QCT or ATL or constraint languages like OCL. For these reasons, the learning of EOL is not considered an issue, it could even be seen as a benefit. Also, no technical knowledge of dynamic web scripts or languages is required, this reduces the knowledge required by a modelling engineer to produce a dynamic web-based application.

However, the approach does shift away from model-driven engineering principles slightly. Most generative approaches utilise a model and subsequent transformations to generate the dynamic script. Our approach currently ignores this model driven approach to the development of the interfaces in favour of a programmatic style that utilises the model driven functions available through the Epsilon platform.

6.2 Performance

Stress and load testing of the alpha test application resulted in an acceptable level of performance for the anticipated usage at BAE Systems. As TDL is a specialised area, it is not envisaged that more than 10 users would use the application concurrently. The stress test results shown in Table 1 show that this application provides adequate performance for 50 users. Studies suggest a web user is willing to accept an 8-10 second delay in loading a page [15,16]. However, there is some supporting research that suggests that under some conditions 30 seconds is an upper limit [16,17]. Therefore, the standard deviation coupled with the average load time for 100 users is likely to be unacceptable.

The results do demonstrate that the approach is not suitable for request intensive applications, such as Google or Amazon, as the weight of requests would

Table 1. Stress Test Results (Users per Minute)

Users	Requests	Min	Max	Avg	σ	Avg File Size (B)	Failure Rate
10	1565	45	13058	1110	2650.502	16362	0.3%
25	3711	55	30262	2649	6217.821	17489	0.3%
50	8057	52	69979	5041	13194.568	15922	0.5%
100	15426	77	130983	11184	27084.301	16715	0.8%

(Load Time (ms) spans the Min, Max, Avg, σ columns.)

degrade performance significantly. Load testing also discovered a performance bottleneck during the first query of a template. This overhead was observed as the models were loaded in the java virtual machine memory. For large models like the prose document, this can take in excess of five minutes. However, subsequent calls to the templates do not suffer as the models are already in memory.

All the tests were performed using Tomcat and the Java Virtual Machine in their default setting with the exception of increased heap size. Performance enhancements to Tomcat [18] and the virtual machine, are expected to result in only a slight improved performance.

7 Conclusions

The alpha test application discussed in Sec. 5.2 has demonstrated that the approach of using Epsilon Generation Language with Apache Tomcat is a plausible solution. It provides a reflective template driven method to producing dynamic web content from EMF models. By using the Epsilon framework, dynamic web scripts can be produced which require no generation of supplementary code. This reduces the amount of duplicated code. Whilst Epsilon is a new langugae to learn, it provides a benfit in providing a range of model management functions that utilise the same core EOL language.

The performance testing in Sec. 6.2 has shown the solution is suitable when using small to medium models with a small number of concurrent users (<50), such as the scenario discussed at BAE Systems. For large scale models and high concurrent request applications, the performance degrades to unacceptable levels. This performance degradation is an issue for ongoing further research.

References

1. U.S. Department of Defense. Department of defense interface standard - tactical data link (tdl) 16 - message standard. Technical Report MIL-STD-6016C, US Department of Defense (2004)
2. Holmes, C., Johnson, J., Riaz, A.: Tactical data links - a description of the supporting models. Technical Report SEIC-RP-0531, BAE Systems (2007)
3. Zeigler, B.: Simulation-based testing of emerging defense information systems. Presentation (April 2006), http://tinyurl.com/ycwfdbz

4. Eclipse Foundation. Epsilon eclipse modeling gmt component, http://www.eclipse.org/gmt/epsilon
5. Clowes, D., Dawson, R., Probets, S., Johnson, J., Holmes, C.: Pilot studies in using the semantic knowledge of information in large technical documents to aid user navigation. In: Proc. European Conference on Knowledge Management 2008 (2008)
6. Gómez, J., Cachero, C.: Information modeling for Internet applications. In: OOH Method: extending UML to model web interfaces, pp. 144–173. Idea Group Inc, IGI (2002)
7. Koch, N.: Software Engineering for Adaptive Hypermedia Systems: Reference Model, Modeling Techniques and Development Process. PhD thesis, LMU Munich (2000)
8. Ceri, S., Fraternali, P., Bongio, A.: Web modeling language (webml): a modeling language for designing web sites. Computer Networks 33(1-6), 137–157 (2000)
9. Moreno, N., Vallecillo, A.: Towards interoperable web engineering methods. Journal of the American Society for Information Science and Technology 59(7), 1073–1092 (2008)
10. Cáceres, P., Marcos, E., Vela, B., Juan, R.: A mda-based approach for web information system. In: Development, Proceedings of Workshop in Software Model Engineering (2004)
11. Kolovos, D.S., Paige, R.F., Polack, F.A.C.: The epsilon object language. In: Rensink, A., Warmer, J. (eds.) ECMDA-FA 2006. LNCS, vol. 4066, pp. 128–142. Springer, Heidelberg (2006)
12. Rose, L.M., Paige, R.F., Kolovos, D.S., Polack, F.A.C.: The epsilon generation language (egl). In: Proc. European Conference in Model Driven Architecture, ECMDA (2008)
13. Sun Microsystems. Jsr-000315 java servlet 3.0 specification, January 2009. This is an electronic document. Date retrieved: June 9 (2009)
14. Epsilon Eclipse Modeling GMT component. Using egl as a server-side scripting language in tomcat, http://www.eclipse.org/gmt/epsilon/doc/articles/egl-server-side/
15. Palmer, J.: Designing for web site usability. IEEE Computer 35, 102–103 (2002)
16. Nah, F.F.: A study on tolerable waiting time: how long are web users willing to wait? Behaviour & Information Technology 23(3), 153–163 (2004)
17. Selvidge, P.R., Chaparro, B.S., Bender, G.T.: The world wide wait: Effects of delays on user performance. International journal of Industrial Ergonomics 29, 15–20 (2002)
18. Chopra, V., Li, S., Genender, J.: Professional Apache Tomcat 6. In: Performance Tuning, pp. 561–584. Wrox Publishing Inc. (2007)

Requirements Analysis and Modeling with Problem Frames and SysML: A Case Study

Pietro Colombo[1], Ferhat Khendek[1], and Luigi Lavazza[2]

[1] Department of Electrical and Computer Engineering, Concordia University
1455, de Maisonneuve W., Montreal, Quebec, Canada H3G 1M8
[2] Dipartimento di Informatica e Comunicazione, Università dell'Insubria
Via Mazzini 5, 21100 Varese – Italy
{colombo,khendek}@encs.concordia.ca,
luigi.lavazza@uninsubria.it

Abstract. Requirements analysis based on Problem Frames is getting an increasing attention in the academic community and has the potential to become of relevant interest also for industry. However the approach lacks an adequate notational support and methodological guidelines, and case studies that demonstrate its applicability to problems of realistic complexity are still rare. These weaknesses may hinder its adoption. This paper aims at contributing towards the elimination of these weaknesses. We report on an experience in analyzing and specifying the requirements of a controller for traffic lights of an intersection using Problem Frames in combination with SysML. The analysis was performed by decomposing the problem, addressing the identified subproblems, and recomposing them while solving the identified interferences. The experience allowed us to identify certain guidelines for decomposition and re-composition patterns.

Keywords: Requirements analysis, Problem decomposition, Problem composition, Problem Frames, SysML.

1 Introduction

Problem Frames (PFs) [1] are a sound requirement analysis approach that aims at driving the analyst from the phase of problem description, where the characteristics of the problem and its requirements are defined, to the specification of a machine that satisfies the requirements. PFs support both context and structural analysis, i.e., they support both the definition of the characteristics of the problem to be solved, and the decomposition of the original problem into simpler sub-problems.

An important weakness of PFs is the lack of an adequate linguistic support. In fact, PFs are not equipped with a unique and clear way for modeling requirements, the behavioral aspects of problem domains and the specification of the machine. Therefore, analysts have to choose a suitable notation to model both the given domain behavior and the required behavior. In order to address this issue, the authors proposed the integration of the PFs with UML [3, 15] and SysML [2]. The experience illustrated in [3] showed that UML does not support the modeling of requirements at the correct level of abstraction, while SysML [2] addresses all the weakness of UML. In [2] we discuss the SysML support for the context analysis of basic problems, illustrating how SysML constructs can be used to represent PFs concepts.

In this paper we tackle the structural analysis of a realistic problem, a controller for traffic lights of a four way road intersection, for an early evaluation of an extended approach combining PFs and SysML. Our extended approach is illustrated through a case study involving guidelines and criteria that drive the decomposition of a problem and the re-composition of the resulting sub-problems at requirements and machine specifications level.

This work is a first step towards a systematic and a more formal approach to the decomposition and re-composition mechanisms for handling realistic size problems using PFs and SysML.

The rest of the paper is organized into four sections. Section 2 describes briefly how the SysML notation can support the PFs methodology. Section 3 presents the extended approach through the case study and illustrates its analysis and specification by decomposing the problem into simpler sub-problems according to proposed criteria, analyzing these individually and recomposing their descriptions. Section 4 discusses related work. Section 5 discusses lessons learned, draws some conclusions and presents some ideas for future work.

2 Supporting Problem Frames with SysML

PFs can be effectively supported by an external notation like SysML. The complete set of guidelines and motivations that show how the requirements engineering approach could take advantage of the usage of SysML are discussed in [2]. In what follow we briefly summarize some activities of the PFs methodology showing how these can be supported by SysML.

- *Problem analysis*: the problem context is decomposed into domains, and shared phenomena are identified. Domains and phenomena are represented by means of Blocks and defined using Block Definition Diagrams (*bdd*) showing the entities of the problem context.
- *Problem definition*: the domain blocks are instantiated and interconnected using an Internal Block Diagram (*ibd*).
- *Requirements definition*: user requirements and properties associated with domains are defined by means of Requirements diagrams (*req*) and refined by means of Parametric Diagrams (*par*), State Machine Diagrams (*stm*), Sequence Diagrams (*seq*) and Activity Diagrams (*act*).
- *Domain refinement*: domain descriptions are refined using SysML diagrams like *bdd* and *ibd* to support domain decomposition into simpler structures, and *stm*, *act*, *par* and *seq* diagrams to define behaviors.

SysML improves the specification part and the usability of the analysis approach, but does not help in scaling it up as it does not affect aspects such as the decomposition and re-composition of problems.

3 Extended Approach Combining Problem Frames and SysML

In this section we introduce the case study and illustrate how its analysis can be effectively supported by an extended approach combining PFs and SysML. Because of lack of space we present only some of the problem diagrams for the static aspects of the problems and some SysML diagrams for the requirements specification.

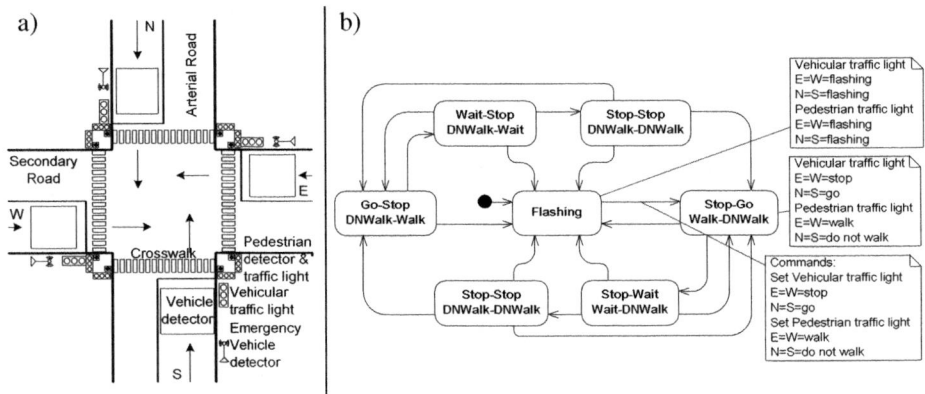

Fig. 1. a) The intersection topography, b) The sequence of commands and phases

3.1 The Case Study

The intersection controller manages the traffic lights for cars and pedestrian traffic at a four way intersection. The controller reacts to events such as the pressing of a presence button at a crosswalk, vehicles transit, emergency vehicles approaching the intersection, commands issued by an operator via a console, and operates vehicle and pedestrian traffic lights that are positioned next to the intersection.

The controller operates a system composed of two approaches partitioned into distinct semi-approaches: N, S, E, W, each of which is characterized by zebra crossing and is equipped with vehicle and pedestrian traffic lights, vehicle and pedestrian presence detectors, and also detectors that reveal emergency vehicles that are approaching or leaving the intersection (see Fig. 1a). The controller is also provided with a console that allows an operator to configure the operating mode of the controller and to set the states of the traffic lights.

The intersection controller has to operate the states of the traffic lights according to the criteria introduced by the "Semi actuated", "Manual" and "Preempted" operating mode (discussed later). In addition, the intersection controller has to verify that the current state of the traffic lights complies with the last command sent, reacting suitably. The commands sent by the controller cause the change of state of the system. The admissible progress is described (in Fig. 1b) by means of a *stm* as a sequence of commands and "phases" (i.e., combinations of states of the traffic lights). For the sake of simplicity vehicles can only go straight: no lefthand or righthand turns are allowed.

The problem diagram [1] shown in Fig. 2 describes the domain of the problem by presenting 1) the involved machine and problem domains, 2) the phenomena that are

Requirements Analysis and Modeling with Problem Frames and SysML: A Case Study 77

shared by such domains, and 3) the requirements that predicate on the domains' phenomena. The system is composed of the following domains:

- Pedestrian presence detector: A device that forwards to the controller the requests of a pedestrian (i.e., the pressure of the button) to cross a zebra crossing.
- Vehicle presence detector: A device that monitors the presence and passage of vehicles. It generates events indicating that 1) no vehicle is passing for some time, 2) a vehicle is waiting in queue, 3) a vehicle has crossed the sensible area.
- Emergency Vehicle Detector: a device that notifies the intersection controller whenever an emergency vehicle is approaching and when it has crossed the intersection and is moving away.
- Pedestrian Traffic Standard and Vehicular Traffic Standard: a traffic light that receives the *go*, *stop*, *wait* and *flash* events from the controller and sets its lamps. It informs the controller of the current state (i.e., go, stop, wait, flashing), and of configuration errors through continuous flows of data and by means of error codes that specify for instance burn bulbs.
- Manual Override: this device receives requests from an operator to set the phases of the system and to set the operating mode of the controller, and sends such requests to the intersection controller.

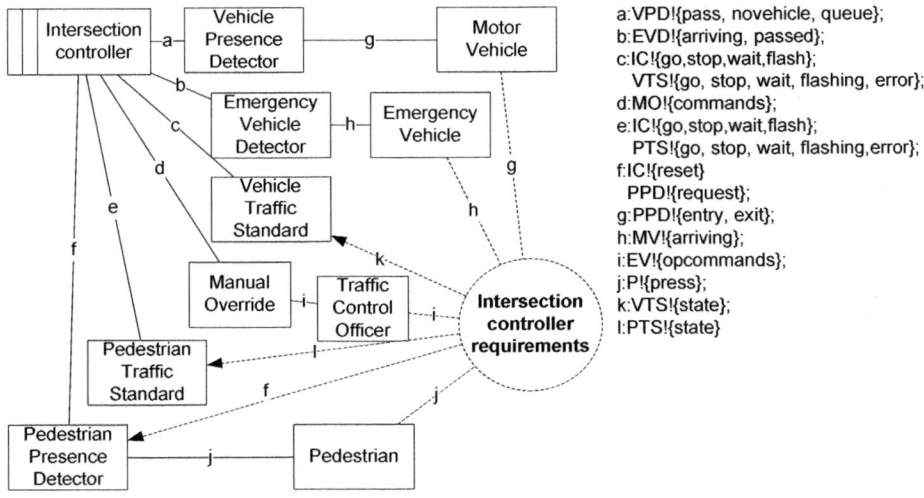

Fig. 2. The problem diagram describing the domain of the problem

3.2 Decomposition of the Problem

The problem is too complex to be analyzed and modeled as a basic frame. The key to mitigate this complexity is decomposition.

Decomposition is not only an approach to the solution of a problem, but also a process that helps the analyst understanding and analyzing the problem itself [1]. Decomposition aims at projecting original large problem into simpler and smaller sub-problems in a recursive manner, until sub-problems that fit basic problem frames are identified. The solution of each sub-problem will contribute to the solution of the whole problem.

Given a certain problem, it may be decomposed in different ways. Decomposition criteria usually depend on the characteristics of the problem and on the knowledge and experience of the analyst. The aim is to generate sub-problems whose description and solution is as simple as possible, and that are also simple to re-compose.

We propose to apply a general decomposition criterion based on the identification of the sequential and parallel activities executed in the context of the original problem. At any given time, the controller can operate a single operating mode. The controller operates the traffic lights alternating a sequence of different operating modes depending on specific conditions. Other activities –like monitoring the state of the traffic lights– are performed in parallel with the control.

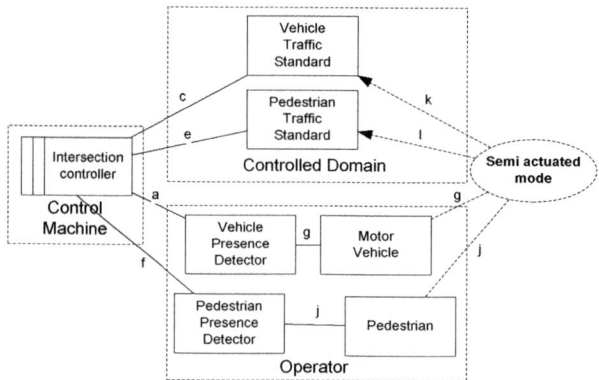

Fig. 3. Semi-actuated mode problem diagram

3.2.1 Semi Actuated Mode

In this operating mode the approaches at the intersection have different priorities. Vehicle detectors in the minor street (EW) notify the presence of vehicles to the controller. The intersection controller must operate the traffic lights so that the minor approach can receive a green light only when traffic is present. When no traffic is on the minor street or a timeout expires, the green lights of the main road (NS) have to be switched on again. Requests of the pedestrians to anticipate the Walk signal may shorten the duration of the waiting phase. As described in Fig. 3, this sub-problem can be modeled as a Commanded Behavior frame [1] that contains a projection of the domains of the original problem. The requirements constrain the state of the traffic lights according to the requests issued by pedestrians and by the presence of vehicles. Transitions triggered by the operator when exiting (entering) the state *Flashing* specify when the traffic light are turned on (off). Transitions triggered by the "after" clause fire when a minimum timeout is expired. More specifically, *WaitD* and *SafetyD* timeouts are imposed for safety reasons, while *GoD* depends on the priority of the approach.

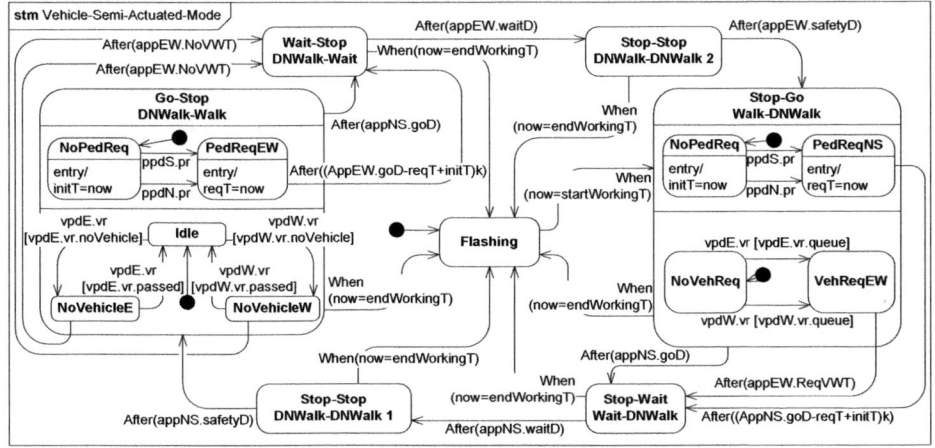

Fig. 4. The requirements of the Semi-actuated mode problem

The duration in the states with the "Go" signal (composite states) can be less than *GoD* when a pedestrian with a "Do not walk" signal requests to cross the street, or there are vehicles that are waiting for the "Go" signal on the secondary approach, or no vehicle has passed on the secondary approach for a given time.

The machine specification, i.e. the behavior of the intersection controller that satisfies the requirements of the sub-problem, is described by means of a *stm* diagram that features the same set of states and transitions as the one used to describe the requirements. Transitions have the same triggering conditions, but –unlike in Fig. 4– they generate "commands" to change the state of the traffic lights. The *stm* is not shown here due to lack of space.

3.2.2 Manual Mode

In this operating mode an operator controls the evolution of the phases. He/she interacts with a dedicated console determining the length of the phases characterized by the "Go" signal, and establishing which will be the next phase. As in the previous operating mode, the transitions between some phases are constrained by safety timeouts and cannot be shortened or overridden by the commands of the operator.

Also this sub-problem is an instance of the Commanded Behavior Frame (Fig. 5). The requirements of the sub-problem are described by means of the *stm* diagram of Fig. 6. For instance, if the current phase is *Stop-Wait Wait-DNWalk* and an emergency vehicle is approaching on the street that has the "Wait" signal, the operator can impose the "Go" signal setting the *Stop-Go Walk-DNWalk* phase.

The specification of the machine could be provided by using a *stm* (not reported here for space reasons) similar to the one that presents the requirements. Like in the Semi-actuated mode, also in this case the only differences between the *stms* concern the signals that are generated at transition firing time.

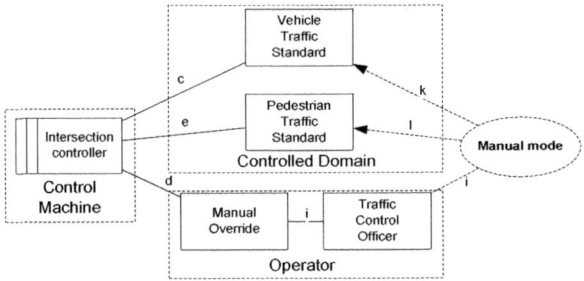

Fig. 5. Manual mode problem diagram

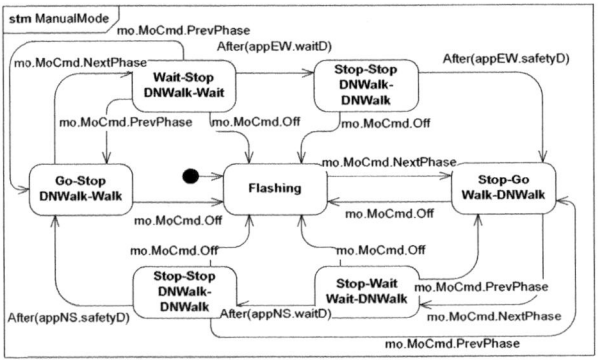

Fig. 6. Manual mode problem requirements

3.2.3 Preempted Mode

In this operating mode the traffic lights are operated in a way such that the roads where emergency vehicles are approaching get the "Go" signal as soon as possible. Emergency detectors determine the presence (and the direction) of emergency vehicles.

The controller has to switch to "Stop" all the traffic lights with the exception of the ones of the approach where the vehicle that triggered the preemption sequence is arriving.

The preempted sequence terminates when the detectors inform the controller that the emergency vehicle has crossed the intersection. Whenever the preempted sequence is enabled, all the requests from the pedestrians and the signals from the vehicle detectors are ignored. The problem is characterized by a Commanded Behavior Frame (not shown for lack of space). The requirements of the problem, described using two parallel state machines, are shown in Fig. 7. The first machine keeps track of the presence of emergency vehicles, while the second one, depending on the current phase, establishes the preempted sequence.

The evolution of the machines is synchronized by the shared variables *EVNS* and *EVEW*, which keep track of emergency vehicles on a given approach, and by events *startEmergency* and *stopEmergency*, which specify when the preempted sequence starts and stops, respectively. The first *stm* introduces four states that depict the

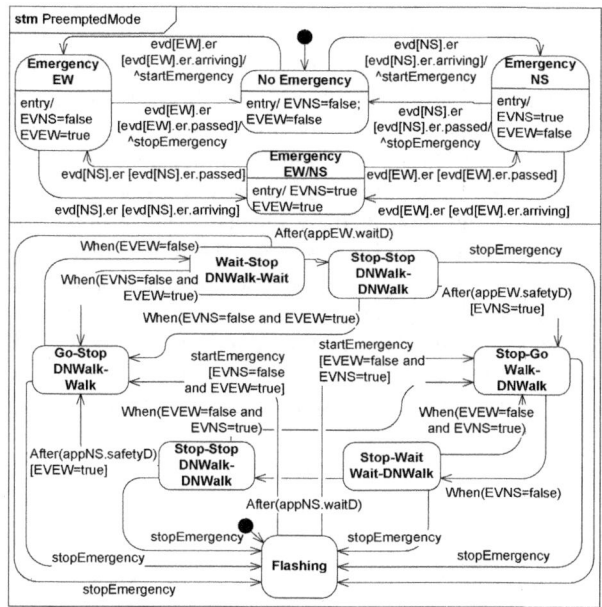

Fig. 7. Preempted mode requirements

following situations: no emergency, emergency on the approach EW, on the NW one, or on both the approaches. The previously mentioned shared variables are updated depending on the current state, while the events are generated when the state *NoEmergency* is entered and exited.

The second *stm* describes the preempted sequence. Whenever an emergency starts (notified by the corresponding event), a new phase that is determined according to the position of the emergency vehicle (shared variables *EVEW* and *EVNS*) is enabled.

As soon as all the emergency vehicles have crossed the intersection the preempted sequence is terminated by returning to the initial state.

The machine specification is not significantly different from the requirements and is not shown due to lack of space.

3.2.4 Traffic Light State Check

The intersection controller has to check whether the current state of the traffic lights is the one expected as a result of the received commands. The control is mediated by the local controllers of the traffic lights that in case of malfunction inform the intersection controller of the error type. When a malfunction that may compromise the safety of the system is reported, the controller has to impose the phase *Flashing*. When minor errors are detected, a description of the problem must be logged.

The problem is characterized by two distinct requirements with respect to the monitoring of the traffic light conditions and the control of their state, respectively. Hence, the problem is decomposed into two distinct parallel sub-problems: an Information display problem [1], which deals with monitoring the states of the traffic lights and a Controlled behavior problem, which defines the reaction of the controller.

The auditing sub-problem is illustrated in the Problem diagram of Fig. 8.

The requirements are defined using the *act* diagram shown in Fig. 9. It defines an action named *CheckTL* that takes as input, as a continuous flow, the information on the traffic lights state and compares them with the last issued commands. Safety threatening misbehaviors cause *Alarm* events to be generated; minor problems are logged. The machine specification is given as an act diagram equivalent to the one used to define the requirements, but it is not shown here due to lack of space.

The second sub-problem, described by means of the problem diagram shown in Fig. 10, defines the effects of the signal *Alarm*. The requirements for the problem are defined using a state machine diagram composed of states representing the phases of the system, and transitions, triggered by the event *Alarm*, allowing the passage from each phase to the *Flashing* one. The requirements *stm* is similar to the ones that illustrate the operating modes and is not reported for space reasons. Also the machine specification is not shown since substantially equivalent to the requirements.

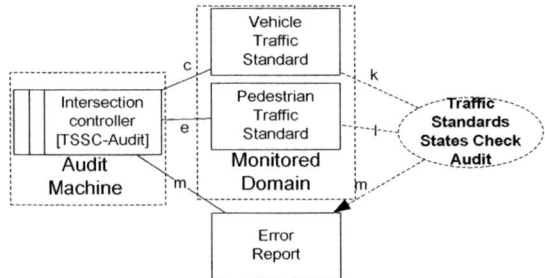

Fig. 8. Misbehaviors auditing sub-problem

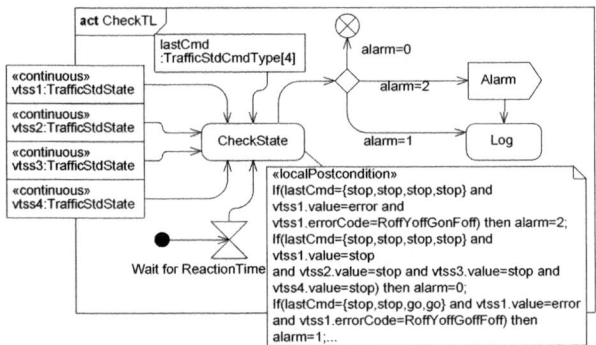

Fig. 9. Monitoring the states

3.3 Composition of Problems

Once the sub-problems have been identified, analyzed and a machine specification has been provided for each of them, their descriptions have to be recomposed. The goal is to define a unique machine specification that, once connected to the involved problem domains, satisfies both the requirements of each sub-problem and additional constraints that aim at addressing possible inconsistencies among the sub-problems. The analyst has to take into account the relationships between the sub-problems and how they overlap and interact. Such interactions occur whenever multiple sub-problems share domains and phenomena.

The correctness of the composition is the subject of composition concerns, which deal with conflicts and interferences that may affect both *indicative* and *optative* descriptions [1]. The concerns aim at addressing conflicts and interferences by introducing priority criteria, mutual exclusion and scheduling mechanisms.

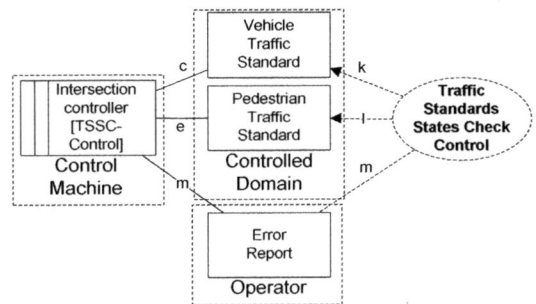

Fig. 10. Reacting to misbehaviors

Composition strategies are subject to the choices operated at decomposition time, hence, in what follow we propose two patterns that guide the composition of sequential and parallel problems, respectively.

3.3.1 Composition of Sequential Problems

The intersection controller operates in a single operating mode at a time. In the previous sections we have identified and described the single sub-problems representing the operating modes of the controller. We have also provided a machine specification for each sub-problem. The composition of these sub-problems requires coordinating the transition between operating modes by synchronizing their machines.

We propose to tackle the problem by means of a Composition Frame [4]. We define the composition by means of a new problem, named Operating Mode Coordinator (OMC), illustrated in the Problem diagram of Fig. 11.

The problem is characterized by the union of problem and machine domains of the sub-problems describing the operating modes. According to the Composition Frame, the machines of the sub-problems, labeled with the initial letter of the sub-problems' name ([SA] for Semi Actuated Mode, [MM] for Manual Mode, [PM] for Preempted mode) are considered given domains [1]. No phenomenon is shared by the machines of the sub-problems and by any other problem domains. According to the Composition frame, we introduce also a new machine, labeled OMC, which filters the connections between the machines of the sub-problems and the problem domains, specifying an interface composed of the union of all the existing shared phenomena. The OMC machine has to behave in a way such that it satisfies the coordination requirements by interacting with the other domains and machines.

The application of the Composition frame suggests a way to organize the composition of the problem, but it does not drive the resolution of the interferences between sub-problems. Interferences depend on the characteristics of the specific sub-problems to be composed, and must be addressed according to priority, mutual exclusion and scheduling principles defined by new requirements. In our case, such requirements can be formulated by considering the pre-conditions that enable an operating mode. Both the requirements and machine specifications of the sub-problems describing the operating modes define *Flashing* as initial phase.

However, the system can be in a different state when a mode change occurs, and we have to assure that the change of mode does not cause losing the current phase. In fact, the new mode has to start by resuming the current phase of the previous operating mode. This requirement is particularly relevant in case of emergency. Suppose that the emergency vehicle is arriving on an approach that has already the "Go" signal: the change of mode has to cause no change of the current phase. The new requirements, reported in Fig. 12, also constrain how and when it is possible to change the operating mode: in case the system is operating in semi-actuated mode and an emergency vehicle is approaching the intersection, it is required to automatically enable the Preempted mode.

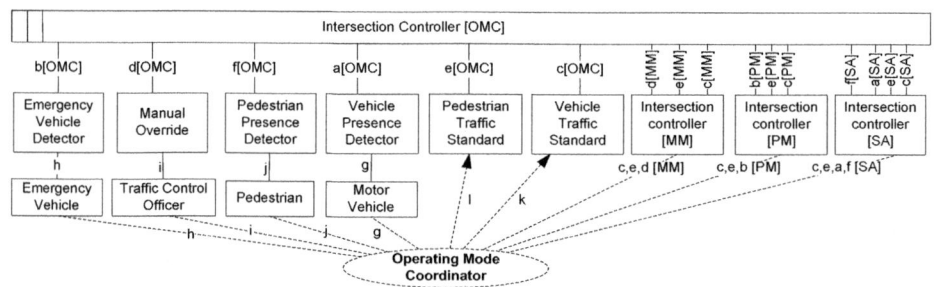

Fig. 11. OMC Problem diagram

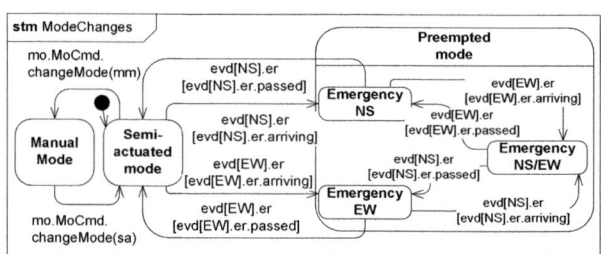

Fig. 12. Mode changes requirements

The last phase before enabling the preempted mode becomes the first phase of the preempted sequence. When the emergency is over, the controller has to return to the previous operating mode. The evolution of the stm is determined by events controlled by domains and observed by the machine of the OMC problem. These events are forwarded to the machines of the different sub-problems, which, in turn, generate commands that trigger the transitions between phases. Fig. 13 shows a small portion of the resulting *stm*, which considers the transition from the phase Stop-Go Walk-DNWalk to Stop-Wait Wait-DNWalk. Notice that the events "NextPhase", "Pr", and "Vr" generated by the console, pedestrian or vehicle detectors are forwarded to the machines of the sub-problems, which react generating signals that may enable a new phase. The machine specification differs from the requirements only for the commands to set the state of the traffic lights and it is not illustrated here because of lack of space.

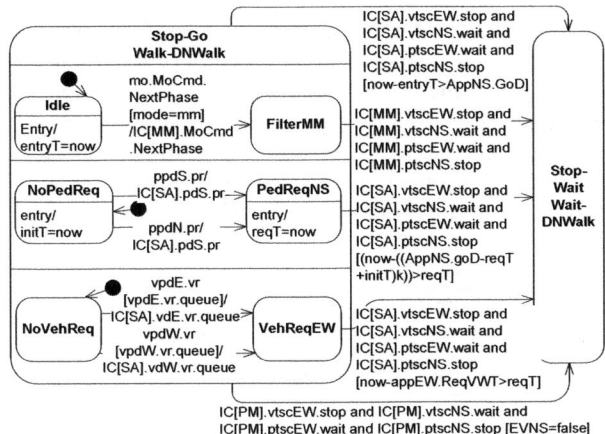

Fig. 13. A view on the *stm* of the requirements

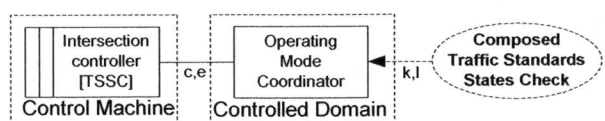

Fig. 14. TSSC Problem diagram

3.3.2 Composition of Parallel Problems

Once the sequential sub-problems have been re-composed, we can consider the interaction with the parallel sub-problems. We need to define the nature of the interaction, establishing whether parallel sub-problems may trigger behaviors described in other sub-problems and addressing possible interferences and conflicts. The State check problem is active in every operating mode.

A preliminary description of the problem –considered as "standalone"– has been given in Section 3.2.4. Now we have to consider its integration with the OMC one.

Hence, we introduce a new problem (illustrated in Fig. 14) characterized by a new integration machine -named Intersection Controller [TSSC]- and a new domain -named Operating Mode Coordinator- that contains the problem domains of the standalone TSSC sub-problems, and all the domains of the OMC (i.e., those that appear in

Fig. 11). This new integrated problem is modeled as a Required Behavior Frame (Fig. 14). The machine of the new problem constrains the connections of the OMC sub-machine with the traffic lights domains, by setting the phase *Flashing* whenever an event *Alarm* is generated. The new machine is characterized by the same interface as the machines of the "standalone" sub-problems TSSC-Audit and TSSC-Control (see Fig. 8 and Fig. 10).

The requirements of the composed problem specify the union of the required properties illustrated in the sub-problems OMC, TSSC audit and TSSC Control, and also additional constraints that address interferences among these sub-problems. Interferences may exist whenever different domains control the same phenomena, for instance, between the sub-problems TSSC Control, which describes the reaction of the controller in case of a malfunction, and OMC, which describes the coordination of the operating modes. For instance, an interference occurs when a serious error concerning the current state of the traffic lights is detected by the controller, which would react by setting the phase *Flashing*, and at the same time an emergency vehicle approaches the intersection, thus causing the intersection controller to switch to the Preempted mode and to force the transition to the phase that favors the crossing of the emergency vehicle: the two target phases are different!

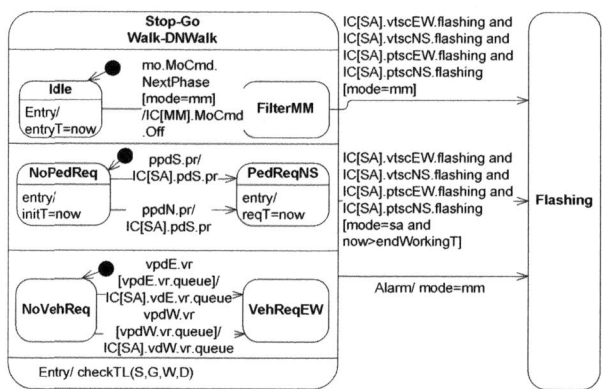

Fig. 15. A view on the stm of the requirements

Hence, whenever an event *Alarm* is generated, it is required to set the Manual operating mode, thus preventing the automatic change of mode and phase.

The requirements of the problem are described by means of the *act* diagram that illustrates the requirements of the TSSC Auditing problem (see Fig. 9), and a *stm* that extends the one used for describing the requirements of the OMC problem. Such a *stm* integrates the transitions of the *stm* of the TSSC Control problem, and also the management of the monitoring activity and the change of mode. Fig. 15 presents a portion of the resulting *stm* which shows that whenever a phase is enabled (and during the whole phase), the current state of the traffic lights is monitored by the action *CheckTL*. The phase *Flashing* can be reached from each phase through transitions that set the Manual mode once triggered by the event *Alarm*. Since the machine specification is not substantially different from the requirements it is not shown here.

4 Related Work

In the literature, requirements analysis and specification approaches based on PFs are usually applied to simple case studies. Only a few papers tackle their applicability to more or less realistic case studies. As a consequence, there is no evidence of the scalability of the analysis approaches. Among these few works, [11] shows the application of PFs to the modeling of the requirements of an online financial system. The same case study has been revisited in [12], describing different decomposition criteria that brought to the identification of different sub-problems and to the proposal of new basic frames. In [10] PFs are used for the analysis of a geographic application. [6] describes the usage of PFs to model the requirements of a system monitoring the transportation of dangerous goods. All the aforementioned works propose decomposition criteria that depend on the characteristics of the analyzed problems, and that cannot be easily abstracted to derive general criteria. On the contrary, the work reported in this paper introduces patterns that can be applied to different problems and domains.

Only a few research works propose (de)composition techniques at problem level. KAOS [7] and the NFR framework [8], together with PFs, are the techniques focusing on problems instead of solutions. However, both KAOS and NFR are goal based approaches and do not explicitly focus on domain properties.

Composition issues have been addressed by several aspect-based approaches [9], but they essentially focus on design and implementation issues. [13] is one among the few aspect oriented papers that address inconsistencies and conflicts among non functional requirements, but it does not address the decomposition of requirements.

Most of the research works found in the literature focus on formal techniques to merge behaviors or to deal with inconsistencies at model level [13]. Although these works focus on the solution space, some of the proposed techniques could be combined with PFs by redefining their scope at problem level. For instance, in [5] a formal approach for composing system behaviors defined as finite state automata is proposed. Such a technique could be adapted to support a (semi-) automatic composition of machine specifications defined using state machines.

5 Discussion and Lessons Learned

The work reported in this paper contributes to the evaluation of the applicability of PFs to case studies of realistic complexity. The experience has shown that PFs can help achieving a complete and clear comprehension of the requirements of the system. It has also confirmed that PFs can benefit from the modeling support of SysML. Although some of the benefits may not be evident from the few diagrams shown in the paper because of the lack of space, SysML modeled well both the structural and behavioral characteristics of the problem domains. It effectively supported the modeling of domains that represent non-pure SW components and the modeling of continuous behaviors (e.g., the monitoring of Fig. 9). SysML is also very promising with respect to scalability. It provides a full support for the decomposition and the projection of domains and phenomena using *bdd* and *ibd* diagrams, views and allocation mechanisms.

The modeling effort would range reasonable to small: PFs mitigated the effort by favoring the application of an incremental process. For instance, the modeling of the recomposed problem machines reused several parts of the specifications of the starting sub-problems. In order to further ease the re-composition we are studying techniques that allow automating the composition of activities like the merging of behaviors described with *stm* diagrams both at requirements and machine specification level.

All the identified frames were easily modeled; diagrams that expressed requirements, specifications and problem domains characteristics at the right level of abstraction and with an intuitive and expressive notation were easily created.

The case study also showed that the decomposition driven by the identification of parallel and sequential sub-problems mitigated the complexity of the original problem. However, such criteria do not help addressing a typical PFs based analysis: the same decomposition choices applied to the requested functionalities or to the machine responsibilities may results in different problems. The patterns facing the re-composition helped in addressing inconsistencies between the sub-problems. However, they represent one possible solution to the (de)composition. We need to identify multiple guidelines to drive the analysis and to refine and generalize them through a thorough analysis of several case studies.

We retain that both the analysis and the modeling could be further facilitated by general analysis guidelines to use PFs, and also by ready to use modeling elements representing frames and other basic concepts. Such elements are the base of a framework for the analysis of complex problems. This experience helped us identifying research directions for the framework definition. In order to better support the modeling we are working towards the definition of a SysML profile for PFs. We have also defined a meta-model for PFs and a tool, built on such a meta-model. This tool supports the analysis of problems using PFs [15]. We are planning to enrich this tool with a transformation engine capable of generating skeletons models of the SysML profile for PFs. The predefined guidelines will ease and speed up the learning of the approach by practitioners in requirements analysis and UML modeling. The proposed framework may ease and speed up the adoption of PFs by practitioners.

References

1. Jackson, M.: Problem Frames - Analysing and Structuring Software Development Problems. Addison-Wesley/ACM Press (2001)
2. Colombo, P., Del Bianco, V., Lavazza, L., Coen-Porisini, A.: A methodological framework for SysML: a Problem Frames-based approach. In: 14th Asia-Pacific Software Engineering Conference, APSEC 2007 (2007)
3. Lavazza, L., Del Bianco, V.: Combining Problem Frames and UML in the Description of Software Requirements. In: Baresi, L., Heckel, R. (eds.) FASE 2006. LNCS, vol. 3922, pp. 199–213. Springer, Heidelberg (2006)
4. Laney, R., Barroca, R., Jackson, M., Nuseibeh, B.: Composing Requirements Using Problem Frames. In: Int. Conf. on Requirements Engineering, RE 2004 (2004)
5. Mizouni, R., Salah, A., Kolahi, S., Dssouli, R.: Merging partial system behaviours: composition of use-case automata. Software, IET 1(4) (2007)

6. Colombo, P., del Bianco, V., Lavazza, L.: Using Problem Frames to Model the Requirements of a System for Monitoring Dangerous Goods Transportation. In: 3rd Int. Work. on Advances and Applications of Problem Frames, IWAAPF 2008 (2008)
7. van Lamsweerde, A.: Goal-Oriented Requirements Engineering: A Guided Tour. In: 5th International Symposium on Requirements Engineering, RE 2001 (2001)
8. Chung, L., Nixon, B.A., Yu, E., Mylopoulos, J.: Non-Functional Requirements in Software Engineering. Kluwer Academic Publishers, Dordrecht (2000)
9. Elrad, T., Filman, R., Bader, A. (Guest eds.): Special Issue on Aspect Oriented Programming. Communications of the ACM 44(10) (2001)
10. Nelson, M., Alencar, P., Cowan, P.: Informal description and analysis of geographic requirements: an approach based on problems. SoSyM 6(3) (2007)
11. Cox, K., Phalp, K.: From process model to problem frame - a position paper. In: Int. Work. on Requirements Engineering: Foundation for Software Quality, REFSQ 2003 (2003)
12. Cox, K., Phalp, K., Bleistein, S., Verner, J.: Deriving requirements from process models via the Problem Frames approach. Information and Software Technology 47(5), 319–337 (2005)
13. Rashid, A., Moreira, A.M.D., Araujo, J.: Modularisation and Composition of Aspectual Requirements. In: AOSD 2003 (2003)
14. Colombo, P., del Bianco, V., Lavazza, L., Coen-Porisini, A.: Towards a Meta-model for Problem Frames: Conceptual Issues and Tool Building Support. In: 4th Int. Conf. on Software Engineering Advances, ICSEA 2009 (2009)
15. Lavazza, L., Del Bianco, V.: A UML-based Approach for Representing Problem Frames. In: 1st International Workshop on Advances and Applications of Problem Frames (IWAAPF), an ICSE 2004 Workshop, Edinburgh, May 24 (2004)

Generative Technologies for Model Animation in the TOPCASED Platform

Xavier Crégut[1], Benoit Combemale[2], Marc Pantel[1],
Raphaël Faudoux[3], and Jonatas Pavei[1,4]

[1] Université de Toulouse, IRIT - France
Firstname.Lastname@enseeiht.fr
[2] Université de Rennes 1, IRISA, France
Firstname.Lastname@irisa.fr
[3] ATOS Origin, Toulouse - France
Firstname.Lastname@atosorigin.com
[4] Universidade Federal de Santa Catarina - Brazil

Abstract. Domain Specific Modeling Languages (DSML) are more and more used to handle high level concepts, and thus bring complex software development under control. The increasingly recurring definition of new languages raises the problem of the definition of support tools such as editor, simulator, compiler, etc. In this paper we propose generative technologies that have been designed to ease the development of model animation tools inside the TOPCASED platform. These tools rely on the automatically generated graphical editors of TOPCASED and provide additional generators for building model animator graphical interface. We also rely on an architecture for executable metamodel (i.e., the TOPCASED model execution metamodeling pattern) to bind the behavioral semantics of the modeling language. These tools were designed in a pragmatic manner by abstracting the various model animators that had been hand-coded in the TOPCASED project, and then validated by refactoring these animators.

Keywords: Generative technologies, Model animation, Model execution, Metamodeling pattern.

1 Introduction

Model Driven Engineering plays a key role in the development of safety critical systems by providing early Validation & Verification (V&V) activities for generic and domain specific models. It is thus mandatory to be able to build easily V&V tools dedicated to each Domain Specific Modeling Language (DSML). We will present in this paper some experiments conducted in the TOPCASED project on the use of generative technologies for graphical model animation tools. In order to design these technologies, we first defined a generic framework for implementing the model execution engines [1], this framework relies, on the one hand, on a metamodeling pattern [2] that extends the classical language definition metamodel with execution related metatypes and attributes; and on the other hand on a generic "discrete event" execution engine. The handling of each discrete event is represented as an endogenous model transformation (i.e., with the same source and target metamodel) that modifies only the attributes of the execution specific metatypes. This framework has been used to implement several model animators in TOPCASED using JAVA and SMARTQVT as transformation languages. Then, these animators were refactored in order to make commonalities explicit, and generation patterns were proposed in order to ease their development. In a last step, the specific parts of the animators were extracted from the first versions and integrated in the generated ones in order to validate our proposal.

Our presentation will rely on the SIMPLEPDL DSML, a toy process description language derived from SPEM. SIMPLEPDL has been designed in TOP-CASED as a simple yet representative use case for teaching and experimenting MDE generative technologies for V&V [3,4]. These technologies have been validated through complete use cases in TOPCASED such as SYSML/UML state machine and SAM[1] model animators.

We will first present the TOPCASED project, the SIMPLEPDL use case and the requirements expressed for model animators by industrial end users for the design of safety critical systems. Then the contributions of this paper are the key facts about the framework for model animation in TOPCASED that relies on: a) a metamodeling pattern for expressing model execution related metatypes; b) a discrete event system execution kernel and c) the use of endogenous model transformation for defining the handling of a specific event in the execution of a model. Then we show how generative technologies were introduced in order to factor out the common parts of the various model animators that had been hand-coded in the first versions of TOPCASED. Finally, we conclude on the current state of our experiments, and we give insights on our future work.

2 The TOPCASED Toolkit

2.1 The TOPCASED Project

TOPCASED[2] (*Toolkit In OPen source for Critical Applications & SystEms Development*) [5] is a project started in 2005 from the French "Aerospace Valley" cluster, dedicated to aeronautics, automotive and space embedded systems. TOPCASED aims at defining and developing an open-source, Eclipse-based, modular and generic CASE environment. It provides methods and tools for the developments of safety critical embedded systems. Such developments will range from system and architecture specifications to software and hardware implementation through equipment definition.

In this purpose, TOPCASED provides both domain specific (as SAM) and general purpose modeling languages (such as SYSML/UML, AADL, EAST-ADL,

---

[1] SAM is a DSML used at Airbus in the A350WB program for specifying inter-system interfaces, mode automata and early design level protocols.
[2] http://www.topcased.org

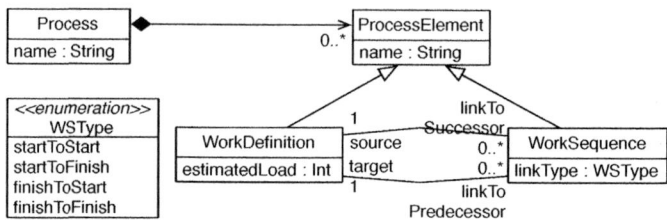

Fig. 1. Domain Definition Metamodel (DDMM) of SimplePDL

SDL, etc.) and associated tools like graphical and text editors, documentation and code generators, validation through model animation, verification through model checking, version management, traceability, etc.

TopCased relies on Model Driven Engineering (MDE) generative technologies to build all these tools for all these languages. It is thus an MDE platform both for building system models and for building the platform itself. MDE technologies used in TopCased for defining and tooling languages are centered around Ecore[3] and configuration models taken as inputs by generative tools (e.g. graphical editor generator).

2.2 Use Case

To illustrate the MDE approach used in TopCased, we rely on a simplified process description language called SimplePDL. SimplePDL is deliberately simplified to avoid overloading this presentation with useless details.

A metamodel is used to define the concepts (metaclasses) of the domain addressed by the DSML and the relationships between them (references). We call it the *Domain Definition MetaModel, DDMM*. The DDMM of SimplePDL is shown on figure 1. It defines the concepts of process (*Process*) composed of process elements (*ProcessElement*) that can be either a work definition (*WorkDefinition*) or a work sequence (*WorkSequence*). Work definitions are the activities that must be performed during the process. A work sequence defines a dependency relationship between two work definitions. The second work definition can be started or finished only when the first one is already started or finished according to the value of the attribute *linkType*.

A metamodel defines only an abstract syntax which is not adequate for human beings. Graphical concrete syntaxes are often a better way to create and manipulate DSML models. TopCased provides a graphical editor generator based on the description of the desired editor. Fig. 2 shows the generated SimplePDL graphical editor. For SimplePDL, one has to define how the SimplePDL concepts are graphically presented (as vertices or arcs) and to explain how to update the SimplePDL model when the graphical elements are created or changed.

---

[3] Ecore is the metalanguage of Eclipse Modeling Framework, www.eclipse.org/modeling/emf

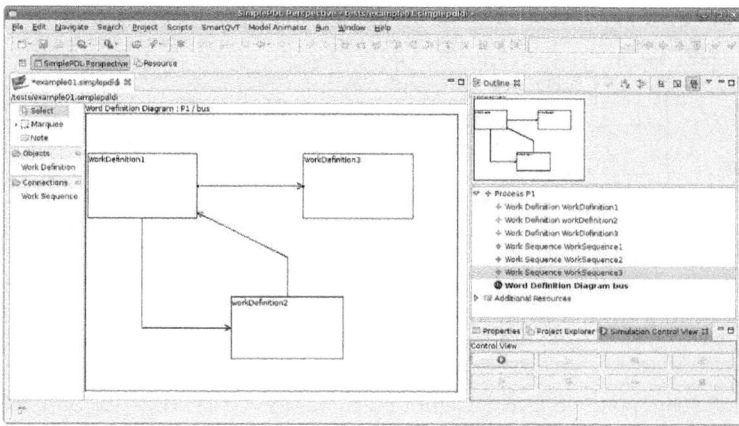

Fig. 2. SimplePDL Graphical Editor Generated with TopCased

2.3 Motivations for Model Animators

The use of DSML allows to introduce early V&V activities at the modeling stage, long before the end product is developped. Here are some key aspects extracted from TopCased end users requirements for model animation :

- Modeling is an error prone activity. A model animator allows the designer to check that the produced model really expresses the expected behavior. This is a validation that the model is a correct rendering of what the designer had in mind.
- The system design team needs to check that the proposed system fits the end user needs. A model animator allows to organise demonstrations of the system behavior connected to realistic system Human Machine Interface (HMI) and thus add the user in the loop. This is a validation that the specification is a correct rendering of the end user needs.
- Early models are usually an approximation of the final system that does not fit all the requirements, it is thus difficult to use exhaustive model verification tools that will detect a large number of errors that are due to the incomplete nature of these early models. Model animation allows to design interactively the verification scenario that fits the current state of the models. This is a partial verification of the appropriate parts of the model with respect to some specific requirements.
- Many behavioral verification tools rely on the semantics of the DSML. This semantics is usually specified by the DSML designer based on informal end users needs. A model animator allows the end user to play with this semantics and check that it really fulfills its needs. It is thus a good tool to validate the DSML definition.

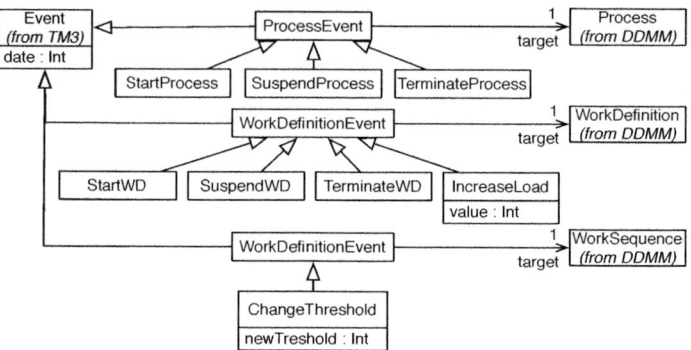

Fig. 3. One possible Event Definition MetaModel (EDMM) for SimplePDL

3 Model Execution in the TopCased Toolkit

The TOPCASED toolkit targets executable DSML. Thus, it must provide means to define their executable semantics. A metamodeling pattern has been defined to capture all the data required to execute a model and a framework is provided based on this pattern. Model execution is then the core building block to add animation facilities for a DSML.

3.1 A Metamodeling Pattern for Model Execution

When we want to simulate a process, that is to execute one of its models, we first have to understand and define what are the interactions between the model and its environment. For SimplePDL, it is possible to start or finish a work definition or record the load already spent on a work definition. The user may also want to specify the meaning of a precedence constraint and thus add a threshold on a work sequence that could be changed during process enactment. All these interactions are external events generated by the environment that will induce changes on the model itself. These external events are captured in the *Event Definition MetaModel, EDMM* (Fig. 3). An event has several attributes. For example, the event "*start a work definition*" takes the targeted work definition as attribute. The event "*increase work load*" has two attributes, the targeted work definition and the load increment.

The next step is to define scenarios as a set of ordered external events. They may be defined interactively during the animation itself or before the execution starts (batch simulation). A scenario is used to drive the execution. Starting from a model and a scenario, the execution produces an output trace of all the events that occurred during the execution (including external events and also possible internal events triggered by the handling of the other events by the semantics). Traces and scenarios are defined in the *Trace Management MetaModel* (*TM3*, Fig. 4).

The concepts captured in the *DDMM* are not sufficient to animate a model. For instance, some events may require additional informations. For example,

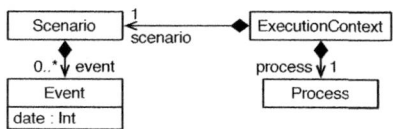

Fig. 4. Trace Management MetaModel (TM3)

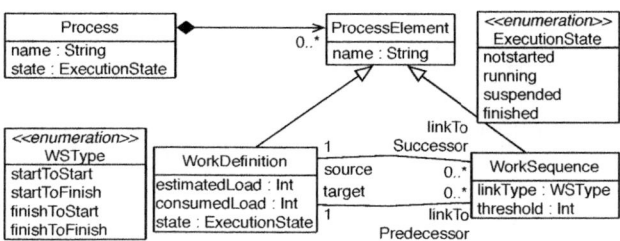

Fig. 5. State Definition MetaModel (SDMM) merged with the DDMM of SIMPLEPDL

the event *"increase work load"* means that the load of a work definition has to be recorded. We also have to be able to decide whether an activity can be started or not. So we have to know the state of its preceding activities. Thus, we propose to define a *State Definition MetaModel SDMM* that captures all the data required during an execution. On Fig. 5, new data have been directly added on the *DDMM*: *loadConsumed* and *state* on *WorkDefinition*, *state* on *Process* and *threshold* on *WorkSequence*. In fact they are defined in the SDMM that "completes" the DDMM. This may be achieved using the *merge* operator defined in MOF specification [6]. So, several SDMM may be defined for the same DDMM, each corresponding to a different execution semantics.

The four previous metamodels DDMM, SDMM, EDMM and TM3 constitute the architectural part of the metamodelling pattern that we have implemented in TOPCASED to support model execution. The execution semantics is still lacking. Its purpose is to define how the SDMM model evolves when a concrete event from the EDMM model occurs. Before describing that aspect, we present the TOPCASED framework for model execution based on this pattern.

3.2 The TOPCASED Framework for Model Execution

TOPCASED provides a framework for model execution based on the previous metamodelling pattern. It is composed of a generic core — independent of any DSML — (top of Fig. 6) that has to be specialized for a given DSML (bottom of Fig. 6).

The framework only depends on the runtime events defined for the DSML in the EDMM. The execution engine is built from three main components: Agenda, Driver and Interpreter. The first two components implement a discrete event computation model, based on the elements in the TM3 metamodel. They are thus generic and independent of any particular executable modelling language. The

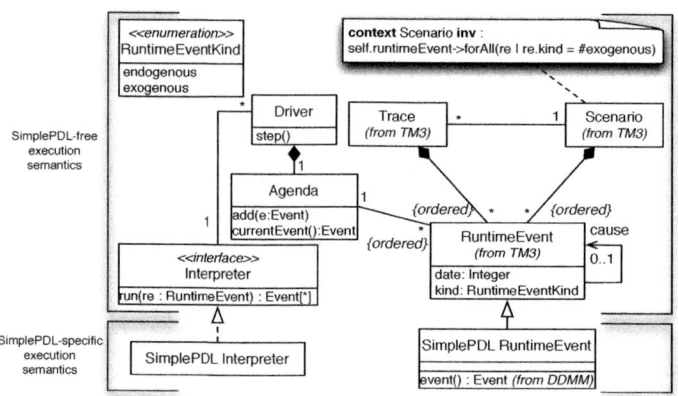

Fig. 6. Framework for Model Execution

Agenda stores the runtime events corresponding to one particular execution. Runtime events are ordered according to their occurring date. At the beginning of the execution, the Agenda instance is initialized with all the events contained in the scenario to be run. The Agenda provides the API required by the Driver to handle the events (e.g., to establish the next runtime event, to add a new runtime event).

The Driver controls the execution. It constitutes the interface with external components (mainly the Control Panel) thanks to a dedicated API, which allows both batch and interactive execution. Its step method consists in getting the next runtime event from the agenda and asking the Interpreter to handle it. The generated endogenous runtime events are then stored in the agenda.

Finally, the Interpreter abstracts the different possible semantics of the pluggable executable modelling language. Its run method interprets runtime events, updates the dynamic information of the model, and returns the list of generated endogenous runtime events. Obviously, the Interpreter is specific to the modelling language and supports its own semantics. It thus has to be specialized for the considered DSML.

The previous classes are the core of the framework. A generic user interface is developed on top of it. It is composed of an interactive *Control Panel* that emulates the environment and allows to add new runtime events into the Agenda. The SDMM model is displayed on the graphical visualization developed for the graphical editors. It is based on the notification facilities provided by the underlying EMF framework and the Adapter pattern to change the color of the graphical elements. These changes of graphical properties were sufficient to animate SysML/UML state machines or SAM models but had to be enhanced for SIMPLEPDL (see section 4).

3.3 Operational Semantics

The last part consists in implementing the *Intepreter* class to define the execution semantics. According to the concrete event received as parameter of the run method, one has to describe how the SDMM model evolves. In the first version of the TopCased animators, the run method was hand-coded using Java and the EMF API. Then, it has been written using SmartQVT, an open source transformation language that implements the OMG QVT specification and generates Java code that facilitates its integration in the TopCased framework. The main benefit of using SmartQVT is to ease the navigation on model elements as discussed in the next section.

Based on these technologies, model animators were implemented for SysML/ UML state machines and SAM models. The interactions with the end user and the graphical editors were hand-coded in Java. As these languages were quite similar one to the other, we developed a model animator for SimplePDL in order to reveal additional requirements. These implementations were abstracted in order to detect common patterns that could be generated thus leading to the following proposals.

4 Generative Tools and Extensions to the Animator's Core

Model animators are composed of three main parts: *semantics*, *controllers* and *animator* which have to be developed for each new DSML. Semantics implements the execution semantics. Controllers allows the user to inject new runtime events. Animator is responsible for allowing the user to inspect the execution. It relies on visualisation tools to display dynamic information and a control panel to drive the animation. In the first versions of TopCased model animators, these components were hand-coded. Our purpose for this work was to develop generative tools that accelerate the development of new animators by generating as much as possible parts of these tools. The first results of these experiments are presented here after.

4.1 Multiple Semantics Definition

In the actual architecture, one has to implement the Interpreter interface and its run method to define the DSML execution semantics. The code then generally starts with a big switch that selects and executes the reaction corresponding to the concrete event received as parameter of the run method. Furthermore, when writing the code implementing the reaction, one has to access the model. It would be helpful to add new helper methods on the model (EDMM and SDMM) to facilitate this. As these methods are specific to the semantics being implemented and because several semantics could be implemented for the same DSML, it is not a good idea to pollute the DDMM or SDMM with all those helper methods. A better solution is to implement the Visitor pattern.

We have defined a new plugin called org.topcased.semantics that provides two interfaces (considered as Eclipse extension points). The first one is called Semantics and uses overloading to specify one run method for each possible concrete event defined in the EDMM. The second interface is called Dispatcher and contains one single method dispatch(RuntimeEvent event, Semantics semantics). These two interfaces correspond to the Visitor and Visitable elements of the Visitor pattern. They are independent of any DSML.

The *Dispatcher* interface has only to be implemented once for each DSML. In fact it is generated from the EDMM model using Acceleo[4]. It implements the *accept* method that is normally present on the *Visitable* elements. In doing so, no change is required on the EDMM. The implementation of Dispatcher's dispatch method is a big switch on the concrete type of the runtime event that selects and executes the right run method of the semantics received as parameter. As the class is generated (like the *Semantics* and *Dispatcher* interfaces), there is no risk of missing some cases.

Then, defining a new execution semantics for a given DSML simply consists in implementing the Semantics interface. It is then possible to register several semantics for the same DSML. The user may then choose which one will be executed. For example, it would be possible to define a semantics that only handles start and finish events and a more precise one that also handles increments of work loads and thresholds.

The Visitor pattern could also be generated for the DDMM (and SDMM) models. The semantics defined on SimplePDL is rather easy to implement because most of the events only imply changes on the target element and do not require heavy navigation on the model. Nevertheless, *WorkDefinition*'s start and finish events require to check whether the states of the previous work definitions are consistent with the constraints defined on the corresponding work sequences. If the semantics had been implemented using Java/EMF, it would be useful to write such helper methods as new instances of the *Visitor* interface. But, as we rely on high level transformation languages such as SmartQVT or ATL, this pattern is useless. Indeed, such languages already provide the possibility to define new operations on the metaclasses of the models they manipulate.

4.2 Hierarchical Runtime Events

Using a model animator is useful to see the evolution of the model being executed. Nevertheless, the presentation of all the states and events and the associated navigation can be quite complex. It is thus mandatory to provide a functionality close to the *step into/step over* behavior of program debuggers. When debugging a program, step into shows the code of the called method and the execution of each of its instructions, one at a time. On the contrary, step over executes the method call in one step and only the final state is seen.

The same kind of mechanism is useful for model animation. For example, in the case of UML state charts, one transition is triggered by an UML event. An action may be associated to this transition. The action may even be a compound action composed of several actions. It means that when the transition is fired, it will generate a new internal runtime event to run the associated compound action and then other internal events, one for each action of the compound action

---

[4] http://www.obeo.fr/pages/acceleo

and so on. The user may want to see the effect for each individual action or only the result of firing the transition.

The solution we provide is based on hierarchical events. When an internal event is created it is considered as being generated by a parent event (either an external event or an internal one). When executing an event, the user can then decide to execute only that event (step into) or also its sub-events (step over).

This new functionality is not useful for the semantics implemented for SimplePDL, but would be required if we had hierarchical work definitions. We could also slightly change the semantics so that an activity whose load consumed is at 100% and all precedence constraints are fulfilled is automatically terminated. In this case, "*Change consumed load*", "*Start WorkDefinition*" or "*Finish WorkDefinition*" events may trigger new "*Terminate a WorkDefinition*" on the current activity or the activities depending on this one. Using step into and step over, the user could see individual changes to the model or only the final state of each work definition.

Hierarchical events are a more general solution than the previous one used for SysML/UML and SAM based only two levels of events (steps and micro-steps).

4.3 Improvement of the Model Graphical Visualization

The previous model animators in the TopCased project only allowed to change graphical properties (like color, font, etc.) of graphical elements representing DDMM elements. For example, to animate UML state charts, current states were shown in red and fireable transition were displayed in green. Unfortunately, changing only graphical properties is not enough to display all the information that is managed in the SDMM. We have thus enhanced the visualisation for the model animator. The basic idea is to rely on the basic graphical editor and to add decorations to represent information added in the EDMM. Fig. 7 shows the new SimplePDL animator. The work load of a *WorkDefinition* is represented as a progress bar. An icon in the upper right corner of a *WorkDefinition* shows its state (not started, runing, finished or interrupted). The threshold of a *WorkDefinition* and the *linkType* are displayed on the arcs that link the *WorkDefinition*.

The decoration mechanism is already provided as an extension point by the GMF[5] library. The work has thus mainly consisted in adding decoration such as progress bars, labels, figures, etc. on the elements of the graphical representation and relying on EMF notifications to update the graphical representations on changes on the SDMM model.

For the moment, this work is done manually. We are now working on a generator that would allow the end-user to define the decoration he/she wants to have and then to produce the enhanced animator.

4.4 Controllers for Event Creation

The last enhancement described in this paper concerns the controllers that allow the user to inject new runtime events in the simulation. For UML state machines

---

[5] The Eclipse Graphical Modeling Framework,
http://www.eclipse.org/modeling/gmf

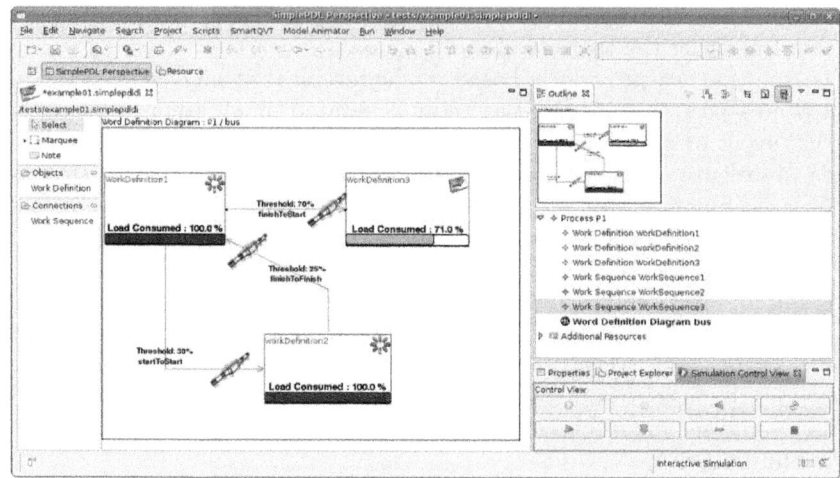

Fig. 7. Visualization of animated models by decorating the graphical editor

animators, a common controller had been defined. It mainly consists in collecting all the UML events[6] that could trigger transitions on the animated model. Those UML events were displayed in a list from which the user chooses the UML event to inject.

In the case of SimplePDL, runtime events have a target (a Process, a WorkDefinition or a WorkSequence) and may require parameters. For instance, IncreaseWDLoad targets a *WorkDefinition* and has an additional attribute corresponding to the value of the increment. In the same way, the newThreshold attribute of *ChangeWSThreshold* stores the new value of the threshold of a targeted *WorkSequence*.

Using Acceleo to perform model to text transformations, we have generated dialogs to display the possible runtime events and the associated parameters that have to be typed in. It is generated from the EDMM model. This dialog may be displayed from the contextual menu after having selected an element on the graphical visualisation. Obviously, only the events that have this type of element as target are selected.

4.5 Refactoring of Existing Animators

The above proposals have been applied to the existing model animators that had been hand coded in TOPCASED. The generators were applied on the metamodels following the execution pattern without any changes. Then the elementary semantics actions were cut and pasted from the previous implementation to the

---

[6] UML events are different from runtime events from the EDMM. Indeed the UML EDMM defines one runtime event called *InjectUMLEvent* which consists in injecting a UML event that will then be used to evolve the UML state machine (firing transitions).

generated skeletons. This refactoring was done in less than one day for each model animator and provided identical tools with better visualisation capabilities thus validating our proposal.

5 Related Works

Several tools support editions and simulations of models, described for example in an automata-like notation. Let us mention, among the more popular ones: *Sildex* [7], *StateMate* [8], *Uppaal* [9], the *Stateflow* module [10] in *Matlab/Simulink*, *Scilab/Scicos* [11], the Finite State Machine (FSM) model of computation of *Ptolemy II* [12], and the UML State Machine [13]. These tools provide graphical visualization of simulations highlighting active states and fireable transitions, coupled with means to visualize and record execution traces. Nevertheless, these tools embed their own hard-coded semantics for a given DSML, and there are important development work without possible reuse. In another way, we address in this paper a generative approach, specifying a DSML based tool for model animator definition of any DSMLs.

Sadilek, Wachsmuth et al. have followed a similar purpose in the EPROVIDE project: bestow a DSML with execution power [14,15,16]. Their framework allows to express the semantics of DSML using various technologies (including JAVA, PROLOG, ASM, QVT). They have experimented its use for PetriNet and SDL DSMLs. The dynamic informations are added to the metamodels in an ad-hoc manner depending on the use case, thus it does not allow to rely on generative technologies. Developers of graphical model animators are required to explicitly rely on APIs requiring a bit more work.

Soden, Eichler et al. have proposed the MXF (Model eXecution Framework) eclipse project [17] in order to define the M3Action graphical semantics description language. The EPROVIDE and TOPCASED projects are parts of the official potential technology users in the project and we plan to commit our metamodeling pattern for executable DSML and the associated generative tools in this context. We plan to provide implementation language specific adapter generators linked to EPROVIDE in that context.

6 Conclusion

The tools presented in this paper were the first results of the experiments in TOPCASED on generative technologies for model animator. We are currently extending that work in several directions:

- Common programming language debugger provides sophisticated conditional breakpoints facilities, we propose to rely on OCL in order to define conditional breakpoints that would stop the execution as soon as a property becomes false.
- Behavioral models properties usually encompass both static properties that must be satisfied at each step of the execution, and temporal properties that

relates the various steps of an execution. The use of TOCL would allow to define conditional breakpoints triggered by sequences of events and not only state contents.
- The current semantics does not provide a step-back facility. The user must start again from the begining if he wants to jump back in time. In order to avoid to store all the intermediate states of the model, we propose to rely on a bi-directional semantics implementation.
- graphical decorations for model animation are currently hand-coded. We propose to define an animation configuration model derive from the graphical editor configuration model to specify the decorators that must be added for a given semantics.

Acknowledgement

This work was partially supported by the french government DGCIS through the FUI TOPCASED project. The authors wish to thank P. Farail and J.-P. Giacometi from Airbus for their helpful comments, and the team from Atos Origin for their intensive development work in TOPCASED.

References

1. Combemale, B., Crégut, X., Giacometti, J.P., Michel, P., Pantel, M.: Introducing Simulation and Model Animation in the MDE TOPCASED Toolkit. In: ERTS (2008)
2. Combemale, B., Rougemaille, S., Crégut, X., Migeon, F., Pantel, M., Maurel, C., Coulette, B.: Towards rigorous metamodeling. In: MDEIS, pp. 5–14. INSTICC Press (2006)
3. Combemale, B., Crégut, X., Garoche, P.L., Thirioux, X., Vernadat, F.: A Property-Driven Approach to Formal Verification of Process Models. In: Enterprise Information System IX, Springer, Heidelberg (2008)
4. Bendraou, R., Combemale, B., Crégut, X., Gervais, M.P.: Definition of an executable spem 2.0. In: APSEC, pp. 390–397 (2007)
5. Farail, P., Gaufillet, P., Canals, A., Camus, C.L., Sciamma, D., Michel, P., Crégut, X., Pantel, M.: The TOPCASED project: a toolkit in open source for critical aeronautic systems design. In: ERTS (2006)
6. Object Management Group, Inc.: Meta Object Facility (MOF) 2.0 Core Specification, Final Adopted Specification (January 2006)
7. Winkelmann, K.: Formal Methods in Designing Embedded Systems - The SACRES Experience. In: Formal Methods in System Design, vol. 19, pp. 81–110. Springer, Heidelberg (2001)
8. Harel, D., Naamad, A.: The STATEMATE semantics of Statecharts, vol. 5(4), pp. 293–333. ACM Press, New York (1996)
9. Behrmann, G., David, A., Larsen, K.G., Möller, O., Pettersson, P., Yi, W.: Uppaal - Present and Future. In: Proceedings of the 40th IEEE Conference on Decision and Control (CDC 2001), Orlando, Florida, USA (2001)
10. Colgren, R.: Basic Matlab Simulink and Stateflow. In: American Institute of Aeronautics and Astronautics. AIAA Education Series (2007)

11. Campbell, S.L., Chancelier, J.P., Nikoukhah, R.: Modeling and Simulation in Scilab/Scicos. Springer, Heidelberg (2005)
12. Lee, E.A.: Overview of the Ptolemy project. Technical Memorandum UCB/ERL no M03/25, University of California at Berkeley (2003)
13. Dotan, D., Kirshin, A.: Debugging and testing behavioral uml models. In: OOPSLA Companion, pp. 838–839. ACM, New York (2007)
14. Wachsmuth, G.: Modelling the operational semantics of domain-specific modelling languages. In: Lämmel, R., Visser, J., Saraiva, J. (eds.) Generative and Transformational Techniques in Software Engineering II. LNCS, vol. 5235, pp. 506–520. Springer, Heidelberg (2008)
15. Sadilek, D.A., Wachsmuth, G.: Prototyping visual interpreters and debuggers for domain-specific modelling languages. In: Schieferdecker, I., Hartman, A. (eds.) ECMDA-FA 2008. LNCS, vol. 5095, pp. 63–78. Springer, Heidelberg (2008)
16. Sadilek, D.A., Wachsmuth, G.: Using grammarware languages to define operational semantics of modelled languages. In: Brakhage, H. (ed.) GI-Fachtagung 1975. LNCS, vol. 33, pp. 348–356. Springer, Heidelberg (1975)
17. Soden, M., Eichler, H.: Towards a model execution framework for eclipse. In: 1st Workshop on Behaviour Modelling in Model-Driven Architecture, pp. 1–7. ACM, New York (2009)

Model-Driven Engineering of Machine Executable Code

Michael Eichberg[2], Martin Monperrus[2], Sven Kloppenburg[1], and Mira Mezini[2]

[1] Kimeta GmbH, Germany
kloppenburg@kimeta.de
[2] Technische Universität Darmstadt, Germany
{eichberg,monperrus,mezini}@cs.tu-darmstadt.de

Abstract. Implementing static analyses of machine-level executable code is labor intensive and complex. We show how to leverage model-driven engineering to facilitate the design and implementation of programs doing static analyses. Further, we report on important lessons learned on the benefits and drawbacks while using the following technologies: using the Scala programming language as target of code generation, using XML-Schema to express a metamodel, and using XSLT to implement (a) transformations and (b) a lint like tool. Finally, we report on the use of Prolog for writing model transformations.

1 Introduction

Programs implementing static analyses of machine-executable code are complex [1,2]. In the terms of Brooks [3], they not only contain intrinsic complexity but also significant accidental complexity. In such programs, several modules are highly interdependent: reading machine-executable code at the byte level, inferring higher-order representation such as control-flow or data-flow graphs, and eventually checking this representation against a property to verify.

Even if these problems are more or less tractable, it is impossible to reuse static analyses across different, yet comparable sets of machine level instructions (e.g. between the Java and the Python sets of bytecodes). However, the ability to write analyses that can be reused across projects is of primary importance in commercial settings. Many industrial projects use multiple languages and technologies and reimplementing basically the same analyses again and again for different languages is not feasible. This state of facts motivated us to design from scratch a static analyses tool in a model-driven manner to improve reuse of analysis components.

So far, we have mentioned four main problems in implementations of static analyses: 1) reading low level formats, 2) inferring higher-order representations, 3) writing the analyses and 4) handling different kinds of executable code. In this paper, we present an architecture that separates all these concerns in different and clearly separated blocks, such that all links from one block to another are implemented using code generation or model transformation. Overall, our contribution is twofold: first, we describe a model-driven architectural blueprint for the application domain of static analysis tools; second, we report on important benefits and drawbacks of using different technologies for the implementation.

The main lessons we have learned from the design and implementation of our model-driven static analysis toolkit are:

- One of the code generators generates Scala code. It seems that this powerful target programming language has much facilitated the implementation of the generator.
- We chose XML-Schema as the implementation technology of the metamodel of executable code. Many, but not all domain-specific constraints could have been implemented with XML-Schema. This confirms the results of [4,5] showing that expressing the static semantics is never straightforward within only a structured metamodel.
- Implementing model transformations in Prolog to express static analyses allows us to write concise and declarative analyses.

The remainder of the paper is structured as follows: Section 2 gives the big picture of our approach. Sections 3 presents the metamodel for specifying bytecode instructions. Section 4 discusses the implementation of analyses. Section 5 lists the lessons we learned. Finally, Section 6 discusses related work and Section 7 concludes the paper.

2 Overview

This section presents the architecture of a new static analysis toolkit that we have been implementing for one year. The architure is designed in a fully model-driven way. First, it is based on three different levels of abstraction, layered in an ontological way as defined by Kühne [6], where the main artifact of each layer is an instance of the upper layer (a meta-layer w.r.t. the lower one.) Second, the architecture uses several times both code generation and model transformation.

Fig. 1 depicts this architecture in terms of the main artifacts and dependencies between them. Boxes represent data (in a larger sense: software to analyze, models, generated code, etc.), and arrows represent relationships between the data (also in a larger sense: generation, transformation, etc.). The three ontological layers are stacked, separated with lines and numbered (from "1" for the most abstract to "3" for the most concrete). The boxes that have a gray background are generated artifacts. We now describe each element at a conceptual level. The details about the technology used and the size and complexity are described in the following sections.

2.1 Meta Layers

Let us now describe the stacked layers of our architecture. We have defined a metamodel for bytecode instructions of virtual machines, which lies in layer #1,

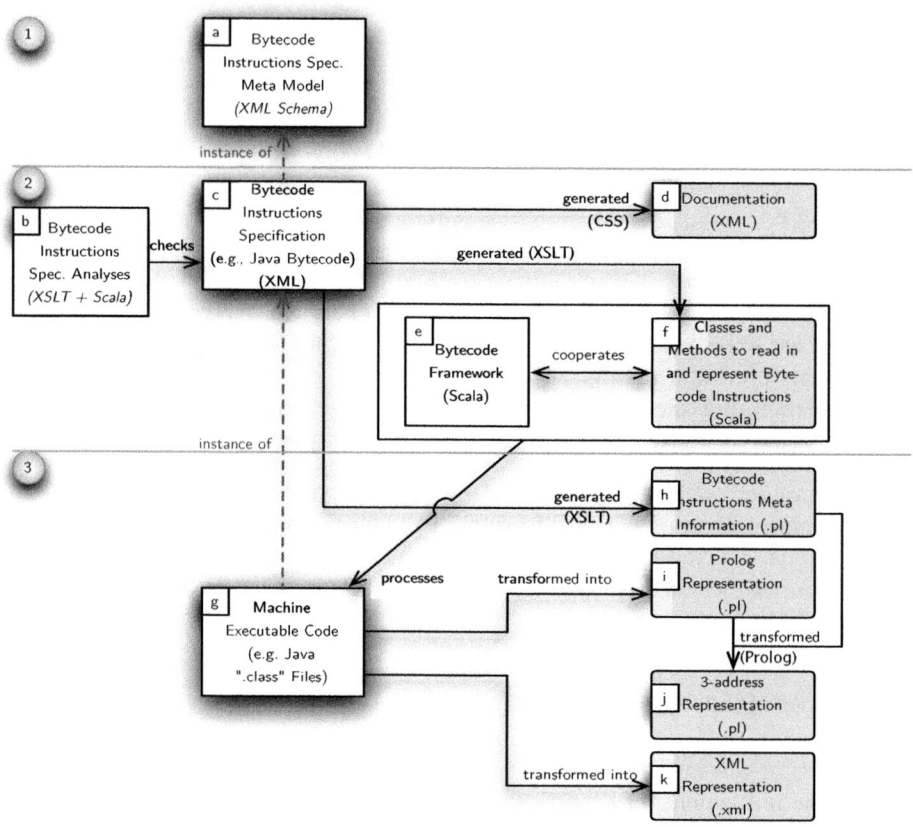

Fig. 1. Overview of the Architecture

at the top of Fig. 1 (a). This metamodel expresses what a bytecode instruction is: type of instruction (e.g. add or remove something to the stack), number of arguments, number of bytes in the machine-level format. This metamodel is further discussed in Section 3. An instance of this metamodel is a specification of bytecodes of a particular virtual machine, for instance, the specification of the Java bytecode instruction set [7] is an instance of the bytecode metamodel. In Fig. 1, an instance is represented in layer #2 as a *Bytecode Instructions Specification* (c). Finally, the software that is analyzed is an instance of a particular bytecode format, and is logically in the lowest layer, numbered #3 (i.e. (g)). If one analyzes Java software, each class file is an instance of the Bytecode Instructions Specification. Note that these three elements are shadowed and linked with dashed arrows "instance of" to emphasize the different levels of abstractions. The other boxes are tools (code generators, model transformations) to manipulate these elements.

2.2 Specification of Bytecode Instructions

The central *Bytecode Instructions Specification* (c) is the input of one domain-specific analysis and three code generators. The domain specific analysis (b) takes the specification as input, and checks whether the specification fulfills certain constraints. For instance, that each opcode only identifies one instruction and its directly related variants. This domain specific analysis is necessary since not all domain-specific constraints can be expressed within the uppermost metamodel.

Also, the *Bytecode Instructions Specification* is used to generate a human-readable and structured documentation of the specification (d). It is also used by two code generators: the first one generates object-oriented classes to read machine-executable code (f) and to represent it in memory with domain classes. This generated code cooperates with a manually written library for static analysis (e). However, note that this piece of code only addresses the concern of reading class files. It is independent of the concern of specifying the analyses themselves. The second code generator generates a library that supports the writing of static analyses called *Bytecode Instruction Meta Information*, (h).

2.3 Specification of Static Analyses

So far, we are able to specify a family of bytecode formats and to generate the tool to read and represent them in a domain-specific manner (i.e. no longer byte arrays, but instance of first-class instructions). Let us now explain how to write static analyses.

Basically, there are two ways to write static analyses, first one can write them directly on top of domain classes using standard programming languages or – as in case of our toolkit – as *declarative* static analyses. To enable writing declarative analyses, the analyzed software is transformed into two different artifacts that both represent the machine executable code at the same granularity. Class files can be transformed either into XML files (k) to write static analyses in an XML based language (e.g. XSLT or XQuery). Additionally, they can also be transformed in a set of Prolog facts (*Prolog Representation* – (i) in Fig. 1).

This set of Prolog facts enables us to write static analyses as Prolog rules which handle the basic facts. Further, these facts are given to a model transformation to obtain a higher-order representation of bytecode, called *3-address Representation* (j). The model transformation is also written in Prolog, using the model of analyzed software (as Prolog facts), and an additional source of information, the *Bytecode Instruction Meta Information* that is obtained automatically from the bytecode specification (and discussed above in Section 2.2). Section 4 provides a more in depth view on the static analyses.

2.4 Recapitulation

The architecture of our static analysis toolkit uses three stacked abstraction levels, one domain specific model validation, three code generators, and three model transformations. The following Sections (3 and 4) describe technical details. Section 5 then exposes the lessons learned in the design and implementation of this architecture.

3   A Meta-Model to Specify Bytecode Instructions

The meta-model for specifying bytecode instructions is called the OPAL Specification Language (OPAL SPL). It enables the encoding of instructions of stack-based intermediate languages, such as, Java Bytecode [7] or CIL Bytecode [8]. OPAL SPL is rich enough to accommodate different bytecode formats and enables the development of analyses and bytecode parsers that are independent of the concrete instance of the specification [9]. To support this goal, the language supports (i) the specification of the type system of the virtual machine which executes the bytecode, (ii) the format of the bytecode instructions and (iii) the specification of the effect on the stack and registers when the instruction is executed. OPAL SPL is focused on specifying the bytecode instruction set and not the complete class file format since the instruction set's structure is more regular and sufficient for developing certain static analyses. The metamodel also supports the declaration of functions (signatures only) to abstract over information that is not directly specified along with an instruction. The functions are implemented manually in a bytecode specific framework ("e" in Fig. 1).

Listing 1 shows the specification of the Java bytecode instruction `getfield` as an instance of the OPAL SPL metamodel: the `getfield` field instruction is an instance of the metaclass "Instruction". Note that this specification uses the functions decl_class_type (Line 4 in Listing 1) and field_type (Line 5) which are declared as part of the specification of the Java instruction set, these functions return the type information related to an object's field.

```
1  <instruction mnemonic="getfield">
2    The variable fieldRef is initialized by information in the class file.
3    <stack> <form>
4      <before><operand type="decl_class_type(fieldRef)"/><rest/></before>
5      <after><operand type="field_type(fieldRef)"/><rest/></after>
6    </form> </stack>
7  </instruction>
```

Listing 1. Specification of the Java Bytecode instruction `getfield` as an instance of the OPAL SPL metamodel

The specification of Java's `if_icmpne` instruction shown in Listing 2 demonstrates some of the features of OPAL SPL. In Line 2-5 the format of the instruction is defined; i.e., how the instruction is stored in a class file. In this case the instruction's opcode (Line 3) is an unsigned byte with the value 161. The opcode is followed by a signed short value representing a branch offset (Line 4). When the instruction is executed it pops two int values and then conditionally branches. The instruction does not push a value onto the stack (Line 10).

```
1  <instruction mnemonic="if_icmpne" transfers_control="conditionally">
2      <format> <sequence>
3          <u1 var="opcode">161</u1>
4          <i2 type="branchoffset" var="branchoffset"/> <!-- relative PC -->
5      </sequence> </format>
6      <stack> <form>
7          <before> <operand type="int_like"/>
8              <operand type="int_like"/>
9              <rest/></before>
10         <after>  <rest/></after>
11     </form> </stack>
12 </instruction>
```

Listing 2. Specification of the Java bytecode instruction if_icmpne as an instance of the OPAL SPL metamodel

4 Writing Static Analyses

Many static analyses can be expressed w.r.t. abstract representations of instructions, thus generalising the algorithm for a family of languages. This section demonstrates, how to express an algorithm to construct a control-flow graph. The model of a bytecode instruction set enables the generation of classes representing each instruction, as well as the reader of the binary format. This program is then used to transform machine executable code to a model of the software. A model transformation transforms it to a set of Prolog facts. For instance, Listing 4 shows the result of the transformation of a simple "Hello World" method (Listing 3) to the corresponding Prolog facts.

```
1 public static void hello(String [] args) {
2     if (args.length == 1) print("Hello " + args[0]) else print("Hello World");
3 }
```

Listing 3. Hello World in Java

```
1 method(cf_1,m_3,'hello',sig([array(class('java/lang','String'))],void),
2              public,abstract(no),final(no),static(yes),...).
3 /*Method Implementation: */
4 /*PC=1-3 */      Put the value 1 and the length of the array on the stack.
5 /*PC=3 */        instr(m_3,3,if_icmpne(13)).  // conditionally jumps to PC=16
6 /*PC=5-14 */     print("Hello "+args[0]);
7 /*PC=15 */       instr(m_3,15,goto_w(4)).
8 /*PC=16-18*/     print("Hello World");
9 /*PC=19 */       instr(m_3,19,return(void)).
```

Listing 4. Result of a Model Transformation from a Java Class File to a Prolog Representation

Let us now assume that we want to calculate the control-flow graph of a method. In this case, it is necessary to identify all instructions that start with basic blocks and to determine the order in which the basic blocks are executed. This requires that all control transfer instructions can be identified and also all instructions that – at runtime – are potentially directly executed after these instructions. As shown in Listing 2, Line 1 the information that the if_icmpne instruction is a control transfer instruction is directly encoded in the bytecode model. Since the instruction is a conditional control transfer instruction, the next instruction is a potential successor instruction and also the instruction where the program counter (PC) is the PC of the if instruction plus the branchoffset.

This meta-information is extracted from the Bytecode Instructions Specification (c) and also transformed to Prolog facts (h), as shown in Listing 5. A generic model transformation to identify a method's basic blocks is shown in Listing 6. The algorithm only assumes that instructions are encoded using a specific syntax (instr(METHOD_ID, PROGRAM_COUNTER, INSTRUCTION)) and, if the instruction is a conditional transfer instruction, that the INSTRUCTION is encoded as follows: MNEMONIC(BRANCHOFFSET, ...). Furthermore, the algorithm uses the meta-information about instructions (Line 4) to identify all control transfer instructions and all potential successor instructions. Hence, the algorithm does not make any assumptions about specific instructions and can provide a foundation for a complete control-flow graph algorithm.

```
1 control_transfer(if_icmpne,conditionally). % "conditionally" is defined by OPAL SPL
2 control_transfer(goto_w,always). % "always" is defined by OPAL SPL
3 control_transfer(return,caller). % "caller" is defined by OPAL SPL
```

Listing 5. Meta-information Related to Control Transfer (They are generated as Prolog facts from the Bytecode Instructions Specification)

```
1 bb_start_instr(MID,0) :- instr(MID,0,_). % the first instr. starts a basic block
2 bb_start_instr(MID,PC) :-
3   instr(MID,CurrentPC,Instr),
4   Instr =.. [Mnemonic|_],control_transfer(Mnemonic,T), T \= 'no',
5   ( ( PC is CurrentPC + 1, instr(MID,PC,_)); % ... if "PC" is valid
6     ( T = 'conditionally',
7       Instr =.. [_,Branchoffset|_], PC is CurrentPC + BranchOffset
8   ) )
```

Listing 6. Model transformation in Prolog to identify the method's basic blocks

5 Lessons Learned

In this section, we report on important lessons that we have learned when realizing the discussed architecture.

Overall Approach: Having an explicit meta-model [9] for specifying bytecode instructions did prove useful. First, given the XML-Schema numerous tools were available that facilitate writing documents according to the XML-Schema. These tools provide code completion and immediately report violations of the defined structure. Additionally, having a schema helped us to get a consistent specification of the Java Bytecode instructions. Several times during the development of the framework we did have to extend and adapt the meta-model to accommodate for the specifics of further instructions. Given the meta-model we were able to rethink and adapt parts of it while being sure to understand the impact on the instructions that have been specified so far, i.e., having an explicit meta-model made it easier to change and extend it since it is possible to assess the impact of changes. Given the meta-model also facilitated the development of generic analyses since it is well-defined which information is generally available. If the specification is only implicitly available one is tempted to look at the concrete instance of it; e.g., the specification of Java bytecode instructions, and to make wrong assumptions about the information that will be common to all instantiations.

Checking Specifications: XML-Schema enables us to express syntactic and, to some extent, semantic constraints which are useful to validate concrete bytecode specifications. However, using XML-schema it is not possible to prevent or detect more complex errors. For example, to make sure that a sequence of instructions is parseable, every instruction has to have a prefix path that uniquely identifies the instruction.[1] In case of the if instruction shown in Listing 2 the opcode uniquely identifies the instruction. But, in case of some other instructions it is necessary to read multiple values before it is possible to identify the (variant of) the instruction. Using XSLT we were able to efficiently implement an analysis (basically using XPath expressions) that checks that every instruction has a unique prefix path. But, implementing a type checker in XSLT worked out to be too troublesome due to XPATH / XSLT's lack of support of other data structures than lists of nodes. We decided to use Scala for this task. The combination of XML-Schema, XSLT and Scala to fully express the static semantics of our bytecode metamodel is heavyweight. However, to our knowledge and at the time of implementing our architecture, there was no metamodeling paradigm that was powerful enough to express all kinds of constraints in a concise and elegant manner.

Overall, writing a lint like tool for OPAL SPL provided two significant benefits. First, we were able to find numerous errors early on. Second, it helped us designing the language, because writing the analyses requires to take the perspective of the user of the language. This helps to identify issues that are relevant when the specification language is used later on. The effect of writing analyses on the design of the language seems to be roughly comparable to the effect of writing test cases early on.

Scala as the Target Language for Code Generation: From our experience using Scala (compared to, e.g., Java) as the target language for code generation is beneficial. Scala offers the following features that are of particular interest:

---

[1] In Java Bytecode the instructions do not have the same length, further some instructions even have a flexible length.

flexible syntax, case classes, type inference, implicit type conversions, semicolon inference, an expressive type system, built-in support for XML and tuple types. In the following, we discuss some of these features to highlight the effect on the code generator.

The flexible and concise syntax of Scala is exemplified by class and constructor definitions. Some code that defines a class that inherits from another class and which defines a field that cannot be changed and is publicly available is shown in Listing 7.

```
1  class ANEWARRAY ( val cmpType : ReferenceType ) extends Instruction {... }
```

Listing 7. Definition of the class ANEWARRAY in Scala

If we compare this class definition with a corresponding class definition in Java (cf. Listing 8) the number of parts that are dynamically generated is much smaller. In Scala, the name of the class (ANEWARRAY), the name of the variable (cmpType) and the variable's type (ReferenceType) occur exactly once. In case of Java, the name of the generated class, and the type of the field both appear twice. The field's name even appears four times. Hence, in case of Scala three parts are generated while in case of Java eight would need to be generated. This advantage of Scala is directly reflected in the code generator, it is correspondingly less complex.

```
1  public class ANEWARRAY extends Instruction {
2      public final ReferenceType cmpType;
3      public ANEWARRAY(ReferenceType cmpType) { this.cmpType = cmpType; }
4      ...
5  }
```

Listing 8. Class definition in Scala

A similar advantage is offered by Scala's case classes. Case classes are Scala's way to allow pattern matching on objects. Basically, for case classes the scala compiler generates default implementations of the equals and hashCode methods that operate on the object's state and not on its reference. Furthermore, factory methods are provided to create objects of the particular type and functionality is provided to take the objects apart to enable pattern matching. To get this functionality it is just required to add the keyword case in front of a class declaration (cf. Listing 9). If we would need to generate the corresponding code, the generator would be orders of magnitude more complex.

```
1  case class ANEWARRAY ...
```

Listing 9. Case Class

To sum up, from our experience a language, such as Scala, that provides advanced language features (e.g., higher-order functions, advanced type systems) does make developing a generator easier. Writing the generator will require less code and more errors in the generated code will be detected early on. Overall, the generator will be more comprehensible and maintainable. Many features of Scala that sometimes are considered "syntactic sugar" were, however, at least as important when developing the generators. As outlined above, semicolon inference, case classes, and implicits support also made the generators less verbose. We are confident that the features proposed for the upcoming versions of Scala (e.g., named arguments and default arguments) will further strengthen the position of Scala as a target language for code generation.

Handling XML-based code generators with Scala: In our architecture, Scala is not only used as target language, but also as an implementation language of certain generators. As shown in Fig. 1 (Artifact (k)), our framework supports an XML representation of bytecode. The functionality to transform the bytecode into XML is provided by Scala classes. Thanks to Scala's built in support for XML, writing a Scala program that generates XML is facilitated.

For instance, the Scala code that generates the XML representation of the if_icmpne instruction is shown in Listing 10. The method body toXML contains an XML pattern which contains values to be replaced (e.g. pc.toString). Thanks to Scala, there is no need to explicitly creates nodes of the generated XML document or to enclose the generated text in print-like statements.

```
1  def toXML(pc : Int) =
2    <if_icmpne pc={ pc.toString }>
3      <branchoffset value={ branchoffset.toString }/>
4    </if_icmpne>
```

Listing 10. Excerpt of Scala Code that Transforms Java Bytecode into XML

To conclude this section, Table 1 sums up the lessons that we learned while designing and implementing a model-driven static analysis toolkit. These findings are rarely explicitly stated in the literature and supported by empirical facts.

Table 1. Main lessons learnt while implementing a model-driven static analysis toolkit

#	Short description
1	Having explicit layers of abstraction helps to identify generic and specific parts.
2	The mature tool support for XML and XML-Schema is really useful for modeling and metamodeling (e.g. code completion).
3	XML-Schema can only be used to only express a small part of the static semantics of a real-world metamodel.
4	XSLT is a pragmatic and good choice to express most of the static semantics of a metamodel implemented with XML-Schema.
5	The need for expliciting the static semantics has a positive impact on the metamodel structure.
6	Using Scala as target language of a code generator ends up in a more readable, maintainable and concise generator.
7	The syntactic support of Scala for writing/reading XML files simplifies the implementation of XML based code generators.

Especially, to our knowledge, there is little work explaining the pros of using a powerful and high level language (such as Scala) as a target language of a code generator (see [10]).

6 Related Work

This paper presents a successful application of the model-driven principles to the domain of static-analysis. Although model-driven architecture has been applied to the development of a wide range of domains, e.g. simulation [11] or multi-agent systems [12], we are the very first to report on its use for static-analyses of programs.

However, both our motivations (extensibility and reuse) and the idea of using modeling to facilitate the implementation of static analyses were alread raised in survey papers. For instance, Jackson and Rinard [1] coined the term *"model-driven code analysis"*. They emphasize on the need for explicit models in analysis. We are going further: in our approach, we handle: (i) explicit models of types of machine code (Section 3), (ii) explicit models of programs (Section 3) and (iii) explicit models of analyses (written declaratively in Prolog, see Section 4). Also, note that Binkley [2] also states that writing static analyses is difficult as well as designing them as flexible.

Evans and Larochelle [13] presented a lightweight and extensible static analysis. The design of their tool anticipated the support for new checks and annotations. On the contrary, in our approach, all new analyses are supported in a standard way, with no special ad hoc tool. For instance, one can write a new analysis for the bytecode specification (Section 3) as an XSLT program, or a bytecode analysis using Prolog.

The research on reverse engineering has investigated for a long time the need for parsing and understanding software. Rugaber proposes a generic solution called *"model-driven reverse engineering"* [14]. While our main goal is not reverse engineering, we also manipulate program models. Hence, it seems to be straightforward to use our toolchain for reverse-engineering which would be another proof of the flexibility of the approach.

Finally, it is important to differentiate between metamodels of source code and metamodels of machine executable code. They are not at the same level of abstraction. For instance, Strein et al. [15] presented a metamodel for program analysis. While we share similar motivations (extensibility and performance of analyses), their metamodel is much closer to the program structure of the source code with goals such as vizualisation. On the contrary, we reason at the level of the execution machine, with other kinds of verification such as pointer analysis. The same argument applies for [16] in which Störrle uses Prolog not to represent machine code but high-level models.

7 Conclusion

Engineering machine-executable code to write static analyses is a complex task. To tame this complexity, we experimented with the design and implementation of a new static analysis toolkit following a model-driven architecture. We are the first to report on a concrete design and implementation of a model-driven tool chain for implementing static analyses of machine executable code. We managed to obtain a system that is loosely coupled and that allows us to reuse code and semantics across different types of machine-level code (different bytecode instruction sets).

Furthermore, this experiment showed that XML based technologies (XML-Schema, XSLT, XSLT, Scala support for XML) nicely fit together in a model-driven architecture and that using an advanced, high-level language as target of a code generator leads to a more clean and concise code generator.

References

1. Jackson, D., Rinard, M.: Software analysis: A roadmap. In: Proceedings of the Conference on The Future of Software Engineering, pp. 133–145 (2000)
2. Binkley, D.: Source code analysis: A road map. In: Future of Software Engineering (FOSE 2007), Washington, DC, USA, pp. 104–119. IEEE Computer Society, Los Alamitos (2007)
3. Brooks, F.: No silver bullet: Essence and accidents of software engineering. IEEE computer 20(4), 10–19 (1987)
4. Garcia, M.: Formalizing the well-formedness rules of EJB3QL in UML+ OCL. In: Kühne, T. (ed.) MoDELS 2006. LNCS, vol. 4364, p. 66. Springer, Heidelberg (2007)
5. Strembeck, M., Zdun, U.: An approach for the systematic development of domain-specific languages. Software: Practice and Experience 39(15) (2009)
6. Kuehne, T.: Matters of (meta-) modeling. Software and System Modeling 5(4), 369–385 (2006)
7. Lindholm, T., Yellin, F.: The Java Virtual Machine Specification, 2nd edn. Addison-Wesley, Reading (1999)
8. ISO/IEC Geneva, Switzerland: Information technology – Common Language Infrastructure (CLI) Partitions I to VI. ISO/IEC 23271:2006(E) edn. (2006)
9. Eichberg, M., Sewe, A.: Encoding the java virtual machine's instruction set. In: Proceedings of the Fifth Bytecode Workshop. Electronic Notes in Theoretical Computer Science. Elsevier, Amsterdam (to appear)
10. Kelly, S., Tolvanen, J.P.: Domain-Specific Modeling: Enabling Full Code Generation. John Wiley & Sons, Chichester (2008)
11. Monperrus, M., Jaozafy, F., Marchalot, G., Champeau, J., Hoeltzener, B., Jézéquel, J.M.: Model-driven simulation of a maritime surveillance system. In: Proceedings of the 4th European Conference on Model Driven Architecture Foundations and Applications (ECMDA 2008), vol. 13. Springer, Heidelberg (2008)
12. Pavon, J., Gomez-Sanz, J., Fuentes, R.: Model driven development of multi-agent systems. In: Proceedings of the European Conference on Model Driven Architecture - Foundations and Applications, ECMDA 2006 (2006)
13. Evans, D., Larochelle, D.: Improving security using extensible lightweight static analysis. IEEE Software (2002)
14. Rugaber, S., Stirewalt, K.: Model-driven reverse engineering. IEEE Software 21(4), 45–53 (2004)
15. Strein, D., Lincke, R., Lundberg, J., Löwe, W.: An extensible meta-model for program analysis. IEEE Transactions on Software Engineering 33, 592–607 (2007)
16. Störrle, H.: A prolog-based approach to representing and querying software engineering models. In: Proceedings of the Workshop on Visual Languages and Logic (VLL 2007), pp. 71–83 (2007)

eSPEM – A SPEM Extension for Enactable Behavior Modeling

Ralf Ellner[1], Samir Al-Hilank[2], Johannes Drexler[2], Martin Jung[2], Detlef Kips[1,2], and Michael Philippsen[1]

[1] University of Erlangen-Nuremberg, Computer Science Department 2, Programming Systems Group, Martensstr. 3, 91058 Erlangen, Germany
{ralf.ellner,philippsen}@cs.fau.de

[2] Develop group Basys GmbH, Am Weichselgarten 4, 91058 Erlangen, Germany
{alhilank,drexler,jung,kips}@develop-group.de

Abstract. OMG's SPEM – by means of its (semi-)formal notation – allows for a detailed description of development processes and methodologies, but can only be used for a rather coarse description of their behavior. Concepts for a more fine-grained behavior model are considered out of scope of the SPEM standard and have to be provided by other standards like BPDM/BPMN or UML. However, a coarse granularity of the behavior model often impedes a computer-aided enactment of a process model. Therefore, in this paper we present eSPEM, an extension of SPEM, that is based on the UML meta-model and focused on fine-grained behavior and life-cycle modeling and thereby supports automated enactment of development processes.

Conventions in This Paper

Names of meta-classes, packages, and properties are printed in *italics*, names of model elements in `monospaces`, and names of a model element's meta-class are **boldface**. Whenever we refer to SPEM or UML without explicitly specifying a version, we mean SPEM Version 2.0 [1] and UML Version 2.2 [2].

The figures in this paper show meta-elements (e.g., meta-classes, packages, and associations) initially defined in SPEM or UML and their instances (model elements) with a white background and thin lines. Meta-elements that are introduced by eSPEM and their instances are shown with a light gray background and thicker lines. Figures showing parts of the eSPEM refer to the merged, flat meta-model and therefore do not show qualified names. For sake of readability, attributes, operations, and constraints of meta-classes are omitted in the figures unless we refer to them.

SPEM clearly distinguishes between processes and methods. This is reflected in the meta-model with different meta-classes for identical or similar concepts (e.g., *TaskDefinition* for a method and *TaskUse* for a process). Whenever we do not specifically name a meta-class (e.g., *Task* instead of either *TaskDefinition* or *TaskUse*), we are referring to both the method and the process meta-classes.

1 Introduction

Developing software systems in international teams spanning several organizations requires well-defined software development processes (SDP) [3,4]. In order to efficiently define and execute SDPs, one needs 1) a process modeling language (PML) that is rich enough for automatic SDP enactment, 2) an easy-to-use process modeling environment (PME) that is flexible enough for different project categories, and 3) a process execution environment (PEX) that can be adapted to be integrated into existing development tool chains. To be useful for practitioners, there are some well-known requirements PMLs must fulfill [5,6,3]. Exploiting our numerous experience from real-life development projects, we enhance these PML requirements gaining the following list of requirements that a well-integrated combination of PML, PME, and PEX has to fulfill:

- Scalability. The PML used to describe an SDP must work for large as well as small processes.
- Decomposability. Subprocesses and their interfaces with compound processes can be defined.
- Adaptability. Tailoring a given process description to the needs of a defined project must be straightforward.
- Testability. Plausibility checks can be performed automatically on a process description to help in designing SDP models, to supervise their enactment, and to ease CMMI and SPICE auditing [7,8].
- Easy-to-digest formalism. An easy-to-digest formalism is needed because in the past complex formalisms have prevented fine-grained development process models from being adopted by practitioners (see for example [3]).
- Executability. The PML can be directly interpreted by a machine or otherwise mapped to another executable language.
- Automatic process enactment. Using the SDP model formulated in a PML as an input, the PEX supports and guides stakeholders in their work according to the process. It triggers certain activities on time, e.g., it invokes the tools the developers need to open artifacts, and controls the delivery of artifacts.
- Integration. Tools that are already used by developers must be integrated into the PEX.
- Electronic process guide. The SDP documentation actively guides developers by providing information that is sensitive to the task context at hand.
- Automatic audit trail. The PEX automatically keeps track of changes to artifacts as well as progress and conformance of a project with respect to the SDP.

Many of the PMLs known from literature can only partially fulfill the requirements listed above. SPEM (Software and Systems Process Engineering Metamodel) defined by the OMG [1] constitutes a promising approach. As SPEM is based on UML Infrastructure and defines a graphical notation, it is easy to pick up by practitioners, and is considered an ideal basis for SDP modeling. SPEM adequately fulfills the mentioned requirements for a PML except one: executability [9].

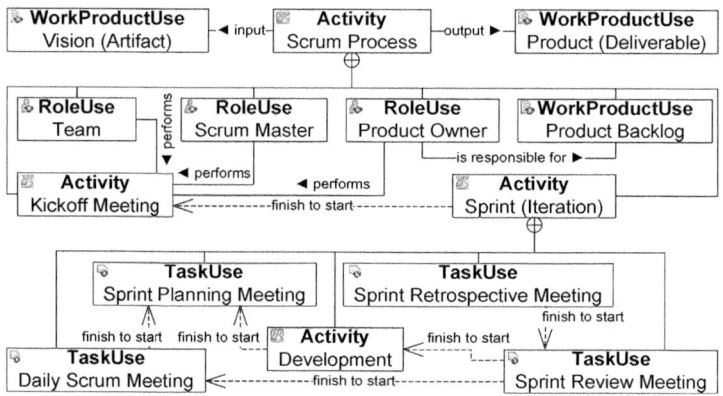

Fig. 1. A SPEM model for the WBS of Scrum

To understand what is required for executability, consider Fig. 1 that demonstrates how SPEM can be used to describe the static structure of an SDP. It shows – with some omissions due to readability – the work breakdown structure (WBS) of the Scrum [10] SDP. However, the problems shown in this example are not specific to Scrum but apply to SDP modeling with SPEM in general.

Many static SDP concepts can be easily expressed in SPEM: *Roles* like Team or Scrum Master may perform work like the *Activity* Kickoff Meeting. *Activities* may have *WorkProducts* as parameters, may be decomposed into sub-activities, and contain further SDP elements. The basic execution order of *Activities* and *TaskUses* is given by precedence edges (e.g., finish to start). *Roles* may also be responsible for certain *WorkProducts*. When considering the requirements listed above, there are at least three types of problems:

First, SPEM does not provide its own behavior modeling approach but leaves the integration of behavior modeling languages up to implementers of the specification [1, Sect. 10, p. 69]. However, without fine-grained behavior modeling concepts for proactive and reactive control, no reasonable support can be provided by a PEX that enacts the process. The SPEM standard suggests UML (*Activities* and *StateMachines*) [2] or BPDM/BPMN [11] as candidates. For interfacing behavior modeling languages SPEM provides several generic meta-classes as depicted in Fig. 2.

In our approach we use the behavior modeling concepts from UML. Their notation is common and therefore easy to pick up by practitioners. It includes constructs that are necessary for a precise behavior modeling of SDPs (e.g., *StateMachines*) but are not available in BPDM/BPMN. Although UML does provide the constructs required for a fine-grained modeling of the behavior of SDPs (e.g., asynchronous events and decisions), the SPEM concept for interfacing with behavior modeling languages is cumbersome to use.

Considering Fig. 2, it is obvious that *Roles* may trigger *Transitions* but cannot directly trigger *Events* or execute *Actions*. Consequently, when using this

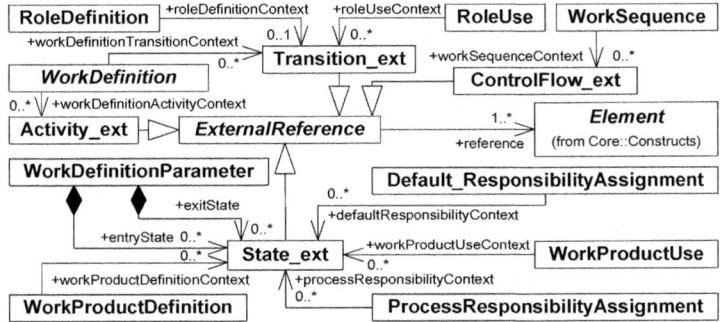

Fig. 2. Behavior model integration in SPEM package *ProcessBehavior* [1, Fig. 10.1]

behavior interfacing mechanism from SPEM, constructs for reactive control (e.g., events and decisions) cannot be sufficiently integrated into the SDP model.

SPEM uses a set of *States* to describe the life-cycle of a *WorkProduct* instead of a *StateMachine*. This contradicts our requirement of an easy-to-digest formalism because it complicates modeling and requires additional consistency rules. In order to avoid these drawbacks of the proposed behavior integration concept from SPEM, we will provide our own solution, combining the advantages of the static process structure modeling features offered by SPEM with the convenient behavior modeling concepts of UML.

Second, experience in industrial development projects shows that in most cases the *Tasks* performed throughout a process are not completely known in advance, but have to be determined and planned when the process is already being executed (e.g., [10]). Another problem exists: Creating, planning, and executing *Tasks* often happens at different points during a process (e.g., in Scrum tasks of a sprint are created and planned in the `Sprint Planning Meeting` and executed during `Development`). In SPEM *Tasks* are always instantiated and executed right away. Thus, the stakeholders cannot be sufficiently supported when planning or working with dynamically created *Tasks*.

Third, modern agile SDPs tend to be used with a wide variety of different development methods without changing the process itself (e.g., the `Sprint Planning Meeting` in Scrum can be used with many different estimation methods). SPEM supports a separation between process and methods using meta-classes that act as proxies for meta-classes representing method elements (e.g., *TaskUse* is a proxy for a *TaskDefinition*). However, a proxy may reference at most one method element. Consequently, changing the target of the proxy also requires changing the process part of the model using SPEM's tailoring concept and raises the modeling effort to adapt a SPEM-based process to a project's needs.

Due to these three issues (behavior modeling support, planning support, and configuration support) many SDPs (e.g., Scrum, Open Unified Process (OpenUP) [12], and V-Modell®XT [13]) cannot be sufficiently modeled with SPEM. Moreover, without such a fine-grained modeling of SDP concepts the stakeholders cannot be sufficiently guided and supported by a PEX that uses the SDP model as its input. We address these shortcomings in this paper and present eSPEM, a CMOF-based extension of SPEM and the UML Superstructure, that enables the mentioned automatic enactment of SDPs and adequately fulfills all requirements listed above. Additionally, eSPEM also provides solutions for other issues, e.g., instance feature support (*Properties* and *Operations*), enhanced *Kinds*, and detailed *WorkProduct* structure modeling. However, we cannot discuss these solutions in this paper due to space restrictions.

The subsequent paper is organized as follows: Section 2 addresses the three main issues of SPEM and presents our solutions. In Sect. 3, we apply eSPEM to SDPs used in industry, followed by a detailed comparison to other existing approaches in Sect. 4. In Sect. 5, we conclude with a brief outlook at the next steps of our project towards a fully automated enactment of SDP models.

2 Proposed Solution

First, we will show how we substitute behavior interfacing concepts of the original SPEM with our more fine-grained approach. We will then present the additional extensions introduced to enhance SDP enactment support. For complexity reasons, the figures presented in this section only reflect parts of eSPEM.

2.1 Detailed Behavior Description

eSPEM provides a drop-in replacement package *ProcessBehavior*, that contains meta-classes and associations to reference *Behaviors* of the UML Superstructure from *WorkDefinitions* in SPEM. Figure 3 shows how this is done for *Activity*[1]. Other types of work in eSPEM (e.g., *TaskDefinition*) reference a *Behavior* in the same way.

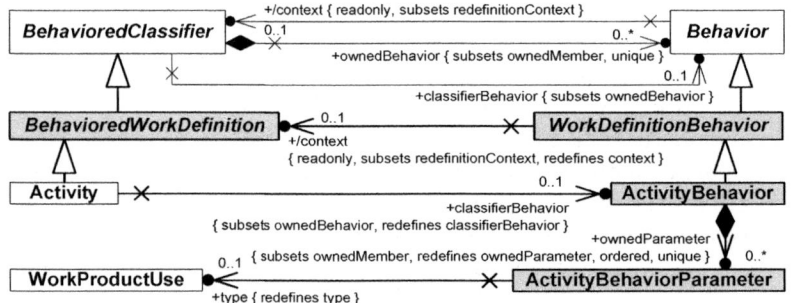

Fig. 3. *Activity* and associated *Behavior* in eSPEM

BehavioredWorkDefinition is the base class of all meta-classes that represent work. It inherits from *BehavioredClassifier* and *WorkDefinition* (not shown).

---

[1] A cross indicates a non-navigable association, and a dot indicates ownership of the association end by the opposite meta-class (UML 2.2 notation).

WorkDefinitionBehavior has the same structure and operational semantics as an *Activity* in UML.

The constructs presented in this section allow for an integration of the basic behavior modeling concepts from UML such as control and object flows, decisions, loops, and events for the different types of work in SPEM. However, we still need a way to express which *Roles* trigger events or make decisions.

2.2 Integration of Roles

Roles play an important part in SDP modeling. Figure 4 shows how eSPEM integrates roles into the behavior modeling concept. *Execution* is a *Relationship* that associates a *Role* for example with an *ActivityNode* (e.g., *DecisionNode* and *SendSignalAction*) and expresses that this *Node* is executed by the *Role*. Thus, it is now possible to specify that a decision is made or an asynchronous *Event* is triggered by a particular *Role*.

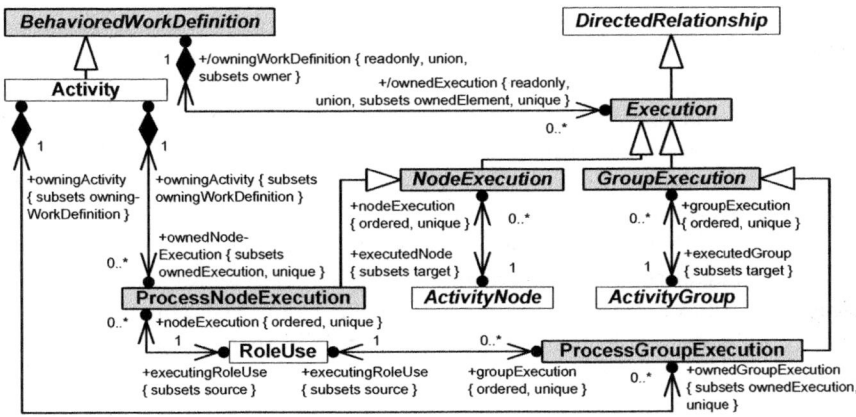

Fig. 4. *Roles* added to behavior modeling concept

Roles may also execute entire *ActivityGroups* to express that a *Role* executes all *Nodes* within that *ActivityGroup*. We added this concept because in UML an *ActivityPartition* (swimlane), which is an instantiable sub-class of *ActivityGroup*, provides no support for being executed by more than one *Element*. However, in SDPs there are often several roles executing the same work unit. This concept of eSPEM reduces the modeling effort and keeps the formalism easy-to-digest.

2.3 State Machines

We consider the use of *StateMachines* for *WorkProduct* life-cycle modeling to be a generic, detailed, and perfectly enactable approach. It outperforms concepts for *WorkProduct* life-cycle modeling found in other approaches (for example *WorkProductStatus* in SEMDM [14] that is a simple enumeration without formally

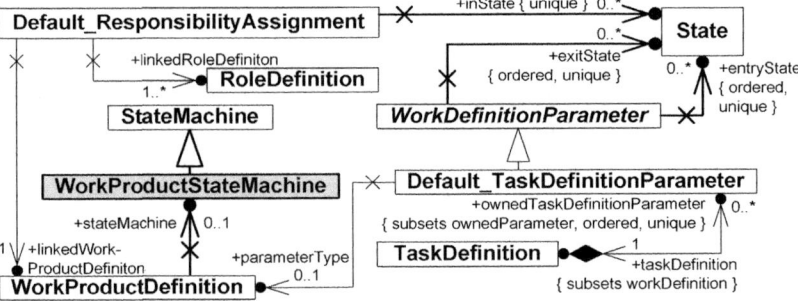

Fig. 5. *StateMachines* for *WorkProducts* in eSPEM

defined transitions). As mentioned above, interfacing *StateMachines* from SPEM is cumbersome and contradicts an easy-to-digest formalism. We integrate *State-Machines* for *WorkProduct* life-cycle modeling as shown in Fig. 5.

In eSPEM a *WorkProduct* may reference a specialized UML *StateMachine* that already groups a consistent and well-defined set of *States* and *Transitions*. With our concept for integrating *Roles* into the behavior model it is now also possible to specify which *Role* may trigger a *Transition* in the life-cycle model of a particular *WorkProduct* (e.g., who is allowed to approve a document). This supports automatic audit trails, one of our key requirements.

From SPEM we adopted the two association properties *entryState* and *exitState* of *WorkDefinitionParameter* that form the set of entry and exit states that are allowed. These constraints can be checked by a PEX and so increase the assessability of the enacted process.

Using the behavior model integration concept from eSPEM it is also possible to specify a life-cycle for all types of work in eSPEM (e.g., *TaskDefiniton*) using *StateMachines*. In practice, the life-cycle model is typically used for work that is not further decomposed (*TaskDefiniton*), is usually rather simple (e.g., created, running, or finished), and administered by a PEX or a dedicated bug tracking tool when the SDP is enacted.

2.4 Scheduling of Dynamically Created Tasks

Software development is often a creative process in which not all details are known a priori. This includes tasks that are usually created and planned while the process is already enacted. Although it would be possible to remodel the SDP whenever tasks are planned or new tasks are added, this approach suffers from the fact that the process description is no longer reusable across projects. We believe that an SDP model should reflect that tasks are dynamically created, planned, and executed at some potentially different point during an SDP. Due to its focus, SPEM neither provides support to define rules for planning tasks nor does it distinguish between the point of creation and the point of execution of tasks in a process.

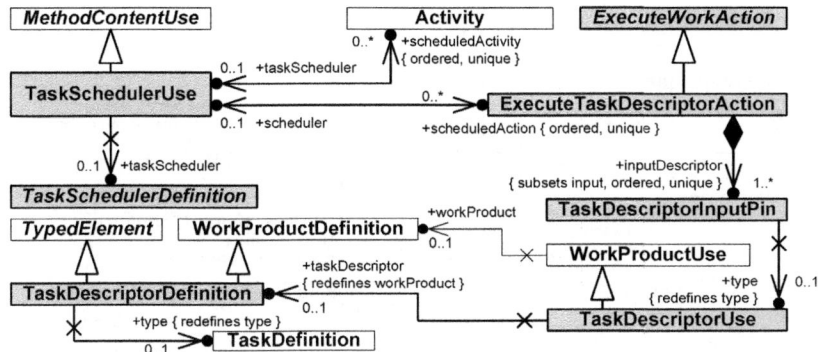

Fig. 6. *TaskScheduler* and *ExecuteTaskDescriptorAction* in eSPEM

To support this, we added the meta-class *TaskScheduler* in eSPEM. A *TaskScheduler* is responsible for planning *Tasks* that may be dynamically created during the process.

In eSPEM an *Activity* may have a *TaskScheduler* associated that is responsible for scheduling the *Activities* and *TaskUses* within the WBS of the *Activity*, as shown in Fig. 6. To be compatible with the process, the *TaskScheduler* of an *Activity* must respect the precedence that is given by *WorkSequence* relationships and the behavior model of the *Activity*.

TaskSchedulers can also be used in the behavior model. An *ExecuteTaskDescriptorAction* takes the union of all sets of *Tasks* that arrive at its *TaskDescriptorInputPins* and delegates their scheduling to an associated *TaskScheduler*. The control flow returns from the *ExecuteTaskDescriptorAction* either when all *Tasks* are performed or when the *TaskScheduler* determines the end of the invocation. This concept allows for a separation between the instantiation and execution of *Tasks* using *ObjectFlows* to denote their "way" through the process.

With the concept presented in this section we added the ability of rule based ordering of *Tasks*, and a separation between instantiation and execution of *Tasks* in eSPEM.

2.5 Configuration of Processes

As outlined in Sect. 1, a significant effort has to be taken, when the target of a proxy in a process shall be changed. This is a quite common use case, e.g., when several suitable methods might be used for executing a task within a process. Choosing from these methods should be possible during process execution without enforcing any remodeling, tailoring or changing the underlying process model.

To reduce the modeling effort, we added the meta-class *ProcessToMethodMapping* in eSPEM, as shown in Fig. 7. A *ProcessToMethodMapping* expresses a possible mapping between a *MethodContentUse* and a corresponding *MethodContentElement*. Instantiable sub-classes of *ProcessToMethodMapping* exist for *Tasks* (see Fig. 7), *Roles*, *WorkProducts*, and *TaskSchedulers*. *ProcessToMethodMappings*

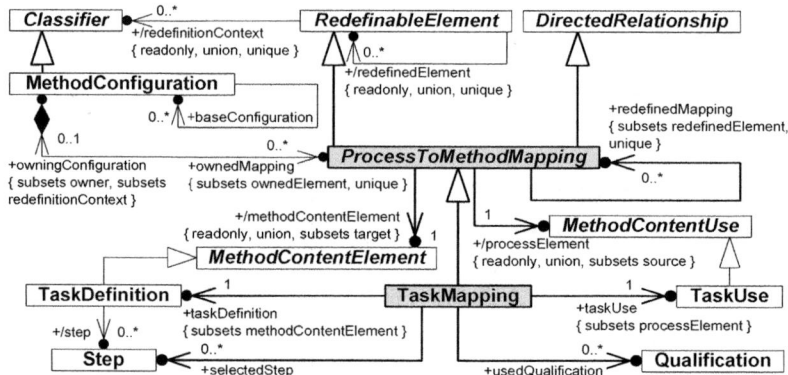

Fig. 7. *ProcessToMethodMapping* and *TaskMapping* in eSPEM

are composed into a *MethodConfiguration* that reflects one valid set of mappings between *MethodContentUses* and *MethodContentElements*. As a result only one proxy with its relationships must be modeled within a process for every possible configuration. Furthermore, the proxy needs no knowledge about its actual implementation because the mapping is separated from the proxy. This results in another benefit of our solution: The integration of new methods with existing processes is easier because the process does not need to be altered, which in turn eases evolution of already executed processes. Compatibility between the proxy and its implementation is ensured by additional OCL constraints we added in eSPEM. However, these are not discussed in this paper due to space restrictions.

2.6 Tool Support

In addition to the extension of SPEM itself we also implemented eSPEMs abstract syntax using the Eclipse Modeling Framework (EMF) [15]. This already enables precise modeling of SDPs. Furthermore, we implemented eSPEMs concrete syntax for *MethodContentElements*, *WorkDefinitionBehaviors* and *Actions*, and *StateMachines* using the Graphical Modeling Framework (GMF) [16] as diagram editors that work with our abstract syntax implementation of eSPEM. Both implementations are integrated into a PME that is used to model eSPEM-based SDPs [17]. Our PME also reuses parts of the Eclipse Process Framework (EPF) [18], which aims to be a PME for SPEM 2.0. Using our PME, we modeled two SDPs (Scrum and OpenUP) used in industry to test the usability of the constructs we added to eSPEM.

3 eSPEM Applied to SDPs

This section provides examples of how to use eSPEM to model aspects of SDPs that cannot be modeled with SPEM. In all these examples we use a mixture of standard UML and eSPEM notation.

3.1 Modeling the Behavior of SDPs

Figure 8 gives an overview of the Scrum behavior modeled with eSPEM (some elements are omitted). The `Product Owner` decides at the beginning of each `Sprint` whether to release the product or not. Depending on his decision either a `Development Sprint` or `Release Sprint` has to be performed next. With eSPEM we model this by means of a *DecisionNode*. A PEX that enacts this SDP model is now able to ask a person playing the role of the `Product Owner` what type of `Sprint` shall be performed and – depending on the answer – choose the right sub-process to guide and support the `Team`. Other SDPs require decisions as well, e.g., decisions that have to be taken when new risks are identified in the OpenUP or the V-Modell.

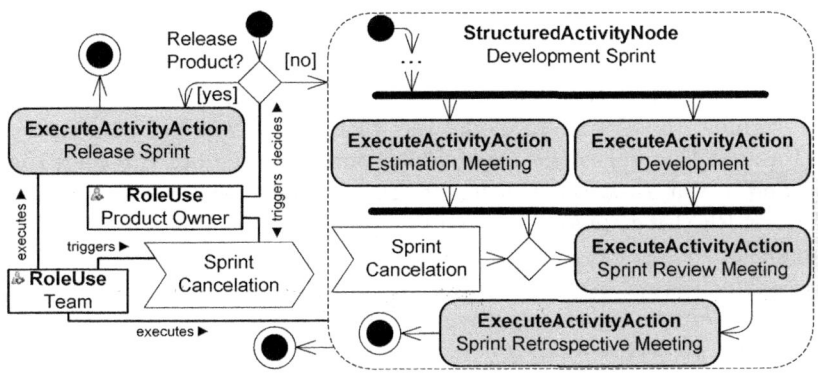

Fig. 8. Scrum behavior model with different *Executions*

Asynchronous *Events* are required by many SDPs. Typical examples are: 1) adding a new item to the `Risk List` (when using OpenUP or the V-Modell), 2) Changing `System-Wide Requirements` (when using the OpenUP), or 3) cancellation of a `Sprint` by the `Product Owner` or the `Team` (when using Scrum). With eSPEM this can be modeled using a *Send-/ReceiveSignalAction* which the corresponding *RoleUse* (e.g., `Product Owner`) triggers (see Fig. 8). A PEX can use this information to provide for example a button in a GUI to trigger this signal and execute the behavior to cancel the sprint.

3.2 Scheduler in SDP Behavior Models

Many SDPs require that *Tasks* are created and planned during enactment, e.g., *Tasks* on the `Work Items List` of the OpenUP and *Tasks* defined in a `Work Order` of the V-Modell. Scrum also requires planning of *Tasks*, e.g., in the course of the `Sprint Planning Meeting` *Tasks* are created, prioritized, and planned using the `Sprint Backlog`. Figure 9 shows how we can model this example using eSPEM. The `Sprint Backlog` is an output *Parameter* of the `Sprint Planning Meeting`. The character C within the *Pin* indicates that it is created during

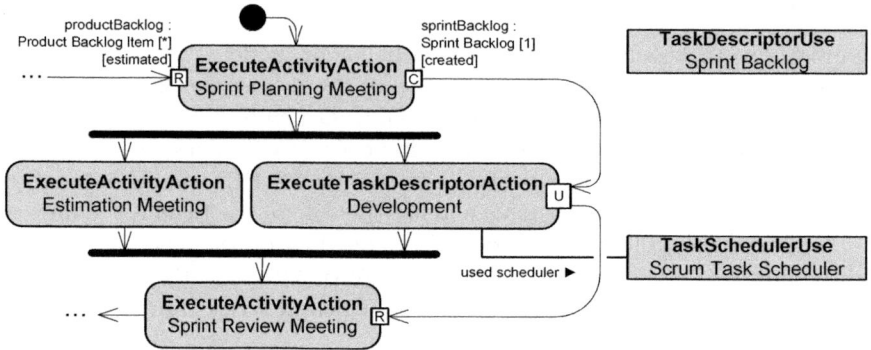

Fig. 9. Scrum behavior model with *Scheduler*

that meeting (*ParameterEffectKind::create*). *Tasks* from the Sprint Backlog are executed by the Team during the rest of the Sprint using their priority for scheduling. In eSPEM we model this with the *ExecuteTaskDescriptorAction* Development that takes the *ObjectFlow* containing the Sprint Backlog as an input and uses a *TaskScheduler* Scrum Task Scheduler for scheduling.

With eSPEM it is possible to model rules for scheduling *Tasks*. We can also distinguish between the point of instantiation and execution of *Tasks* during the process, which is not possible in SPEM. Based on this SDP model, a PEX can dynamically create tasks and provide suggestions, e.g., for the execution order of *Tasks* and project workers who could perform these *Tasks*.

3.3 Configuring an SDP

SPEM distinguishes between process and methods. In order to get a complete SDP, methods have to be integrated with the process using a configuration. Figure 10 shows parts of two possible configurations for the *TaskUse* Integrate and Create Build from the OpenUP. The configuration Default OpenUP provides a basic build management setup (*TaskDefinition* Integrate and Create Build) using the contained mapping. The configuration OpenUP with CI provides extra steps to setup an continuous integration (CI) build (*TaskDefinition* Setup CI Build). Other SDPs require our enhanced configuration support as well, e.g., to configure the Process Modules of the V-Modell®XT for the different project type variants (e.g., Project (Acquirer) with One Supplier and Project (Acquirer) with Several Suppliers). eSPEM's configuration support can also be used when modeling Scrum, e.g., to define different types of scheduling strategies for *Tasks* executed during Development (e.g., based on the priority of *Tasks* or to optimize workload of the project workers).

4 Related Work

Since Osterweil's original approach of process programming [19], many PMLs have been proposed. Acuña and Ferré [4] discuss several of these PMLs and

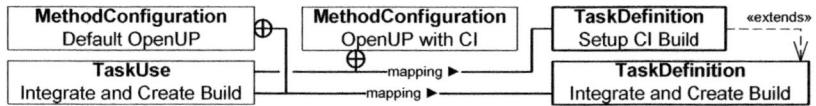

Fig. 10. Different OpenUP configurations

corresponding tools. Gruhn [3] demonstrates why the approaches were not accepted in industry and derives requirements for successful SDP modeling and execution environments. These requirements are addressed by our approach.

Standards like BPMN [11] or WS-BPEL [20] and its extension for People [21] were created to model and enact business processes. Although these approaches provide a reasonable behavior modeling and enactment concept, they do not provide other constructs from SDPs, e.g., roles, guidelines, responsibility assignments, and tools, that have to be modeled by means of BPEL variables or cannot be modeled at all. However, without these constructs a PEX cannot fulfill our requirements, i.e., a comprehensive EPG or integration of existing tools is hard to realize. Additionally, these approaches do not support a formally defined, fine-grained life-cycle modeling for artifacts or task scheduling. eSPEM provides a tightly integrated, fine-grained behavior modeling approach that supports the mentioned constructs from SDPs.

Bendraou et al. [22] present an extension of the SPEM standard called xSPEM and focus on SDP validation using timed Petri nets. xSPEM also adds *Events* for SPEM-*Activities* but lacks a fine-grained behavior modeling approach with decisions, life-cycles as well as task scheduling.

Seidita et al. [23] extend SPEM to support the modeling of agent oriented methodologies [24] but do not define a fine-grained behavior modeling concept.

Both extensions do not address the incomplete configuration support of SPEM, as we do.

Another meta-model driven approach for describing development methodologies is the ISO/IEC standard SEMDM [14]. It does not use OMG's strict meta-modeling approach but uses the power type pattern [25]. This pattern was adopted for meta-modeling in the domain of software development methodologies by Henderson-Sellers and Gonzalez-Perez [26]. The rationale for using the power type pattern is to be able to define instance features within the meta-model, which is not supported when using strict meta-modeling. However, SEMDM does not provide a standardized notation, which clearly contradicts an easy-to-digest formalism. Additionally, SEMDM lacks a fine-grained behavior modeling concept. Similar to [27,28], we use *Kinds* in a model library (not in the meta-model) to specify common instance properties for a set of model elements.

The concept of rule-based task execution for SDPs has been studied before. Heimann et al. [29] present DYNAMITE, which is based on instance level task nets. DYNAMITE uses PROGRES [30] for rule-based transformations of whole subgraphs within task nets. This already allows for a basic scheduling of tasks. However, DYNAMITE does neither support modeling additional properties for tasks nor does it support modeling roles. Thus, some scheduling strategies are hard to implement, e.g., a priority based scheduler that requires a property *priority* for the tasks it schedules, or scheduling strategies that consider the qualifications of roles that project workers play. eSPEM does support roles and instance features and therefore *TaskScheduler* implementations are able to use the additional information to get more accurate scheduling results.

Using UML for modeling SDPs is a common approach. Bendraou et al. [9] compare six UML-based languages for modeling SDPs including SPEM 1.1, SPEM 2.0 [1], UML4SPM [31], and other approaches [32,33,34]. We will give a short comparison of these approaches with eSPEM in the following.

Closest to our work is UML4SPM [31]. UML4SPM is based on SPEM 1.1 and UML 2.0 behavior modeling concepts. In [35] UML4SPM is mapped to WS-BPEL for enactment support. As mentioned, WS-BPEL cannot fulfill our requirements. A more recent approach to gain enactment support for UML4SPM is shown in [36]. In this paper the authors present an execution model based on the OMG proposal for an executable UML subset [37], as well as an implementation of the execution model for UML *Activity* and *Actions* using Kermeta [38]. This enables an execution and simulation of UML4SPM-based models. However, UML4SPM is based on SPEM 1.1 and therefore does not provide sophisticated tailoring and configuration support. Additionally, UML4SPM does not use *StateMachines* for life-cycle modeling.

Chou [33] uses a subset of UML 1.4 activity and class diagrams in combination with a proprietary object-oriented process programming language. The approach suffers from the fact, that code in the low-level programming language is not derived from the diagrams.

Di Nitto et al. [32] propose a UML 1.3-based framework to model SDPs. They do not extend the UML meta-model or use stereotypes. The framework elements, e.g., `SoftwareActivity`, are instances of the UML meta-class *Class*. However, using plain *Classes* is a major drawback of this approach because all process elements have the same notation and semantics.

Franch et al. [34] present PROMENADE, an extension of the UML 1.x metamodel, and add essential concepts for SDP modeling, i.e., roles, tasks, and documents. However, they do not add dedicated relationships, e.g., responsibility assignments that are available in eSPEM.

Engels et al. [39] show how the concepts in UML can be used for process modeling. However, essential concepts of SDP modeling are missing in UML, e.g., work products and responsibility assignments. This results in an incomplete and imprecise SDP description.

Other approaches use UML and extensions through stereotypes for SDP modeling [40] or SPEM itself [1]. This allows to use standard UML modeling tools and the behavior modeling concepts from UML. However, several other problems arise. Stereotypes change the semantics of UML elements when being applied to them but have no influence on the language structure as defined by the UML meta-model. Consequently, "type-safety" and multiplicities of common relationships for SDP modeling (e.g., responsibility assignments and relationships between work products) must be re-implemented (e.g., as constraints for the stereotypes). This contradicts our requirement of an easy-to-digest formalism and limits the support that a general purpose UML modeling tool can give when creating or editing model elements with stereotypes.

5 Conclusion and Future Work

Given our requirements, the current SPEM standard has a few issues that we have identified by modeling exemplary SDPs. With eSPEM we have provided an extension of SPEM that addresses the identified issues. eSPEM supports a fine-grained behavior and life-cycle modeling, definition of task scheduling strategies, and an enhanced configuration support. None of the approaches known from literature does support all of the features in eSPEM that we consider to be required for precise modeling and reasonable enactment support of SDPs.

Our future work will focus on an enhanced tool support for eSPEM. This includes a full implementation of eSPEM's concrete syntax and additional tooling to improve usability of our PME. In addition to that, we will also work on implementing a PEX for eSPEM-based SDP models. Research in this field will include the formal definition and implementation of the operational semantics of eSPEM's behavior model, integration of existing tools and their data formats, traceability support for artifacts, and process evolution. Providing the combination of a PME and a PEX will also allow to empirically evaluate the impact of computer-aided process enactment on real development projects, and an adaption of eSPEM by practitioners.

References

1. Object Management Group: Software & Systems Process Engineering Meta-Model Specification Version 2.0 (April 2008)
2. Object Management Group: Unified Modeling Language: Superstructure Version 2.2 (February 2009)
3. Gruhn, V.: Process Centered Software Engineering Environments – A Brief History and Future Challenges. Annals of Software Engineering 14(1-4), 363–382 (2002)
4. Acuña, S.T., Ferré, X.: Software Process Modelling. In: Proc. World Multiconf. on Systemics, Cybernetics and Informatics, Orlando, FL, pp. 237–242 (2001)
5. Conradi, R., Jaccheri, M.L.: Process Modelling Languages. In: Derniame, J.-C., Kaba, B.A., Wastell, D. (eds.) Promoter-2 1998. LNCS, vol. 1500, pp. 27–52. Springer, Heidelberg (1999)
6. Jaccheri, M.L., Baldi, M., Divitini, M.: Evaluating the requirements for software process modeling languages and systems. In: Process support for Distributed Team-based Software Development (PDTSD 1999), Orlando, FL, pp. 570–578 (1999)
7. CMMI Product Team: CMMI for Development Version 1.2. Carnegie Mellon University – Software Engineering Institute, Pittsburgh, PA (August 2006)
8. ISO/IEC: ISO/IEC 15504-5:2006 – Information technology – Process Assessment – Part 5: An exemplar Process Assessment Model (March 2006)
9. Bendraou, R., Jezequel, J.M., Gervais, M.P., Blanc, X.: A Comparison of Six UML-Based Languages for Software Process Modeling. IEEE Transactions on Software Engineering 99 (2009) (PrePrint)

10. Schwaber, K., Beedle, M.: Agile Software Development with Scrum. Pearson Studium, London (2008)
11. Object Management Group: Business Process Modeling Notation Version 1.2 (January 2009)
12. Balduino, R.: Open Unified Process (OpenUP). Technical report, Eclipse Process Framework Project (2007)
13. V-Modell®XT Authors: V-Modell®XT, Version 1.3 (Feburary 2009), http://www.v-modell.iabg.de/
14. ISO/IEC: ISO/IEC 24744:2007 – Software Engineering – Metamodel for Development Methodologies (February 2007)
15. Steinberg, D., Budinsky, F., Paternostro, M., Merks, E.: EMF: Eclipse Modeling Framework, 2nd edn. Addison-Wesley, Longman (2009)
16. Gronback, R.C.: Eclipse Modeling Project: A Domain-Specific Language (DSL) Toolkit. Addison-Wesley, Longman (2009)
17. University of Erlangen-Nuremberg, Research Group Applied Software Engineering: Integrated Tool Chain for Meta-model-based Process Modelling and Execution (March 2010), http://pswt.cs.fau.de/EN/research/IWKMMASWEP/
18. Eclipse Foundation: Eclipse Process Framework Project (EPF) (March 2010), http://www.eclipse.org/epf/
19. Osterweil, L.J.: Software processes are software too. In: Proc. 9th Intl. Conf. on Software Engineering, Monterey, CA, pp. 2–13 (1987)
20. OASIS: Web Services Business Process Execution Language Version 2.0. (April 2007)
21. Active Endpoints Inc., Adobe Systems Inc., BEA Systems Inc., IBM Corp., Oracle Inc., and SAP AG: WS-BPEL Extension for People (BPEL4People), Version 1.0. (June 2007)
22. Bendraou, R., Combemale, B., Crégut, X., Gervais, M.P.: Definition of an Executable SPEM 2.0. In: Proc. 14th Asia-Pacific Software Engineering Conf., Nagoya, Japan, pp. 390–397 (2007)
23. Seidita, V., Cossentino, M., Gaglio, S.: Using and Extending the SPEM Specifications to Represent Agent Oriented Methodologies. In: Proc. Agent-Oriented Software Engineering IX, 9th Intl. Workshop, Estoril, Portugal, pp. 46–59 (2008)
24. Henderson-Sellers, B., Giorgini, P.: Agent-Oriented Methodologies. Idea Group (2005)
25. Odell, J.J.: Power types. J. of Object-Oriented Programming 7(2), 8–12 (1994)
26. Henderson-Sellers, B., Gonzalez-Perez, C.: The Rationale of Powertype-based Metamodelling to Underpin Software Development Methodologies. In: Proc. 2nd Asia-Pacific Conf. on Conceptual Modelling, Newcastle, Australia, pp. 7–16 (2005)
27. Firesmith, D., Henderson-Sellers, B.: The OPEN Process Framework: An Introduction. Addison-Wesley, Longman (2002)
28. Brinkkemper, S.: Method Engineering: engineering for information systems development methods and tools. Information Software Technology 38(4), 275–280 (1996)
29. Heimann, P., Joeris, G., Krapp, C.A., Westfechtel, B.: DYNAMITE: Dynamic Task Nets for Software Process Management. In: Proc. 18th Intl. Conf. on Software Engineering, Berlin, Germany, pp. 331–341 (1996)
30. Schürr, A.: Rapid Programming with Graph Rewrite Rules. In: Proc. USENIX Symp. on Very High Level Languages, Santa Fee, NM, October 1994, pp. 83–100 (1994)
31. Bendraou, R., Gervais, M.P., Blanc, X.: UML4SPM: A UML2.0-Based Metamodel for Software Process Modelling. In: Briand, L.C., Williams, C. (eds.) MoDELS 2005. LNCS, vol. 3713, pp. 17–38. Springer, Heidelberg (2005)

32. Di Nitto, E., Lavazza, L., Schiavoni, M., Tracanella, E., Trombetta, M.: Deriving executable process descriptions from UML. In: Proc. 24th Intl. Conf. on Software Engineering, New York, NY, pp. 155–165 (2002)
33. Chou, S.C.: A Process Modeling Language Consisting of High Level UML-based Diagrams and Low Level Process Language. J. of Object Technology 1(4), 137–163 (2002)
34. Franch, X., Ribó, J.M.: A Structured Approach to Software Process Modelling. In: Proc. 24th EUROMICRO Conf., Washington, DC, vol. 2, pp. 753–762 (1998)
35. Bendraou, R., Sadovykh, A., Gervais, M.P., Blanc, X.: Software Process Modeling and Execution: The UML4SPM to WS-BPEL Approach. In: Proc. 33rd EUROMICRO Conf. on Software Engineering and Advanced Applications, Lübeck, Germany, pp. 314–321 (2007)
36. Bendraou, R., Jezéquél, J.M., Fleurey, F.: Combining Aspect and Model-Driven Engineering Approaches for Software Process Modeling and Execution. In: Wang, Q., Garousi, V., Madachy, R., Pfahl, D. (eds.) ICSP 2009. LNCS, vol. 5543, pp. 148–160. Springer, Heidelberg (2009)
37. Object Management Group: Semantics of a Foundational Subset for Executable UML Models RFP (April 2005)
38. Muller, P.A., Fleurey, F., Jezéquél, J.M.: Weaving Executability into Object-Oriented Meta-languages. In: Briand, L.C., Williams, C. (eds.) MoDELS 2005. LNCS, vol. 3713, pp. 264–278. Springer, Heidelberg (2005)
39. Engels, G., Förster, A., Heckel, R., Thöne, S.: Process Modeling using UML. In: Dumas, M., van der Aalst, W., ter Hofstede, A. (eds.) Process-Aware Information Systems, pp. 85–117. John Wiley & Sons, Chichester (2005)
40. Jäger, D., Schleicher, A., Westfechtel, B.: Using UML for Software Process Modeling. In: Nierstrasz, O., Lemoine, M. (eds.) ESEC 1999 and ESEC-FSE 1999. LNCS, vol. 1687, pp. 91–108. Springer, Heidelberg (1999)

Adding Abstraction and Reuse to a Network Modelling Tool Using the Reuseware Composition Framework

Jendrik Johannes[1] and Miguel A. Fernández[2]

[1] Technische Universität Dresden, Nöthnitzer Str. 46, 01187 Dresden, Germany
`jendrik.johannes@tu-dresden.de`
[2] Department of Broadband Service Platforms, Telefónica R&D, Valladolid, Spain
`mafg@tid.es`

Abstract. Domain-specific modelling (DSM) environments enable experts in a certain domain to actively participate in model-driven development. Developing DSM environments need to be cost-efficient, since they are only used by a limited group of domain experts. Different model-driven technologies promise to allow this cost-efficient development. [1] presented experiences in developing a DSM environment for telecommunication network modelling. There, challenges were identified that need to be addressed by other new modelling technologies. In this paper, we now present the results of addressing one of theses challenges—abstraction and reuse support—with the Reuseware Composition Framework. We show how we identified the abstraction and reuse features required in the telecommunication DSM environment in a case study and extended the existing environment with these features using Reuseware. We discuss the advantages of using this technology and propose a process for further improving the abstraction and reuse capabilities of the DSM environment in the future.

1 Introduction

Domain-specific modelling (DSM) environments enable experts in a certain domain to actively participate in model-driven software development (MDSD)—even if they lack experience in software engineering or software modelling. Since such environments are only used by a limited group of experts, the development needs to be cost-efficient. This can be achieved by developing DSM environments with model-driven technologies instead of implementing them by hand.

[1] presents experiences gained in developing such a DSM environment for telecommunication experts at Telefónica. There, the Graphical Modeling Framework (GMF) [2] was used to develop a graphical editor as core of the environment. [1] identified challenges for technologies that were not met by the tooling used so far. One of the identified challenges is *abstraction and reuse*. That is, supporting domain experts to create abstract views of complex models and to develop reuseable model components.

In this paper, we now report on the results in addressing the *abstraction and reuse* issue with another modelling technology—the Reuseware Composition Framework[1]. Reuseware is founded on Invasive Software Composition [3] and extensions of it [4,5]. It is based on the Eclipse Modeling Framework (EMF) [6] and integrates into the Eclipse platform. It also has a component for integrating with GMF. Therefore, we used Reuseware to extend the existing domain-specific network modelling environment [1] that is based on Eclipse, EMF and GMF.

The core of the network modelling DSM environment is a domain-specific language (DSL) based on the Common Information Model (CIM) [7] that is a Distributed Management Task Force (DMTF)[2] standard for systems, networks, applications and service definition. The graphical editor of the DSL, which was the main part of the DSM environment as presented in [1], is directly based on an Ecore[3] metamodel that represents a large part of the CIM standard.

In the MODELPLEX project[4], Telefónica defined a case study in which they not only use the CIM-based DSL for telecommunication network modelling, but also formulate abstraction and reuse concerns [9]. Driven by this case study, we developed abstraction and reuse tooling for the DSM environment with Reuseware. During the process, we realised that many design decisions require feedback from the domain experts. Therefore, rapid prototyping and continuous updating of the DSM environment, based on that feedback, is needed. Consequently, we propose a development process for abstraction and reuse features of a DSM environment that is also applicable for other environments than the network modelling tool. We discuss how this development process can be implemented with the model-driven technologies we used.

This paper is structured as follows. Section 2 motivates the need for abstraction and reuse in DSM environments and introduces the network modelling case study. It further shows the features we developed, driven by the case study, with Reuseware. In Sect. 3 we present the development process for improving the DSM environment and Sect. 4. presents conclusions from this work.

2 Abstraction and Reuse Support in the DSM Environment for Network Modelling

In this section, we first motivate the need for reuse and abstraction mechanisms in DSM environments for complex domains. We then show the setup of the case study we conducted and explain the abstraction and reuse features we developed, driven by the case study, for the network modelling tool with Reuseware.

2.1 Reuse and Abstraction in a DSM Environment

A DSM environment is the tooling for a domain-specific language (DSL). A DSL is used to reduce the complexity arising when developing software systems

---

[1] http://reuseware.org
[2] http://www.dmtf.org
[3] Metamodelling language of EMF; conforms to OMG's EMOF [8] standard.
[4] http://www.modelplex.org

using a general-purpose language (GPL) such as UML or Java. Unlike a GPL, a DSL focuses on a particular problem domain and contains a relatively small number of constructs that are immediately identifiable to domain experts and allows them to construct concise models capturing the design of the system at an appropriate level of abstraction. While typical DSLs are small languages with a manageable number of concepts, a DSL that embodies a standard vocabulary of a larger domain is a complex language with a large number of concepts. This complexity eventually compromises the very aims against which the DSL was built in the first place: domain focus and conciseness.

The metamodel and the graphical editor [1] developed on the basis of the Common Information Model (CIM) [7] represent such a complex DSL. While this language is a DSL in the sense that it provides dedicated constructs for the telecommunication domain, its size in terms of the number of constructs and features is comparable to that of a GPL such as the UML—the CIM standard defines more than 1500 concepts.

However, the domain for which CIM is designed can be split into more specialised domains where not all details of CIM are required in each of them. The classical MDSD approach would be to construct new DSLs that provide abstractions over and above the constructs provided by CIM. This means that different DSLs, all in the telecommunication domain, are created for different abstraction levels and are combined in an MDSD process.

To employ this approach, one has to identify the abstraction levels and decide which DSLs, and with which constructs, have to be created. This is an iterative process, since a DSL has to be tested and used by the domain experts to evaluate its usefulness and improve it. Updating one DSL alone can be costly when the associated tooling needs to be adapted manually, which is often the case with today's DSL development technology as experienced in the development of tooling for the original CIM-based DSL [1]. This cost would even increase if multiple DSLs, which are connected in an MDSD process, are updated and co-evolved.

Instead of using a classical MDSD approach as described above, we develop abstraction tooling for CIM using model composition. This is done by defining a *composition system* with Reuseware. As we will discuss in Sect. 3, this solution can be used as 1) an alternative for the classical MDSD approach, 2) prototyping for finding the DSLs in the classical approach (and thus avoiding costs of evolution) and 3) basis for implementing the classical approach.

2.2 Case Study Setup

We extended the network modelling DSM environment with abstraction and reuse support driven by a case study defined by Telefónica [9]. For the case study, Telefónica defined a model of a typical ADSL service network configuration for their customers consisting of 52 model elements. An excerpt of the model, displayed in the graphical editor of the DSM environment, is shown in Fig. 1. After the model was defined, the domain experts at Telefónica marked and named parts of the model that can be abstracted into a single concept on a higher abstraction level and reused at different places in the model. For

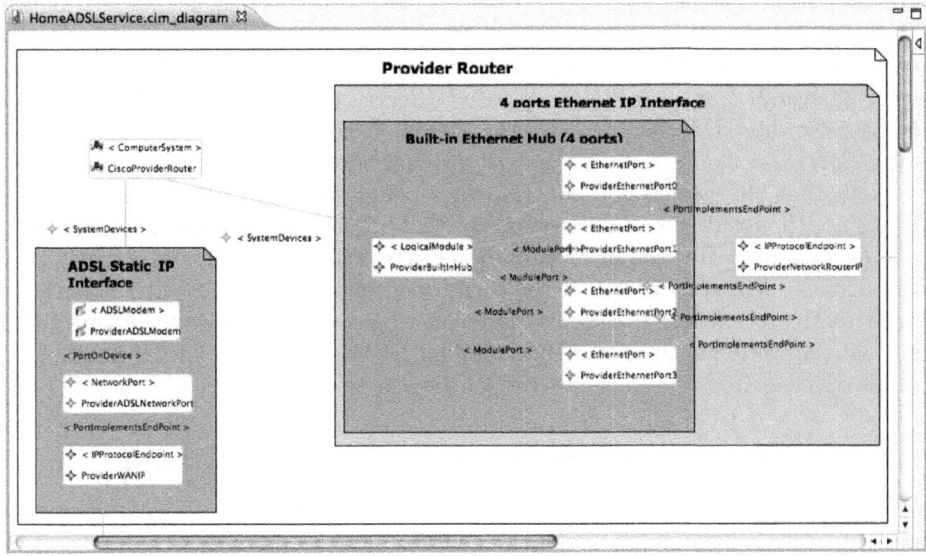

Fig. 1. An excerpt from a CIM model of an ADSL service network topology (provided by Telefónica R&D for the MODELPLEX project [9])

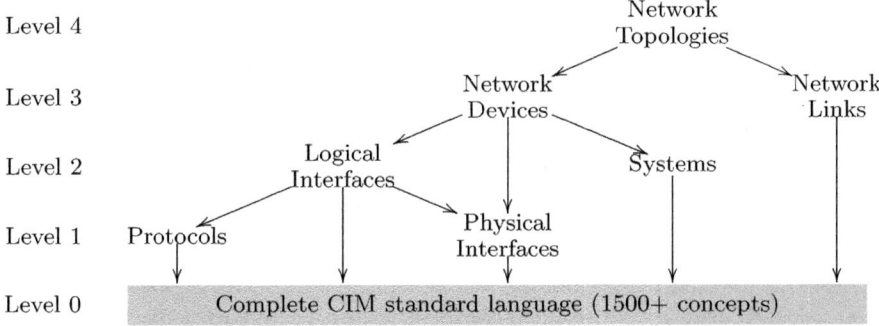

Fig. 2. Abstraction levels and component types for network models

the marking they used notes with different colours. These are only parts of the graphical syntax and do not change the meaning of the underlying model. In addition, for each concept they marked, they provided a list of attributes that need to be visible on a higher abstraction level.

The concepts were then grouped into seven specialised domains (Protocols, Physical Interfaces, Logical Interfaces, Systems, Network Devices, Network Links, Network Topologies) that reside on different abstraction levels (Levels 1–4) as summarised in Fig. 2. For each specialised domain and/or each abstraction level, a separate DSL could potentially be defined. Between the different specialised domains, dependencies can be identified (arrows in Fig. 2). They express which domains from a lower abstraction level are used to express concepts of a higher abstraction level. We note that in principle concepts of Level x can be represented by concepts of Level $x-1$. However, certain concepts of higher abstraction levels (Level 2, 3 or 4) are also expressed directly with concepts of Level 0. This is, because the CIM standard (Level 0) itself, offers constructs of low (e.g. *EthernetPort*) but also high (e.g. *System*) abstraction.

Note that the levels, domains and dependencies between them as shown in Fig. 2 are the results of a first case study. Using DSM tools based on these results and doing more case studies with more models, will most likely extend and alter the results—which can lead to the mentioned evolution costs when the results are directly manifested in DSLs. Therefore, we present a Reuseware composition system that extends the network modelling DSM environment with abstraction and reuse features as an alternative solution in the following.

2.3 Analysis and Decomposition of the Case Study Model

We used the Reuseware Composition Framework to define a *composition system* and integrate it into the DSM environment for network modelling. A composition system defines how users of the system—domain experts in our case—can define and compose model components. In Reuseware, a composition system is defined based on an existing DSL to extend it with abstraction and reuse features, while preserving the existing tool support for the DSL. The user is then able to define model *fragments* using the existing editor of the DSL. Such fragments can then be composed graphically by defining *composition programs* in a graphical editor provided by Reuseware with the possibility to reuse one fragment several times in one or different composition programs. Reuseware then interprets the composition programs to merge the fragments to complex models that can again be inspected using the existing DSL editor.

In our case, we defined a composition system for the CIM-based DSL driven by the requirements specified in the case study model (cf. Fig. 1). In the first step, the model was decomposed into fragments following the decomposition suggestions marked in the model. Second, initial composition programs were defined using Reuseware's graphical composition program editor. At this point, the composition programs did not yet contain the composition definitions. Third, we constructed a composition system that allows the composition of CIM fragments in an easy and intuitive way such that domain experts can use it. Finally, we adjusted the fragments to the composition system and completed the composition programs such that they recompose the original case study model.

Figure 4 shows the fragments and composition programs that are the decomposed version of the part of the case study model that is shown in Fig. 1. The three rows in the figure correspond to the abstraction Levels 1–3 (from bottom to top). On Level 1, we have the *BuiltInEthernetHub* fragment, which is a Physical Interface modelled in the CIM-based DSL, and the *IP* fragment, which is a *Protocol* also modelled in the CIM-based DSL. On Level 2, three CIM models are defined. Two Logical Interfaces and one System. The first Logical Interface—*EthernetIPInterface*—is a composition program that contains the

	fragments	avg. no. of model elements	comp. programs	avg. no. of fragments in comp. prgr.	reused
Level 4 NW Topologies	0	n.a.	1	8.00	0
Level 3 NW Devices	0	n.a.	4	3.25	4
Network Links	2	1.00	0	n.a.	4
Level 2 Logical Interfaces	1	3.00	3	2.67	6
Systems	1	1.00	0	n.a.	4
Level 1 Physical Interfaces	3	3.00	0	n.a.	4
Protocols	5	2.60	0	n.a.	7
Total	12	2.42	8	3.63	29

Fig. 3. Fragments of the case study

two Level 1 fragments. On the contrary, the second—*ADSLStaticIPinterface*—is directly modelled in the CIM-based DSL. The *System* fragment is also modelled in the CIM-based DSL. On Level 3, we then have one composition program—*ProviderRouter*—that composes the three Level 2 fragments.

An overview of all fragments and composition programs we obtained by decomposing the complete case study model that consists of 52 elements, is given in Fig. 3. In total, 12 fragments and 8 composition programs were defined. In average, each fragment contains 2.42 model elements which means that a total of 29 model elements were created in the CIM-based DSL. In the original model, 52 elements were modelled, which means that 44% of the case study model can be created by reusing fragments instead of modelling in the CIM-based DSL. To enable domain experts to perform this composition and reuse of CIM model fragments, we defined a composition system with Reuseware that is presented in the following.

2.4 Re-composition of the Case Study Model Using the CIM Composition System

Since the composition system for CIM models should extend the existing tooling (the graphical editor of the CIM-based DSL and the Reuseware composition program editor) we introduce five prefixes (+, %, ?, *, -) that can be prepended to attribute values of model elements to define the *composition interface* of a CIM model fragment. A composition interface points at the parts of a model fragment that are exported to be connected with parts of other model fragments in composition programs. The prefixes are explained in the following on the example of Fig. 4.

Looking at the two Level 1 models (Fig. 4; bottom row), we can see that the BuiltInHub element in the *BuiltInEthernetHub* fragment is prefixed with + and named +BuiltInHub. + exports the element to the composition interface and lets it appear with the name of the element (in this case BuiltInHub). This can be seen in the *EthernetIPInterface* composition program on Level 2 (1st in middle row). Similar is done with the IP element in the *IP* fragment. Furthermore, we

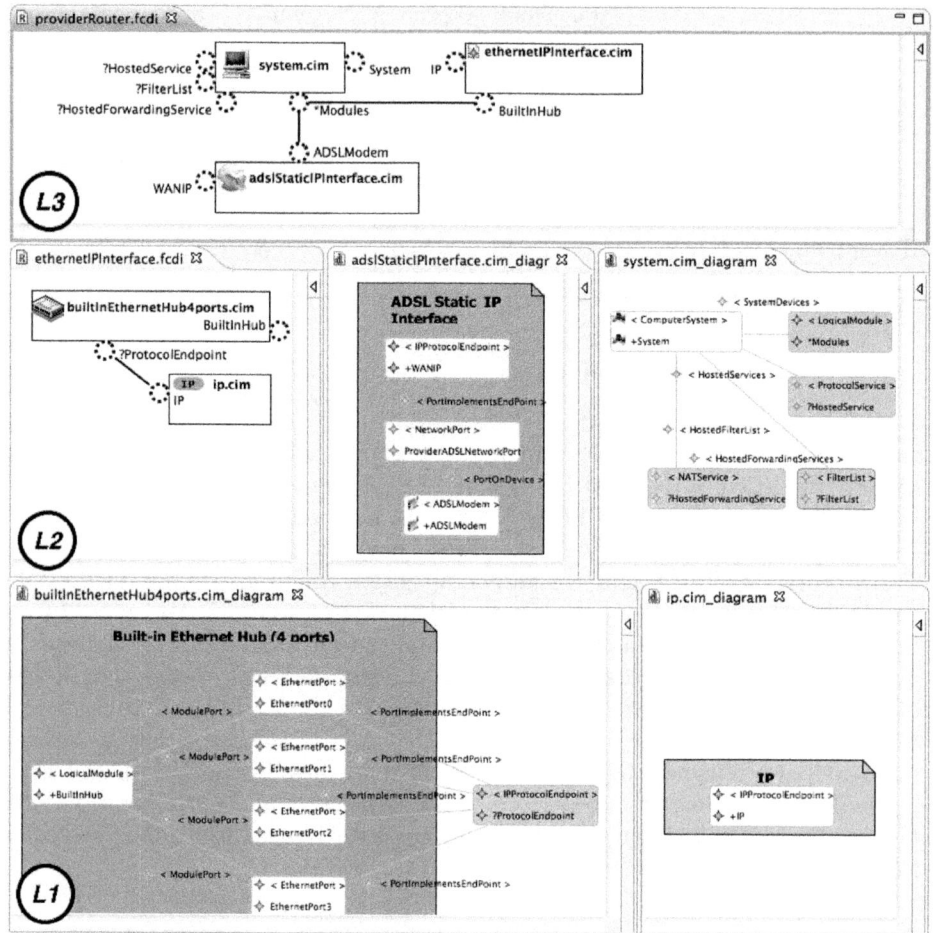

Fig. 4. Fig. 1 decomposed into fragments and composition programs on Levels 1–3

add a new element (depicted in orange) to the *BuiltInEthernetHub* that we name ?PrototcolEndpoint and connect to other elements in the fragment. ? is used to define a variation point. That is, this is not an element with meaning, but only a placeholder. It will be replaced or removed during composition.

The composition program *EthernetIPInterface* (1st in middle row) on Level 2 can now make use of the composition interface. Concretely, the exported IP element is linked to the ?PrototcolEndpoint variation point. Executing the invasive composition yields an *EthernetIPInterface* fragment that is equal to the corresponding part of the original use case model (cf. Fig. 1). In the *ADSLStaticIPInterface* fragment, we declare two elements to be exported using + (WANIP and ADSLModem). In the *System* fragment, we also export the System element, add three variation points (using ?) and add the extension point *Modules* (using *). In contrast to a variation point, an extension point defined by *

Computer System %System		
	Property	Value
Core	Description	%Description
Appearance	Element Capabilities	
	Element Name	+System
	Element Setting Data	
	Enabled Default	Enabled
	Hosted Dependency	
	Hosted Filter List	Filter List ?FilterList
	Hosted Services	Protocol Service ?Hc
	Identifying Descriptions	
	Install Date	
	Name	%System

Fig. 5. Properties of the System model element (cf. Fig. 4 middle)

system.cim : org/modelplex/...2/systems/system/system.cim		
	Property	Value
Core	▼*ExtensionPoints	
Appearance	*Modules	-
	▼%Description	
	value	This is a Cisco 800 Series Router
	▼%System	
	value	CiscoProviderRouter

Fig. 6. Properties of the Level 2 fragment *system.cim* (cf. Fig. 4 top)

allows for multiple extensions and needs to be explicitly removed by using – in a composition program.

Using the exports, variation points and extension points defined in the fragments of Level 1 and 2, the *ProviderRouter* composition program on Level 3 can now be enriched with the composition links that are required to construct a *ProviderRouter* CIM model that is equal to the corresponding part of the original case study model (cf. Fig. 1 top).

Furthermore, the % prefix is used in all fragments to export attributes to the composition interface. Figure 5 shows this exemplarily for the System element in the *System* fragment (middle row on the right in Fig. 4). We can see that there are many attributes, which is typical for all elements in a CIM model. Therefore, as many attributes as possible should be set to default values if sufficient and only a limited set should be exported to the next abstraction level. Here, we export the Description attribute by setting it to %Description. The value followed after % defines the name of the attribute on the next abstraction level (here Description). The ElementName attribute is also exported to an attribute System, because + is exported by default. Furthermore, the Name attribute (not to confuse with ElementName) is exported to the attribute System (by using %System). This means that settings to System on the next abstraction level will set both attributes (Name and ElementName) to the same value.

The exported attributes can be modified in the properties of a corresponding fragment instance in a composition program. Figure 6 shows these attributes for the instance of the *System* fragment in the *ProviderRouter* composition program (top row in Fig. 4). We can see that both exported attributes—%Description and %System—are set. The %System attribute (which maps to ElementName on the lower abstraction level) is set to CiscoProviderRouter which means that the +System element is not re-exported. For re-exporting it, we would need to set the attribute to +CiscoProviderRouter. The properties also list all extension points, which is only *Modules in this case. An extension point can be removed if it should be no longer visible on the next abstraction level by setting it to -, which we do in the case of *Modules here.

Another feature to improve the user experience is the specification of icons that are then shown on fragments in composition programs. In the CIM composition system, domain experts can specify icons themselves by placing them next to the fragments they develop.

Using the composition system, we were able to recompose the complete original case study model from the fragments (cf. Fig. 3) that were created from it based on the decomposition proposed by the domain experts (cf. Fig. 1). As mentioned, 44% of the model consists of reused fragments compared to complete manual modelling.

The features of this CIM composition system give the domain experts a lot of freedom. They can introduce new fragments at will and design their composition interface and their look in composition programs individually. They can also introduce new abstraction levels without modifying any language, tooling or composition systems, since all CIM models on abstraction levels higher than 0 are composition programs. Thus, the presented composition system is useful in particular in the early stages of building a DSM environment to find appropriate abstraction levels. Of course, the composition programs expose certain parts of the generic Reuseware tooling. Thus, for certain abstractions it might become desirable to hide more of the composition system and Reuseware to the domain experts, which we will discuss in the following.

3 A Process for Introducing and Improving Reuse and Abstraction in DSM Environments

This paper presented the extension of the DSM environment for network modelling with abstraction and reuse support. For this, we have developed a composition system with Reuseware as a less cost-intensive alternative to developing a set of DSLs for different abstraction levels and connect them via transformations, which would have been the classical MDSD approach. The composition system was developed with relatively little effort—the complete system definition consists of only 103 lines of textual specification in Reuseware specific languages for composition system definition.[5] Nevertheless, the system, as described in Sect. 2.4, was integrated into the DSM environment and directly used by domain experts. They can now use the additions in the DSM environment to introduce new abstraction levels as required.

---

[5] Specifications, case study model, fragments and composition programs can be obtained from http://reuseware.org/index.php/Reuseware_Application_CIM.

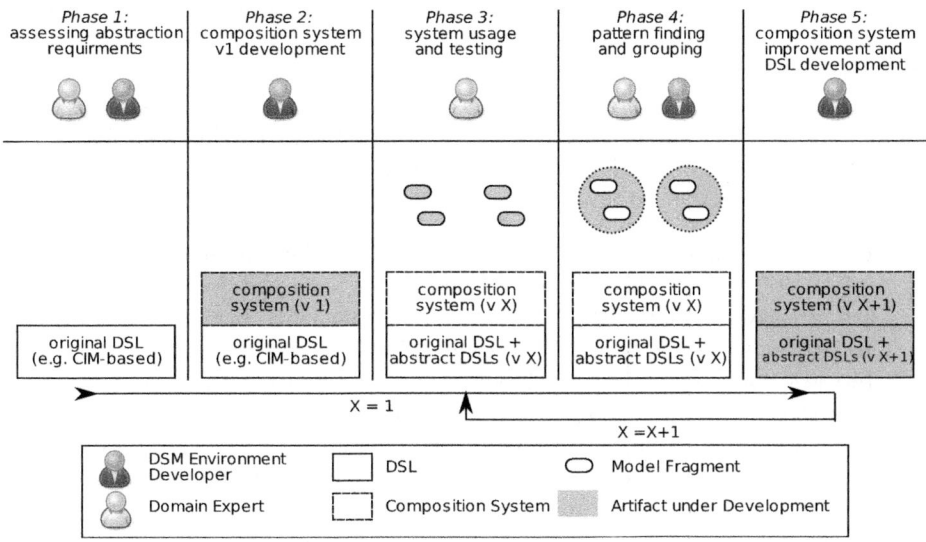

Fig. 7. Process for obtaining a DSM environment for a complex DSL

Still, there are also (potential) drawbacks in using the developed composition system over the classical MDSD approach. First, the flexibility we gave to the composition system inherently comes with the danger that it again threatens the simplicity and abstraction we wanted to introduce with the it in the first place. Since the domain experts control the composition interfaces themselves to a large degree, they might overload the interface of components or design them too restrictive, which would make fragments hard or impossible to reuse. Second, the tooling (in particular the user interface), which is only a thin layer on top of Reuseware, can never be as highly customised or adjusted to other platforms and technologies as individual DSLs can be.

These drawbacks, however, only apply in certain scenarios. For example, when new users that only work on one particular abstraction level are introduced to the DSM environment often, which justifies the costs of developing customised tools for them; or when people have to work on specific platforms with resource restrictions that can not be met by the Reuseware tooling. To answer such questions for the CIM case, we need to perform more case studies and, most importantly, get feedback from the domain experts on these questions.

Because this feedback from domain experts is of high importance for the whole idea of DSL building, we claim that creating a flexible composition system for an existing complex DSL, as the one shown in this paper for the CIM-based DSL, is a good first step to build abstraction and reuse facilities on top of the existing complex DSL. Even if we switch to a classical MDSD approach later, the composition system is an inexpensive way to obtain a first prototype that can then be used and tested by the domain experts to collect feedback on what the correct abstraction levels are. With this we can obtain the final DSM environment which may consist of the composition system or a set of DSLs (on the correct abstraction levels) or a combination of both.

To support this claim, we propose the following process to continue the development of the DSM environment for network modelling with different abstraction levels that can also be used for developing DSM environments for other domains. The process, consisting of five phases, is visualised in Fig. 7:

1. In the first phase, the developer of the DSM environment collects initial information about desired abstraction levels from the domain experts who are already familiar with the complex existing DSL. In the Telefónica case study this was done in form of markings in the case study model (cf. Fig. 1).
2. In the second phase, the developer designs the first composition system version that is flexible enough to cover all abstraction and reuse requirements identified in step one, but is customised enough such that it can be used by domain experts. For the network modelling DSM environment, this composition system was shown in Sect. 2.4.
3. In the next phase, the domain expert uses the composition system, creates fragments and gives feedback. The developer can give support in this phase. We started this phase for the CIM-based DSL when we created the fragments and composition programs in Sect. 2.3.
4. In phase four, the fragments and composition programs are analysed to find common patterns and to group the fragments following these patterns. From these patterns, the developer can derive restrictions and default behaviour for the composition system or identify constructs for abstract DSLs and refine the abstraction levels. In the CIM composition system for instance, it turned out that `EndPoint` elements (used e.g. several times in Fig. 4) are nearly always exported because they mark places where components are connected in the physical world. Thus one useful refinement of the composition system might be to export `EndPoint` elements by default.
5. In the last phase, the developer improves the composition system based on the results from the previous phase or builds abstract DSLs that replace (parts of) the composition system. The result is then given to the domain experts. It is either the final DSM environment or a next prototype and phase three to five are repeated.

If the abstraction levels are manifested and the customisation capabilities of the composition system are not sufficient, the developer can decide to build abstract DSLs with other technologies. One way he can go to keep the costs of this low is to use generative technologies for the DSL tooling such as EMFText [10] or EuGENia [11] that allow the generation of textual or graphical editors with minimal effort. Transformations between the new DSLs can be realised using a model transformation approach or reusing the already existing composition system. We presented this idea in [12].

4 Conclusion

In this paper, we used Reuseware to add abstraction and reuse support to a domain-specific modelling environment for telecommunication networks. With this, we addressed one of the missing features of the environment identified in [1]. Judging by the case study we performed, Reuseware provides the necessary means to extend the environment with the desired features with acceptable effort.

Performing the case study, we realised that several iterations for the DSM environment are necessary to find which abstraction and reuse features make the domain experts' work most efficient. Therefore, we proposed an iterative development process that focuses on collecting feedback from domain experts and performing rapid prototyping with Reuseware. In the future, we need to realise this process in larger case studies to improve the DSM environment.

Acknowledgments

This research has been co-funded by the European Commission in the 6th Framework Programme project MODELPLEX contract no. 034081 (www.modelplex.org).

References

1. Evans, A., Fernández, M.A., Mohagheghi, P.: Experiences of Developing a Network Modeling Tool Using the Eclipse Environment. In: Paige, R.F., Hartman, A., Rensink, A. (eds.) ECMDA-FA 2009. LNCS, vol. 5562. Springer, Heidelberg (2009)
2. Gronback, R.C.: Eclipse Modeling Project: A Domain-Specific Language (DSL) Toolkit. Pearson Education, London (April 2009)
3. Aßmann, U.: Invasive Software Composition. Springer, Heidelberg (April 2003)
4. Heidenreich, F., Henriksson, J., Johannes, J., Zschaler, S.: On Language-Independent Model Modularisation. In: Katz, S., Ossher, H., France, R., Jézéquel, J.-M. (eds.) Transactions on Aspect-Oriented Software Development VI. LNCS, vol. 5560. Springer, Heidelberg (2009)
5. Henriksson, J.: A Lightweight Framework for Universal Fragment Composition— with an application in the Semantic Web. PhD thesis, TU Dresden (January 2009)
6. Steinberg, D., Budinsky, F., Paternostro, M., Merks, E.: Eclipse Modeling Framework, 2nd edn. Pearson Education, London (January 2009)
7. Distributed Management Task Force Inc. (DMTF): Common Information Model Standards (January 2010), http://www.dmtf.org/standards/cim
8. Object Management Group: MOF 2.0 Core Specification (January 2006), http://www.omg.org/spec/MOF/2.0
9. MODELPLEX Project: Deliverable D1.1.a (v3): Case Study Scenario Definitions (March 2008), http://www.modelplex.org
10. Heidenreich, F., Johannes, J., Karol, S., Seifert, M., Wende, C.: Derivation and Refinement of Textual Syntax for Models. In: Paige, R.F., Hartman, A., Rensink, A. (eds.) ECMDA-FA 2009. LNCS, vol. 5562. Springer, Heidelberg (2009)
11. Kolovos, D.S., Rose, L.M., Paige, R.F., Polack, F.A.: Raising the Level of Abstraction in the Development of GMF-based Graphical Model Editors. In: Proc. of 3rd MISE Workshop @ ICSE (May 2009)
12. Johannes, J., Zschaler, S., Fernández, M.A., Castillo, A., Kolovos, D.S., Paige, R.F.: Abstracting Complex Languages through Transformation and Composition. In: Schürr, A., Selic, B. (eds.) MODELS 2009. LNCS, vol. 5795. Springer, Heidelberg (2009)

Model-Based Development of Automotive Electronic Climate Control Software

Rupesh Kakade, Mohan Murugesan, Bhupal Perugu, and Mohanan Nair

Vehicle Controls Software, General Motors Technical Centre India Pvt. Ltd.,
ITPL, 560066 Bangalore, India
{Rupesh.Kakade,Mohan.Murugesan,Bhupal.Perugu}@gm.com,
Mohanan.Nair@gm.com

Abstract. With increasing complexity of software in today's products, writing and maintaining thousands of lines of code is a tedious task. Instead, an alternative methodology must be employed. Model-based development is one candidate that offers several benefits and allows engineers to focus on the domain of their expertise than writing huge codes. In this paper, we discuss the application of model-based development to the electronic climate control software of vehicles. The *back-to-back* testing approach is presented that ensures flawless and smooth transition from legacy designs to the model-based development. Simulink report generator to create design documents from the models is presented along with its usage to run the simulation model and capture the results into the test report. Test automation using model-based development tool that support the use of unique set of test cases for several testing levels and the test procedure that is independent of software and hardware platform is also presented.

Keywords: Control law, Framework model, Doc block, Legacy designs, S-function, Back-to-back testing, Test automation.

1 Introduction

With increasing market competition, reduced time-to-market for products and growing complexity of algorithms, mechanics and electronics, it has become necessary to explore new development methodologies. Model-based development is one methodology that offers several benefits which have made it favorite among the automotive and industries alike such as aerospace [1]. Majority of software in industries is no longer hand-written in C or assembly language, but developed in the form of graphical models using model-based development tools such as MATLAB™, Simulink®, Stateflow® or similar tools [1]. The production code is automatically generated and ported into the hardware – the Electronic Control Unit (ECU).

In this paper, we have discussed several benefits of using model-based development for the Electronic Climate Control (ECC) software of the vehicles. The approach using S-functions that facilitates *back-to-back* testing of the legacy designs in handwritten C and the graphical models is described. Also discussed is the use of Simulink Report Generator™ to create a detailed design document and the simulation test report with the user specified test inputs from the models. Furthermore, the test automation using model-based development tools is presented that allows a set of test cases with systematic selection to be used over different testing levels and for different software architecture and hardware platform.

The following section describes the model-based development of the ECC software using MATLAB, Simulink and Stateflow. It also details various challenges faced and benefits gained in the process. The section 3 describes the approach of *back-to-back* testing that ensures flawless and smooth transition from legacy designs to model-based development. Also described is the test automation applied to several testing levels. Section 4 concludes the paper.

2 Designs Using Model-Based Development Technique

Model-based development begins with the development of graphical models by application experts [2]. There are several tools such as MATLAB/Simulink/Stateflow/ Rhapsody which can be used for development of graphical models. The requirements can also be in the form of executable graphical model to aid better understanding of the application. The graphical models can be simulated to analyze the performances of software much earlier in the development cycle that is, before the hardware for example, the Electronic Control Unit (ECU) is available, which help to ensure thorough quality assurance of software [3]. Furthermore, the closed-loop simulation of model gives the *first best guess* for design parameters such as calibration data, filter coefficients, etc. that can be fine tuned subsequently. For more complex application such as engine management system, model-based development tool allows engineers to build models for several functionalities independently and interlink them at the framework model using the referencing capability of the tool. When the design of the framework model is complete with all referenced models, the production code can be generated using the model-based development tool such as the Embedded Real-Time (ERT) coder from MATLAB. Tools are available that help engineers customize the automatically generated production code to make it run on a particular hardware. For example, the ERT coder lets engineers to customize the automated code generation process via Target Link Compiler (TLC) file. It also allows automated code generation to be customized to support integration of generated code and the existing hand-written C code. This feature is particularly beneficial when migrating to model-based development while maintaining the capability to deliver software on-time for the products nearing their production.

Furthermore, with the use of Simulink report generator tool, a detailed design document from the models can be created along with snapshots of the model to aid better understanding of the implementation among the software developers. The report generator can also be used to run the graphical simulation model with the user given test cases and generate a document capturing the test results.

In the following sections we have described the model-based development of the ECC software that used tools from The MathWorks[TM] - MATLAB[®], Simulink[®], Stateflow[®], ERT, Legacy Code Tool (LCT) and Simulink Report Generator[TM].

2.1 Electronic Climate Control Application

The development of the ECC project began in 1996, when the model-based development was not matured enough for industrial applications. The project began with design of the algorithms from scratch for the core control algorithms of vehicle's Heating, Ventilation, and Air-Conditioning (HVAC) system such as compressor speed control, evaporator air temperature control, mixed-air temperature control, and cabin air temperature control, to name a few. The earlier designs by application experts were in hand-written C mainly from their field experience with minimal documents. The development methodology therefore, demanded not only the domain knowledge but also the software coding expertise which at best led to increased development cost. Design documents were also hand-written as no automatic report generator is available to document the designs in C. This led to developers with expertise in their areas of work with minimal or no overlap, thereby reducing the quality of communication. Furthermore, the earlier development cycle didn't allow testing of software before the hardware is available. This led to delay in the product's time to market and less than thorough testing of the integrated software. Also, the testing of integrated software on the test bench, windows-based simulator and vehicle to find minute design flaws was at best expensive and likely not practical for more complex algorithms.

Simultaneous to the development of the ECC software, due to its promising benefits when compared to a physical sensor in the car, development was undertaken for a sophisticated algorithm that calculates, in real-time the air temperature throughout the vehicle interior by using the effects of ambient temperature, sun load, heat-transfer mechanisms – conduction, convection and radiation [4]. Performance evaluation of such a complex algorithm needed a platform earlier in the development cycle before the hardware is available. Also, the ECC software is needed to be deployed for all General Motors (GM) vehicles worldwide. Therefore the reusability of the production software with minimal changes specific to a vehicle program/project was desired. With the advent and promising benefits of model-based development tools such as MATLAB®, it was decided to migrate the earlier hand-written C designs to model-based development while maintaining the capability to deliver the software for vehicles nearing their production.

Engineers used the model-based development tools- Simulink and Stateflow to design algorithms and test them under various failure conditions before hardware is available. Due to the referencing capability of the tool [3], it was possible to design models for the complex algorithms independently and interlink them at a common Simulink framework level. A Simulink framework model therefore consists of only references to the several models, connections between the referenced models the interface to the algorithms which are still in hand-written C and I/O interface. This is illustrated in Fig. 1 which shows a top most level of the model for *control_airquality* algorithm on the right and a Simulink framework model on the left with references to several models including *control_airquality*. Furthermore, the closed-loop simulation consisting of the model for control law and the plant gave a *first best guess* for the design parameters such as PID gains, filter coefficients, etc. which can be fine tuned subsequently. Such an approach allowed for smooth migration to the model-based

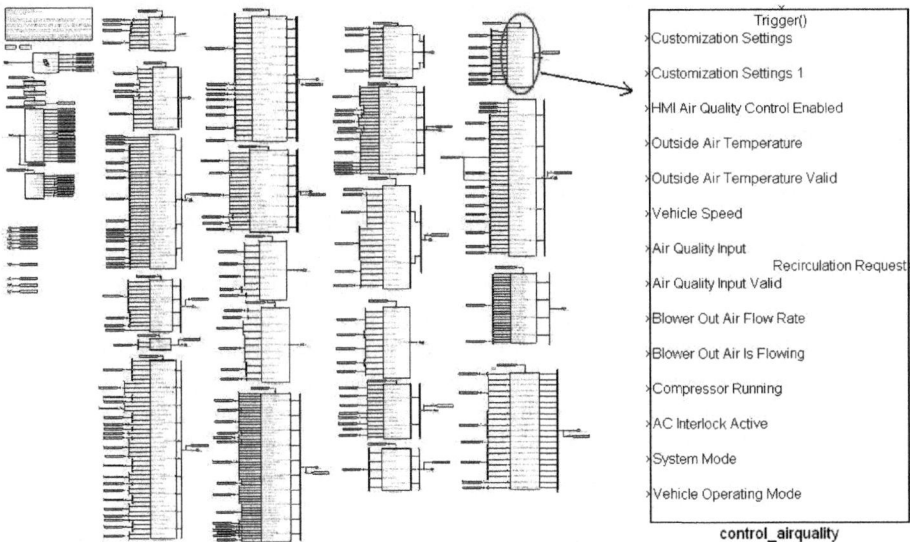

Fig. 1. Simulink framework model that consist of references to several models developed independently. Also shown on the right is the top most level of the model for *control_airquality* algorithm.

development with guarantee to ensure timely delivery of integrated software for vehicles nearing their production. The integration of existing algorithms hand-written in C and model-based designs also included customizing the target link compiler (TLC) file used for production code generation by embedded real-time (ERT) coder. For example, inputs to the Simulink designs from hand-written C codes were automatically resolved to the appropriate C function calls. Furthermore, these models are reused with relatively small amount of calibration changes across several vehicle programs worldwide.

The graphical nature of the Simulink models and Stateflow charts aid to better understanding of the design than reading a thousands of lines of hand-written C code. The simulation capability of the graphical model helps identify the design flaws much earlier in the development cycle that is, before the hardware is available. Furthermore, the use of Simulink Report Generator^{TM} to create a detailed design document helped to understand the designs developed by other software developers. This improved communication among the team members as the collaborative development of the ECC software involved members from India, North America and Europe.

The correctness of conversion of hand-written C algorithms into the models was measured using exactitude of performances of C code and the model. With the use of model-based development, it was possible to perform such verification at the Simulink level that is, much before the system software is ported into the ECU. The simulation model consisting of the model for control law and its environment is developed in the Simulink framework without any physical hardware components. The simulation model is then modified to include hand-written C code in the form of S-function in the Simulink framework. The S-function and the model for control law are therefore subjected to the same simulated environment and test inputs to aid easy comparison of performances. This resulted in engineers feel confidence on the model developed from the existing hand-written C code.

2.2 Simulink Report Generator

Simulink Report Generator™ is used to create design documents for Simulink® and Stateflow® models developed by engineers' located in India, North America and Europe. The design documents are produced in a standard form (.doc, .pdf and .html) that can be distributed to the team members to understand designs created by others [5]. During the development phase of the model design information is included with the use of *Doc Blocks* (documentation blocks from the Simulink® library) at various subsystems of the model. A common framework of the Simulink report generator is used to generate a design document. Since the doc blocks are embedded into the model, any updates to the model could be easily reflected back to the corresponding doc blocks and a fresh design document for the model can be generated with just a click of the button. Furthermore, a design document for the Simulink® framework model consisting of multiple models with interlinks between them can be generated the same way it is generated for an individual model.

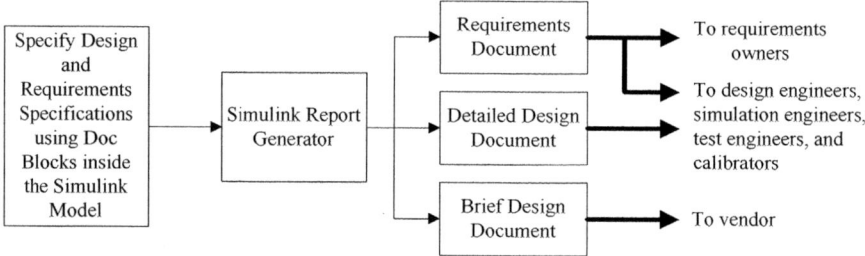

Fig. 2. Simulink® report generator can be used to systematically select the doc blocks with appropriate contents to generate report for different users such as requirements owners', engineers', and vendor, if Original Equipment Manufacturer (OEM) and vendor are working in collaboration

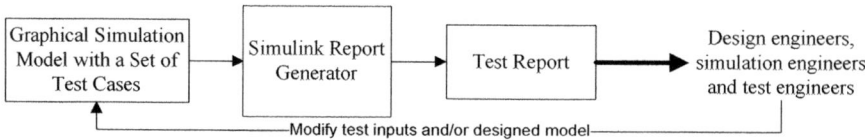

Fig. 3. Simulink report generator tool can run the graphical simulation model with the user specified test inputs and document the results into the test report

The report generator tool offers various features to generate document. The prominent features used for the ECC software development cycle are mentioned below.

1. Snapshots of the implementation can be captured in a document which can highlight interlink between the implementation and the requirement
2. A set of calibration for the model or system software can be published at the end of the document to aid calibrators.
3. A list of model inputs and outputs can be published at the end of the document to aid simulation and test engineers.
4. Documents for different set of people for example, design engineers, requirement owners, and engineers' at vendor can be created from a single model. For example, a requirements document can be created by using doc blocks containing requirements, a brief design document can be created by omitting doc blocks containing requirements and detailed design information. Similarly, the doc blocks with detailed design information are used when creating a design document required by the developers and the other team members. This is particularly an interesting feature when software is designed by the Original Equipment Manufacturer (OEM) in collaboration with supplier or vendor. This feature is depicted in Fig. 2.
5. If table-data is used in implementing the design, graph of the table-data can be included in the design document.
6. Finite State Machine (FSM)'s can be explained in the design document with their states and the transition conditions between the states. The report generator tool can also include description provided by the software developer for the states and the transition conditions between the states.
7. The document in html form has traceability tags that can be used for easy navigation throughout the report.
8. The Simulink report generator also creates Web views that are visual replicas of the models viewable in a Web browser. These Web views can be navigated the same way models are navigated and look exactly the same as the models viewed in Simulink and Stateflow editors. Apart from navigating to a specific subsystem, it is also possible to view properties of blocks, subsystems and signals. Furthermore, like design or requirements documents, Web views can be shared with users who do not have access to MATLAB [5].
9. The simulation model with the user specified test inputs can be run by the report generator tool and the test results at MiL and *back-to-back* levels of testing can be captured in the report [5]. This feature is illustrated in Fig. 3.

3 Testing in Model-Based Developments

About a decade ago, testing automotive designs comprised primarily of four well-understood areas: (1) electromagnetic compatibility (EMC) tests, (2) electrical tests (short-circuits, voltage-current levels, loading effects), (3) environmental tests (testing under extreme conditions), and (4) field tests (on proving ground or test roads) [1]. The functional testing of the algorithms was not possible until the design was complete and hardware (also referred to as Electronic Control Unit (ECU)) was available. By *'design was complete'* we mean the object code was available and ready to flash into the ECU. Since automotive development is an interdisciplinary system that consists of software, electrical, mechanical, and/or hydraulic components inextricably entwined, such test methods as mentioned above are at best expensive and time consuming (often leading to delay in delivery of product to market). Furthermore, the functional complexity of the algorithms was comparatively low therefore functional testing was not mandatory [1]. However, with increasing complexity of designs to make the best products in the market with ever increasing competition, belief on the use of only such test methods is likely not practical and would lead to less than thorough quality assurance standards.

Model-based development tools such as MATLAB/Simulink/Stateflow® allow engineers to develop graphical test models that are not only easy to understand but also powerful enough to express complex algorithms. Such an approach allows for validation of the designs under various failure conditions at an early stage of the development that is before the hardware is available. Simulation of such models allow engineers to find a common functional understanding at an early stage of the development. It also reduces product's time to market by validating designs up front prior to implementation [1]. Due to its distinct advantages, there is a new trend in automotive industry and industries alike such as aerospace, towards model-based development. Majority of software components are no longer hand-written in C or assembly code but modeled with MATLAB/Simulink/Stateflow® or similar tools. Engineers are also working on conversion of algorithms from its *legacy* C form to Simulink/Stateflow models. This process marked the initial phase of transition to model-based development. Engineers' focus in this phase is to reproduce the functional performances of C code from the models while maintaining the capability to deliver the latest software to the products such as vehicles in automotive industry, which are nearing the production. The exactitude of software developed from models and that from hand-written C can be measured using model-based development tool such as MATLAB/Simulink®. Legacy Code Tool (LCT) of MATLAB/Simulink® is used by engineers' to create S-functions that allow including the hand-written C-code (associated source and header files) into the simulation model. The authors' would like to refer this method of software testing as *back-to-back* testing because it allows engineers' to subject the original C code and the model to the same test inputs and the test environment, and measure the performances using a single simulation model.

3.1 Back-to-Back Testing

The correctness of initial stage of transition (conversion from the handwritten C) to mode-based development is measured using exactitude of performances of C code and the model. The performances are quantified as the steady-state response and the transient (or rate of) response of the algorithm when subjected to a specific set of test inputs. The beauty of model-based development is that, such testing is performed before the software is integrated and ported into the ECU. Simulation model is prepared that is, the model and its environment (interaction with other software algorithms and hardware – sensors, actuators and plant) are simulated in the Simulink® framework without any physical hardware components. Such a simulation testing is commonly referred to as *Model-in-the Loop (MiL)* testing [1]. The MiL testing is extended to *back-to-back* testing by modifying the simulation model to include S-function for the C code into the Simulink® framework. The S-function (in effect, the C code) and the simulation model are subjected to a common simulated environment to allow engineers get confidence in the model developed from the hand-written C code. The example is illustrated in Fig. 4; the gray block on the top shows the S-function block to include the existing C code for linear interpolation. The Simulink model and the S-function are subjected to the same test input and the results are shown in Fig. 5. Furthermore, the use of legacy code tool of MATLAB® can be extended to include the S-function for the auto-generated production code in the simulation model and perform *back-to-back* testing with respect to auto-generated code. Such a step of verification can be considered necessary if an unqualified model development tool is used for automated code generation or the qualified model development tool is used but is customized to suit an individual application [1]. It is worth to note that, the production code is always generated for the software framework with all the algorithms implemented and integrated than for each algorithm design independent from the others.

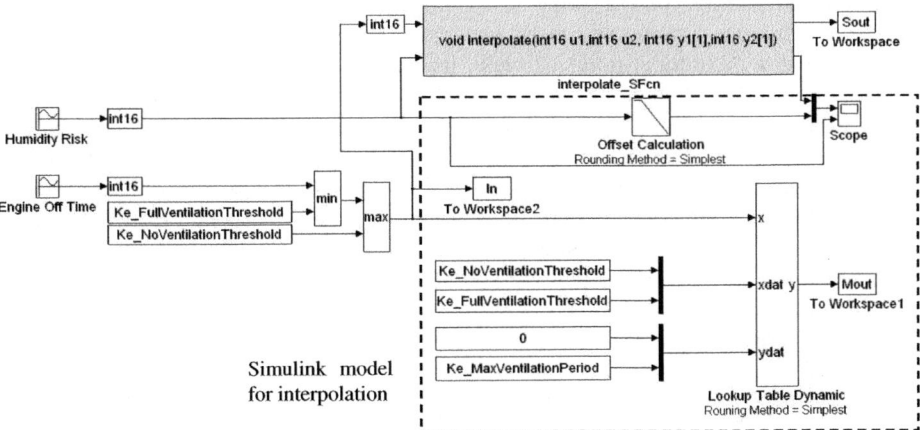

Fig. 4. Simulation model for *back-to-back* testing of the Simulink design and the S-function used to include an existing C code for linear-interpolation

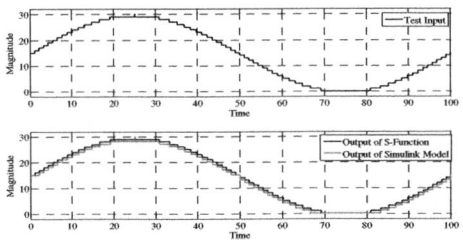

Fig. 5. Test results of *back-to-back* testing for linear-interpolation with sinusoidal input. The difference in the output from the model and S-function are clear seen.

Between the initial stage of the model development (from the legacy C code, or textual or other form of requirements) and the integration followed by porting of software into the ECU there are several intermediate stages of both the integration and testing. These include *Software-in-the-Loop* (SiL) testing where the integrated or the system software and the simulated environment runs on the platform such as Windows- or Linux-based desktop machines, *Hardware-in-the-Loop* (HiL) testing where software runs on the ECU, however the environment around the ECU is still a simulated one, *System bench or test rig* where the environment consists of physical components, and *In-car* level of testing [1]. Since the functionality of the system should remain invariable and independent of the integration and testing, relevant test cases designed should also be invariable throughout the different levels of integration and testing. In order to maximize the reuse, test cases can also be designed to remain invariable for various platforms, for example, ECUs from various vendors with likely different micro-controller, compiler, hardware drivers, etc. On one hand this reduces the effort of test case design tremendously and, on the other hand, allows for easy comparison of test results between the different levels of integration and testing, and across different platforms. Comparison of test results between several levels of integration and testing for the same test inputs also aid to easy traceability of flaw. Although having a common set of test cases for several testing levels may sound trivial from a theoretical point of view, its feasibility is not certain because the test procedures and test languages are different for different levels of testing and for one particular platform from others [1]. Furthermore, with ever increasing competition in the market and its close interaction with customers, before final release of an automotive product there are interim releases of the integrated software or the system. It means that the same tests have to be repeated over and over again over the development cycle of the product. Test automation is therefore necessary as the manual test workload would be at best expensive and likely not practical.

3.2 Test Automation

Different levels of testing have different test procedures and test languages. HVAC engineers at GM India use MATLAB m-scripts for MiL level of testing, xml-data for SiL level of testing on Windows desktop machines and CAN Application Programming Language (CAPL) scripts for HiL level of software testing. Furthermore, there can be a different platform for each vendor. At present, the ECC software has the support of three vendors with two different platforms. Repeating the same tests manually over different testing levels and for different platforms is time consuming and likely not practical, and may lead to less than thorough quality assurance standards.

Software testing of automotive products often requires test cases with a precise sequence of time-related events, especially for power-train and chassis systems. For example, recirculation of air within the vehicle interior is allowed for a maximum duration from few minutes to half an hour. Vehicle interior then needs to be aired out by exchanging inside stale air with outside fresh air. This sequence is repeated until the persistent request for recirculation of cabin air exists.

Furthermore, a couple of testing levels involve interaction of system software with physical components such as electrical, mechanical, and/or hydraulic. Physical components can fail and the software has to detect such failures and compensate for them in a robust way. Detecting and reporting of failures is handled by diagnostic part of the system software. On the other hand, testing at MiL and SiL does not need design

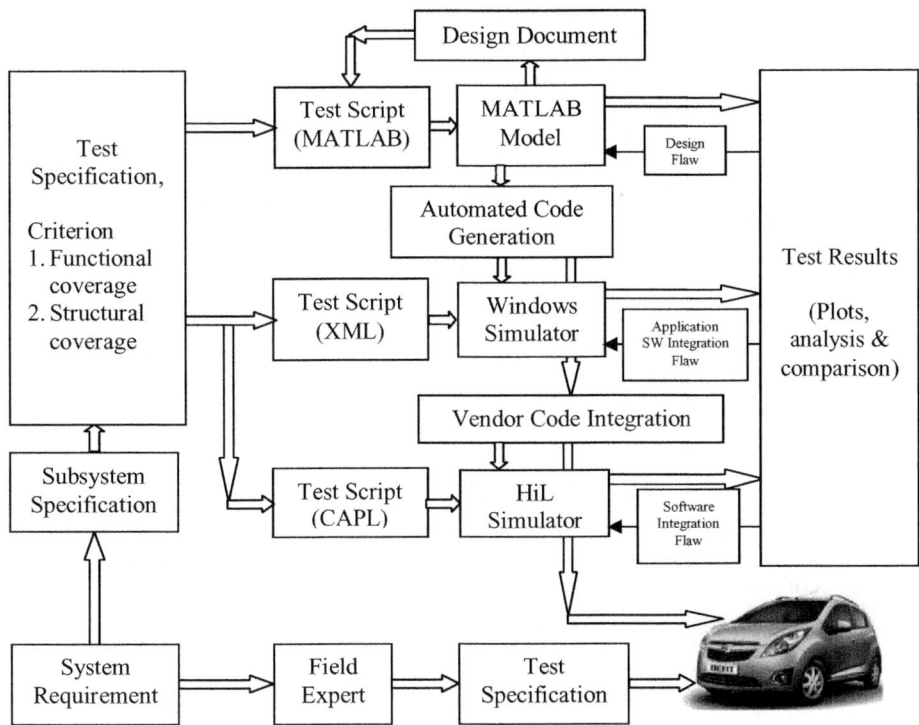

Fig. 6. Test procedure illustrating a set of test cases used with systematic selection over the several testing levels

of test cases for interaction between the model or system software and the physical components because the environment for model or system software is simulated, anyway with no physical components. A test procedure therefore must support systematic selection of test cases especially when there are hundreds or thousands of test cases.

The only way to consider all such scenarios is automation. As a general principle, test cases shall be independent of the underlying software architecture and the test and software platform. Fig. 6 illustrates the test automation at GM India and is explained in the following.

Design of Test Cases using Model-Based Development Tool. Test cases are designed using MATLAB® m-scripts and/or Simulink®. The test cases are designed using the functional system requirements often available as a requirements document or model. Since the test cases are designed using a real-time tool, the Simulink, a sequence of the test data or events is obtained with the time information. Furthermore, it is possible to import measurement data obtained from in-car or field testing into the test cases. MATLAB scripts are designed to generate a graphical representation of the test inputs using the Simulink Signal Builder for ease of understanding the test inputs. Simulation model is then run using the report generator tool and results are captured in the test report for further analysis. The test report also gives a summary of passed and failed test cases. With test automation, changes in the design are easily handled and can be tested in a short time thereby, reducing the time required by software development cycle drastically.

Compiling Test Cases into a Platform-Independent Form. Test cases are compiled using m-script into the Microsoft® Excel spreadsheet. Spreadsheets are independent of the software architecture and the test platform.

Test Execution
1. *Model-in-the-Loop (MiL)* and *back-to-back* testing. A set of test cases designed using m-scripts and Simulink® is used as the test input for the simulation model. Test inputs are exported to Excel spreadsheets so that they can be used over the several levels of testing and for hardware platform.
2. *Software-in-the-Loop (SiL)* testing. System software and the simulated environment with no connection to physical components runs on the Windows desktop machine. Selected test cases are exported from spreadsheet to xml-data which is used as the test input by the system software.
3. *Hardware-in-the-Loop (HiL)* testing. Selected test cases are imported into the CAPL script so that they can be used as test inputs by the system software ported into the ECU with a simulated environment surrounding it.

3.3 Impact of Change in Software Architecture on Testing

With ever growing software technology, in future it may be required to use new software architecture. If software design ignores such a consideration as change in software architecture, the whole design may need to be worked out again. With model-based development, it is possible to design core algorithms independent of the software architecture. However, software for interface to the physical components such as sensors and actuators needs to be designed by considering the software architecture. This is depicted in Fig. 7 which illustrates that the core algorithm is independent of the software architecture and also shows that the interfaces to the physical components are automatically generated using the MATLAB m-script.

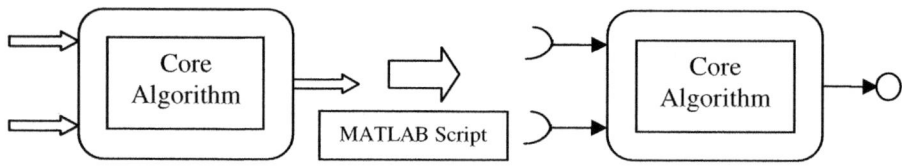

Fig. 7. Core algorithm software designed independent of the software architecture

4 Conclusion

The graphical models are high level abstraction of the designs which allow engineers to focus on the domain of their expertise instead of writing thousands of lines of code. With its several benefits such as validation of software up front prior to the availability of the hardware, reusability, improved communication among team members, etc model-based development promises its widespread use across industrial applications. The closed-loop simulation of models gives a *first best guess* of the design parameters such as filter coefficients, PID gains, calibration data, etc. Early simulation of the designs improved the quality of final product. Migrating to the model-based development can be assured with the presented *back-to-back* testing method. Model-based development allows possible automation at several stages of the development cycle which would reduce the product's time to market drastically.

Acknowledgments. Authors would like to thank Mr. Narayana Bhyravajhula and Mr. Krishnan CMC for their scrutiny of the paper.

References

1. Bringmann, E., Kramer, A.: Model-based Testing of Automotive Systems. In: International Conference on Software Testing, pp. 485–493 (2008)
2. Knight, J.C.: Future Trends of Software Technology and Applications Model-Based Development. In: 30th Annual International Computer Software and Applications Conference, vol. 1, p. 18 (2006)
3. Marsh, P.: A Model of Control – Graphical Modeling, IET Computing & Control Engineering (2006)
4. User story: GM Engineering Europe Develops HVAC Controller for GM Vehicles Using Model-Based Design (2009), http://www.mathworks.com
5. Simulink Report Generator 3 (2006), http://www.mathworks.com

Example-Based Sequence Diagrams to Colored Petri Nets Transformation Using Heuristic Search

Marouane Kessentini[1], Arbi Bouchoucha[1], Houari Sahraoui[1], and Mounir Boukadoum[2]

[1] DIRO, Université de Montréal
{kessentm,bouchoua,sahraouh}@iro.umontreal.ca
[2] DI, Université du Québec à Montréal
mounir.boukadoum@uqam.ca

Abstract. Dynamic UML models like sequence diagrams (SD) lack sufficient formal semantics, making it difficult to build automated tools for their analysis, simulation and validation. A common approach to circumvent the problem is to map these models to more formal representations. In this context, many works propose a rule-based approach to automatically translate SD into colored Petri nets (CPN). However, finding the rules for such SD-to-CPN transformations may be difficult, as the transformation rules are sometimes difficult to define and the produced CPN may be subject to state explosion. We propose a solution that starts from the hypothesis that examples of good transformation traces of SD-to-CPN can be useful to generate the target model. To this end, we describe an automated SD-to-CPN transformation method which finds the combination of transformation fragments that best covers the SD model, using heuristic search in a base of examples. To achieve our goal, we combine two algorithms for global and local search, namely Particle Swarm Optimization (PSO) and Simulated Annealing (SA). Our empirical results show that the new approach allows deriving the sought CPNs with at least equal performance, in terms of size and correctness, to that obtained by a transformation rule-based tool.

Keywords: Model transformation, Petri nets, Sequence diagrams, Search-based software engineering.

1 Introduction

Model Transformation plays an important role in Model Driven Engineering (MDE) [1]. The research efforts by the MDE community have produced various languages and tools, such as ATL [2], KERMETA [3] and VIATRA [4], for automating transformations between different formalisms. One major challenge is to automate these transformations while preserving the quality of the produced models [1, 6].

Many transformation contributions target UML models [1, 6]. From a transformation perspective, UML models can be divided into two major categories: static models, such as class diagrams, and dynamic models, such as activity and state diagrams [7]. Models of the second category are generally transformed for validation and simulation purposes. This is because UML dynamic models, such as sequence diagrams (SDs) [7], lack sufficient formal semantics [8]. This limitation makes it difficult to build automated tools for the analysis, simulation, and validation of those models [9]. A widely accepted approach to circumvent the problem uses concomitant formal representations to specify the relevant behavior [11]; Petri Nets (PNs) [10] are well suited for the task. PNs can model, among others, the behavior of discrete and concurrent systems. Unlike SDs, PNs can derive new information about the structure and behavior of a system via analysis. They can be validated, verified, and simulated [11]. Moreover, they are suitable for visualization (graphical formalism) [11]. These reasons motivate the work to transform UML SDs to PNs.

SD-to-PN transformation may be not obvious to realize, due to two main reasons [29]. First, defining transformation rules can be difficult since the source and target languages have constructs with different semantics; therefore, 1-to-1 mappings are not sufficient to express the semantic equivalence between constructs. The second problem is the risk of a state explosion [11]. Indeed, when transformation rules are available for mapping dynamic UML models to PNs, systematically applying them generally results in large PNs [11]. This could compromise the subsequent analysis tasks, which are generally limited by the number of the PNs' states. Obtaining large PNs is not usually related to the size of the source models [29]. In fact, small sequence diagrams containing complex structures like references, negative traces or critical regions can produce large PNs. To address this problem, some work has been done to produce reduction rules [35].

In this paper, we explore a solution based on the hypothesis that traces of valid transformations of SD-to-PN (performed manually for instance), called transformation examples, can be used by similarity to derive a PN from a particular SD. In this context, our approach, inspired by the Model-Transformation-by-Examples (MTBE) school [12, 13, 14], helps define transformations without applying rules. Because it reuses existing valid model transformation fragments, it also limits the size of the generated models.

More concretely, to automate SD-to-PN transformations, we propose to adapt, the MOTOE approach [14, 15]. MOTOE views a model transformation as an optimization problem where solutions are combinations of transformation fragments obtained from an example base. However, the application of MOTOE to the SD-to-PN transformation problem is not straightforward. MOTOE was designed for and tested with static-diagram transformations such as class-diagrams-to-relational schemas [14, 15]. The transformation of a dynamic diagram is more difficult [8] because, in addition to ensuring structural (static) coherence, it should guarantee behavioral coherence in terms of time constraints and weak sequencing. For instance, the transformation of a SD message depends on the order (sequence) inside the diagram and the events within different operands (parallel merge between the behaviors of the operands, choice between possible behaviors, etc.).

This paper adapts and extends MOTOE to supports SD-to-CPN transformation. The new version, dMOTOE, preserves behavioral coherence. We empirically show that the new approach derives the correct models, and that the obtained CPNs have a significantly lower size than those obtained with a rule-based tool [16] taken for comparison.

The remainder of this paper is structured as follows. In section 2, we provide an overview of the proposed approach for automating SD-to-CPN transformations and discuss its rationale in terms of problem complexity. Section 3 describes the transformation algorithm based on the combined PSO and SA search heuristics. An evaluation of the algorithm is explained and its results are discussed in Section 4. Section 5 is dedicated to the related work. Finally, concluding remarks and future work are provided in section 6.

2 SD-to-CPN Transformation Overview

A model transformation takes a model to transform as input, the *source model*, and produces another model as output, the *target model*. In our case, the source model is a UML sequence diagram and the target model is a colored Petri net. First, we describe the principles of our approach and discuss the rationale behind given the complexity of the transformation problem.

2.1 Overview

dMOTOE takes a SD to transform and a set of transformation examples form an example base as inputs, and generates an equivalent CPN as output. The generation process can be viewed as selecting the subset of the transformation fragments (mapping traces) in the example base that best matches the constructs of the SD according to a similarity function. The outcome is a CPN consisting of an assembly of building blocks (formally defined below). The quality of the produced target model is measured by the level of conformance of the selected fragments to structural and temporal constraints, *i.e.*, by answering the following three questions: 1) Did we choose the right blocks? 2) Did they fit together? 3) Did we perform the assembly in the right order?

As many block assembly schemes are possible, the transformation process is a combinatorial optimization problem where the dimensions of the search space are the constructs of the SD to transform. A solution is determined by the assignment of a transformation fragment (block) to each SD construct. The search is guided by the quality of the solution in terms of its internal coherence (individual construct vs. associated blocks), external coherence (between blocks) and temporal coherence (message sequence).

To explore the solution space, the search is performed in two steps. First, we use a global heuristic search by means of the PSO algorithm [18] to reduce the search space size and select a first transformation solution. Then, a local heuristic search is done using the SA algorithm [19] to refine this solution. In order to provide the details of our approach, we define some terms.

A *construct* is a source or target model element; for example, messages or objects in a SD. An element may contain *properties* that describe it such as its name. Complex constructs may contain *sub-constructs*. For example, a message could have a guard that conditions its execution.

A *Transformation example* (TE) is a mapping of constructs from a particular SD to a CPN. Formally, we view a TE as a triple <SMD, TMD, MB> where SMD denotes the source model (SD in our case), TMD denotes the target model (optimal CPN in our case), and MB is a set of mapping blocks that relate subsets of constructs in SMD to their equivalents in TMD. The *Base of examples* is a set of transformation examples. The transformation examples can be collected from different experts or by automated approaches.

Each TE is viewed as a set of blocks. A ***block*** defines a transformation trace between a subset of constructs in the source model and a subset of constructs in the target model. Constructs that should be transformed together are grouped into the same block. For example, a message *m* that is sent from an object $\underline{A}$ to an object $\underline{B}$ cannot be mapped independently from the mapping of $\underline{A}$ to $\underline{B}$. In our examples, blocks correspond to concrete traces left by experts when transforming models. They are not general rules as they involve concept instances (*e.g.*, a message *m*) instead of concepts (*e.g.*, message concept). In other words, where transformation rules are expressed in terms of meta-models, blocks are expressed in terms of concrete models.

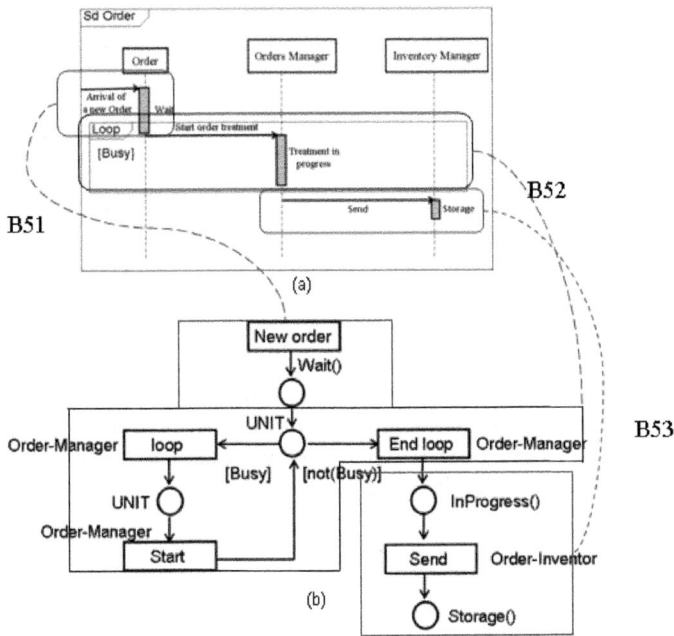

Fig. 1. (a) Example of SD (source model) and (b) his equivalent CPN (target model)

In a SD-to-CPN transformation, blocks correspond to transformation traces of loops (*loop*), alternatives (*alt*), concurrent interactions (*par*), *activation boxes*, and *messages* (see UML2.0 SD specification for more details about these constructs [7]). In the case where the constructs are imbedded, a single block is created for the higher-level construct. Blocks can be derived automatically from the transformation trace of the whole model.

An example of a SD-to-CPN transformation is presented in Figure 1. For legibility reasons, we present an example containing only one complex fragment *loop*. In the validation section, we will use more complex SDs that involve different CPN constructs. The SD in Figure 1.a contains 10 constructs that represent 3 objects, 3 messages, 1 loop and 3 activation boxes. Three blocks are defined[1]: B_{51} for message *Arrival of a new Order* and activation box *Wait*, B_{52} for the loop with guard *[Busy]*, message *Start order treatment*, and activation box *Treatment in progress*, and B_{53} for message *Send* and activation box *Storage*. Notice that only one block is defined in B_{52} as the activation box is inside the loop.

In block B_{51}, for example, *Arrival of a new Order* was transformed by an expert into the transition *New order* and *Wait* into the place *Wait()* (Figure 1.b).

To manipulate them more conveniently, the models (source or target) are described by sets of predicates, each corresponding to a construct (or a sub-construct) type. The order of writing predicates is important in the case of a dynamic model. The predicate types for SDs are:

```
Object (ObjetName, ObjetType);
Message (MessageType, Sender, Receiver, MessageName, ActivityName);
Activity (ActivityName, ObjectName, Duration, MessageNumber);
Loop (StartMessageName, EndMessageName, ConditionValue);
Par (StartMessageName, EndMessageName, ConditionValue, ConditionType);
```

Similarly, those of CPN are:

```
Place (PlaceName);
Transition (TransitionName);
Input(TransitionName, PlaceSourceName)
Output(TransitionName, PlaceDestinationName)
```

For example, the message *Arrival of a new Order* in Figure 1.a can be described by

```
Message (Synchronic,_, Order, ArrivalOfNewOrder, Wait);
```

The predicate indicates that *Arrival of a new Order* is a synchronic message sent to Order (with "_" meaning no sender) and connected to activation box *Wait*. Mapping traces are also expressed using predicate correspondences with the symbol ":". In Figure 1.b, for instance, block B_{51} is defined as follows:

```
Begin B51
Message (Synchronic, _, Order, ArrivalOfNewOrder, Wait). : Transition
   (NewOrder, Coulor1), Input(NewOrder, _), Output(NewOrder, Wait).
Activity (Wait, Order, 10, 2). :  Place (Wait).
End B51
```

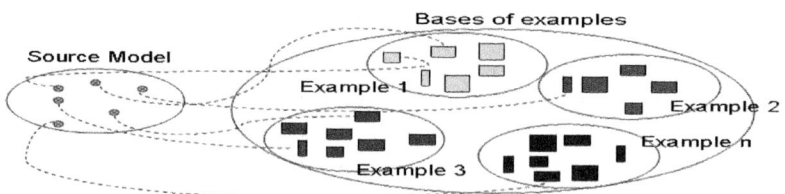

Fig. 2. Transformation solution as blocks-to-constructs mapping

---

[1] For traceability purpose, blocks are sequentially numbered. For instance, the 3 blocks of this example TE_i are B_{51} to B_{53}. Those of TE_{i+1} are B_{54} to B_{xx}, and so on and so forth. When a solution is produced, it is easy to determine which examples contributed to it.

In the absence of transformation rules, a construct can be transformed in many ways, each having a degree of relevance. A SD M_i to transform is characterized by its description SMD_i, i.e., a set of predicates. Figure 2 shows a source model with 6 constructs to transform represented by circles. A transformation solution consists of assigning to each construct a mapping block transformation possibility from the example base (blocks are represented by rectangles in Figure 2). A possibility is considered to be adequate if the block maps a similar construct.

2.2 Transformation Complexity

Our approach is similar to case-based reasoning [21] with the difference that we do not select and adapt the whole transformation of a similar SD. Instead, we combine and adapt fragments of transformations coming from the transformations of several SDs.

The transformation of a SD M_i with n constructs, using a set of examples that globally define m possibilities (blocks), consists of finding the subset from the m possibilities that better transforms each of the n constructs of M_i. In this context, m^n possible combinations have to be explored. This value can quickly become huge.

If we limit the possibilities for each construct to only blocks that contain similar constructs, the number of possibilities becomes $m_1 \times m_2 \times m_3 \times \ldots \times m_n$ where each $m_i \leq m$ represents the number of blocks containing constructs similar to construct i. Although the number of possibilities is reduced, it could still be very large for big SDs. A sequence diagram with 50 constructs, each having 8 or more mapping possibilities, necessitates exploring at least 8^{50} combinations. Considering these magnitudes, an exhaustive search cannot be used within a reasonable time frame. This motivates the use of a heuristic search when a more formal approach is either not available or hard to deploy.

3 Heuristic-Based Transformation

We describe in this section the adaptation of two heuristics, PSO [18] and SA [19], to automate SD-to-CPN transformation. These methods each follow a generic strategy to explore the search space. When applied to a given problem, they must be specialized by defining: (1) the coding of solutions, (2) the operators that allow moving in the search space, and (3) the fitness function that measures the quality of a solution. In the remainder of this section we start by giving the principles of PSO and SA. Then, we describe the three above-mentioned heuristic components.

3.1 Principle

To obtain a more robust optimization technique, it is common to combine different search strategies in an attempt to compensate for deficiencies of the individual algorithms [20]. In our context the search for a solution is done in two steps. First, a global search with PSO is quickly performed to locate the portion of the search space where good solutions are likely to be found. In the second step, the obtained solution is refined with a local search performed by SA.

PSO, *Particle Swarm Optimization,* is a parallel population-based computation technique proposed by Kennedy and Eberhart [18]. The PSO swarm (population) is represented by a set of K particles (possible solutions to the problem). A particle i is defined by a position coordinate vector X_i, in the solution space. Particles improve themselves by changing positions according to a velocity function that produces a translation vector. The improvement is assessed by a fitness function.

The particle with the highest fitness is memorized as the global best solution (*gbest*) during the search process. Also, each particle stores its own best position (*pbest*) among all the positions reached during the search process. At each iteration, all particles are moved according to their velocities (Equation 1). The velocity V_i' of a particle i, depends on three factors: its inertia corresponding to the previous velocity, its *pbest*, and the *gbest*. Factors are weighted respectively by W, C_1, and C_2. The importance of the local and global position factors varies and is set at each iteration by a random function. The weight of inertia decreases during the search process. The derivation of V_i' is given by Equation 2. After each iteration, the individual *pbest*s and the *gbest* are updated if the new positions bring higher qualities than the ones before.

$$X_i' = X_i + V_i' \tag{1}$$

$$V_i' = W \times V_i + C_1 \times rand\,() \times (pbest_i - X_i) + C_2 \times rand\,() * (gbest - X_i) \tag{2}$$

The algorithm iterates until the particles converge towards a unique position that determines the solution to the problem.

Simulated Annealing (SA) [19] is a local search algorithm that gradually transforms a solution following the annealing principle used in metallurgy. Starting from an initial solution, SA uses a pseudo-cooling process where a pseudo temperature is gradually decreased. For each temperature, the following three steps are repeated for a fixed number of iterations: (1) determine a new neighboring solution; (2) evaluate the fitness of the new solution; (3) decide on whether to accept the new solution in place of the current one based on the fitness function and the temperature value. Solutions are accepted if they improve quality. When the quality is degraded, they can still be accepted, but with a certain probability. The probability is high when the temperature is high and the quality degradation is low. As a consequence, quality-degrading solutions are easily accepted in the beginning of process when the temperatures are high, but with more difficulty as the temperature decreases. This mechanism prevents reaching a local optimum.

3.2 Adaptation

To adapt PSO and SA to the SD-to-CPN transformation problem, we must define the following: a solution coding suitable for the transformation problem, a neighborhood function to derive new solutions, and a fitness function to evaluate these solutions.

As stated in Section 2, we model the search space as an n-dimensional space where each dimension corresponds to one of the n constructs of the SD to transform. A solution is then a point in that space, defined by a coordinate vector whose elements are blocks numbers from the example base assigned to the n constructs. For instance, the transformation of the SD model shown in Figure 3 will generate a 7-dimensional space that accounts for the two objects, three messages and two activities. One solution is this space, shown in Table 1, suggests that message *CheckDriver* should be transformed according to *block B_{19}*, activity *Positioning*, according to *block B_7*, etc.

Thus concretely, a solution is implemented as a vector where constructs are the dimensions (the elements) and block numbers are the element values.

The association between a construct and a block does not necessarily mean that a transformation is possible, *i.e.*, the block perfectly matches the contest of the construct. This is determined by the fitness function described in subsection 3.2.3.

The proposed coding is valid for both heuristics. In the case of PSO, as an initial population, we create *k* solution vectors with a random assignment of blocks. Alternatively, SA starts from the solution vector produced by PSO.

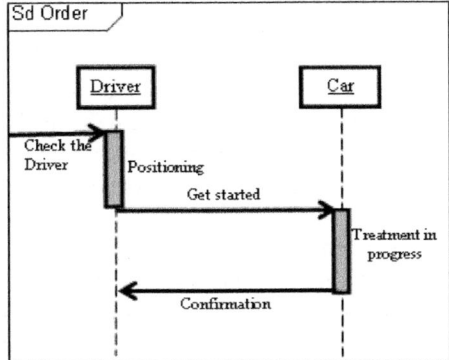

Fig. 3. Example of source model

Table 1. Solution representation

Dimensions	Constructs	Block numbers
1	Message(CheckDriver)	B19
2	Activity(Positioning)	B7
3	Message(GetStarted)	B51
4	Activity(Treatment)	B105
5	Message(Confirmation)	B16
6	Object(Driver)	B83
7	Object(Car)	B33

Change Operators. Modifying solutions to produce new ones is the second important aspect of heuristic search. Unlike coding, change is implemented differently by the PSO and SA heuristics. While PSO sees change as movement in the search space driven by a velocity function, SA sees it as random coordinate modifications.

In the case of PSO, a translation (velocity) vector is derived according to equation 2 and added to the position vector. For example, the solution of Table 1 may produce the new solution shown in Figure 4. The velocity vector V has a translation value for each element (real values). When summed with the block numbers, the results are rounded to integers. They are also bounded by 1 and the maximum number of available blocks.

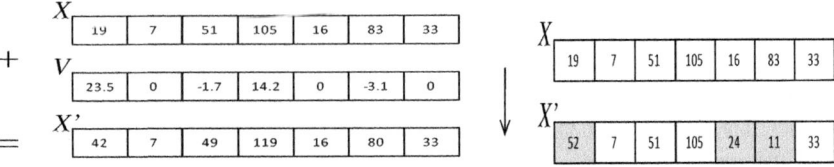

Fig. 4. Change Operator in PSO   **Fig. 5.** Change Operator in SA

For SA, the change operator randomly chooses l dimensions ($l < n$) and replaces their assigned blocks by randomly selected ones from the example base. For instance, Figure 5 shows a new solution derived from the one of Table 1. Constructs 1, 5 and 6 are selected to be changed. They are assigned respectively blocks 52, 24, and 11 instead of 19, 16, and 83. The other constructs remain unchanged. The number of blocks to change is a parameter of SA (three in this example). In our validation, we set it to 4 considering that the average number of constructs per SD is 36.

Fitness Function. The fitness function allows quantifying the quality of a transformation solution. As explained in the previous paragraph, solutions are derived by random assignment of new blocks to some constructs. The quality of a transformation solution is then the sum of the individual transformation qualities of the n constructs of the SD. To evaluate if assigned block B_i is a good transformation possibility for construct C_j, the fitness function first evaluates the **adequacy**, *i.e.*, does B_i contains a construct C_k from the same type as C_j? if the answer is "no", the assigned block is unsuitable. Otherwise, the fitness function checks the three following coherence aspects: (1) **internal coherence** (what is the degree of similarity between C_j and C_k in terms of properties?), (2) **external coherence** (to what extent the transformation proposed by B_i contradicts the transformations of constructs related to C_j?), and (3) **temporal coherence** (to what extent the transformation proposed by B_i preserves the temporal constraints of message sequences in SD?). The fitness function is formally defined as follows:

$$f = \sum_{j=1}^{n} a_j \times (ic_j + ec_j + tc_j) \qquad (3)$$

where a_j is the adequacy of assigning B_i to C_j (1 if B_i is adequate, 0 otherwise), and ic_j, ec_j, and tc_j are respectively the internal, external, and temporal coherences of the assignment. ic_j is defined as the ratio between the number of parameters of the predicate P_j representing C_j that match the parameters of the associated construct in block B_i and the total parameters of P_j.

Consider the SD example shown in Figure 3. Message *GetStarted* is defined by predicate `Message(Synchronic, Driver, Car, GetStrated, Positioning)`. This predicate indicates that the message *GetStarted*, which is *synchronic*, is sent by object *Driver* to *Car* from the activity *Positioning*. The solution in Table 1 assigns the block B_{51} to this message. Block B_{51} is described in section 2.1 as follows:

```
Begin B51
Message (Synchronic, _, Order, ArrivalOfNewOrder, Wait). : Transition
   (NewOrder, Coulor1), Input(NewOrder, _), Output(NewOrder, Wait).
Activity (Wait, Order, 10, 2). : Place (Wait).
End B51
```

The adequacy a_3 of the transformation of *GetStarted* (3rd construct) is equal to 1 because block B_{51} also contains predicate *message* (*ArrivalOfNewOrder*). The parameters of the two messages are similar except for the sender which is not an object in the case of *ArrivalOfNewOrder*. As a result, internal coherence ic_3=4/5=0.8 (four parameters that match over 5).

For external coherence ec_j, let $RCons_j$ be the set of constructs related to C_j and $RConsM_{ij}$, the subset of constructs in $RCons_j$ whose transformations are consistent with the one of C_j, *i.e.*, we compares the transformation proposed by the block assigned to C_j with the ones suggested by the blocks assigned to the related constructs. ec_j is calculated as the ratio between $RConsM_{ij}$ and $RCons_j$.

In our example, *GetStarted* involves three constructs (sender, receiver, and activity). According to B_{51}, only *Positioning* activity is related (has a predicate) and should be transformed into a place similarly to *Wait* activity. In the solution of , the construct *Positioning* is assigned the block B_7 (dimension 2 of the solution vector). This block is defined as follows:

```
Begin B7
Message (Asynchronic, User, Printer, NewPrint, Progress). : Transition
   (NewPrint, Coulor7), Input(NewPrint, _), Output(NewPrint, Progress).
Activities (Progress, Printer, 8, 1). : Place (Progress).
End B7
```

According to B_7, *Positioning* should also be mapped to a place. Thus there is no conflict between B_{51} and B_7, and ec_3=1 (1/1).

tc_j represents the temporal coherence. It reflects the time constraint specific to dynamic models. To preserve the temporal coherence, we ensure that the transformation of elements that are contiguous to C_j preserve the temporal semantics. To this end, we first consider the block B_{inc} that includes C_j and the blocks B_{pre} and B_{fol} that respectively precedes and follows B_{inc}. Although the model to transform is not in the example base, we identify blocks with only the source part according to the rules given in Section 2.1. Then we consider the block B_i, assigned to C_j by the evaluated solution, and the two blocks B_{pre_i} and B_{fol_i} preceding and following B_i. tc_j is obtained by comparing B_{pre} to B_{pre_i}, B_{inc} to B_i, and B_{fol} to B_{fol_i}. For example, let $P_{pre}(k)$ be the predicate having the kth position in B_{pre} and $P_{pre\_i}(k)$ be the predicate having the kth position in B_{pre_i}, the number of pairs of predicates $PMatch(B_{pre}, B_{pre\_i})$ that match in the two blocks is defined as

$$\left|\{(P_{pre}(k), P_{pre\_i}(k)) | P_{pre}(k) = P_{pre\_i}(k)\}\right| \qquad (4)$$

tc_i is then defined as follows:

$$tc_j = \frac{|PMatch(B_{pre}, B_{pre\_i})| + |PMatch(B_{inc}, B_i)| + |PMatch(B_{fol}, B_{fol\_i})|}{\max(|B_{pre}|, |B_{pre\_i}|) + \max(|B_{inc}|, |B_i|) + \max(|B_{fol}|, |B_{fol\_i}|)} \qquad (5)$$

Figure 6 shows an example of the calculation of tc_j. Going back to the example of message *GetStarted*, to derive the tc_3, we identify in the SD to transform two blocks: B_s which contains *GetStarted* and B_{s-1} which precedes B_s. Consequently, block B_{51} will be compared to B_s. B_s contains a message followed by an activity and another message. B_{51} contains a message followed by an activity. Then, two pairs of predicates match and the max size between the two blocks is 3. As B_{51} has no preceding block, we consider that no match exists with B_{s-1}, and the corresponding max size is that of B_{s-1}, i.e., 2 for the message and the activity. Finally, as B_s has no following block, no match exists with B_{52}, which follows B_{51}. We take then as max size, the size of B_{52} (3 corresponding to the loop, the message, and the activity). According to equation 5, $tc_3=(0+2+0)/(2+3+3)=0.25$. This temporal coherence factor is standard and works with any combined fragments of SDs.

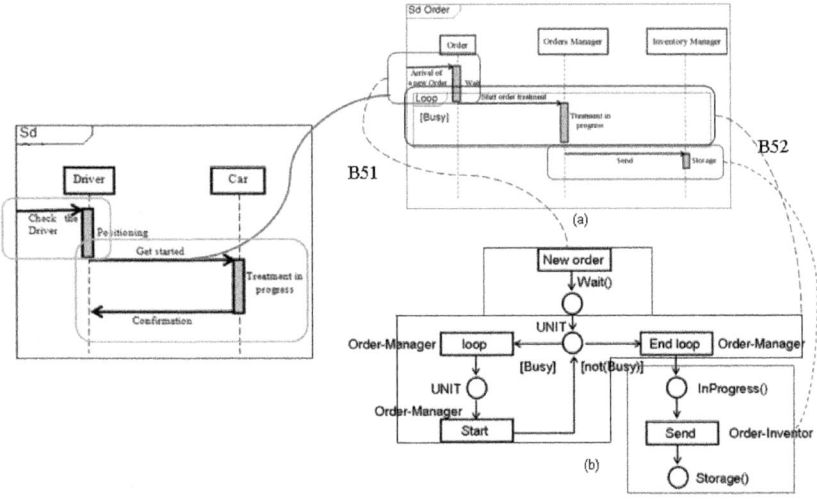

Fig. 6. Temporal coherence

The fitness function does not need a considerable effort to be adapted for other transformations (e.g. state machine to PNs). However, the block definition must be adapted to the semantics of the new transformation.

4 Validation

To evaluate the feasibility of our approach, we conducted an experiment on the transformation of 10 UML sequence diagrams[2]. We collected the transformations of these 10 sequence diagrams from the Internet and textbooks and used them to build an example base EB = {<SD_i, CPN_i> | i=1,2,...,10}. We ensured by manual inspection that all the transformations are valid. The size of the SDs varied from 16 to 57

---

[2] The reader can find in this link www.marouane-kessentini.com/ecmfa2010 all the materials used in our experiments.

constructs, with an average of 36. Altogether, the 10 examples defined 224 mapping blocks. The 10 sequence diagrams contained many complex fragments: *loop, alt, opt, par, region, neg* and *ref*.

To evaluate the correctness of our transformation method, we used a 10-fold cross validation procedure. For each fold, one sequence diagram SD_j is transformed using the remaining 9 transformation examples. Then, the transformation result for each fold is checked for correctness using two methods: automatic correctness (*AC*) and manual correctness (*MC*). Automatic correctness consists of comparing the derived CPN to the known CPN, construct by construct. This measure has the advantage of being automatic and objective. However, since a given SD_j may have different transformation possibilities, *AC* could reject a valid construct transformation because it yields a different CPN from the one provided. To prevent this situation, we also perform manual evaluation of the obtained CPN. In both cases, the correctness is the proportion of constructs that are correctly transformed.

In addition to correctness, we compare the size of the obtained CPNs with the ones obtained by using the rule-based tool WebSPN for mapping UML diagrams to CPN [16]. The size of a CPN is defined by the number of constructs.

Figure 7 shows the correctness for the 10 folds. Both automatic and manual correctness had values greater than 90% in average (92.5% for *AC* and 95.8% for *MC*). Although few examples were used (9 for each transformation), all the SDs had a transformation correctness greater than 90%, with 3 of them perfectly transformed.

Figure 7 also shows that, in general, the best transformations are obtained with smaller SDs. After 36 constructs, the quality degrades slightly but steadily. This may indicate that the transformation correctness of complex SDs necessitates more examples in general. However, the largest and most complex SD (57 constructs and 19 complex fragments) has a *MC* value of 96%.

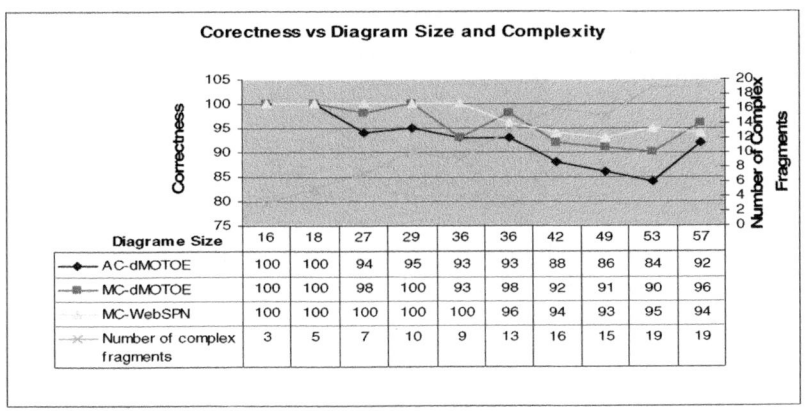

Fig. 7. Correctness of the transformations

In addition, our results show that the correctness of our transformations is equivalent that of WebSPN. Another interesting finding during the evaluation is that, in some cases, a higher fitness value does not necessarily imply higher transformation correctness. This was the case for the transformations of SD_3 (fitness of 82% and *MC*

= 98%) and SD_5 (fitness of 92% and MC = 93%). This is probably due to the fact that we assign the same weight to simple constructs such as messages and complex constructs such as loops in the fitness function. Indeed, temporal coherence is more difficult to assess for complex constructs.

Manual inspection of the generated CPNs showed that the different transformation errors are easy to fix. They do not require considerable effort and the majority of them is related to the composition of complex fragments. For example, as we did not have an example that mapped two *alts* situated in a *loop*, the optimization technique used one that contained only one *alt* in a *loop*. Almost the same errors were made by WebSPN, including the case of two *alts* in a *loop*.

When developing our approach, we conjectured that the example-based transformation produce CPNs smaller than the one obtained by systematic rule application. Table 2 compares the obtained CPN sizes by using dMOTOE and WebSPN for the 10 transformations. In all cases, a reduction in size occurs when using dMOTOE, with an average reduction of 28.3% in comparison to WebSPN. Although the highest reduction corresponded to the smallest SD, the reductions for larger diagrams were important as well (*e.g.*, 39% for 36 constructs, 38% for 39 constructs, and 29% for 76 constructs). These reductions should be viewed in the context of the correctness equivalence between our approach and WebSPN.

Table 2. CPN size comparison

Size(WebSPN)	Size(dMOTOE)	Variation
22	13	41%
36	22	39%
39	24	38%
43	31	28%
51	36	30%
50	39	22%
56	39	30%
53	44	16%
58	52	10%
76	54	29%
Average Reduction :		28.3%

The obtained results confirm our assumption that systematic application of rules results in CPNs larger than needed and that reusing valid transformed examples attenuates the state explosion problem.

As for execution time, we ran our algorithm on a standard desktop computer (Pentium CPU running at 2 GHz with 2 GB of RAM). The execution time was of the order of a few seconds and increased linearly with the number of constructs, indicating that our approach is scalable from the performance standpoint.

5 Related Work

The work proposed in this paper crosscuts two main research areas: model transformation and traceability in the context of MDD.

In [5], five categories of transformation approaches were identified: graph-based [22], relational [23], structure-driven [24], direct-manipulation, and hybrid. One conclusion to be drawn from studying the existing MT approaches is that they are often based on empirically obtained rules [25].

Recently, traceability gained popularity in model transformation [26]. Usually, trace information are generated manually and stored as models [27]. For example, Marvie et al. [28] propose a transformation composition framework that allows the manual creation of linkings (traces). In the studied approaches and frameworks based on traceability, trace information is used in general for detecting model inconsistency and fault localization in transformations. On the other hand, dMOTO uses traces to automate the transformation process.

More specifically, in the case of SD-to-PN, several approaches were proposed in addition to WebSPN. In [29], the authors describe a meta-model for the SD-to-PN mapping. It defines rules involving concepts of the meta-models representing respectively sequence diagrams and Petri nets. One of the limitations of this approach is that temporal coherence is not addressed explicitly. Additionally, the meta-model representing the rules tends to generate large PNs, as noticed by the authors. In [11], a set of rules to transform UML 2.0 SDs into PNs is proposed. The goal is to animate SDs using the operational semantics of PNs. In our case, we can generate the structure of the targeted CPN in an XMI file that can be used as input for some simulation tools like CPN tools [38]. Other UML dynamic diagrams are also considered for the transformation to PNs. For example, use case constructs are mapped to PN using a multi-layer technique [8].

There are other research contributions that concentrate on supporting validation and analysis of UML statecharts by mapping them to Petri nets of various types [36, 37]. Unlike our approach, this work uses information extracted from different UML diagrams to produce the Petri nets. A general conclusion on the transformation of dynamic models to PNs is that, in addition to the fact that no consensual transformation rules are used, a second step is usually required to reduce the size of the obtained PNs.

dMOTOE uses the "by example" principle to transform models, but what we propose is completely different from other contributions to model transformation by example (MTBE). Varro and Balogh [12, 13] propose a semi-automated process for MTBE using Inductive Logic Programming (ILP). The principle of their approach is to derive transformation rules semi-automatically from an initial prototypical set of interrelated source and target models. Wimmer et al. [30] derive ATL transformation rules from examples of business process models. Both works use semantic correspondences between models to derive rules, and only static models are considered. Moreover, in practice, a large number of transformation learning-examples may be required to ensure that the generated rules are complete and correct. Both approaches provide a semi-automatic generation of model transformation rules that needs further refinement by the user. Also, since both approaches are based on semantic mappings, they are more appropriate in the context of exogenous model transformations between different metamodel. Unfortunately, the generation of rules to transform attributes is not well supported in most MTBE implementations. Our model is different from both previous approaches to MTBE. We do not create transformation rules to transform a source model, directly using examples instead. As a result, our approach is independent from any source or target metamodels.Recently, a similar approach to MTBE, called Model Transformation By Demonstration (MTBD), is proposed [34]. Instead of the MTBE idea of inferring the rules from a prototypical set of mappings, users are asked to demonstrate how the model transformation should be done by directly editing (e.g., add, delete, connect, update) the model instance to simulate the model transformation process step by step. This approach needs a large number of simulated patterns to give good results and, for instance, MTBD cannot be useful to transform an entire source model.

6 Conclusion

In this paper, we propose the approach dMOTOE, to automate SD-to-CPN transformation using heuristic search. dMOTOE uses a set of existing transformation examples to derive a colored Petri net from a sequence diagram. The transformation is seen as an optimization problem where different transformation possibilities are evaluated and, for each possibility, a quality is associated depending on its conformance with the examples at hand.

The approach we propose has the advantage that, for any source model, it can be used when rules generation is difficult. Another interesting advantage is that our approach is independent from source and target formalisms; aside from the examples, no extra information is needed. Moreover, as we reuse existing transformations, the obtained CPN are smaller than those obtained by transformation rules.

We have evaluated our approach on ten sequence diagrams. The experimental results indicate that the derived CPNs are comparable to those defined by experts in terms of correctness (average value of 96%). Our results also reveal that the generated CPNs are smaller than the ones generated by the tool WebSPN [16].

Although, the obtained results are very encouraging, many aspects of our approach could be improved. Our approach currently suffers from the following limitations: 1) in the case of SD-to-PNs transformation, it provides less clean semantics than a rules-based approach; 2) coverage of complex fragments examples is needed for completeness and to ensure consistently good results; 3) the base of examples is difficult to collect especially for complex and not widely used formalisms; 4) the fitness function could weight complex constructs more heavily when evaluating a solution. In addition, a validation on a larger example base is in project to better assess the adaptation capability of the approach, and we can compare the sizes of the reachability graph of the produced CPNs by dMOTOE and WebSPN in order to treat the richer behaviors (in fact, a bigger net is not necessarily worse in some cases). In a broader perspective, we plan to experiment and extend dMOTOE to other transformations involving dynamic models: code generation (model-to-code), refactoring (code-to-code), or reverse-engineering (code-to-model).

References

1. France, R., Rumpe, B.: Model-driven Development of Complex Software: A Research Roadmap. In: ICSE 2007: Future of Software Engineering (2007)
2. Jouault, F., Kurtev, I.: Transforming models with ATL. In: Bruel, J.-M. (ed.) MoDELS 2005. LNCS, vol. 3844, pp. 128–138. Springer, Heidelberg (2006)

3. Muller, P., Fleurey, F., Jezequel, J.M.,et al.:: Weaving executability into object-oriented meta-languages. In: Briand, L.C., Williams, C. (eds.) MoDELS 2005. LNCS, vol. 3713, pp. 264–278. Springer, Heidelberg (2005)
4. Varró, D., Pataricza, A.: Generic and meta-transformations for model transformation engineering. In: Baar, T., Strohmeier, A., Moreira, A., Mellor, S.J. (eds.) UML 2004. LNCS, vol. 3273, pp. 290–304. Springer, Heidelberg (2004)
5. Czarnecki, K., Helsen, S.: Classification of model transformation approaches. In: OOSPLA 2003, Anaheim, USA (2003)
6. Ehrig, H., Ehrig, K., de Lara, J., Taentzer, G., Varró, D., Varró-Gyapay, S.: On the Correspondence Between Conformance Testing and Regular Inference. In: Cerioli, M. (ed.) FASE 2005. LNCS, vol. 3442, pp. 175–189. Springer, Heidelberg (2005)
7. Booch, G., Jacobson, I., Rumbaugh, J.: The Unified Modeling Language Users Guide. Addison Wesley, Reading (1998)
8. Saldhana, J., Shatz, S.M.: UML Diagrams to Object Petri Net Models: An Approach for Modeling and Analysis. In: SEKE 2000, July 2000, pp. 103–110 (2000)
9. Lilius, J., Paltor, I.P.: vUML: A Tool for Verifying UML Models. In: ASE 1999 (1999)
10. Murata, T.: Petri Nets: Properties, Analysis, and Applications. Proceedings of the IEEE 77(4), 541–580 (1989)
11. Ribeiro, O.R., Fernandes, J.M.: Some Rules to Transform Sequence Diagrams into Coloured Petri Nets. In: Jensen, K. (ed.) CPN 2006, Aarhus, Denmark, October 2006, pp. 237–256 (2006)
12. Varro, D.: Model transformation by example. In: Nierstrasz, O., Whittle, J., Harel, D., Reggio, G. (eds.) MoDELS 2006. LNCS, vol. 4199, pp. 410–424. Springer, Heidelberg (2006)
13. Varro, D., Balogh, Z.: Automating Model Transformation by Example Using Inductive Logic Programming. ACM Symposium, 2007 In: SAC (2007)
14. Kessentini, M., Sahraoui, H., Boukadoum, M.: Model Transformation as an Optimization Problem. In: Czarnecki, K., Ober, I., Bruel, J.-M., Uhl, A., Völter, M. (eds.) MODELS 2008. LNCS, vol. 5301, pp. 159–173. Springer, Heidelberg (2008)
15. Kessentini, M., Sahraoui, H., Boukadoum, M.: Search-based Model Transformation by Example. Submitted to SoSym (under review)
16. Distefano, S., Scarpa, M., Puliafito, A.: Software Performance Analysis in UML Models. FIRB-Perf 2005: 115-125, https://mdslab.unime.it/webspn/mapping.htm
17. Jensen, K.: Coloured Petri Nets. Basic Concepts, Analysis Methods and Practical Use. Basic Concepts. Monographs in Theoretical Computer Science, vol. 1 (1997)
18. Kennedy, J., Eberhart, R.C.: Particle swarm optimization. In: Proc. IEEE Intl. Conf. on Neural Networks, pp. 1942–1948 (1995)
19. Kirkpatrick, D.S., Gelatt, J., Vecchi, M.P.: Optimization by simulated annealing. Science 220(4598), 671–680 (1983)
20. Kelner, V., Capitanescu, F., Léonard, O., Wehenkel, L.: A hybrid optimization technique coupling an evolutionary and a local search algorithm. J. Comput. Appl. Math (2008)
21. Aamodt, A., Plaza, E.: Case-Based Reasoning: Foundational Issues, Methodological Variations, and System Approaches. AIC 39–52 (1994)
22. Andries, M., Engels, G., Habel, A., Hoffmann, B., Kreowski, H.-J., Kuske, S., Kuske, D., Plump, D., Schürr, A., Taentzer, G.: Graph Transformation for Specification and Programming. Technical Report 7/96, Universität Bremen (1996)
23. Akehurst, D.H., Kent, S.: A Relational Approach to Defining Transformations in a Metamodel. In: Jézéquel, J.-M., Hussmann, H., Cook, S. (eds.) UML 2002. LNCS, vol. 2460, pp. 243–258. Springer, Heidelberg (2002)

24. Interactive Objects Software GmbH, Project Technology, Inc. MOF 2.0 Query/Views/Transformations RFP, Revised Submission
25. Egyed, A.: Heterogeneous Views Integration and its Automation, Ph.D. Thesis (2000)
26. Galvão, I., Goknil, A.: Survey of Traceability Approaches in Model-Driven Engineering. In: EDOC 2007, pp. 313–326 (2007)
27. Jouault, F.: Loosely coupled traceability for atl. In: ECMDA 2005(2005)
28. Marvie, R.: A transformation composition framework for model driven engineering. Technical Report LIFL-2004-10, LIFL (2004)
29. Ouardani, A., Esteban, P., Paludetto, M., Pascal, J.-C.: A Meta-modeling Approach for Sequence Diagrams to Petri Nets Transformation. In: ESMC 2006 (2006)
30. Wimmer, M., Strommer, M., Kargl, H., Kramler, G.: Towards model transformation generation by-example. In: HICSS-40 Hawaii International Conference on System Sciences
31. Harman, M., Jones, B.F.: Search-based software engineering. Information & Software Technology 43(14), 833–839 (2001)
32. Seng, O., Stammel, J., Burkhart, D.: Search-based determination of refactorings for improving the class structure of object-oriented systems. In: GECCO 2006, pp. 1909–1916 (2006)
33. Harman, M.: The Current State and Future of Search Based Software Engineering. In: Proceedings of ICSE 2007, Minneapolis, USA, May 20–26 (2007)
34. Sun, Y., White, J., Gray, J.: Model Transformation by Demonstration. In: Schürr, A., Selic, B. (eds.) MODELS 2009. LNCS, vol. 5795, pp. 712–726. Springer, Heidelberg (2009)
35. Uzam, M.: The use of Petri net reduction approach for an optimal deadlock prevention policy for flexible manufacturing systems. Int. J. Adv. Manuf. Technol. 23, 204–219
36. Hu, Z., Shatz, S.M.: Mapping UML Diagrams to a Petri Net Notation for System Simulation (SEKE), Banff, Canada, June 2004, pp. 213–219 (2004)
37. Bernardi, S., Donatelli, S., Merseguer, J.: From UML Sequence Diagrams and StateCharts to analysable Petri Net models. In: WOSP 2002, Rome, Italy, pp. 35–45 (July 2002)
38. http://wiki.daimi.au.dk/cpntools/cpntools.wiki

Model Search: Formalizing and Automating Constraint Solving in MDE Platforms

Mathias Kleiner[1], Marcos Didonet Del Fabro[2], and Patrick Albert[2]

[1] Arts et Metiers ParisTech, CNRS, LSIS Laboratory, France
mathias.kleiner@ensam.eu
[2] IBM Software Group, France
{marcos.ddf,albertpa}@fr.ibm.com

Abstract. Model Driven Engineering (MDE) and constraint programming (CP) have been widely used and combined in different applications. However, existing results are either ad-hoc, not fully integrated or manually executed. In this article, we present a formalization and an approach for automating constraint-based solving in a MDE platform. Our approach generalizes existing work by combining known MDE concepts with CP techniques into a single operation called model search. We present the theoretical basis for model search, as well as an automated process that details the involved operations. We validate our approach by comparing two implemented solutions (one based on Alloy/SAT, the other on OPL/CP), and by executing them over an academic use-case.

1 Introduction

The combination of models and constraints is well-known and widely used in software engineering. On the one hand, the model-driven engineering (MDE) approaches have been using constraint languages (like OCL[21]) to further specify metamodels. Many constraint-based tools such as [15,10] have been developed, mainly for model checking and animation. However, in most of these approaches, constraint-solving is an external operation that can hardly be automated (in terms of input generation and output retrieval), and usually relies on solver-dependent tasks. On the other hand, part of the constraint programming (CP) approaches have aimed at extending the search engines with higher-level language support, either to obtain solver-independent languages [19], or to solve object-oriented/relational problem definitions[5,2,27].

Typical MDE solutions require chaining operations of different nature, such as extractions, injections or transformations. However, the explicit scope of CP-based operations remains vague. We believe they can be seen as model operations with combinatorial properties (see [17] for an application scenario). The CP-solving operation thus needs to be model-driven, fully automated and integrated with existing MDE tools.

In this paper, we therefore present a formalization of CP-solving tasks within a solver-independent MDE process chain. We define it as a first-class model-driven operation called *model search*. Our solution generalizes existing approaches with an identified set of elementary operations and model-based inputs and outputs. The operations cover the whole model search chain, from the data definition to the solver execution and data re-injection.

We validate our approach by implementing it based on two well know solvers: Alloy/SAT [5] and OPL/CP [8]. We also apply both chains on an academic example of software product lines and discuss the results.

This paper is organized as follows. In section 2, we introduce model-driven engineering and constraint programming. In Section 3, we describe the model search approach and we present formal definitions for it. In Section 4, we present a solver-independent MDE integration for model search. In Section 5, we present two implementations of the presented chain using known solvers. Experiments on an application use case are provided in Section 6, and Section 7 discusses related and future work.

2 Context

2.1 Introduction to MDE and Model Transformation

Model Driven Engineering considers models, through multiple abstract representation levels, as a unifying concept. The central concepts that have been introduced are terminal model, metamodel, and metametamodel. A terminal model is a representation of a system. It captures some characteristics of the system and provides knowledge about it. MDE tools act on terminal models expressed in precise modeling languages. The abstract syntax of a modeling language, when expressed as a model, is called a metamodel. The relation between a model and the metamodel of its language is called *conformsTo*. Metamodels are in turn expressed in a modeling language for which conceptual foundations are captured in an auto-descriptive model called metametamodel.

The main way to automate MDE is by executing operations on models. For instance, the production of a model Mb from a model Ma by a transformation Mt is called a model transformation. The OMG's Query View Transform (QVT) [20] defines a set of useful model operations and proposes clues on how they should be implemented. As a mean to provide interoperability with tools from non-MDE environments (often referred to as *technological spaces*), special model operations (often called *injection/extraction*) allow for data exchange (usually through serializing/parsing) [14].

We use in this article the model definitions introduced in [6]:

Definition 1 (model). *A model M is a triple $< G, \omega, \mu >$ where:*

- *G is a directed multigraph,*
- *ω is a model (called the reference model of M) associated to a graph G_ω*
- *μ is a function associating nodes and edges of G to nodes of G_ω*

Definition 2 (conformsTo). *The relation between a model and its reference model is called conformance and noted conformsTo (or abbreviated C2).*

Definition 3 (metametamodel). *A metametamodel is a model that is its own reference model (i.e.it conforms to itself).*

Definition 4 (metamodel). *A metamodel is a model such that its reference model is a metametamodel.*

Definition 5 (terminal model). *A terminal model is a model such that its reference model is a metamodel.*

As stated by the previous definitions, the notion of reference model is independent from the absolute modeling levels. For instance, both the MOF metametamodel and the UML metamodel are reference models (respectively of the UML metamodel and of a UML (terminal) model). Therefore, the conformance relation is also level-independent and can simply be checked by the existence of a function μ between the graphs of a model and its reference model.

2.2 Constrained Metamodels

The notion of constraints is closely tight to MDE. Engineers have been using constraints to complete the definition of metamodels for a long time, as illustrated by the popular combination UML/OCL. Constraints can be, for instance, checked against one given model in order to validate it. In our approach we will always consider that the metamodels on which we wish to conduct CP solving potentially have constraints attached. We propose the following to formally define such combination:

Definition 6. *A constrained metamodel CMM is a pair $< MM, C >$ where MM is a metamodel and C is a set (a conjunction) of predicates over elements of the graph associated to MM. C is an oracle that, given a model $M =< G, MM, \mu >$, returns true (noted $C(M)$) iff M satisfies all the predicates.*

Definition 7. *A model M conformsTo a constrained metamodel CMM if and only if $C(M)$.*

Many languages can be used to define predicates (i.e. constraints), with different levels of expressiveness. OCL supports operators on sets and relations as well as quantifiers (universal and existential) and iterators. In this article, we will be using an OCL-compatible extension (OCL+ [9]) that focuses on metamodel static constraints. OCL+ is itself defined by a metamodel (available as KM3 [6]) and a parser (generated with TCS [7]).

2.3 Introduction to Constraint Programming

Constraint programming (CP) is a declarative programming technique to solve combinatorial (usually NP-hard) problems. A constraint, in its wider sense, is a predicate on elements (represented by variables). A CP problem is thus defined by a set of elements and a set of constraints. The objective of a CP solver is to find an assignment (i.e a set of values for the variables) that satisfy all the constraints. There are several CP formalisms and techniques which differ by their expressiveness, the abstractness of the language and the solving algorithms. In this article we will focus on the language part, i.e what kind of elements and constraints can be represented and reasoned about. In order to narrow the scope, we introduce two important CP formalisms: SAT (boolean SATisfiability problem) and CSP (Constraint Satisfaction Problem). Associated solvers and their (higher-level) language will be presented in Section 5.

The SAT formalism. SAT problem is to decide if, for a given boolean formula, each boolean variable can be given an assignment such that the formula evaluates to true. SAT is known as being a NP-complete problem[1].

Definition 8 (SAT instance). *A SAT instance S is defined by $S = (\mathcal{X}, \mathcal{C})$ where $\mathcal{X}$ is a set of boolean variables and $\mathcal{C}$ is a set of clauses. A clause is a finite disjunction of literals and a literal is either a variable or its negation.*

The CSP formalism. CSP extends SAT in that it does not restrict variable domains to binary values.

Definition 9 (CSP instance). *A CSP instance is well-defined by a triplet $< X, D, C >$:*

- *X is a finite set of variables $X_1, ..., X_n$*
- *D is a finite set of domains $D_1, ..., D_n$ where D_i is a set of possible values for X_i*
- *C is a finite set of constraints where each constraint is an assertion on a subset of $X = X_j, ...X_k$ defined by a subset of $D_j, ..., D_k$*

Solving a CSP consists in assigning a value V_i of the domain D_i to each variable X_i such that it satisfies all the constraints in C.

3 Model Search

Deterministic rule-based model transformations are not sufficient for different MDE scenarios, such as model animation or model automatic generation, because they cannot handle combinatorial parts of operations chain. For instance, in [17], the MDE scenario uses a CP-based technique for a part of the process in which the input model needs to be automatically completed. In this section, we present *model search* as a first-class MDE operation for handling such combinatorial tasks.

3.1 Relaxed Metamodels and Partial Models

In order to formally define model search, we first define a set of notions that relate to constrained metamodels.

Definition 10 (Relaxed metamodel). *Let $CMM = <MM, C>$ be a constrained metamodel. $CMM_r = <MM_r, C_r>$ is a relaxed metamodel of CMM (noted $CMM_r \in Rx(CMM)$) if and only if $G_{MM_r} \subseteq G_{MM}$ and $C_r \subseteq C$.*

In other words, a (minimal) relaxed metamodel can be obtained by the removal of all constraints: minimum cardinalities are set to zero, attributes are optionals and predicates are removed. Computing such a relaxed metamodel can obviously be done easily with existing (meta)model transformation techniques. We call this operation *relaxation*.

Definition 11 (Partial model, p-conformsTo). *Let $CMM = <MM, C>$ be a constrained metamodel and M a model. M_r p-conformsTo CMM if and only if it conforms to a metamodel CMM_r such that CMM_r is a relaxed metamodel of CMM ($CMM_r \in Rx(CMM)$). M_r is called a partial model of CMM.*

3.2 Model Search

Definition 12 (Model search). *Let $CMM = <MM, C>$ be a constrained metamodel, and $M_r = <G_r, MM_r, \mu_r>$ a partial model of CMM. Model search is the operation of finding a (finite) model $M = <G, MM, \mu>$ such that $G_r \subseteq G$, $\mu_r \subseteq \mu$ (embedding i.e $\forall x \in Gr, \mu(x) = \mu_r(x)$), and M conformsTo CMM.*

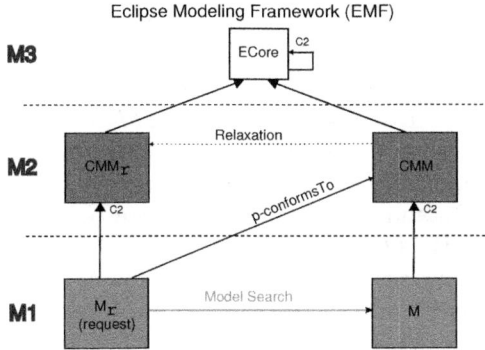

Fig. 1. Model search

This MDE operation is illustrated in Figure 1. We consider model search as a model transformation where the source (metamodel and model) is an instance of a non-deterministic (combinatorial) problem and the target model is a solution (if any exists). From the CP point of view, the target metamodel acts as the constraint model whereas the source model (the request) is a given partial assignment that needs to be extended.

4 A Solver-Independent MDE Integration

As introduced in the previous Section, the goal of model search is to generate a complete and valid model M of a constrained metamodel CMM out of a

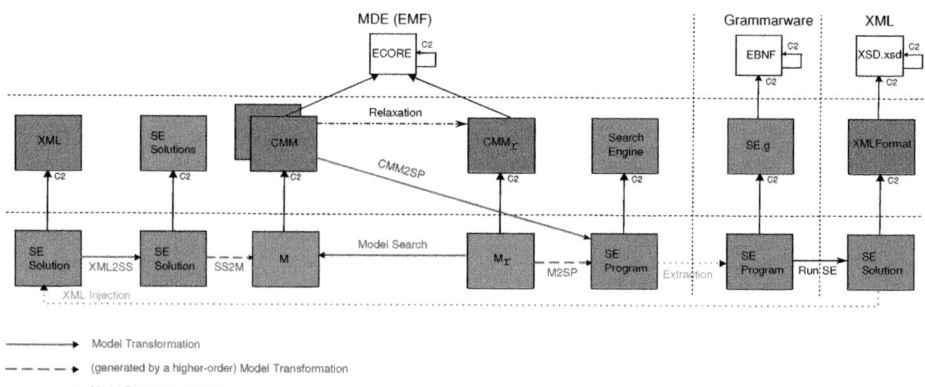

Fig. 2. Model search integration

partial (possibly empty) model M_r (the *request*). Figure 2 illustrates the whole process in a model-driven engineering framework. This process is composed of 5 main tasks.

1) Search problem generation: this task, illustrated by the $CMM2SP$ transformation, expresses the constrained metamodel as a model conforming to the search engine metamodel. However, the $CMM2SP$ arrow in Figure 2 is a simplified view of the process, since there are actually two source models (represented by the doubled square) as input to the transformation. Figure 3 illustrates the complete generation process. The metamodel MM contains the structural constraints, such as cardinality and lower bounds. However, typical model search applications require more complex domain constraints. These domain constraints, which are not part of standard ECORE, are expressed in the constraint model C, which conforms to the OCL metamodel.

The difficulty of expressing a constrained metamodel in the search engine language is highly dependent on the abstraction level and the basic elements offered by the language. Differences between search engines and implementation issues will be thoroughly discussed in Section 5.

2) Search data generation: this task is illustrated by the $M2SP$ transformation. It takes the request model M_r as input and generates the input data that will be used by the search engine. However, this transformation is metamodel-specific, i.e., there is one $M2SP$ per input metamodel. To avoid writing one transformation for every metamodel MM, a higher-order transformation (HOT) is defined. The HOT takes MM as input and produces the transformation $M2SP$, using the transformation language as target metamodel.

It is important to note that most of the search engines do not separate the problem and the data definition: they are expressed all together using the same language. For that reason, the input data and the problem definition are merged. This is a straightforward task, since there are no overlapping elements.

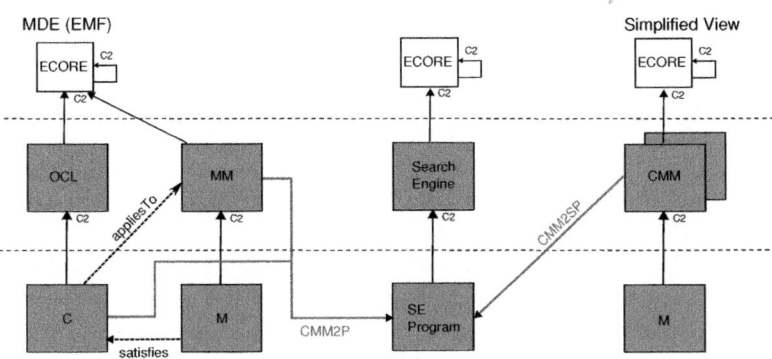

Fig. 3. Generation of the problem definition

3) Engine program extraction: this task extracts the search engine model into its executable format.

4) CP search: the generated search program is executed in the search engine. When the search succeeds (i.e there is at least one solution), we obtain a solution model in the search engine output format. The most common formats are XML or plain-text files.

5) Solution injection: this last task is to inject the resulting solution produced by the search engine as a model of the original metamodel MM. We have illustrated this tasks by two transformations, $XML2SS$ and $SS2M$. Although those transformations could be merged, we have considered that the engine generates an XML file. As a result, it is natural to decompose the operation into two tasks: expressing the XML model as a model of a metamodel of the search engine solutions, then transform it to a model of MM. For the same reasons as the $M2SP$ transformation, $SS2M$ is generated using a HOT, which takes MM as source and generates a transformation from SS to MM.

ECORE vs KM3. The presented process assumes the use of EMF's Ecore (from the Eclipse modeling project) as the metametamodel. Effective implementations, as the ones described later in this article, define the metamodels using the KM3 language[6]. Since KM3 offers automatic translation to Ecore, the conversion from one framework to another does not introduce any difficulty.

5 Implementation Alternatives

The presented chain is solver-independent. We materialize such chain using two technologies. However a number of difficulties arise with implementations, because of the solvers languages lack of expressiveness or the formalisms inherent limitations. We discuss in this section the difficulties that we identified for each of the two formalisms presented in Section 2.3 combined with state-of-the-art solvers: OPL/CSP and Alloy/SAT.

5.1 Implementation with Alloy/SAT Solver

The SAT paradigm has clear limitations: it requires a finite set of boolean variables and only offers a low-level predicate language (only negation, disjunction and conjunction are supported). However, [5] introduced an expressive relational language with a built-in compilation that allows the use of many recent SAT solvers. We will thus use Alloy as our target search engine language in order to ease the transformation definition.

Alloy, which can be seen as a subset of the Z language [13], allows for expressing complex predicates using atoms (indivisible elements), sets (of atoms), relations, quantifiers (universal or existential), operators for relations traversal, etc. However, due to the properties of SAT problems, Alloy cannot be considered as a true first-order logic solver. Indeed, to be able to translate the problem into SAT, a *scope* needs to be given to each set, that limits the number of atoms that can be contained in the set.

In Alloy, every element is either an atom or a relation but the language is exclusively based on relations. Indeed, a set is itself a relation from an atom to the contents of that set (which in turn are also atoms). The main artifacts that we will manipulate in the Alloy language are:

- *Signatures*, declarations of sets, for which the body may contain fields as *relations* to other signatures. Attributes are treated the same as any relation. Scalars, as for signatures, are treated as sets of atoms. Signatures also support a form of inheritance.
- *Facts*, declarations of predicates, with quantifiers and an important number of logical, scalar and set operators available.

Generic expression of constrained KM3 metamodels. We developed a metamodel of the Alloy language containing the necessary constructs to represent KM3 metamodels and OCL+ constraints. Figure 4 shows an overview of the metamodel. The complete metamodel is written in KM3. We also developed a TCS parser generator allowing to inject/extract between the textual version of the language and our metamodel. Both the metamodel and the TCS are freely available, submitted as a TCS use case (under the form of an Eclipse project), and can be downloaded from [4]. The OCL+ metamodel is also written in KM3, its metamodel and TCS are freely available and can be downloaded from [9]. An overview is presented in Figure 5.

On this basis, we defined a mapping from KM3 to Alloy and developed the corresponding transformation, using ATL (AtlanMod Transformation Language), a QVT-like model transformation language and tool [11]. An excerpt of the mapping is presented in Table 1. In short, KM3 classes are mapped to Alloy signatures, KM3 attributes and references are mapped to Alloy fields, references properties are turned into facts. We also developed an ATL transformation from OCL+ to Alloy so as to express metamodel constraints. An informal excerpt of these mappings are presented in Table 1. Both the transformations are merged into a unique transformation using two source models and able to resolve the links between the constraints and the metamodel elements on which they apply.

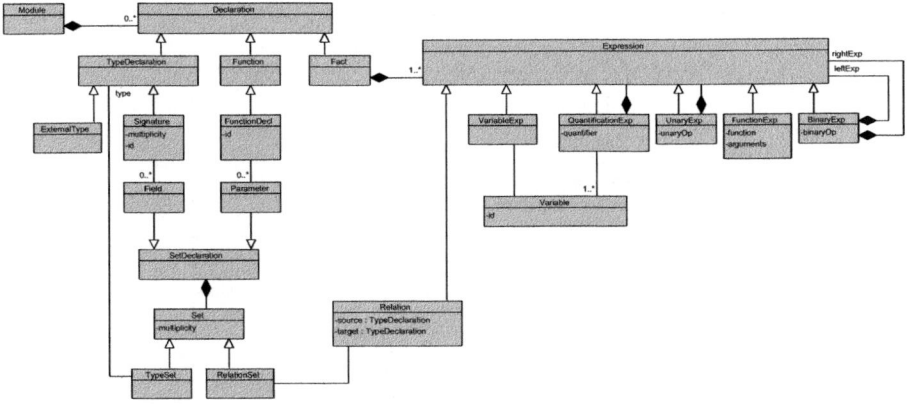

Fig. 4. Overview of the Alloy metamodel

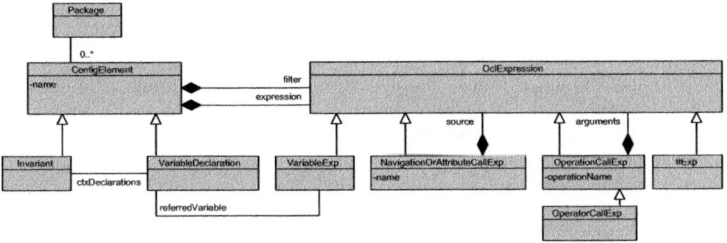

Fig. 5. Overview of the OCL+ metamodel

This combined transformation corresponds to the *CMM2SP* of Figure 2. It is freely available, submitted as an ATL use case (under the form of an Eclipse project), and can be downloaded from [18].

The whole project is a partial implementation (all but the two high-order transformations) of the model search process presented in Section 4, using Alloy as the search engine. Thanks to its language expressiveness, Alloy bridges the gap between constrained metamodels and low-level languages. As an open-source tool, it is a viable alternative with only few drawbacks.

5.2 Implementation with OPL/CP Solver

OPL (Optimization Programming Language) [28] is a language part of the IBM ILOG ^{TM}OPL-CPLEX^{TM}development bundle [8], which is an IDE for developing CP and optimization models. The OPL programs are executed by the IBM ILOG^{TM}CP Optimizer engine. The OPL language has a clear separation between the input data (booleans, integers, sets, strings, tuples, and others) and the decision variables (integers and arrays of integers). It offers as well a set of logical and arithmetic expressions on those elements. These features - together

Table 1. Excerpt of the mapping from KM3 and OCL+ to Alloy concepts

KM3 concept	Alloy concept
Metamodel	Module
DataType	ExternalType
Class	Signature
Attribute	Field
Reference	Field
StructuralFeature multiplicity	Quantifier or Fact
Reference containment	Fact
Reference opposite	Fact
OCL+ concept	**Alloy concept**
Invariant	Fact and QuantificationExpression
Invariant declarations	QuantificationExpression variables
VariableDeclaration	Variable
VariableExp	VariableExpression
IfExp	ImpliesExpression
NavigationOrAttributeCallExp	NavigationExpression
OperatorCall	BinaryExpression
OperationCall (size)	SetCardinalityExpression
OperationCall (isIn)	ComparisonExpression
OperationCall (others)	ExternalFunction

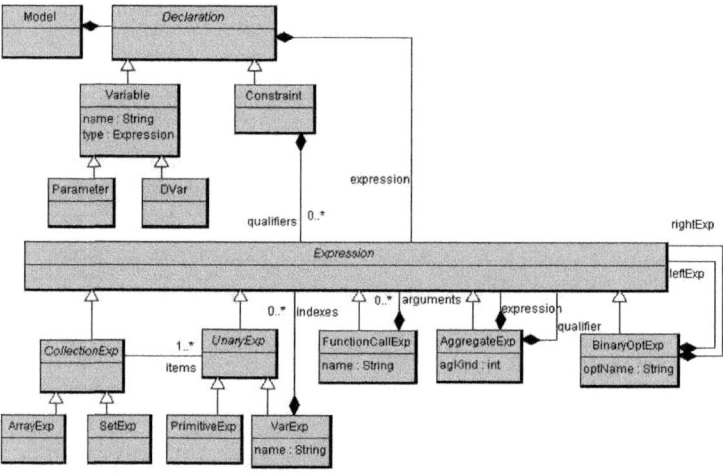

Fig. 6. Extract of the OPL metamodel

with the possibility of defining universal quantifiers over variables - enables the reutilization of the optimization models over different data.

We have developed an OPL metamodel based on the definition from [8] (see an extract on Figure 6). The main structures used are the following:

- *Expressions*: combination of logical and arithmetical expressions, functions, aggregates (sum, union, max and min) and (indexed) variables.
- *Input parameters*: the input (fixed) data. A parameter may be initialized from a data set or it can be calculated using any kind of expression.
- *Decision variables*: the decision variables are scalars or arrays of integers and doubles. The decision variables may considered the "output data", i.e.,

Table 2. Excerpt of the mapping from KM3 and OCL+ to OPL

KM3 concept	OPL concept
Metamodel	Model
DataType	Type
Class	Integer set
Attribute	PrimitiveType set and integer array
Reference	Integer set and integer bi-dimensional array
StructuralFeature multiplicity	Aggregate expression
Reference containment	Global uniqueness constraint
Reference opposite	Equality constraint
OCL+ concept	**OPL concept**
Invariant	ForAll constraint
Invariant declarations	ForAll qualifiers
VariableDeclaration	Qualifier expression
VariableExp	VarExp
NavigationOrAttributeCallExp	Indexed variable exp
OperatorCall (arithmetic and logical)	BinaryOptExp + operator type
OperationCall (size)	AggreateExp
OperationCall (isIn)	AggregateExp and indexed variable
OperationCall (others)	FunctionCall
CollectionExp	Combination of aggregate expression

the values of the decision variables are assigned based on a set of constraints and on the input data.
- *Constraints*: constraints are logical expressions that are written as an arbitrary composition of expressions, input parameters and decision variables. These constraints must be respected during the solver execution.

Generic expression of constrained KM3 metamodels. We have applied the same approach as for the Alloy/SAT tool: we have developed an OPL metamodel in KM3 and a TCS parser generator for the injection/extraction between the OPL textual version and the model[1]. The mapping from constrained KM3 into OPL has a higher conceptual mismatch (model-based vs integer-based) than the one into Alloy. An excerpt of the mapping is presented in Table 2.

The transformation has three major set of rules. First, the KM3 model is transformed into the input parameters. Second, the KM3 metamodel is transformed into the output decision variables. The KM3 metamodel is transformed twice because of the difference of expressiveness between the OPL input parameters and the decision variables. The decision variables are restricted to integers and array of integers. Finally, the constraints are transformed into OPL constraints compatible with the input and output variables. The arithmetical, logical and comparison expressions are translated into their equivalent counterparts in OPL. The navigation expressions are translated into indexed decision variables, where the index is the calling expression. Then, the collection expressions are transformed into aggregates.

6 Application and Experiments

In this section, we describe an effective application of the approach on a Software Product Lines (SPL) use case. First, we briefly present the context of SPL and

---
[1] The complete OPL metamodel/TCS and the transformation from KM3/OCL+ are not freely available.

the considered problem. Then, we compare the results of the two implementation alternatives presented in Section 5.

6.1 Search in Software Product Lines

The goal of SPL [22] is to create a shared model for a given application domain, which acts as a basis to generate a set of derived products. The specificities of each product are defined by features satisfying the needs of a particular application. These features contain explicit variation points, which guide the generation of the final products.

The first step in a SPL chain is to define a model of the shared domain. A domain model contains a set of characteristics and components that are common for a class of applications, plus a set of variation points. The variation points may be expressed in terms of choices of possible values or in terms of user constraints. Each combination of variation point may generate a distinct product (a process called *derivation*). In other words, finding and generating all the possible products satisfying a set of constraints in a SPL is a model search problem. The domain model and the variation points are expressed in terms of a constrained metamodel.

In our example we need to generate classes that handle the execution of watches (this use case is an adaptation from [23]). We want to generate 5 different kinds of watches: 1) one simple watch, 2) one with alarm, 3) one with sound alarm, 4) one with sound and visual alarm and 5) one with visual alarm. We provide below a simple KM3 metamodel for this SPL problem:

```
package watches {
  class Root {
    reference classifiers[1-10] container : Class;
  }
  abstract class Class {
    reference methods[1-15] container : Method oppositeOf class;
  }
  class Watch extends Class {
      reference class : Class oppositeOf methods;
  }
  abstract class Method { }
  class DisplayTime, Start, StartAlarm, StartSoundAlarm,
      StartVisualAlarm, Stop, StopAlarm extends Method {}
}
```

However, not all combinations of methods are allowed. The derived models should respect the following constraints. 1) the *DisplayTime* and *Start* methods are mandatory; 2) if there is a *Start*, there is a *Stop*; 3) if there is a *StartAlarm*, there is a *StopAlarm*; 4) if there is a *StartSoundAlarm*, there is a *StartAlarm*; 5) if there is a *StartVisualAlarm*, there is a *StartAlarm*. We show below one constraint in OCL+, Alloy and OPL, respectively.

```
context Class inv : methods.exists ( m | m.oclIsTypeOf(Start) ) ;
fact { all c : Class | some m : c.methods | m in Start }
forall(c in classes)(sum(m in methods) (c_m[c][m] > 0 && m in start)) >=1;
```

6.2 Results

We executed an Alloy/SAT and an OPL/CP chain in a Intel Core Duo, 2.53GHz, 3GB of RAM and 32 bit processor, with the same metamodel and the same set of constraints. We used Alloy 4.1.10 with the default SAT4J [26] solver and OPL 6.2 with the CP solver. The CMM2SP for Alloy transformation produced an Alloy program with 107 lines and the CMM2SP for OPL produced an OPL program with 131 lines.

The initial setting for executing the solvers is the standard setting of both tools. However, in the Alloy case, the bit-width is increased to 6 (the default is 4), to be able to represent the cardinalities of the references *classifiers* and *methods*. OPL/CP has a largest integer default of $2^{31} - 1$. We used the same input, i.e., one element per class, (1 Root, 1 Watch, 1 Start, 1 Stop, 1 StopAlarm, 1 StartAlarm, 1 DisplayTime, 1 StartVisualAlarm and 1 StartSoundAlarm).

Both engines produced the combination of methods shown in Figure 7. Despite being simple, this example enables the visualization of all the solutions produced and the implication of the input constraints in the output models.

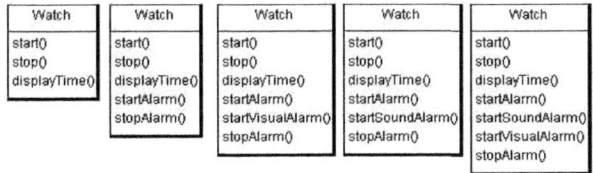

Fig. 7. Produced watches

Both transformation chains produced equivalent solutions from the same specification. The operations are called automatically (sequentially) by an Apache-Ant script. The Alloy program is then translated by the built-in compiler into a SAT predicate (923 lines) with 753 vars, 79 primary vars and 1271 clauses. The extraction plus the execution were executed in 0,19 seconds. The OPL program is transformed and executed by the CP engine in-memory, so the number of lines of the problem is not accessible. The problem definition has 8 variables and 300 constraints. It was executed in 0,11 seconds. The high difference in the number of variables is due to the expressiveness of the outputs: boolean-based vs integer-based. The conceptual mismatch between OCL+ and OPL is higher than from OCL+ and Alloy, which provides an expressive language based on relations and logic.

The clear separation of the problem definition from the input data in OPL - and the existence of universal quantifiers - enables defining a $CMM2SP$ for OPL transformation independent of the input data. In particular, it is not necessary to unfold all the variables and loops.

The metamodels of both tools have been designed to work directly with the TCS parser. Therefore, some syntactical constructs would deserve a semantical analysis to completely check the validity of a textual input during model injections. This 2-step parsing process is left for future work.

To summarize, we were able to execute model search on both tools by implementing the modeling operations of the chain. Despite differences on the solver capabilities, the tools produced the expected results, showing the applicability of our approach. Automatic generation of the problem did not here generate an extra performance overhead compared to a manual definition. Considering the complexity of constrained search, this should however be validated on larger problems.

7 Related and Future Work

To the best of our knowledge, this article presents a first formal definition of *model search* as a deep integration of constraint programming in the MDE conceptual framework. However, this work can be linked to other recent developments that apply optimization techniques to solve MDE problems. For example, [16] describes transformation as an "Optimization Problem", this is very close to our approach, though in this case the optimization engine is not used during the transformation. The goal is rather to find a good transformation starting from a small set of available examples. A large share of the work of Jules White relates to our approach. The CURE system - for Configuration Understanding and REmedy [12] - for example, transforms a configuration into a set of constraints, automating the diagnosis of invalid configurations or the adapting of existing configurations to fulfill new requirements. Our approach also differs from SPL-dedicated solutions, such as [24], because we do not target a specific application domain. Based on some preliminary work, we believe that the SPL as a whole will benefit from the model search approach.

More generally, the many bridges that have been built between CP and MDE in the past years can be divided in two categories:

The CP community that works on modeling has started focusing on the DSL (Domain Specific Languages) approach for providing specific modeling languages, see [19] or [25], while preserving the so-called "solver independence", or supporting object-oriented or relational problem definitions [5,2,27]. Although they usually do not provide MDE integration, these languages have a higher expressiveness and adapted engine support, therefore easing the transition from metamodeling languages.

The MDE community has been using constraint languages to further specify metamodels or transformation rules, while constraint-based tools such as [15,10] were developed mainly for model checking and validation. More recently, constraints have been considered to specify transformations or extend their capabilities [3]. Most of these tools depend on a specific solver/language. Moreover, the MDE integration is incomplete either because the inputs/outputs for the engine cannot be directly generated/retrieved or because they do not use model-driven transformations. Finally, partial assignments (i.e non-empty input models) are usually not taken into account.

In this respect, this article presents both a formalization and generalization of these approaches. Existing tools can be seen either as partial implementations, components or goal-specific usage of model search. By formalizing model search as a first-class model operation, we allow for comparison and integration into MDE platforms.

As future work, we plan to release the higher-order model transformations needed to complete the whole presented process. One of them allows to transform models to partial instances of the considered problem, and the other to transform the search results into a MDE format (*M2SP* and *SS2M* in Figure 2). We also plan to further validate the two implementations on a set of industrial and academic use cases[2]. At the theoretical level, our model search theory and process can naturally be extended to a general model transformation scheme (i.e with different source and target metamodels), which would expand the scope of transformations through an implementation of Relational-QVT.

8 Conclusion

In this article, we presented and formalized the use of constraint-based search engines in MDE platforms as a novel model operation called *model search*. Besides the presented theoretical foundations, we also described a MDE solver-independant process chain to realize model search, demonstrated its validity with two implementations (resp. Alloy/SAT and OPL/CSP), and discussed the results through experiments on an academic SPL use case. The presented approach generalizes existing work about constraints resolution in MDE, allows the complete automation of the process and provides a basis to develop and compare different alternatives. It simplifies the use of constraint solvers in model-based software engineering at two levels: a shared knowledge representation (constrained graph-based models), and a generic process in that one implemented chain is reusable for any application scenario.

Acknowledgments. This article has been partially funded by ANR Idm++ project.

References

1. Cook, S.A.: The complexity of theorem-proving procedures. In: STOC, pp. 151–158. ACM, New York (1971)
2. Felfernig, A., Friedrich, G., Jannach, D., Zanker, M.: Configuration knowledge representation using uml/ocl. In: Jézéquel, J.-M., Hussmann, H., Cook, S. (eds.) UML 2002. LNCS, vol. 2460, pp. 49–62. Springer, Heidelberg (2002)
3. Petter, A., Behring, A., Muhlhauser, M.: Solving constraints in model transformations. In: Paige, R.F. (ed.) ICMT 2009. LNCS, vol. 5563, pp. 132–147. Springer, Heidelberg (2009)
4. Alloy usecase (2010), http://www.lsis.org/kleinerm/MS/Alloy_mm.html
5. Jackson, D.: Automating first-order relational logic. In: FSE, pp. 130–139 (2000)

---

[2] We have successfully applied the approach to parse English sentences[17].

6. Jouault, F., Bézivin, J.: Km3: A dsl for metamodel specification. In: Gorrieri, R., Wehrheim, H. (eds.) FMOODS 2006. LNCS, vol. 4037, pp. 171–185. Springer, Heidelberg (2006)
7. Jouault, F., Bézivin, J., Kurtev, I.: TCS: a DSL for the specification of textual concrete syntaxes in model engineering. In: GPCE, pp. 249–254. ACM, New York (2006)
8. IBM ILOG CPLEX Development Bundle (December 2009), http://www-01.ibm.com/software/integration/optimization/cplex-dev-bundles/
9. OCL+ usecase (2010), http://www.lsis.org/kleinerm/MS/OCLP_mm.html
10. Cabot, J., Clarisó, R., Riera, D.: Umltocsp: a tool for the formal verification of uml/ocl models using constraint programming. In: ASE, pp. 547–548 (2007)
11. Jouault, J., Kurtev, I.: Transforming Models with ATL. In: Bruel, J.-M. (ed.) MoDELS 2005. LNCS, vol. 3844, pp. 128–138. Springer, Heidelberg (2006)
12. White, J., Schmidt, D.C., Benavides, D., Trinidad, P., Ruiz-Cortez, A.: Automated diagnosis of product-line configuration errors in feature models. In: Software Product Lines Conference (SPLC 2008), Limmerick, Ireland (2008)
13. Spivey, J.M.: The Z Notation: a reference manual (2001)
14. Kurtev, I., Bezivin, J., Aksit, M.: Technological spaces: An initial appraisal. In: International Symposium on Distributed Objects and Applications (2002)
15. Gogolla, M., Büttner, F., Richters, M.: Use: A uml-based specification environment for validating uml and ocl. Sci. Comput. Program. 69(1-3), 27–34 (2007)
16. Kessentini, M., Sahraoui, H.A., Boukadoum, M.: Model transformation as an optimization problem. In: Czarnecki, K., Ober, I., Bruel, J.-M., Uhl, A., Völter, M. (eds.) MODELS 2008. LNCS, vol. 5301, pp. 159–173. Springer, Heidelberg (2008)
17. Kleiner, M., Albert, P., Bezivin, J.: Parsing sbvr-based controlled languages. In: Schürr, A., Selic, B. (eds.) MODELS 2009. LNCS, vol. 5795, pp. 122–136. Springer, Heidelberg (2009)
18. Model search (2010), http://www.lsis.org/kleinerm/MS/ModelSearch-Alloy.html
19. Nethercote, N., Stuckey, P.J., Becket, R., Brand, S., Duck, G.J., Tack, G.: Minizinc: Towards a standard cp modelling language. In: Bessière, C. (ed.) CP 2007. LNCS, vol. 4741, pp. 529–543. Springer, Heidelberg (2007)
20. Object Management Group. Meta Object Facility (MOF) 2.0 Query/View/Transformation (QVT) Specification, version 1.0 (2008)
21. OCL 2.0 specification (2008), http://www.omg.org/spec/OCL/2.0/
22. Clements, P., Northrop, L.: Software Product Lines: Practices and Patterns, 1st edn. Addison-Wesley, Reading (2001)
23. Tessier, P., Servat, D., Gerard, S.: Variability management on behavioral models. In: VaMoS Workshop, pp. 121–130 (2008)
24. Trinidad, P., Benavides, D., Cortés, A.R., Segura, S., Jimenez, A.: Fama framework. In: SPLC, p. 359. IEEE Computer Society, Los Alamitos (2008)
25. Chenouard, R., Granvilliers, L., Soto, R.: Model-driven constraint programming. In: 10th ACM SIGPLAN PPDP, Valence, Spain (2008)
26. SAT4J. A SATisfiability libray for Java (2010), http://www.sat4j.org
27. Junker, U., Mailharro, D.: The logic of (j)configurator: Combining constraint programming with a description logic. In: IJCAI 2003. Springer, Heidelberg (2003)
28. Hentenryck, P.V.: The Optimization Programming Language. MIT Press, Cambridge (1999)

MoPCoM Methodology: Focus on Models of Computation

Ali Koudri, Joël Champeau, Jean-Christophe Le Lann, and Vincent Leilde

ENSIETA
firstname.lastname@ensieta.fr

Abstract. Today, developments of Real Time Embedded Systems have to face new challenges. On the one hand, Time-To-Market constraints require a reliable development process allowing quick design space exploration. On the other hand, rapidly developing technology, as stated by Moore's law, requires techniques to handle the resulting productivity gap. In a previous paper, we have presented our Model Based Engineering methodology addressing those issues. In this paper, we make a focus on Models of Computation design and analysis. We illustrate our approach on a Cognitive Radio System development implemented on an FPGA. This work is part of the MoPCoM research project gathering academic and industrial organizations (http://www.mopcom.fr).

Keywords: MBE, UML, MARTE, COMETA, Models of Computation.

1 Introduction

Recently the market of System-on-Chip (SoC) has grown rapidly. It is expected to worth $56 billion in 2012, which represents almost 24% annual growth rate. As the technology evolves rapidly, according to the Moore's law, entire systems, made of processors, memories or sensors, can now be integrated on SoC. Indeed, only reliable methodologies, based on well-adapted formalisms and tools, can handle the growing design complexity of such systems.

On the one hand, the challenges posed by design of SoC consist mainly in reducing TTM (time-to-market), costs and productivity gap due to the rapid evolution of technologies [1]. To achieve those goals, SoC design methodologies have to tackle co-design issues such as Design Space Exploration, reuse of IPs (Intellectual Property) or Platform Based Design (PBD). On the other hand, Model Based Engineering (MBE) adds valuable contributions to SoC Design [2]: analysis enhancement, communication and traceability improvement, technology breakpoints reduction, platform independent approach, etc.

In this paper, after a quick presentation of the MoPCoM methodology, we emphasize the use of a communication model between the platform elements to clarify the execution model dedicated to receive the application. In this purpose, we propose an extension of MARTE, called COMETA, that abstracts hardware platforms to communication models, i.e. Models of Computation. We illustrate the use of this extension on a industrial design of a Cognitive Radio System implemented on a Xilinx ML-506 FPGA platform.

The paper is organized as follow: the second section provides a general overview of the MoPCoM methodology; the third section discusses the integration of models of computation to the system specification, the fourth section presents illustration and tooling of our methodology, the fifth section places our work in the context of related works, and the conclusion discusses the relevancy of our work.

2 Process and Application Overview

The MoPCoM methodology is a refinement of the MDA Ychart [3] dedicated to Design Space Exploration, reuse of IPs and Platform Based Design [4]. This methodology is based on the use of the UML for MARTE profile (Modeling and Analysis of Real Time Embedded Systems [5]) and has been tooled in the Rhapsody modeling tool. It takes as input functional, non-functional and allocation requirements expressed in SysML complemented by MARTE for non-functional properties expression.

Figure 1 gives an overview of the process, highlighting 3 modeling levels which are detailed in [6]:

- The *Abstract Modeling Level* (AML) is intended to provide the description of the expected level of concurrency and pipeline through the mapping of functional blocks onto an abstract platform,
- The *Execution Modeling Level* (EML) is intended to provide the topology of the execution platform defined in terms of execution, communication or storage nodes in order to proceed to coarse grain analysis,
- The *Detailed Modeling Level* (DML) is intended to provide a detailed description of the platform in order to proceed to fine grained analysis. It

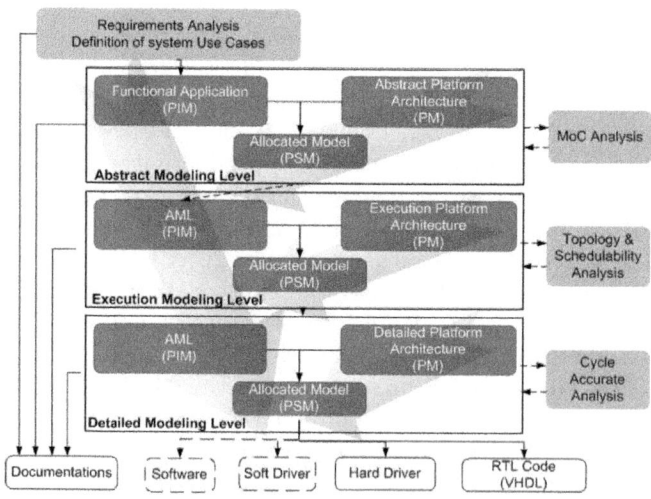

Fig. 1. MoPCoM Process Overview

allows Register Transfer Level (RTL) code generation for hardware (VHDL) and software (C) parts including glue code (drivers).

We illustrate application of the methodology on a Cognitive Radio System. A Cognitive Radio [7,8] is a system that adapts its behavior to enhance the use of electromagnetic spectrum in order to provide a best quality of service for communications handling. Actually, we have applied our methodology on a real use case which consists in locating emitting RF sources in the electromagnetic spectrum, from specification to implementation. This application is used as a reference application in an industrial context. In the next section, we discuss allocation of the functional design (PIM - Platform Independent Model) onto an AML platform, capturing first implementation choices in terms of communication and concurrency.

3 Abstract Modeling Level

Modeling concurrency and communications can be achieved by several means. For instance, concurrency in UML can be expressed at several levels. At the behavioral level, one can use for example AND states (state machines) or fork nodes (activity). At the structural level, the meta-attribute "isActive" of the UML Class bears the notion of concurrent entity. In the MARTE profile, concurrency can be captured through the notion of "RTUnit" which adds real-time features to the UML active class. Unfortunately, execution semantics and communication are not well addressed either in UML or in the MARTE profile. For instance, execution semantics in UML is described informally allowing tool providers the responsibility to define the way models should be executed [9] as well as solving semantic variation points of the UML specification [10]. In MARTE, communications are point-to-point and occur through "RTeConnectors" between "RTUnits" instances in the context of their owning classifier. Even if the MARTE profile allows a better modeling of communications, especially in real time features modeling, we think work of designers could be facilitated if some of the well known communication schemes could be reused and integrated more easily.

Then, more information is required in order to achieve more deterministic execution enabling uniform simulations and analysis. Regarding the lack of UML and MARTE to model MoC, we propose a metamodel called COMETA dedicated to the capture and the analysis of high level MoCs. The goals of this metamodel are: to provide a better separation between computation and communication, to ease decisions related to allocation of the application onto the execution platform, and to preserve the application behavior through allocations in order to ease verification activities.

The aim of the abstract modeling level is to allocate business blocks onto a virtual platform representing choices about concurrency and communication (MoC - Model of Computation) and proceed to relevant analysis like deadlock or starvation detection based on model simulations. Indeed, an AML platform is made of interconnected units of concurrency communicating via specific connectors providing data transport or synchronization services. At this level, the

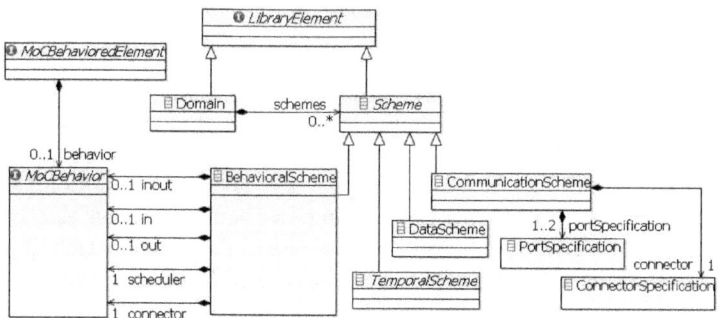

Fig. 2. Excerpt of Domain Definition

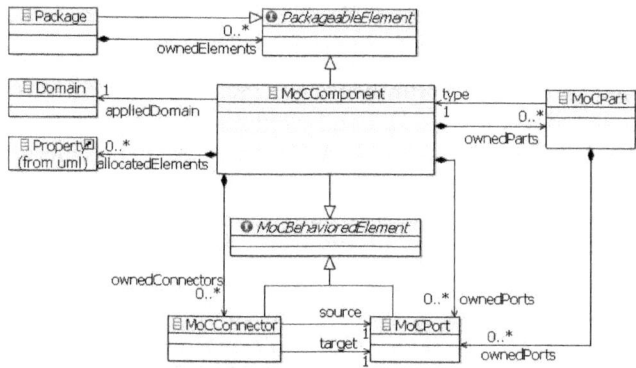

Fig. 3. MoC Component and Domains

platform is considered as an ideal point-to-point network since it does not make any assumption about resource limitations.

MoCs provide different capabilities in terms of design and analysis, and one of the goals of system designers is to select appropriate MoC and proceed to relevant analysis, taking into account heterogeneity of modeled systems. In this context, tools supporting execution of heterogeneous MoCs like Ptolemy [11] are useful to analyze systems combining heterogeneous parts (analog, digital, GALS, etc).

The COMETA extension is dedicated to description and capitalization of MoC domains. A MoC domain gathers the definition of a particular MoC regarding 4 orthogonal concerns (figure 2): the behavioral scheme defines kind of supported behavior (state based, ODE, etc.), the temporal scheme defines the underlying model of time (causal, discrete, continuous, etc.), the data scheme defines the kind of data manipulated (abstract data types, bit vectors, etc.), and the communication scheme defines mechanisms supporting communications and synchronizations. Examples of MoC domains are numerous in the literature, and for the sake of simplicity, we show in this paper how our extension handles the definition and the reuse of the two MoCs that have been used in our experiments: the Concurrent Sequential Process (CSP) and the Kahn Process Network (KPN).

Briefly, in the CSP MoC, each time a producer emits a data, it locks until this data has been consumed by the consumer. At the same time, when a consumer requires a data, it locks until this data has been produced by the producer. In this synchronous model, both read and write operations are blocking. In the KPN MoC, a producer emits its data without worrying if it has been consumed or not. At the same time, when a consumer requires a data, it locks until this data has been produced. In this asynchronous model, the write operation is non-blocking and occurs through infinite fifo while the read operation is blocking.

In our metamodel, the notion of concurrency is reified under the concept of "MoC-Component". A MoC component has the responsibility to adapt parts allocated from the application design with respect to the chosen model of computation. More precisely, a MoC component is a unit of concurrency composed of heterogeneous "MoCParts" interconnected by "MoCConnectors" through "MoCPorts" (figure 3). All those elements define the structural aspect of a model of computation.

Domain applied to a MoC Component binds semantics for each of those structural features. For instance, communication schemes are defined in respect to other orthogonal schemes of the domain, e.g. data, time and behavior and, can be checked through OCL constraints. They define constraints related to communication specification (interfaces and protocols) as well as detailed support mechanisms (FIFO, shared memory, etc.). We show in the next section an example of use of this feature to manage CSP and KPN communications. In this approach, heterogeneity can be handled through the use of ports having different nature on the same MoC component.

4 Experiments and Tooling

The COMETA metamodel has been tooled into the Eclipse environment and we provide a set of transformation rules in order to reuse model execution capabilities provided by the Rhapsody UML modeling tool and its execution framework

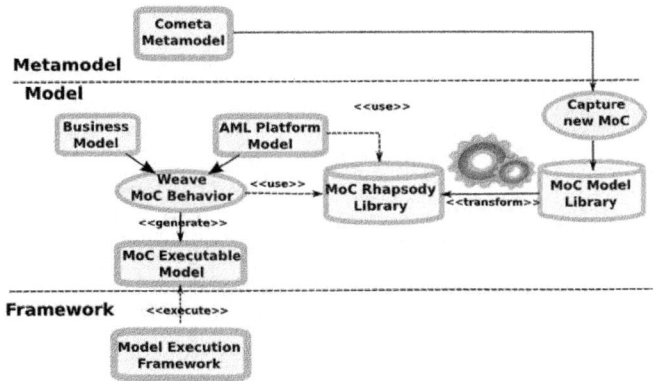

Fig. 4. Flow for Tooling a New MoC

OXF (Object eXecution Framework). The OXF framework provides a discrete event engine onto which several MoCs can be executed. The approach adopted is quite similar to the approach presented in [12] in the context of the SystemC framework. The flow associated to the utilization of the metamodel is summarized in the figure 4.

Initially, a designer captures the properties of a model of computation using the COMETA metamodel. Then, a model-to-model transformation takes as input the captured model and generates a model library of usable and configurable MoC components for the Rhapsody framework. Those components can be then assembled to build an AML Platform which can be woven with the application model to generate an executable model.

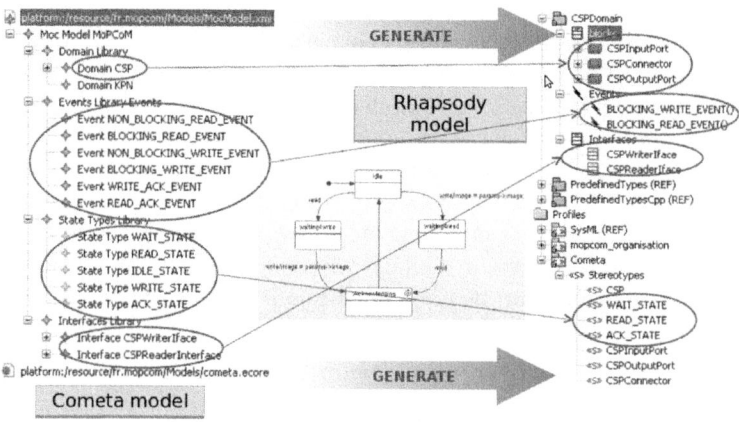

Fig. 5. MoC Library Generation

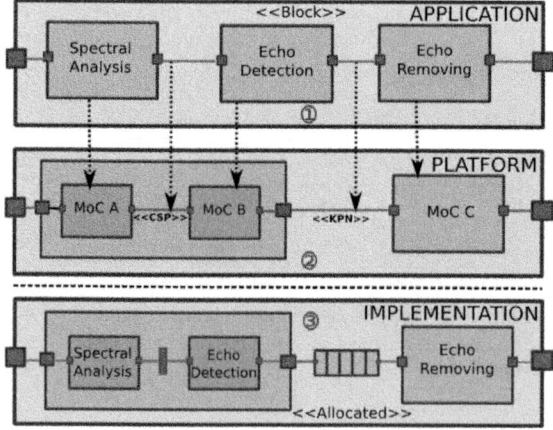

Fig. 6. Functional to AML Platform Allocation

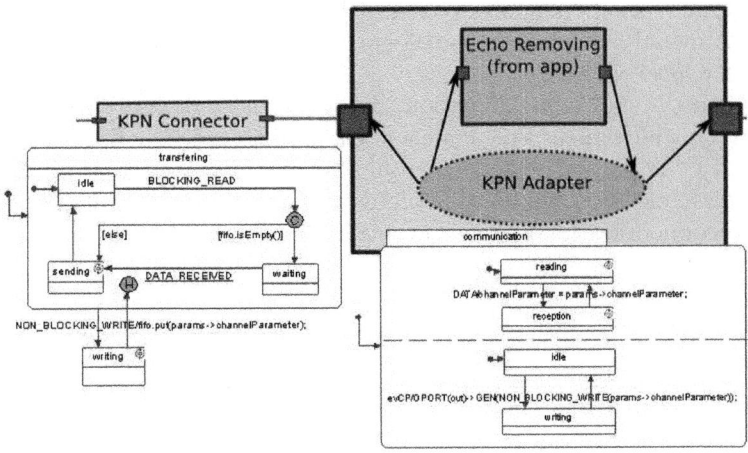

Fig. 7. AML Allocated Platform Excerpt

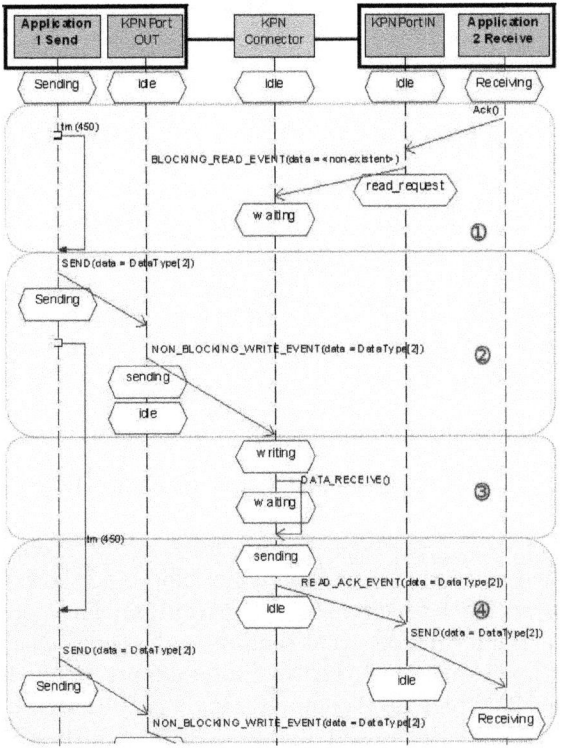

Fig. 8. KPN Simulation with Rhapsody

The figure 5 shows a small excerpt of Rhapsody artifacts generation from a COMETA model. All generated artifacts are directly usable for both design and allocation captures.

The figure 6 shows an allocation of the business design ① onto an AML platform ②, which mixes two models of computation: KPN (Kahn Process Network) and CSP (Concurrent Sequential Process). The allocated platform ③ is generated thanks to a model-to-model transformation and contains additional artifacts (communication and synchronization resources) needed to achieve correct simulations.

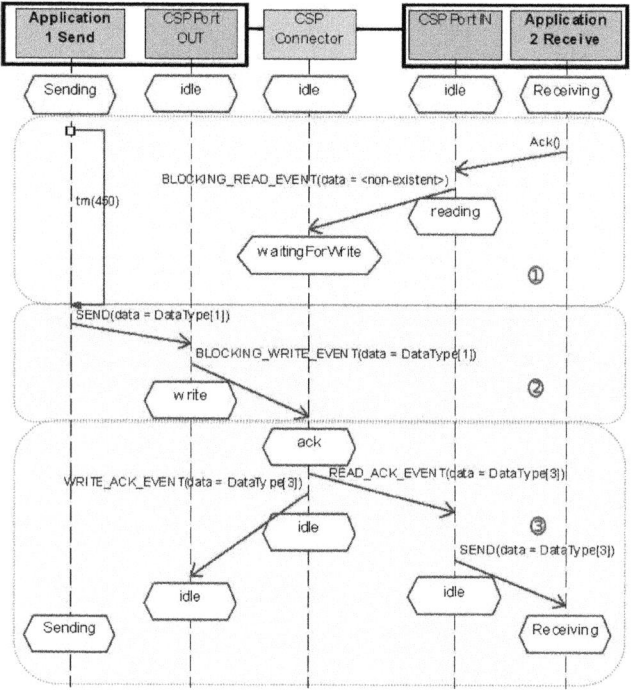

Fig. 9. CSP Simulation with Rhapsody

The figure 7 focuses on the "Echo Removing" block and shows the adaptation of the spectral analysis block to support KPN execution. This generated block acts as a local scheduler and controls event sending and reception as well as execution of allocated functional blocks. The KPN adapter adapts system interfaces to MoC interfaces which exibits high level communication primitives (non-blocking write, blocking read, etc.) and implements high level communication protocols.

For instance, the figures 8 and 9 show traces of 2 different mappings of the same application. The first one targets a platform implementing KPN communications while the second one targets a platform implementing CSP communications. Briefly, in the first figure (KPN), *Application 2* locks until data has been produced by *Application 1* ①. When *Application 1* produces a data ②, it sends it to the connector ③ and continues its job. Then, availability of a new data unlocks *Application 2* which consumes it ④. In the second figure (CSP), *Application 2* locks until data has been produced by *Application 1* ①. When *Application 1* produces a data ②, it locks until the *Application 2* has consumed it ③.

5 Related Works

Transforming customer requirements into implementations making good trade-offs between performance and cost requires relevant analysis activities based on appropriate languages and tools. System-on-Chip are heterogeneous as they generally mix analog or digital sub-systems with different characteristics related to specific domains (signal processing, image processing, etc.). Therefore, such heterogeneity must be handled at design and analysis time using dedicated formalisms and tools through several abstraction levels and well defined processes.

Several approaches have been applied by ESL (Electronic System Level) in order to tackle issues posed by economic laws and rapid evolution of technology. Among them:

- High Level Synthesis [13] aims at transforming high level behavior specification into optimized architecture,
- IP reuse aims at building systems assembling IPs which requires standard interfaces or wrappers [14],
- Platform Based Design [15] consists in configuring a generic platform containing configurable components like microprocessors or FPGA to suit a specific kind of application.

MBE adds valuable contributions to SoC Design: analysis enhancement, communication and traceability improvement, technology breakpoints reduction, etc. Related works on MBE based RTES methodologies and associated tools are numerous. For instance, in [16], the authors present a methodology based on the use of UML and Platform Based Design called Metropolis. They highlight the necessary orthogonalization of several aspects: computation and communication, function and architecture, behavior and performance. They provide a set of stereotypes and a dedicated framework supporting function / platform mapping, refinements and code generation. In [17], the authors present an object oriented methodology based on the use of UML: the HASoC methodology (Hardware and Software Object on Chip). They first provide an abstract model of the system that is executable (uncommitted model) and proceed to the partition into hardware and software parts taking into account implementation constraints (committed model). In [18], the authors combine the visual features of UML with the simulation and debugging features of the SystemC language in a methodology called UPES (Unified Process for Embedded Systems). This "specify-simulate-debug-refine" methodology is based on the use of the UML for SystemC profile and allows users to capture behavioral and structural aspects of the system at several levels of abstraction. The Gaspard methodology [19] is dedicated to Multi-Processors Systems-on-Chip (MPSoC) design. It is based on the use of a dedicated profile called "Gaspard Profile" allowing regular repetitive structure platform modeling. The Gaspard environment provides TLM and RTL code generation and bridges to several analysis tools. Finally, the Harmony/ESW (Embedded System Workflow) [20] is a Rational Unified Process (RUP) based methodology dedicated to RTES design. It describes the rationale that guide RTES development from requirements capture to implementation using SysML [21] and SPT [22] profiles.

According to the MDA specification [3], using models to represent business domain (problem / specification), platform (support of the solution) and allocations (implementations choices) is really helpful because it makes explicit what was previously made implicitly. But as we mentioned in [6], the current MDA specification is mainly related to software development as it represents only one level of abstraction of the platform; and according to the ESL community, there is a need to represent the platform at several levels of abstraction in order to handle design space exploration [23]. Among main issues addressed by the ESL community, choices related to concurrency and communication issues should be explicitly captured by high level Models of Computation. Several approaches have been proposed to handle MoC heterogeneity. For instance, the authors in [16,24] highlight the necessary orthogonalization of several aspects of MoCs: computation and communication, function and architecture, behavior and performance. Additionally, in [2], the authors discuss MoCs and semantics metamodel and show that MBE is a good candidate to address those issues. Actually, Models of Computation are present at each level of abstraction, and from the idea (specification) to the realization (implementation), they exhibit different properties, related to the kind of analysis that has to be performed.

6 Conclusion

In this paper, we have presented our SoC Design Flow based on the use of UML and dedicated profiles. Although some improvements can be done, particularly in the MoCs support, we have shown that MBE techniques, based on the use of UML for MARTE profile, can fit into Co-Design through an example of a Cognitive Radio Application implemented on FPGA. This MBE approach refines the MDA Y-Chart in order to tackle achievements of the ESL community. In addition to the use of the UML for MARTE profile, we have implemented a metamodel called COMETA to specify and tool models of computation.

The following table gives some model metrics for the processed use case (Locate RF Source).

Those metrics compare the number of generated artifacts after allocation to the number of captured artifacts. Those generated artifacts, which handle concurrency and communication schemes, should have been coded by hand, and contribute thus to reduce efforts of engineers to manage MoC related aspects. This work is part of the MoPCoM project (http://www.MoPCoM.fr), gathering

Table 1. Design Metrics

	System	AML	
		Captured	Generated
Blocks	7	7	10
Connectors	9	9	21
Behaviors	9	13	23

academic and industrial organizations and supported by the French Agence Nationale de la Recherche (RNTL 2006 TLOG 022 01), the "Media and Networks" "cluster of clusters" and Brittany and Pays de la Loire regions.

References

1. ITRS: Design. Technical report, International Technology Roadmap For Semiconductors (2007)
2. Sangiovanni-Vincentelli, A., Shukla, S.K., Sztipanovits, J., Yang, G., Mathaikutty, D.A.: Metamodeling: An emerging representation paradigm for system-level design. IEEE Des. Test 26(3), 54–69 (2009)
3. OMG: Mda guide version 1.0.1. Technical report, Object Management Group (2003)
4. Sangiovanni-Vincentelli, A.: Defining platform-based design. EEDesign of EETimes (2002)
5. OMG: Uml profile for marte, beta 1. Technical Report ptc/07-08-04, Object Management Group (2007)
6. Koudri, A., Joël Champeau, D.A., Soulard, P.: Mopcom/marte process applied to a cognitive radio system design and analysis. In: Model Driven Architecture, Foundations and Applications (2009)
7. Mitola Joseph, I.: Cognitive radio for flexible mobile multimedia communications. Mob. Netw. Appl. 6(5), 435–441 (2001)
8. Hachemani, R., Palicot, J., Moy, C.: A new standard recognition sensor for cognitive radio terminals. In: EURASIP 2007, Kessariani, Greece (2007)
9. Varró, D., Pataricza, A.: Metamodeling mathematics: A precise and visual framework for describing semantics domains of UML models. In: Proc. Fifth International Conference on the Unified Modeling Language – The Language and its Applications, pp. 18–33. Springer, Heidelberg (2002)
10. Chauvel, F., Jézéquel, J.M.: Code generation from uml models with semantic variation points. In: Briand, L.C., Williams, C. (eds.) MoDELS 2005. LNCS, vol. 3713, pp. 54–68. Springer, Heidelberg (2005)
11. Buck, J., Ha, S., Lee, E.A., Messerschmitt, D.G.: Ptolemy: a framework for simulating and prototyping heterogeneous systems. IEEE 10, 527–543 (2002)
12. Herrera, F., Sánchez, P., Villar, E.: Modeling of csp, kpn and sr systems with systemc. Languages for system specification: Selected contributions on UML, SystemC, system Verilog, mixed-signal systems, and property specification from FDL 2003, 133–148 (2004)
13. Greg, S., Frank, V., Walid, N.: A code refinement methodology for performance-improved synthesis from c. In: ICCAD 2006: Proceedings of the 2006 IEEE/ACM international conference on Computer-aided design, New York, NY, USA, pp. 716–723. ACM, New York (2006)

14. Koudri, A., Meftali, S., Dekeyser, J.L.: IP integration in embedded systems modeling. In: 14th IP Based SoC Design Conference (IP-SoC 2005), Grenoble, France (2005)
15. Sangiovanni-Vincentelli, A., Carloni, L., Bernardinis, F.D., Sgroi, M.: Benefits and challenges for platform-based design. In: DAC 2004: Proceedings of the 41st annual conference on Design automation, New York, NY, USA, pp. 409–414. ACM, New York (2004)
16. Chen, R., Sgroi, M., Lavagno, L., Martin, G., Sangiovanni-Vincentelli, A., Rabaey, J.: Uml and platform-based design
17. Edwards, M., Green, P.: Uml for hardware and software object modeling. In: UML for real: design of embedded real-time systems, pp. 127–147 (2003)
18. Riccobene, E., Scandurra, P., Rosti, A., Bocchio, S.: Designing a unified process for embedded systems. In: Fourth International Workshop on Model-Based Methodologies for Pervasive and Embedded Software (MOMPES), Braga, Portugal, IEEE Computer Society, Los Alamitos (2007)
19. Piel, E., Attitalah, R.B., Marquet, P., Meftali, S., Niar, S., Etien, A., Dekeyser, J.L., Boulet, P.: Gaspard2: from marte to systemc simulation. In: Proceeedings of the DATE 2008 friday workshop on Modeling and Analyzis of Real-Time and Embedded Systems with the MARTE UML profile (2008)
20. Douglass, B.P.: Real-Time Agility: The Harmony Method for Real-Time and Embedded Systems Development. Addison-Wesley Professional, Reading (2009)
21. OMG: Systems modeling language specification v1.1. Technical Report ptc/2008-05-16, Object Management Group (2008)
22. OMG: Uml profile for schedulability, performance, and time, version 1.1. Technical Report formal/2005-01-02, Object Management Group (2005)
23. Ghenassia, F.: Transaction-Level Modeling with SystemC. Springer, Heidelberg (2005)
24. Jantsch, A.: Modeling Embedded Systems and SoC's. Systems on Silicon (2004)

Dynamic Computation of Change Operations in Version Management of Business Process Models

Jochen Malte Küster[1], Christian Gerth[1,2,*], and Gregor Engels[2]

[1] IBM Research - Zurich, Säumerstr. 4
8803 Rüschlikon, Switzerland
{jku,cge}@zurich.ibm.com
[2] Department of Computer Science, University of Paderborn, Germany
{gerth,engels}@upb.de

Abstract. Version management of business process models requires that changes can be resolved by applying change operations. In order to give a user maximal freedom concerning the application order of change operations, position parameters of change operations must be computed dynamically during change resolution. In such an approach, change operations with computed position parameters must be applicable on the model and dependencies and conflicts of change operations must be taken into account because otherwise invalid models can be constructed. In this paper, we study the concept of partially specified change operations where parameters are computed dynamically. We provide a formalization for partially specified change operations using graph transformation and provide a concept for their applicability. Based on this, we study potential dependencies and conflicts of change operations and show how these can be taken into account within change resolution. Using our approach, a user can resolve changes of business process models without being unnecessarily restricted to a certain order.

Keywords: Model Synchronization, Version Management, Model Transformation.

1 Introduction

Version management of models typically comprises change detection as well as change resolution. Change detection produces a list of change operations which can then be inspected by the user. Within change resolution, the user makes decisions which change operations should be applied in order to produce a consolidated model. Existing approaches to version management of models allow the computation of change operations (e.g. by using technology such as EMF Compare [7]) and provide a set of techniques for model matching under different circumstances (see e.g. [1,11]).

Version management of process models poses specific requirements on change operations: Compound change operations [16,25] are used which always produce a connected process model and abstract from individual edge changes. Position parameters of change operations specify the place where a change is applied, i.e. direct predecessor

---

[*] Funded by the International Graduate School of Dynamic Intelligent Systems at the University of Paderborn.

and successor of the element that is changed. Iterative application of change operations requires a concept of change operations where position parameters are dynamically computed [16] in order to give the user maximal flexibility in the selection of change operations to apply.

If position parameters of change operations are dynamically computed, it has to be ensured that the change operations obtained are applicable on the model and produce again a connected process model. In addition, potential dependencies and conflicts of change operations must be taken into account. Otherwise it can happen that a user applies a change operation which cannot be properly applied, leading to a potentially unconnected model and problems when applying following change operations.

Existing approaches to dependency and conflict computation of change operations rely on the computation of a dependency and conflict matrix which allows to determine whether two operations are dependent [18,14]. These approaches require that change operations are fully specified (i.e. all position parameters are known) and cannot be applied in the situation that parameters are dynamically computed.

In this paper, we distinguish between *fully specified* and *partially specified* change operations (i.e. not all position parameters are known) and study the transition from partially to fully specified operations. For this purpose, we formalize change operations using graph transformation. We introduce the concept of an *applicable* change operation which ensures that a change operation produces a connected model. We establish the concept of an *enabled* operation which does not have any dependencies on another operation. We show that an enabled operation is always applicable and use this result to ensure that a connected process model is produced. We show how dependencies can be efficiently computed even for partially specified change operations based on an underlying decomposition of the process model into a process structure tree [24]. Using this decomposition, also conflict detection between change operations in distributed scenarios can be improved by reducing the number of required operation comparisons.

Throughout the paper, we present the theory for our approach along process models. However, we believe that the fundamental techniques can also be applied for other behavioral models where a tree-based representation of the model can be computed (such as statecharts).

The paper is organized as follows: We first introduce an example scenario where version management of business process models is demonstrated with a set of change operations. We then provide a formal model for change operations in Section 3 and explain our approach for computing position parameters of change operations. This provides the basis for introducing dependencies in Section 4 and conflicts in Section 5. We briefly report about tool support in Section 6 and conclude with related work and conclusions.

2 Business Process Model Version Management

We use business process models as our domain for model version management. In the following, we first introduce an example and then explain our approach which relies on the process structure tree to compute changes.

Figure 1 shows an example business process model V from the insurance domain using Business Process Model Notation (BPMN) [20]: Nodes can be *Activities*,

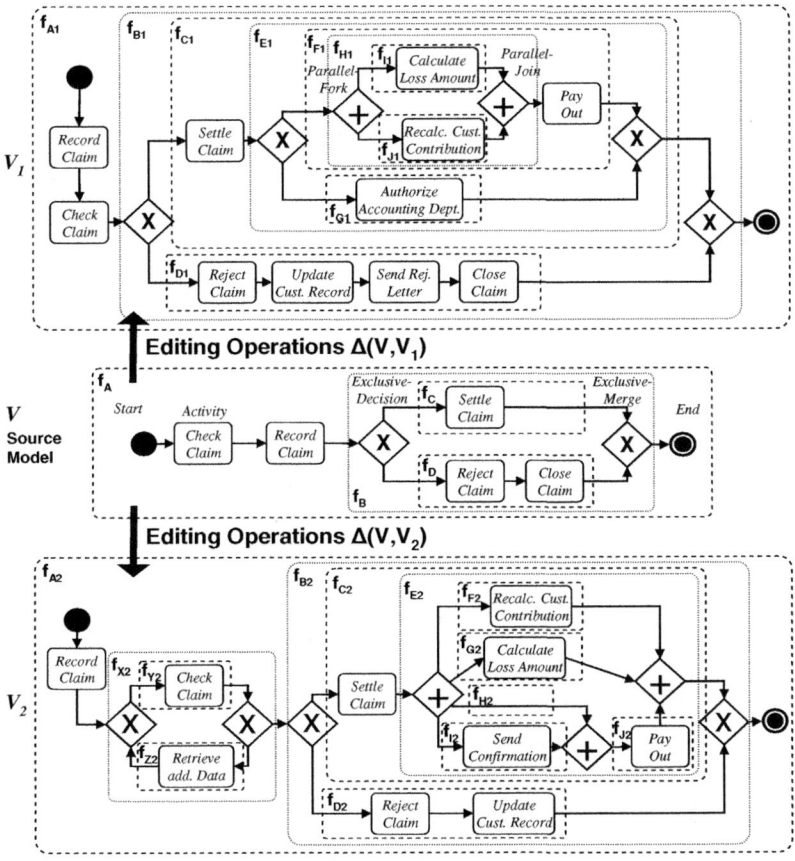

Fig. 1. An example scenario

Gateways, or *Events* such as Start and End. *Gateways* contain Exclusive/Inclusive/Complex Decision and Merge, and Parallel Fork and Join. Nodes are connected by control flow edges. In the example in Figure 1, an insurance claim is first checked, then it is recorded and then a decision is made whether to settle or reject it. Figure 1 also shows a decomposition of the models into fragments (e.g. f_Z, f_X,..), which are non-empty subgraphs in the process model with a single entry and a single exit edge. A fragment can either be an alternative fragment consisting of an Exclusive Decision and an Exclusive Merge node, a concurrent fragment consisting of a Parallel Fork and a Parallel Join node or further types of fragments including unstructured or complex fragments which allow to express all combinations of gateways. For more details about fragment types the reader is referred to [24]. Fragments can be organized into a Process Structure Tree (PST) of the process model [24].

In a distributed modeling scenario, the process model V (Figure 1) might have been created by the process model representative in an enterprise and then stored in a repository for further elaboration. During this elaboration period, two colleagues individually

Change Operation op	Effects on Process Model V	type(op)
InsertActivity(x, a, b)	Insertion of a new activity x (by copying activity y) between two succeeding elements a and b in process model V and reconnection of control flow.	INSERTACT
DeleteActivity(x, c, d)	Deletion of activity x between c and d and reconnection of control flow.	DELETEACT
MoveActivity(x, c, d, a, b)	Movement of activity x from its old position between element c and d into its new position between two succeeding elements a and b in process model V and reconnection of control flow.	MOVEACT
InsertFragment(f_i, a, b)	Insertion of a new fragment f_i between two succeeding elements a and b in process model V and reconnection of control flow.	INSERTFRAG
DeleteFragment(f_i, c, d)	Deletion of fragment f_i between c and d from process model V and reconnection of control flow.	DELETEFRAG

Fig. 2. Change operations for process models [16]

manipulate V to create new versions, e.g., V_1 and V_2. In our approach, changes performed by the colleagues to obtain V_1 and V_2 will be detected and collected in terms of change operations in a change log $\Delta(V, V_1)$ and $\Delta(V, V_2)$.

We have previously proposed change operations for process models [16] as follows: *InsertActivity*, *DeleteActivity* or *MoveActivity* operations allow to insert, delete or modify activities and always produce a connected process model as output. Similarly, *InsertFragment* and *DeleteFragment* operations can be used for inserting or deleting a complete fragment of the process model. Figure 2 shows an overview of the change operations that are supported by our approach. Given an operation op we denote by $type(op)$ the type of the operation and assume the type as indicated in Figure 2. These change operations are computed by comparing the PSTs of two process models and identifying newly inserted, deleted and moved nodes in the PSTs (see [16] for a detailed introduction).

In the case of the elaboration of V into V_1 in our example (Figure 1), we obtain the change operations given in the change log $\Delta(V, V1)$ in Figure 3. These change operations are initially partially specified. For example, for c) *InsertActivity("Pay Out",-,-)* the last two parameters are not defined yet. These parameters which we denote as *position parameters* will be computed dynamically during change resolution.

$\Delta(V, V1)$:
a) MoveActivity("Check Claim", -, -, -, -)
b) InsertFragment(f_{E1}, -, -)
c) InsertActivity("Pay Out", -, -)
d) InsertActivity("Authorize Accounting Dept.", -, -)
e) InsertFragment(f_{H1}, -, -)
f) InsertActivity("Calculate Loss Amount", -, -)
g) InsertActivity("Recalc. Cust. Contribution", -, -)
h) InsertActivity("Update Cust. Record", -, -)
i) InsertActivity("Send Rej. Letter", -, -)

Fig. 3. Change log $\Delta(V, V1)$

The operations in the change log can then be used to create a consolidated model V' out of V, V_1 and V_2. That means, the process model representative in the distributed modeling scenario, will inspect each change and decide which change to apply in order to construct a consolidated model V'. Thereby, he applies the changes in an iterative way and continues to do so until he is satisfied with the resulting model V'. With regards to Figure 1, the process model representative might first apply operation *i) InsertActivity("Send Rej. Letter",-,-)* and then operation *h) InsertActivity("Update Cust. Record",-,-)*. In this approach, the order of operation application leads to different position parameters of the change operations requiring dynamic computation of position parameters.

In contrast to that, fixing the position parameters in advance in terms of fully specified change operations restricts the order of application to one particular order and thereby restricts the user in creating a consolidated version. Figure 4 gives an example,

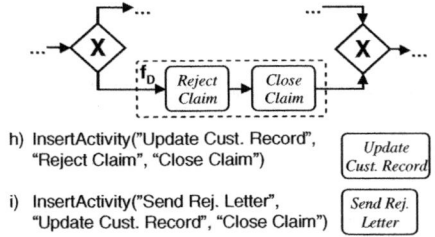

Fig. 4. Fully specified change operations restrict the execution order

assuming that operations h) and i) have not yet been applied. The fully specified operations h) *InsertActivity("Update Cust. Record", "Reject Claim", "Close Claim")* and i) *InsertActivity("Send Rej. Letter", "Update Cust. Record", "Close Claim")* restrict the application order to h), i). In addition, it is not possible to apply only the operation i) *InsertActivity("Send Rej. Letter", "Update Cust. Record", "Close Claim")*.

One requirement for iterative change resolution is that when computing position parameters of change operations it must be ensured that they yield a change operation that can be applied on the process model. Further, a dependency concept for change operations is needed to ensure that only operations that do not depend on other operations can be applied. Otherwise it can happen that applying a change operation leads to a potentially unconnected model and problems when applying following change operations. For example, inserting an activity into a fragment that does not exist yet leads leads to an unconnected activity (and therefore unconnected model) and to problems when later inserting the fragment. Furthermore, in a concurrent modeling scenario as described above, an approach for computing conflicts is required as well. In the following sections, we will present our approach for addressing these problems.

3 Partially and Fully Specified Change Operations

In this section, we formalize change operations using typed attributed graph transformation, distinguishing between fully specified and partially specified ones. Using this formalization, we define whether a fully specified change operation obtained from a partially specified one is applicable on the model.

3.1 Formalization of Change Operations

Each change operation op for a model V can be viewed as a model transformation rule on the model V transforming it to a model V'. A model transformation rule can be formalized as a typed attributed graph transformation rule [13,6,19]. We distinguish between change operation type and a concrete change operation: A change operation type (such as *InsertActivity(x,a,b)*) describes a set of concrete change operations. By replacing the parameters of a change operation type with model elements of the model V and V', a concrete change operation is obtained. Figure 5 b) shows a sequence of concrete change operations.

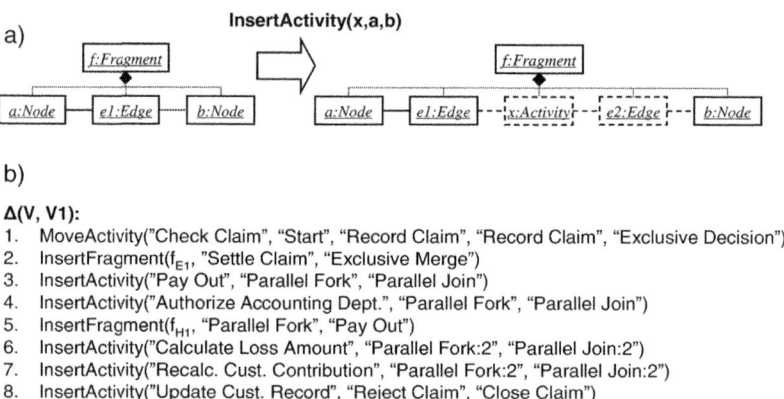

Fig. 5. Change operation type and concrete change operations

The behavior (or semantics) of a change operation type op is specified using a typed attributed graph transformation rule op_r. A typed graph transformation rule $op_r : L \rightarrow R$ consists of a pair of typed instance graphs L, R such that the union is defined. A graph transformation step from a graph G to a graph H, denoted by $G \stackrel{op_r(o)}{\Longrightarrow} H$, is given by a graph homomorphism $o : L \cup R \rightarrow G \cup H$, called occurrence, such that the left hand side L is embedded into G and the right hand side R is embedded into H and precisely that part of G is deleted which is matched by elements of L not belonging to R, and, that part of H is added which is matched by elements new in R. Figure 5 a) shows the typed attributed graph transformation rule for *InsertActivity(x,a,b)*.

The theory of graph transformation provides the basis for defining the semantics of a change operation type as follows: Given a change operation type op together with its rule op_r, a concrete change operation on a model V leading to a model V' conforming to the type op is modelled by a change operation application of the rule op_r to V transforming it to V'. Formally, this is represented by a graph transformation $G_V \stackrel{op_r(o)}{\Longrightarrow} H_{V'}$ where op_r is applied at an occurrence o to the graph G_V leading to a new graph $H_{V'}$ (where G_V and $H_{V'}$ are represented as typed graphs obtained from the models V and V'). We also write $V \stackrel{op}{\Longrightarrow} V'$ or $V \stackrel{op(o)}{\Longrightarrow} V'$. To represent a concrete change operation, we write $op(o)$.

Formally, the occurrence morphism o represents a binding between the change operation type and the models V and V'. It maps nodes and edges of L and R to G and H. An occurrence morphism can be specified by a set of parameters $x_1, ..., x_n$ in the change operation type op and their instantiation in the change operation $op(o)$. We also write $op(x_1, .., x_n)$ for a change operation type and $op(X_1, ..., X_n)$ for a concrete change operation $op(o)$. For each rule op_r, we distinguish between parameters that are preserved, deleted or newly created, so $x_i \in pres(op_r) \cup del(op_r) \cup new(op_r)$.

As an example, consider the change operation type *InsertActivity(x,a,b)* and the change operation *InsertActivity(X,A,B)*. This implies an occurrence morphism mapping x to X, a to A and b to B where X, A, B are model elements in model V and/or V', and x

is newly created whereas a and b are preserved elements. When designing a set of change operation types, we use a shorthand which only includes those elements of the occurrence morphism such that the morphism is uniquely determined. For example, we write *InsertActivity(x,a,b)* instead of *InsertActivity(f,a,e1,b,x,e2)* where $f, a, e1, b, x, e2$ refers to the elements defined in the transformation rule (see Figure 5 a)).

In model version management, an important concept is change operation applicability: Given a change operation $op(X_1, .., X_n)$, we want to reason whether this change operation is applicable to a model V or not:

Definition 1 (Applicable Change Operations). *Let a change operation $op(X_1, .., X_n)$ of a change operation type $op(x_1, .., x_n)$, its rule op_r and a model V be given, with $X_i \in V$ if $x_i \in pres(op_r) \cup del(op_r)$. Then we say that $op(X_1, .., X_n)$ is applicable to V if there exists a model V' with $V \stackrel{op_r(o)}{\Longrightarrow} V'$ for an occurrence o such that $x_i \mapsto X_i \in V$ if $x_i \in pres(op_r) \cup del(op_r)$ and $x_i \mapsto X_i \in V'$ if $x_i \in new(op_r)$. Otherwise, we say that $op(X_1, .., X_n)$ is not applicable on V.*

Figure 5 b) shows examples of applicable and non-applicable change operations. For example, *InsertActivity("Pay Out", "Parallel Fork", "Parallel Join")* is not applicable if *Parallel Fork* and *Parallel Join* do not exist in the model or are not connected by an edge as required by op_r. In other words, the applicability of the change operation *InsertActivity("Pay Out", "Parallel Fork", "Parallel Join")* depends on the chosen position parameters and might also be dependent on the application of another operation. Computing position parameters of change operations is discussed in the following.

3.2 Correct Specification and Computation of Position Parameters

If all parameters of a concrete change operation are specified, we call the change operation *fully specified*. Otherwise, it is called *partially specified*. For example, *InsertActivity(X,-,-)* is a partially specified change operation because only x has been specified and a, b are not specified yet.

Fully specified change operations are obtained from partially specified ones by computing position parameters. In the following, we explain how the PSTs can be used for computing position parameters of change operations. Given two process structure trees $PST(V)$, $PST(V_1)$ and correspondences between their nodes, a joint PST, denoted as $J-PST(V, V_1)$, can be constructed which contains both process structure trees where corresponding nodes have been identified [16]. A J-PST can be annotated with change operations where each change operation is associated to the fragment node in the J-PST in which it occurs. In addition, for *InsertFragment* or *DeleteFragment* operations, we denote with $fragment(op)$ the newly inserted or deleted fragment. Figure 6 shows the annotated J-PST of the example.

When transitioning from a partially specified to a fully specified change operation, we require that parameters are chosen inside the parent fragment of an operation as follows:

Definition 2 (Correct Specification). *Given a partially specified change operation op in a J-PST, a full specification of op is said to be correct, if the position parameters are chosen inside the parent fragment.*

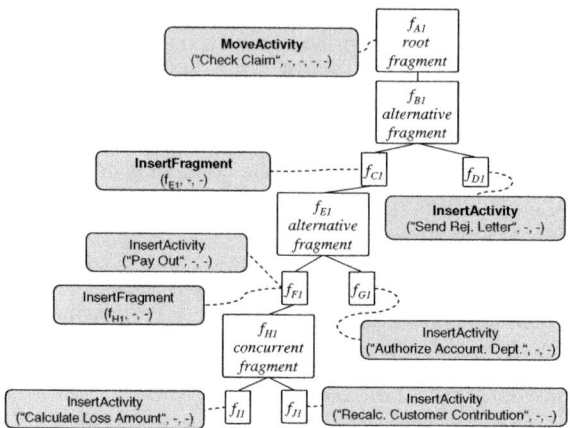

Fig. 6. The J-PST of the example

With regards to Figure 6, a correct full specification of the partially specified operation *InsertActivity("Calc. Loss Amount",-,-)*, e.g., *InsertActivity("Calc. Loss Amount","Parallel Fork$_{H1}$","Parallel Join$_{H1}$")* ensures that the position parameters are chosen inside fragment f_{H1} and not outside.

For applying a partially specified change operation, Algorithm 1 shows how to compute the position parameters. This algorithm starts at the element which is affected by the change operation and then searches backward and forward until a node is reached that exists in both process models.

Although Algorithm 1 always returns a fully specified change operation, this does not ensure that the operation obtained is also correct according to Def. 2. For ensuring their correctness, dependencies between change operations must be taken into account which we will discuss in the next section.

4 Dependencies of Change Operations

In this section, we introduce concepts for dependencies of change operations. We first review dependencies for fully specified change operations and then elaborate on partially specified change operations.

As a fully specified change operation op is formally defined by a graph transformation rule op_r, we can directly apply the dependency concept from graph transformation (see e.g. [4,19,10,14]): Informally, if two changes are dependent, then the second one requires the application of the first one. This is usually the case if the first change creates model structures that are required by the second change. Formally, we define:

Definition 3 (TR-Dependent Change Operations). *Let two fully specified change operations op_1 and op_2 be given such that $V \xRightarrow{op_1} V'$ and $V' \xRightarrow{op_2} V''$. Then we call op_2 transformation rule dependent (TR-dependent) on op_1 if op_2 is not applicable on V and op_2 is applicable on V'.*

Algorithm 1. Computation of position parameters of a change operation op in model V and V_1

Procedure computePositionParameter(op,V,V_1):
$x = op.element$;
{Old Position Parameters of x in Model V}
if op is $DeleteActivity/Fragment$ or $MoveActivity$ **then**
    c = direct predecessor of $x \in V$; d = direct successor of $x \in V$;
{New Position Parameters of x in Model V}
if op is $InsertActivity/Fragment$ or $MoveActivity$ **then**
    a = getPredecessor(x,V,V_1); b = getSuccessor(x,V,V_1);
    if $a, b \neq$ null **then**
        if a is not directly connected to b **then**
            select an edge i between a and b; $a = i.source$; $b = i.target$;
    else
        select an edge i in V in the parent fragment of op; $a = i.source$; $B = i.target$;
return a, b, c, d;

{Computation of Predecessor}
Procedure getPredecessor(x,V,V_1):
determine predecessor p of x in V_1
if p exists in $V \wedge p$ is not affected by a Move operation **then**
    return p;
else
    return getPredecessor(p,V,V_1)
return null;

{Computation of Successor}
Procedure getSuccessor(x,V,V_1):
determine successor s of x in V_1
if s exists in $V \wedge s$ is not affected by a Move operation **then**
    return s
else
    return getSuccessor(s,V,V_1)
return null

Dependencies can be computed for change operations by applying existing theory for establishing a so-called dependency matrix (see [14] for an overview). An entry in this matrix then states the conditions under which two fully specified change operations are dependent.

Dependencies of partially specified change operations cannot be computed using the dependency matrix because parameters are missing. One possibility would be to apply dependency computation only to fully specified change operations, leading to the situation that dependencies are only detected late in the change resolution phase. Another approach is to use the annotated J-PST (see Figure 6) for defining dependencies of change operations as follows:

Definition 4 (J-PST Dependencies and Enabled Change Operations). *Let a J-PST annotated with change operations OPS be given. For each $op \in OPS$, we denote with*

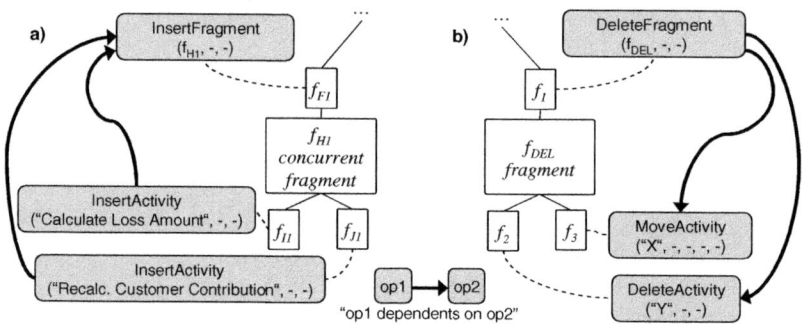

Fig. 7. Dependencies in the J-PST

$depops(op)$ all operations that are dependent on op. We define dependencies on the change operations as follows:

- Let a change operation op be given with $type(op) = INSERTFRAG$ and let OPC be the set of all operations associated to a child of $fragment(op)$. Then every $op_i \in OPC$ is dependent on op and therefore $depops(op) = \{op_i \in OPC\}$.
- Let a change operation op be given with $type(op) = DELETEFRAG$ and let OPC be the set of all operations associated to a child of $fragment(op)$. Then every $op_i \in OPC$ is a prerequisite of op and therefore $op \in depops(op_i)$.

We call a partially specified change operation op **enabled** if $depops(op) = \emptyset$.

The idea behind these dependencies is that a change operation that is dependent on an *InsertFragment* operation can only be applied if the *InsertFragment* operation has previously been applied to create the fragment. Similarly, a *DeleteFragment* operation is dependent on all other operations that affect the fragment deleted. This ensures that first all operations within the deleted fragment are applied before the fragment is deleted. Figure 7 a) shows an extract of the J-PST introduced earlier and the two *InsertActivity* change operations which are both dependent on the *InsertFragment* change operation. Figure 7 b) shows an example for *DeleteFragment* dependencies.

J-PST dependencies yield a dependency concept for change operations that are partially (or fully) specified. J-PST dependencies can be easily computed by traversing the J-PST and, for each fragment, computing dependencies between all operations associated to the fragment and operations associated to the grandfather fragment. J-PST dependencies have the following important property[1] by definition:

Lemma 1 (Acyclic J-PST Dependencies). *Let a J-PST annotated with change operations be given. Then the J-PST dependencies are acyclic.*

In our approach, J-PST dependencies together with the concept of a correct specification can be used to show that an enabled operation is also applicable. The following theorem[1] shows this:

---

[1] Proof sketches for Lemma 1, Theorem 1, and Theorem 2 can be found in [15].

Theorem 1 (Applicability of Enabled Operations). *Let a fragment f in the J-PST together with a change operation op be given. If op is enabled then it is also applicable if its position parameters are computed by Algorithm 1.*

For our application in model version management, it is important to know whether we can run into a dependency when applying fully specified change operations. The following theorem[1] shows that it is sufficient to compute J-PST dependencies if operations are associated to different fragments in the J-PST:

Theorem 2 (TR-Independence). *Let a J-PST annotated with change operations be given and let op_i and op_j be two operations. Assume further that op_i and op_j are attached to different fragments. If op_i and op_j are not J-PST dependent then op_i and op_j are not TR-dependent on each other.*

The previous theorems have the following consequences for iterative change resolution: All enabled operations are applicable which means that there exists a model V' obtained from V when applying an enabled change operation. As all transformation rules of our change operations produce connected process models, V' is always connected. Further, the order in which enabled operations are applied which are contained in different fragments does not matter. Further, by Theorem 1, each enabled operation is always applicable. This ensures that after applying an operation re-computation of position parameters of other operations leads to applicable operations again.

In the next section, we will elaborate on conflicts that can arise when a process model has been changed concurrently by two persons.

5 Conflicts of Change Operations

In this section, we consider conflicts between change operations. Similar to the previous section about dependencies, we first introduce conflicts between fully specified change operations and then show how the J-PST can be used to ease up conflict computation.

Conflicts between change operations arise in scenarios where changes are applied independently on different versions of a process model. Our running example (see Figure 1) illustrates such a scenario where an original process model V is manipulated independently to create two new versions V_1 and V_2.

In general, two changes are in conflict if only one of the two can be applied. This is the case if the two changes involve the same model structure and manipulate it in a different way. Typical conflicting pairs of change operations include the movement of an element in one model (e.g., *MoveActivity("Check Claim",-,-,-,-)*) and its deletion (e.g., *DeleteActivity("Check Claim",-,-)*) in the other model. Formally, we define:

Definition 5 (TR-Conflicting Change Operations). *Let two fully specified change operations op_1 and op_2 be given such that $V \xrightarrow{op_1} V'$ and $V \xrightarrow{op_2} V''$. Then we call op_1 and op_2 transformation rule conflicting (TR-conflicting) if op_2 is not applicable on V' and op_2 is applicable on V.*

Conflicts between fully specified change operations can be computed by applying existing theory, e.g., by establishing a conflict matrix (see [18,14]) which specifies conditions under which two fully specified change operations are conflicting.

In contrast to dependencies, conflicts cannot be computed on partially specified change operations. However, using the J-PST still simplifies the conflict detection by decreasing the number of change operations, which need to be compared. Using the J-PST, conflicts can be computed by inspecting the set of enabled change operations between $\Delta(V, V_1)$ and $\Delta(V, V_2)$, instead of comparing all fully specified operations.

Given two joint process structure trees $J - PST(V, V_1)$, $J - PST(V, V_2)$, we first compute position parameters for enabled operations in the J-PSTs and then use the conflict matrix to identify conflicting operations. In the case that a conflicting operations is assigned to a fragment, all children are also marked as conflicting. Formally, we define conflicts of change operations in the J-PST:

Definition 6 (J-PST Conflicts). *Let two joint process structure trees $J - PST(V, V_1)$ and $J - PST(V, V_2)$, both annotated with operations, be given. Then we define conflicts on the change operations as follows:*

- *Two enabled change operations $op_{V1} \in \Delta(V, V_1)$ and $op_{V2} \in \Delta(V, V_2)$ are conflicting if they are TR-conflicting according to Definition 5.*
- *For two enabled conflicting change operation op_{V1} and op_{V2} of the $type(op_{V1}) = $ INSERTFRAG, DELETEFRAG, let OPC_{V1} be the set of all operations associated to a child of $fragment(op_{V1})$. Then every $op_i \in OPC_{V1}$ is dependent on op_{V2}.*
- *For two enabled conflicting change operation op_{V1} and op_{V2} of the $type(op_{V2}) = $ INSERTFRAG, DELETEFRAG, let OPC_{V2} be the set of all operations associated to a child of $fragment(op_{V2})$. Then every $op_i \in OPC_{V2}$ is in conflict op_{V1}.*

Using the J-PSTs for conflict detection reduces the number of required comparisons to the set of enabled operations. There is no need to compare all operations with each other. Figure 8 gives an example. The $J - PST(V, V_1)$ illustrates the alternative fragment f_{E1} which was inserted into process model V_1 (see our running example in Figure 1) and $J - PST(V, V_2)$ depicts the inserted concurrent fragment f_{E2} in V_2. The change operations *InsertFragment(f_{E1},-,-)* and *InsertFragment(f_{E2},-,-)* that insert these fragments into V_1 and V_2 are enabled and conflicting according to Definition 6, since only one of the operations can be applied in the merged version. Depending on the resolution of this conflict, the child operations contained in these fragments may also be conflicting. Thus, they are marked preventively as conflicting, as required by Definition 6.

In the following theorem[2] we show that the number of conflicts in the J-PST constitute an upper bound for conflicting transformations, i.e. if two operations are not conflicting in the J-PST then they cannot be transformation conflicting.

Theorem 3 (TR-Conflicts are limited by J-PST Conflicts). *Let a J-PST annotated with operations be given and let op_i be an operation. Then no J-PST conflict between op_i and any other op_j induces that op_i is not transformation conflicting.*

Other than for dependencies, conflicts in the J-PST are not an abstraction but only an approximation of conflicts on the transformation rules and provide an upper bound of the overall number of conflicting transformation rules. This means that if two operations are conflicting in the J-PST then they may be giving rise to conflicting transformations

---

[2] A proof sketch for Theorem 3 can be found in [15].

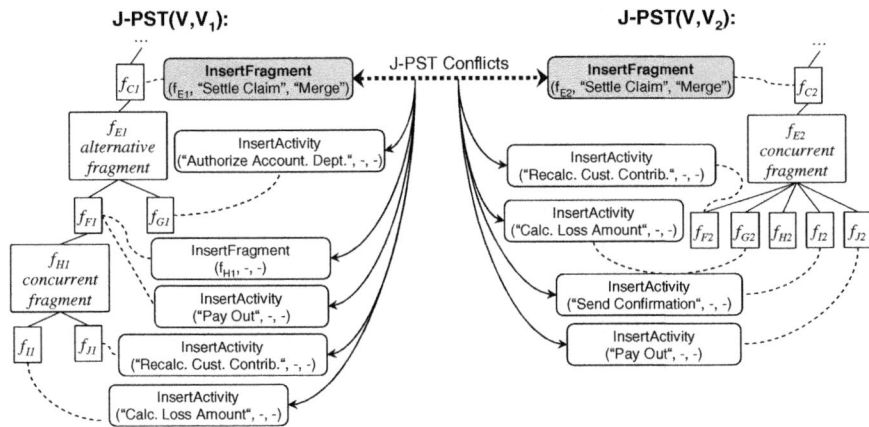

Fig. 8. Conflicts between Change Operations in the $J - PST(V, V_1)$ and $J - PST(V, V_2)$

but this is not always the case. For instance in Figure 8, the resolution of the conflict between the two enabled *InsertFragment(f_{E1},-,-) InsertFragment(f_{E2},-,-)* operations, which is not known prior to resolving the conflict (see [14] for several options of conflict resolution), determines possible conflicts between child operations. To avoid problems, we make all the child operations conflicting and recompute conflicts after resolving the conflict between enabled operations.

6 Tool Support

Our approach has been implemented in a prototype for process model version management in the IBM WebSphere Business Modeler and the IBM WebSphere Integration Developer. For an architectural overview we refer to [9]. In Figure 9 iterative change resolution in the IBM WebSphere Business Modeler is illustrated. In this view, only enabled change operations can be selected and applied, whereas dependent operations are grayed-out. After the application of an enabled operation, the set of enabled operations is recomputed. Conflicts are visualized to the user as soon as a conflicting operations is selected for application. Internally, the prototype uses the algorithms described above for computing position parameters and dependencies of partially specified change operations.

7 Related Work

One area of related work is concerned with model composition and model versioning. Alanen and Porres [1] describe an algorithm how to compute elementary change operations. Kolovos et al. [12] describe the Epsilon merging language which can be used to specify how models should be merged. Kelter et al. [11] present a generic model differencing algorithm. Cicchetti et al. [3] propose a metamodel for the specification and detection of syntactical and semantical conflicts. In the IBM Rational Software Architect [17] or using the EMF Compare technology [7], dependencies and conflicts between versions are computed based on elementary changes. These approaches to model

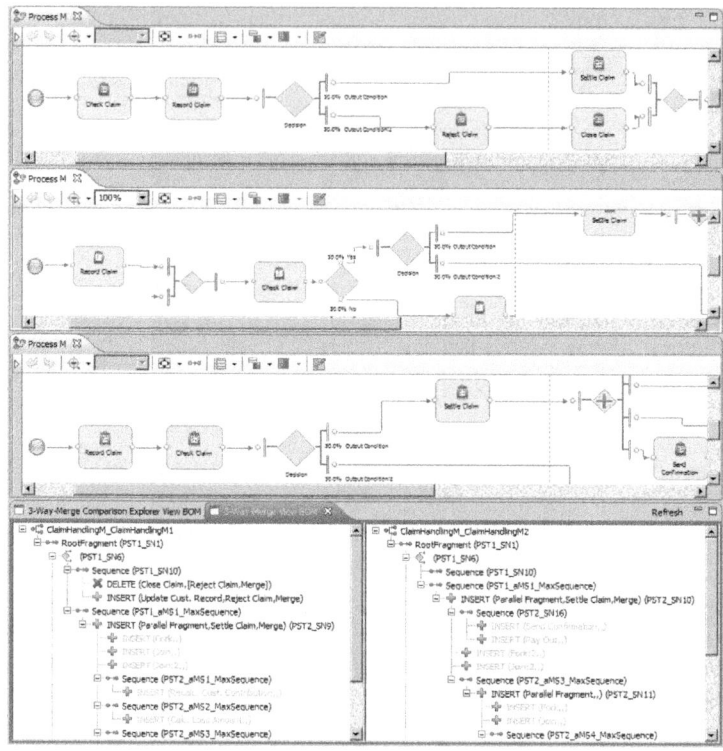

Fig. 9. Screenshot of our prototype in WebSphere Business Modeler

versioning deal with the problem of model merging but they do not make use of a model structure tree (such as our process structure tree). This enables us to compute position parameters for partially specified change operations and thereby realize iterative change resolution.

In the area of software evolution, Fluri et al. [8] describe how to use abstract syntax trees and tree differencing for extracting changes and better understanding change types. Our work uses the process structure trees on the modeling level. One difference can be seen in the way change resolution is performed because on the modeling level more flexibility is needed which is incorporated by the concept of partially specified change operations.

Dependencies of transformation rules have been studied in the literature: Mens et al. [19] analyze refactorings for dependencies using critical pair analysis. They first express refactorings as graph transformations and then detect dependencies using the AGG tool [23]. Graph transformations have also been used extensively for defining and parsing visual languages [21] where rules are used as parsing rules. Further, graph transformation rules have been used in various model transformation approaches (see e.g. [5,2]), as a formal foundation as well as in transformation engines executing a model transformation. In these approaches, a transformation rule is matched and applied along existing theory of graph transformation [4]. In contrast to these approaches, we study dependencies of change operations that are partially specified using J-PST dependencies and establish a relationship to TR-dependencies. In our earlier work [14], we assumed that all change operations are fully specified and in [9] we describe our general architecture.

Within the process modeling community, Rinderle et al. [22] have studied disjoint and overlapping process model changes in the context of the problem of migrating process instances but have not considered dependencies between changes and different forms of change resolution.

8 Conclusion

Version management of process models poses specific requirements on change operations: Typically, a flexible change resolution needs to be supported that does not restrict the user to follow a predefined resolution order of change operations. This requires dynamic computation of position parameters of change operations.

In this paper, we have introduced the concept of a partially specified change operation where position parameters are dynamically computed on demand. We have established a formal model for change operations, based on the theory of graph transformation. We have then introduced an approach for computing dependencies and conflicts of change operations based on an underlying tree-based decomposition of the model. Using our approach enables a user to follow an arbitrary order when resolving changes and reduces the number of comparisons needed for computing dependencies and conflicts.

We intend to transfer the results to other types of models such as statecharts. Further, as our change operations are essentially model transformations with changing parameters it arises the question whether dynamic computation of model transformation parameters are also required in other application scenarios.

Acknowledgements. The authors wish to thank Jana Koehler for valuable feedback on an earlier version of this paper.

References

1. Alanen, M., Porres, I.: Difference and Union of Models. In: Stevens, P., Whittle, J., Booch, G. (eds.) UML 2003. LNCS, vol. 2863, pp. 2–17. Springer, Heidelberg (2003)
2. Biermann, E., Ermel, C., Taentzer, G.: Precise Semantics of EMF Model Transformations by Graph Transformation. In: Czarnecki, K., Ober, I., Bruel, J.-M., Uhl, A., Völter, M. (eds.) MODELS 2008. LNCS, vol. 5301, pp. 53–67. Springer, Heidelberg (2008)
3. Cicchetti, A., Di Ruscio, D., Pierantonio, A.: Managing Model Conflicts in Distributed Development. In: Czarnecki, K., Ober, I., Bruel, J.-M., Uhl, A., Völter, M. (eds.) MODELS 2008. LNCS, vol. 5301, pp. 311–325. Springer, Heidelberg (2008)
4. Corradini, A., Montanari, U., Rossi, F., Ehrig, H., Heckel, R., Löwe, M.: Algebraic Approaches to Graph Transformation Part I: Basic Concepts and Double Pushout Approach. In: Rozenberg, G. (ed.) Handbook of Graph Grammars and Computing by Graph Transformation. Foundations, vol. 1, pp. 163–245. World Scientific, Singapore (1997)
5. Csertán, G., Huszerl, G., Majzik, I., Pap, Z., Pataricza, A., Varró, D.: VIATRA: Visual Automated Transformations for Formal Verification and Validation of UML Models. In: Proceedings ASE 2002, September 2002, pp. 267–270 (2002)

6. de Lara, J., Bardohl, R., Ehrig, H., Ehrig, K., Prange, U., Taentzer, G.: Attributed graph transformation with node type inheritance. Theor. Comput. Sci. 376(3), 139–163 (2007)
7. Eclipse Foundation. EMF Compare, http://www.eclipse.org/modeling/emft/?project=compare
8. Fluri, B., Würsch, M., Pinzger, M., Gall, H.: Change Distilling: Tree Differencing for Fine-Grained Source Code Change Extraction. IEEE Trans. Softw. Eng. 33, 725–743 (2007)
9. Gerth, C., Küster, J.M., Engels, G.: Language-Independent Change Management of Process Models. In: Schürr, A., Selic, B. (eds.) MODELS 2009. LNCS, vol. 5795, pp. 152–166. Springer, Heidelberg (2009)
10. Hausmann, J.H., Heckel, R., Taentzer, G.: Detection of conflicting functional requirements in a use case-driven approach: a static analysis technique based on graph transformation. In: Proceedings ICSE 2002, pp. 105–115. ACM Press, New York (2002)
11. Kelter, U., Wehren, J., Niere, J.: A Generic Difference Algorithm for UML Models. In: Liggesmeyer, P., Pohl, K., Goedicke, M. (eds.) SE 2005, Fachtagung des GI-Fachbereichs Softwaretechnik, LNI, vol. 64, pp. 105–116, GI (2005)
12. Kolovos, D.S., Paige, R., Polack, F.: Merging Models with the Epsilon Merging Language (EML). In: Nierstrasz, O., Whittle, J., Harel, D., Reggio, G. (eds.) MoDELS 2006. LNCS, vol. 4199, pp. 215–229. Springer, Heidelberg (2006)
13. Küster, J.M.: Definition and validation of model transformations. Software and Systems Modeling 5(3), 233–259 (2006)
14. Küster, J.M., Gerth, C., Engels, G.: Dependent and Conflicting Change Operations of Process Models. In: Paige, R.F., Hartman, A., Rensink, A. (eds.) ECMDA-FA 2009. LNCS, vol. 5562, pp. 158–173. Springer, Heidelberg (2009)
15. Küster, J.M., Gerth, C., Engels, G.: Dynamic Computation of Change Operations in Version Management of Business Process Models. IBM Research Report RZ 3763, IBM Zurich Research Laboratory (January 2010), http://www.zurich.ibm.com/~jku/Papers/rz3763.pdf
16. Küster, J.M., Gerth, C., Förster, A., Engels, G.: Detecting and Resolving Process Model Differences in the Absence of a Change Log. In: Dumas, M., Reichert, M., Shan, M.-C. (eds.) BPM 2008. LNCS, vol. 5240, pp. 244–260. Springer, Heidelberg (2008)
17. Letkeman, K.: Comparing and merging UML models in IBM Rational Software Architect: Part 3. A deeper understanding of model merging. IBM Developerworks (2005)
18. Mens, T.: A State-of-the-Art Survey on Software Merging. IEEE Trans. Software Eng. 28(5), 449–462 (2002)
19. Mens, T., Taentzer, G., Runge, O.: Analysing refactoring dependencies using graph transformation. Software and System Modeling 6(3), 269–285 (2007)
20. Object Management Group (OMG). Business Process Modeling Notation (BPMN), http://www.omg.org/spec/BPMN/1.2
21. Rekers, J., Schürr, A.: Defining and Parsing Visual Languages with Layered Graph Grammars. J. Vis. Lang. Comput. 8(1), 27–55 (1997)
22. Rinderle, S., Reichert, M., Dadam, P.: Disjoint and Overlapping Process Changes: Challenges, Solutions, Applications. In: Meersman, R., Tari, Z. (eds.) OTM 2004. LNCS, vol. 3290, pp. 101–120. Springer, Heidelberg (2004)
23. Taentzer, G.: AGG: A Graph Transformation Environment for Modeling and Validation of Software. In: Pfaltz, J.L., Nagl, M., Böhlen, B. (eds.) AGTIVE 2003. LNCS, vol. 3062, pp. 446–453. Springer, Heidelberg (2004)
24. Vanhatalo, J., Völzer, H., Leymann, F.: Faster and More Focused Control-Flow Analysis for Business Process Models Through SESE Decomposition. In: Krämer, B.J., Lin, K.-J., Narasimhan, P. (eds.) ICSOC 2007. LNCS, vol. 4749, pp. 43–55. Springer, Heidelberg (2007)
25. Weber, B., Rinderle, S., Reichert, M.: Change Patterns and Change Support Features in Process-Aware Information Systems. In: Krogstie, J., Opdahl, A.L., Sindre, G. (eds.) CAiSE 2007 and WES 2007. LNCS, vol. 4495, pp. 574–588. Springer, Heidelberg (2007)

Detecting Inconsistencies in Multi-View Models with Variability

Roberto Erick Lopez-Herrejon and Alexander Egyed

Institute for Systems Engineering and Automation
Johannes Kepler University Linz, Austria
{roberto.lopez,alexander.egyed}@jku.at

Abstract. Multi-View Modeling (MVM) is a common modeling practice that advocates the use of multiple, different and yet related models to represent the needs of diverse stakeholders. Of crucial importance in MVM is consistency checking — the description and verification of semantic relationships amongst the views. Variability is the capacity of software artifacts to vary, and its effective management is a core tenet of the research in Software Product Lines (SPL). MVM has proven useful for developing one-of-a-kind systems; however, to reap the potential benefits of MVM in SPL it is vital to provide consistency checking mechanisms that cope with variability. In this paper we describe how to address this need by applying Safe Composition — the guarantee that all programs of a product line are type safe. We evaluate our approach with a case study.

1 Introduction

Extensive experience in software architecture and design has shown the importance and necessity of using multiple, different, and yet related models to represent the perspectives and information needs of diverse system stakeholders throughout the development process. This practice is known as *Multi-View Modeling (MVM)*[1,2,3]. UML is an example of MVM where the different types of diagrams can represent distinct views of the same system.

MVM intrinsically requires *consistency checking* whereby all views must adhere to *consistency rules* that describe the semantic relationships amongst their elements [1,2,3]. A classical example of a consistency rule in UML is that if a sequence diagram has a message m targeting an object of class C, then the class diagram of class C must contain method m.

Variability is the capacity of software artifacts to vary [4], and its effective management is a core tenet of the research in *Software Product Lines (SPL)*[5,6,7]. On one hand, the significant benefits of applying SPL practices have been extensively documented and corroborated both in academia and industry [6,8,7]. On the other, MVM has proven useful for the development of one-of-a-kind systems. Several research works have added variability into UML modeling because of its extensive use in industry and academia [9,10,11]. However, the effective use of MVM in SPL demands mechanisms for consistency checking that cope with variability. To the best of our knowledge, this issue has not been extensively researched.

In this paper we propose *Safe composition* [12], the guarantee that *all* programs that can be composed according to the product line domain constraints are type safe (i.e. they do not have undefined references to structural elements such as classes, methods or fields), as a technique for consistency checking of MVM with variability. To achieve the same guarantee, conventional consistency checking approaches without support for variability would have to be applied to the models of each single member of a product line which is unfeasible even in small SPL as the number of potential feature combinations can grow exponentially.

We use a representative set of UML consistency rules and a feature composition technique to illustrate how safe composition can be used for consistency checking. However, other modeling artifacts, consistency rules and composition techniques can be used. Furthermore, we define a categorization scheme of consistency rules according to the number of artifact types they use and their relation with the composition technique. This categorization enables the identification of conditions where living with inconsistencies is acceptable (and even expected) and others where inconsistencies are not tolerable. To evaluate our approach, we developed a prototype tool and applied it to a case study.

2 Running Example

SPL approaches can be broadly categorized in two main groups depending on how they express variability in software artifacts. In *integrative* approaches, artifacts contain both the common and variable parts. Building a system means keeping the variable parts of the desired features in the artifacts while removing those parts belonging to unselected features [9,13,14]. In *compositional* approaches, variable parts are encapsulated in modular units which are put together according to the features selected for building a system [15,16,17,18][1]. There are several SPL methodologies that advocate a compositional approach, some of them use multiple views [10,20,15]. To illustrate our work, in this section we describe the core concepts of the compositional approach and the example we use throughout the paper.

2.1 Feature Oriented Software Development

Feature Oriented Software Development (FOSD) provides formalisms, methods, languages and tools for building variable, customizable and extensible software [15]. FOSD has been successfully used in several case studies [21,22]. FOSD advocates modularizing *features*, increments in program functionality [23], as the systems building blocks. At the heart of FOSD is a feature algebra that drives the (de)composition of software artifacts [24,16,25,26,27]. A *feature module* contains all the software artifacts, or parts thereof, required for implementing the feature. In other words, feature modules capture the multiple views of a feature.

In FOSD features are composed hierarchically starting from the root element of the corresponding models. Elements that have the same name and type at the same hierarchical level are composed together, elements that do not have a corresponding matching

---

[1] This classification appears with different names in the literature, for example *negative* or *positive* variability respectively[19].

element are copied along hierarchically. We illustrate FOSD composition with our running example as we proceed with the explanation of safe composition in next section. For further details please consult [16,28,29].

2.2 Video on Demand Example

The running example to illustrate our work is a hypothetical product line of video on demand systems. In this systems family, a video on demand (VOD) system can record and/or play videos and can be used with either TV sets or mobile phones. Thus our SPL example contains five features: VOD, Play, Record, TV, and Mobile. In FOSD, each feature is implemented in a feature module which contains all the required software artifacts for its realization. In our example, we use UML class, sequence and state diagrams[2]. Figure 1 shows the diagrams of the five features.

The diagrams of feature VOD are shown in Figure 1(a). The class diagram consists of three classes: Service, Streamer, and Program. These classes have some methods, a navigable association going from Service to Streamer, and one from Streamer to Program. The sequence diagram illustrates a call of method select in a Service object and a call of method stream from Service to Streamer. Lastly, the state machine shows two states in which a Service object can be in. After receiving a select method call a Service object initializes its information. Similarly, after receiving a go method call it starts streaming the video, and finally when it receives a stop it goes to a final state.

Figure 1(b) shows the diagrams of feature Play. This feature has a new class Server, and an association manages with class Streamer whose association end name is handler. The sequence diagram shows a message go from Streamer to Service objects, and a message play from Service object to itself. Notice here that message go is not defined in this feature but in feature VOD. The state machine diagram shows a new state Frozen with new actions resume and pause, as defined in the class diagram of this feature. Note again that action go is not defined in this feature but in feature VOD.

Figures 1(c)-(e) show the diagrams of features Record, TV, and Mobile respectively. Note for instance in feature Record depicted in 1(c) that messages wait is not a method of class Streamer. A similar case occurs in feature TV whose message caption is not a method of its class Program.

3 Detecting Inconsistencies with Safe Composition

Safe composition is the guarantee that programs composed from multi-view feature modules according to the product line domain constraints are type safe, i.e. they do not have undefined references to structural elements such as classes, methods or fields [12]. Current research on this topic has mainly focused on source code artifacts, particularly in FOSD extensions to Java-like languages. As pointed out by Thaker et al., the principles underlying safe composition can be also applied to other artifact types. Our

---
[2] In practice, FOSD feature modules can contain any number of any artifact type (e.g. code, script files, grammars, etc.), for further details consult [15].

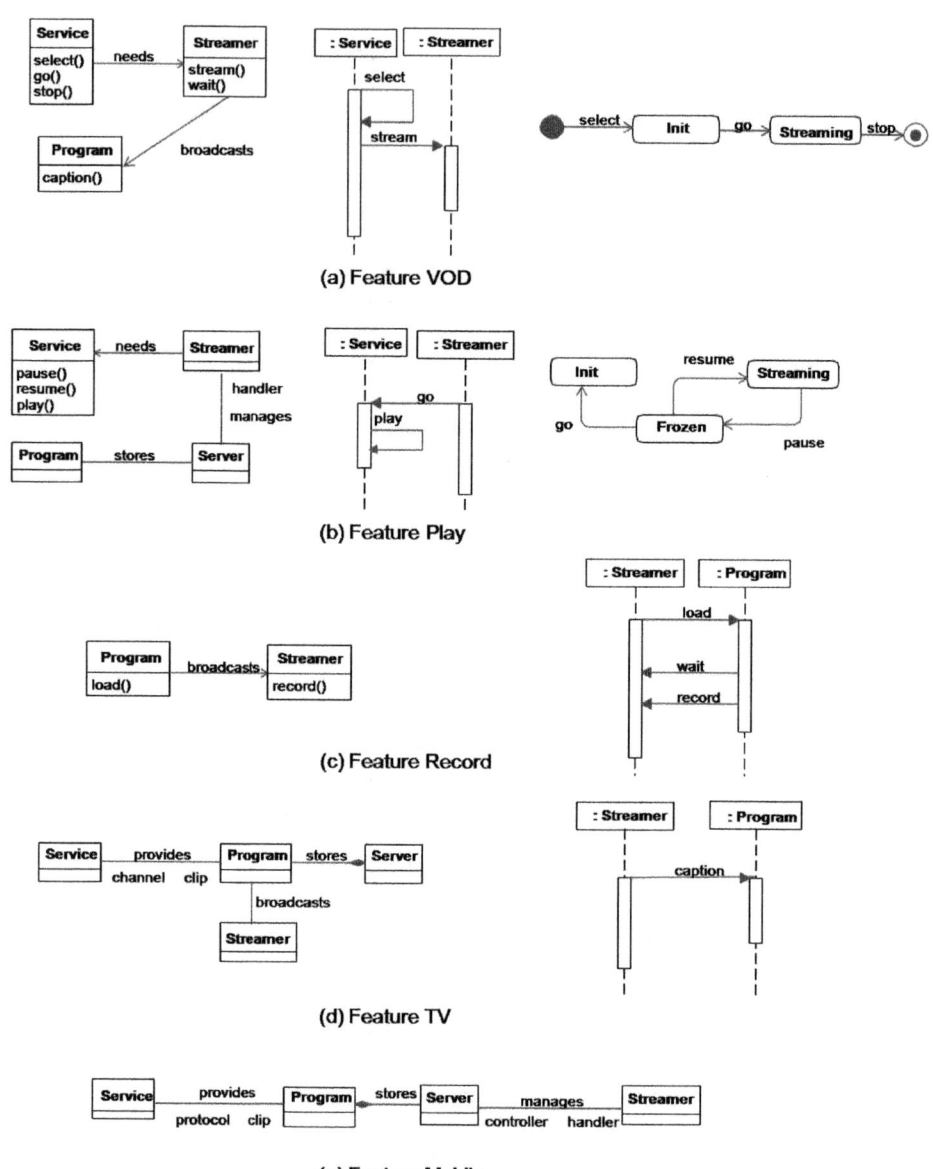

Fig. 1. Features in VOD SPL

work shows how safe composition applies to model artifacts by considering consistency rules that must be met by all composed program models. Safe composition can thus be used to detect inconsistencies not only on a single view (artifact type) but also amongst multiple views and most importantly within and across features.

3.1 Safe Composition Principles

Let us start by giving an example of an application of safe composition. Consider feature Play in Figure 1(b). In this feature, the sequence diagram shows a call to method go from Streamer to Service. Notice that this method is not defined in the class diagram of that feature. Safe composition verifies that *all* valid (according to domain constraints) combinations of features that include feature Play do also include another feature where go is defined (implementation constraints).

Safe composition is based on Czarnecki's et al. observation that implementation constraints should follow from domain constraints [30]. Let PL_f denote the domain constraints and IMP_f denote the implementation constraints of a consistency rule instance. Safe composition uses propositional logic to express and relate these two terms. Because we are interested in verifying that all members of the product line satisfy a given implementation constraint, the following formula should not be satisfiable:

$$\neg(PL_f \Rightarrow IMP_f) \qquad (1)$$

In case it is satisfiable, it would mean that there is a member of the product line that does not meet constraint IMP_f. By using a *satisfiability (SAT)* solver, the violating feature configuration(s) can be identified. This is done for each instance of each implementation constraint we want to verify. We show next how the propositional formulas of PL_f and IMP_f are obtained.

3.2 Obtaining Domain Constraints from Feature Models

Feature models are a standard way to model the common and variable features of SPL and their relationships [31,32]. In these models, features are depicted as labeled boxes and are connected to other features to form a tree. A feature can be classified as: *mandatory* if it is part of a program whenever its parent feature is also part, and *optional* if it may or may not be part of a program whenever its parent feature is part. Mandatory features are denoted with filled circles while optional features are denoted with empty circles both at the child end of the feature relations denoted with lines. Features can be grouped into: *inclusive-or* relation whereby one or more features of the group can be selected, and *exclusive-or* relation where exactly one feature can be selected. These relations are depicted as filled arcs and empty arcs respectively.

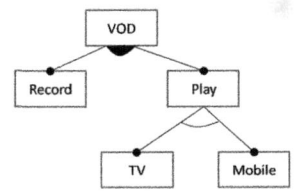

Fig. 2. Example of Feature Model

Figure 2 shows the feature model of our SPL of on-demand video recorders and players. In this hypothetical product line, the root feature VOD provides the basic functionality that the video systems offer. In FOSD, a feature in a feature model closely corresponds to a feature module. Recall that in our example SPL, a video on demand (VOD) system have features Record and Play in an inclusive-or relation, meaning that systems in this product line can: 1) record videos, 2) play videos, 3) record and play videos. Additionally, in those systems with playing capability, the systems either have television screens (TV) or screens of mobile devices (Mobile), corresponding to an exclusive-or relation.

Mapping of Feature Models to Propositional Logic. There exist extensive research on mapping feature models to propositional logic [33,34]. This mapping is summarized in Figure 3. Consider now for example the propositional formula for our model in Figure 2 shown in Equation 2. The first proposition comes from the fact that the root feature is always selected. The second proposition is the application of the inclusive-or rule for features Record and Play, while the last two propositions are the application of the exclusive-or for features TV and Mobile. Thus PL_f for our example is:

$$\begin{aligned}&(VOD \Leftrightarrow true\,)\wedge\\&(VOD \Leftrightarrow Record \vee Play\,)\wedge\\&(TV \Leftrightarrow \neg Mobile \wedge Play\,)\wedge\\&(Mobile \Leftrightarrow \neg TV \wedge Play)\end{aligned} \quad (2)$$

Name	Diagram Notation	Propositional Logic
Mandatory	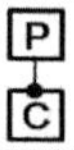 P—C	$P \Leftrightarrow C$
Optional	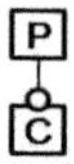 P—C	$C \Rightarrow P$
Exclusive-Or	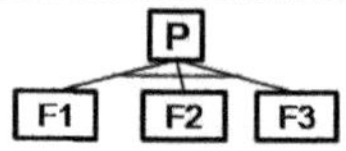 P / F1 F2 F3	$(F1 \Leftrightarrow (\neg F2 \wedge \neg F3 \wedge P)) \wedge$ $(F2 \Leftrightarrow (\neg F1 \wedge \neg F3 \wedge P)) \wedge$ $(F3 \Leftrightarrow (\neg F1 \wedge \neg F2 \wedge P))$
Inclusive-Or	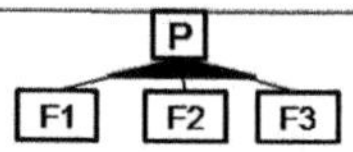 P / F1 F2 F3	$P \Leftrightarrow F1 \vee F2 \vee F3$
Requires	Cross feature arrow	$A \Rightarrow B$
Excludes	Cross feature arrow	$A \Rightarrow \neg B \equiv \neg(A \wedge B)$

Fig. 3. Mapping a feature model to propositional logic

3.3 Using Consistency Rules as Implementation Constraints

Consistency rules describe the semantic relationships that must hold amongst the different elements of the views. Consistency rules can be categorized according to the number of views they involve [35,36]:

- *Intra-view*: Exactly one view or artifact type is used by a rule.
- *Inter-view*: Multiple views or artifact types are used by a rule.

Our extension of safe composition for MVM adds another classification dimension that depends on the number of features involved:

- *Intra-feature*: Only one feature is needed to verify a constraint.
- *Inter-feature*: More than one feature are needed to verify a constraint.

It should be noted here that traditional consistency checking approaches fall into intra-feature category because they do not address variability issues in their models. Safe composition, on the other hand, allows us to extend the scope of current consistency checking approaches to address variability.

Consistency rules are usually specified as well-formedness rules [37], or emerge as standard best practices in certain domains [38,39]. In our previous work, we developed UML/Analyzer, a tool that incrementally checks consistency of UML class, sequence, and state machine diagrams. This tool checks over 30 distinct rules. For our work on safe composition, we selected seven representative structural rules from this set. Next we describe in detail each of the selected rules, their categorization, and use in safe composition with FOSD approach to model composition.

Rule 1. Method parameters should have different names. This rule specifies that in class diagrams the parameter names of methods in classes or interfaces must be unique. Clearly, this is an intra-view rule as it uses only class diagram views.

FOSD model composition. In FOSD, methods are matched based on their signature. This means that if two matching classes with two methods of different signatures are composed, then both methods are copied along to the result. In other words, FOSD does not support the addition of new parameters to methods. Thus, rule 1 is also an intra-feature rule because to validate this constraint it is only necessary to verify the feature where the method is defined. Because it is an intra-feature rule, safe composition does not apply as meeting this constraint is independent of how the feature being checked is composed. Notice however, that if a different composition approach were used that allows adding new parameters when methods are composed, then this rule would be classified as inter-feature.

Rule 2. An interface can only contain public operations. This rule specifies that the methods defined in an interface should have public visibility, i.e. accessible to any code that references it. Rule 2 can also be categorized as intra-view as it only uses class diagram views.

FOSD model composition. In FOSD, access modifiers are not composable. Thus, this rule is also an example of intra-feature rules because it is only required to verify the feature where the method is defined. Because it is an intra-feature rule, safe composition does not apply as meeting this constraint is independent of how the feature being checked is composed. Again, if a different composition approach were used that allows access modifiers to be composed, then this rule would be categorized as inter-feature.

Inter-feature Consistency Rules and Safe Composition. The properties denoted by inter-feature consistency rules make use of safe composition for two distinct purposes: 1) to assert the presence of a structural element that a feature requires, or 2) to assert the exclusion of a structural element that a feature conflicts with. We refer to these two kinds of rules as *requiring* and *conflicting* respectively.

Requiring rules. Let F be a feature that refers a model element e defined in another feature. For a system program that includes feature F, it must therefore also include at least one other feature $\texttt{Freq}_i$ where element e is defined. This is denoted in the following expression[3]:

$$IMP_f \equiv F \Rightarrow \bigvee_{i=1..k} Freq_i \qquad (3)$$

By substituting IMP_f in Equation 1, we obtain the logical expression that is passed to the SAT solver. In this case is the conjunction of all the terms of the features that define an element that feature F requires.

$$\neg(PL_f \Rightarrow IMP_f) \equiv PL_f \wedge F \bigwedge_{i=1..k} \neg Freq_i \qquad (4)$$

When feature F requires an element that is not defined in any other features, that is expression $\bigvee Freq_i$ evaluates to $\texttt{false}$, it means that such element is not defined in the entire product line. This situation is clearly an error and renders unnecessary to verify this constraint with the SAT solver.

Conflicting rules. Let F be a feature that defines a model element e. A feature $\texttt{Fconf}_i$ conflicts with feature F if it has an element d which cannot be present in the same program where element e is also present. Put in different words, because of the conflict between elements e and d, if feature F is selected as part of a system program, then feature $\texttt{Fconf}_i$ cannot be selected. The propositional logic expression is thus:

$$IMP_f \equiv F \Rightarrow \neg(\bigvee_{i=1..k} Fconf_i) \qquad (5)$$

By substituting IMP_f in Equation 1, we obtain the logical expression that needs to be passed to the SAT solver. In this case, they are k disjunctions, one for each feature F has conflicting elements with. Thus it requires k calls to the SAT solver.

$$\neg(PL_f \Rightarrow IMP_f) \equiv \bigvee_{i=1..k} (PL_f \wedge F \wedge Fconf_i) \qquad (6)$$

In the case where feature F has no conflicts with any other features, that is expression $\bigvee Fconf_i$ evaluates to $\texttt{false}$, it is thus unnecesary to evaluate this constraint for element e.

Rule 3. Association ends must have a unique name within the association. This rule specifies that for any given association the names of its ends must not be repeated.

FOSD model composition. To illustrate this rule please consider features Mobile and TV in Figure 1(e) and Figure 1(d) respectively. FOSD composition of the corresponding class diagrams dictates to compose association provides between classes

---

[3] For notational simplicity in the rest of the paper, we overload feature terms such as F or $\texttt{Freq}_i$ to mean propositional logic terms and the set of software artifacts. We make the distinctions explicit when necessary.

Service and Program because their names are the same and their types (association between Service and Program) also match. Notice however that the association end names of class Server are channel and protocol. This name mismatch violates this rule as the association end of Server has more than one name. This means that if feature TV is selected then feature Mobile cannot be selected because of this naming conflict. From this example, for FOSD composition technique, Rule 3 is then an example of intra-view and inter-feature rule.

Consider now feature Mobile Figure 1(e) feature in Play in Figure 1(b). FOSD dictates to compose association manages between Server and Streamer because their matching names and types. The association end of class Streamer is named handler on both features so no naming conflict arises on this class. The association end of class Server is named controller in feature Mobile and it is undefined in feature Play. In FOSD, the composed end name is controller. Therefore, in the composition of this association there is no conflict between features Play and Mobile.

Rule 3 is an example of a conflicting rule because of the naming conflicts in the end names. More formally, and using Equation (5), let F be a feature of the SPL that contains association assoc between classes A and B with respective association end names assoc.A_{name} and assoc.B_{name}[4]. A conflicting feature $Fconf_i$ is then defined as follows:

$Fconf_i$ contains association assoc between classes A and B,
and [(F.assoc.A_{name}≠$Fconf_i$.assoc.A_{name} ∧ F.assoc.A_{name}≠null ∧
$Fconf_i$.assoc.A_{name}≠null) ∨
(F.assoc.B_{name}≠$Fconf_i$.assoc.B_{name} ∧ F.assoc.B_{name}≠null ∧
$Fconf_i$.assoc.B_{name}≠null)]

(7)

In words, this condition establishes that two features conflict in an association if they define non-null names that are different. Applying Equation (5) to the two examples just illustrated, we have that feature Mobile conflicts with feature TV but does not conflict with feature Play. Thus in this example IMP_f ≡ Mobile⇒¬TV.

Rule 4. At most one association end may be an aggregation or composition. This rule specifies that any given association can only have either an aggregation or a composition but not both.

FOSD model composition. As an example, consider features TV and Mobile in Figure 1(d) and Figure 1(e) respectively. Both features have in their class diagrams an association stores between Program and Server. Notice however that the composition lies at different sides of the association. Thus, selecting both features together violates this rule. Clearly because this rule involves only class diagrams and two features it is and example of intra-view and inter-feature rule. Furthermore, it is a conflicting rule because the existence of an aggregation or composition in one feature excludes the existence of another aggregation or composition at another feature.

---

[4] As notational convention we use qualified names to denote containment of elements and subscripts to refer to their values.

More formally, and using Equation (5), let F be a feature of the SPL that contains association assoc between classes A and B. A conflicting feature $Fconf_i$ is then defined as follows:

$Fconf_i$ contains association assoc between classes A and B,
and $[(F.assoc_{type}=$aggregation $\vee F.assoc_{type}=$composition $) \wedge$ (8)
$(Fconf_i.assoc_{type}=$aggregation $\vee Fconf_i.assoc_{type}=$composition $)]$

In words, this condition establishes that two features conflict if an association defines either an aggregation or composition in feature F and on the same association but in feature $Fconf_i$ there is either an aggregation or a composition. Applying Equation (5) give us $IMP_f \equiv$ Mobile$\Rightarrow \neg$TV.

Rule 5. Message action must be defined as an operation in receiver's class. This rule specifies that in a sequence diagram a message action should have a corresponding operation defined in the class diagram of the message receiver's class.

FOSD model composition. As an example for this rule, the sequence diagram of feature Play in Figure 1(b) refers to method go but feature Play does not define it in its class diagram. Thus, every time that feature Play is selected, another feature that defines method go must also be selected. In this example, the class diagram of feature VOD in Figure 1(a) provides such definition and can thus be selected when feature Play is selected. This rule is then an inter-feature rule, and because it involves class diagrams and sequence diagrams an inter-view rule. Furthermore, it is a requiring rule because the existence of a message action demands the existence of a method that defines it in the target class.

More formally, and using Equation (3), Let F be a feature of the SPL that contains message action msg with receiver's class Cls. A requiring feature $Freq_i$ is then defined as follows:

$Freq_i$ contains method msg in class Cls in a class diagram (9)

In words, this condition establishes that a feature whose sequence diagram references a method requires the definition of that method in the class diagram of another feature. Applying Equation (3) thus give us $IMP_f \equiv$ Play$\Rightarrow$VOD.

Rule 6. State machine action must be defined as an operation in owner's class
This rule specifies that in a state machine associated to a class the actions should be operations defined in the class diagram of such class.

FOSD model composition. This rule is similar to Rule 5. Consider now the state machine diagram of feature Play in Figure 1(b) that has transition method go, but again it is not defined in the class diagram of this feature. Thus, whenever feature Play is selected there must be another feature where method go is defined. As we have seen, this method is defined in feature VOD in Figure 1(a). Because this rule involves class and state machine diagrams in more that one feature, it is an example of inter-view and inter-feature rule. Furthermore, it is a requiring rule because the existence of an action in a state machine diagram requires its definition in another feature's class diagram.

More formally, and using Equation (3), Let F be a feature of the SPL that contains a state machine action msg. Let F be a feature module of the SPL that has transition method msg in state machine of class Cls. A requiring feature Freq_i is then defined as follows:

$$\text{Freq}_i \text{ contains method msg defined in class Cls} \tag{10}$$

In words, this condition establishes that a feature that has a state machine diagram that references a method requires the definition of that method in the class diagram of another feature. Applying Equation (3) thus give us $\text{IMP}_f \equiv \text{Play} \Rightarrow \text{VOD}$.

Rule 7. Calling direction of message must match calling direction of association
This rule specifies that if a sequence diagram has a message going from an object of class A to an object of class B then in the class diagram the relationship between both classes should be navigable in that direction.

FOSD model composition. As an example of this rule, consider feature Record in Figure 1(c) that has message load from Streamer to Program. Notice however that in this feature the direction of the association between these two classes is the opposite. Therefore, if feature Record is included there must be another feature that defines a navigable association from Streamer to Program, in our case feature VOD in Figure 1(a). Because this rule involves sequence and class diagrams on multiple feature it is an example of inter-view and inter-feature rule. This rule is requiring because the existence of a message in the sequence diagram demands the existence of an association navigable in the direction of the message in a class diagram.

More formally, and using Equation (3), Let F be a feature of the SPL that contains a message going from an object of class Src to an object of class Tgt. A requiring feature Freq_i is then defined as follows:

$$\text{Freq}_i \text{ contains navigable association from class Src to class Tgt} \tag{11}$$

Applying Equation (3) thus give us $\text{IMP}_f \equiv \text{Record} \Rightarrow \text{VOD}$.

3.4 Analysis

This section summarizes the main insights gained with our application of safe composition for MVM consistency checking.

Safe composition granularity. Table 1 shows the classification of our rules along the two dimensions. Rule 1 and Rule 2 highlight the fact that not all consistency rules are applicable to safe composition. The distinctive characteristic of both rules is that their level of granularity, method parameter names for Rule 1 and access modifiers for Rule 2, falls below the granularity level of FOSD composition. In other words, FOSD composes elements such as methods or classes (coarser granularity) but not their nested elements (finer granularity). This observation is summarized in the following principle:

> *Principle of Safe Composition Granularity: Safe composition is applicable to consistency rules that operate at the granularity level supported by the model composition mechanism.*

Table 1. Classification of consistency rules

	Intra-view	Inter-view
Intra-feature	Rule 1 Rule 2	
Inter-feature	Rule 3 Rule 4	Rule 5 Rule 6 Rule 7

Tolerable and intolerable inconsistencies. Our categorization of consistency rules along two dimensions allows us to further distinguish two types of inconsistencies from a compositional perspective. We call *intolerable* inconsistencies those that arise from violations to rules that are both intra-view and intra-feature because they render features unfit for composition. On the other hand, we call *tolerable* those inconsistencies arising from violations to inter-feature rules because it is expected that they be fixed by composition with other features. Finally, it should be noted that in the sample of consistency rules we analyzed there was no rule categorized as inter-view and intra-feature. In the case of FOSD, this follows in part from the fact that feature composition can add elements to any views.

Multi-feature consistency rules. The inter-feature rules we presented involved only two features. Our consistency checking tool UML/Analyzer uses 34 consistency rules, out of those there are only two rules that can involve more than two features. One of such rules checks that circular inheritance does not occur. A solution would be along the lines proposed by Thaker et al. that would collect the inheritance information by succesively composing all features and relying on the monotonicity of the composition detect the circular references [12]. The implementation of this alternative and its evaluation are part of our future work.

More expressive formal representation and automated rule generation. Currently, our rules have been manually implemented following their OCL description in relation to the FOSD approach for model composition. However, we believe that some (if not all) the implementation could be generated directly from formal rule specifications and the underlying semantics used for model composition. This is a topic of our future research.

3.5 Evaluation

We used the *Graph Product Line (GPL)* [40] as case study for our approach. The features of this product line are basic graph algorithms and data structures. A GPL program is a combination of different algorithms implemented on different data structures. There are implementations of GPL available in several programming languages. The models used in our study were manually drawn in the Eclipse UML editor from a Java version of GPL.

We implemented a prototype tool that uses EMF to parse and gather information from the EMF models [41], and PicoSAT SAT solver to test for satisfiability [42].

Despite of being a short example, we found a total of 298 distinct instances of consistencies rules. When mapped to propositional logic, the FODA model of GPL consists of 22 domain constraints: 5 mandatory, 2 optional, 2 exclusive-or, 1 inclusive-or, 1 excludes, and 11 requires. These domain constraints amounted to 39 propositional clauses when normalized to CNF for use by PicoSAT.

Our experiments showed that the time taken to evaluate consistency rule instances by the SAT solver was negligible (in the magnitud of nanoseconds when run on an Intel Core-Duo at 2.8 GHz) as the number of clauses involved and the number of variables (one for each of the nineteen features) are of relatively small size for what SAT solvers such as PicoSAT can effectively handle. Though encouraging results, the scalability and performance of our approach needs to be more extensively validated with more complex examples of SPL that contain larger models on which to validate more consistency rules instances. Doing that is part of our future work.

4 Related Work

There is a significant amount of related literature. We focus on the research that most closely relates to our work and divide them in three categories.

FOSD Model Composition. Our previous work has shown the applicability of an algebraic representation to describe model composition in *use case slices*, an Aspect-Oriented modeling techniques based on UML diagrams [43], when used for SPL modeling [44]. Work by Umapathy developed basic composition of UML diagrams using XAK, a FOSD composer of XML-based artifacts [45]. Our recent work has shown the applicability of rewriting technologies for composing UML class diagrams exploiting the native support of algebraic properties of operators in Maude [28]. Work by Apel et al. uses superimposition to compose simple UML diagrams that are treated as trees [29]. These technologies are different alternatives to support model composition for FOSD.

Models and Software Product Lines. Product Line UML-based Software engineering (PLUS) [9] is a method that brings FODA ideas to UML. PLUS uses features throughout the entire product line development process, however their boundaries are lost in the model diagrams. In other words, most of the diagrams in this approach show elements that either belong to all the product line or to those of a particular product configuration (i.e. a selected set of features). This is an example of the integrative approach to variability management. Jayaraman and Whittle have developed a compositional approach to PLUS whereby models are modularized in *feature slices*, collections of fragments of UML diagrams, that are composed via graph transformations [10]. To the best of our knowledge their work does not make any provisions for consistency checking of the composed feature slices.

Safe Composition and Well-formedness. Work by Czarnecki et. al uses OCL constraints to specify and verify well-formedness in model templates. In contrast to our work, this is an integrative approach for variability modeling [30]. Work by Kästner et al. follows an integrative approach whereby program elements are annotated with distinct colors to visually indicate the features they belong to [46]. It enforces two simple structural rules to guarantee syntactic correctness of the programs derived.

5 Conclusions and Future Work

In this paper we showed how safe composition principles can be applied for MVM consistency checking in the context of SPL. We used a representative set of UML consistency rules as illustration of our approach. These rules were categorized according to the number of views and their relation to feature composition. Though our work is presented in the context of UML and FOSD, our results can be mapped to other modeling artifacts, constraints, and composition approaches.

We implemented a prototype tool and used it in a case study to evaluate the feasibility of our approach. Performance and scalability were not an issue for this case study. However, these aspects need further assessment with larger and more complex product lines as well as considering more consistency rules. Such an assessment is part of our future work. FOSD composition has been defined as a monotonic operation. Recent work by Kuhlemann relaxes this requirement to consider non-monotonic composition [47]. We plan to investigate alternatives for non-monotonic model composition along the lines of this work. SAT solvers are just one technology used for consistency checking. Because of the incremental nature of feature composition, we will explore the applicability of incremental consistency approaches, like UMLAnalyzer[38,39], to safe composition.

Acknowledgments. We thank Alexander Nöhrer for his help with PicoSAT solver, Leticia Montalvillo for drawing the diagrams used in the case study, and Maider Azanza for her reviews of early drafts. This research was partially funded by the Austrian FWF under agreement P21321-N15 and Marie Curie Actions - Intra-European Fellowship (IEF) project number 254965.

References

1. Finkelstein, A., Kramer, J., Nuseibeh, B., Finkelstein, L., Goedicke, M.: Viewpoints: A framework for integrating multiple perspectives in system development. International Journal of Software Engineering and Knowledge Engineering 2(1), 31–57 (1992)
2. Nuseibeh, B., Kramer, J., Finkelstein, A.: A framework for expressing the relationships between multiple views in requirements specification. IEEE Trans. Software Eng. 20(10), 760–773 (1994)
3. Finkelstein, A., Gabbay, D.M., Hunter, A., Kramer, J., Nuseibeh, B.: Inconsistency handling in multperspective specifications. IEEE Trans. Software Eng. 20(8), 569–578 (1994)
4. Svahnberg, M., van Gurp, J., Bosch, J.: A taxonomy of variability realization techniques. Softw., Pract. Exper. 35(8), 705–754 (2005)
5. Batory, D., Sarvela, J.N., Rauschmayer, A.: Scaling Step-Wise Refinement. IEEE TSE 30(6) (2004)
6. Clements, P., Northrop, L.: Software Product Lines: Practices and Patterns. Addison-Wesley, Reading (2002)
7. Pohl, K., Bockle, G., van der Linden, F.J.: Software Product Line Engineering: Foundations, Principles and Techniques. Springer, Heidelberg (2005)
8. van d Linden, F.J., Schimd, K., Rommes, E.: Software Product Lines in Action: The Best Industrial Practice in Product Line Engineering. Springer, Heidelberg (2007)
9. Gomaa, H.: Designing Software Product Lines with UML. In: From Use Cases to Pattern-Based Software Architectures, Addison-Wesley, Reading (2004)

10. Jayaraman, P., Whittle, J., Elkhodary, A., Gomaa, H.: Model Composition in Product Lines and Feature Interaction Detection Using Critical Pair Analysis. In: Engels, G., Opdyke, B., Schmidt, D.C., Weil, F. (eds.) MODELS 2007. LNCS, vol. 4735, pp. 151–165. Springer, Heidelberg (2007)
11. Käkölä, T., Dueñas, J.C. (eds.): Software Product Lines - Research Issues in Engineering and Management. Springer, Heidelberg (2006)
12. Thaker, S., Batory, D.S., Kitchin, D., Cook, W.R.: Safe composition of product lines. In: Consel, C., Lawall, J.L. (eds.) GPCE, pp. 95–104. ACM, New York (2007)
13. Gomaa, H., Olimpiew, E.M.: Managing variability in reusable requirement models for software product lines. In: Mei, H. (ed.) ICSR 2008. LNCS, vol. 5030, pp. 182–185. Springer, Heidelberg (2008)
14. Zhang, H., Jarzabek, S.: Xvcl: a mechanism for handling variants in software product lines. Sci. Comput. Program.(Hongyu Zhang and Stanislaw Jarzabek) 53(3), 381–407
15. Batory, D.: AHEAD Tool Suite (2008), http://www.cs.utexas.edu/users/schwartz/ATS.html
16. Batory, D.S., Sarvela, J.N., Rauschmayer, A.: Scaling step-wise refinement. IEEE Trans. Software Eng. 30(6), 355–371 (2004)
17. Mezini, M., Ostermann, K.: Variability management with feature-oriented programming and aspects. In: Taylor, R.N., Dwyer, M.B. (eds.) SIGSOFT FSE, pp. 127–136. ACM, New York (2004)
18. Groher, I., Völter, M.: Using aspects to model product line variability. In: Thiel, S., Pohl, K. (eds.) SPLC (2), Lero Int. Science Centre, University of Limerick, Ireland, pp. 89–95 (2008)
19. Groher, I., Völter, M.: Aspect-oriented model-driven software product line engineering. T. Aspect-Oriented Software Development VI 6, 111–152 (2009)
20. Clarke, S., Baniassad, E.: Aspect-Oriented Analysis and Design. In: The Theme Approach. Addison-Wesley, Reading (2005)
21. Trujillo, S., Batory, D., Diaz, O.: Feature Oriented Model Driven Development: A Case Study for Portlets. In: ICSE (2007)
22. Batory, D., O'Malley, S.: The Design and Implementation of Hierarchical Software Systems with Reusable Components. ACM Transactions on Software Engineering and Methodology (TOSEM) 1(4), 355–398 (1992)
23. Zave, P.: Faq sheet on feature interaction, http://www.research.att.com/~pamela/faq.html
24. Lopez-Herrejon, R.E.: Understanding Feature Modularity. PhD thesis, Department of Computer Sciences, The University of Texas at Austin (2006)
25. Batory, D.S., Lopez-Herrejon, R.E., Martin, J.P.: Generating product-lines of product-families. In: ASE, pp. 81–92. IEEE Computer Society, Los Alamitos (2002)
26. Lopez-Herrejon, R.E., Batory, D.S., Lengauer, C.: A disciplined approach to aspect composition. In: Hatcliff, J., Tip, F. (eds.) PEPM, pp. 68–77. ACM, New York (2006)
27. Batory, D.S.: Using modern mathematics as an fosd modeling language. In: Smaragdakis, Y., Siek, J.G. (eds.) GPCE, pp. 35–44. ACM, New York (2008)
28. Lopez-Herrejon, R.E., Rivera, J.E.: Realizing feature oriented software development with equational logic: An exploratory study. In: Vallecillo, A., Sagardui, G. (eds.) JISBD, pp. 269–274 (2009)
29. Apel, S., Janda, F., Trujillo, S., Kästner, C.: Model superimposition in software product lines. In: Paige, R.F. (ed.) ICMT 2009. LNCS, vol. 5563, pp. 4–19. Springer, Heidelberg (2009)
30. Czarnecki, K., Pietroszek, K.: Verifying feature-based model templates against well-formedness ocl constraints. In: Jarzabek, S., Schmidt, D.C., Veldhuizen, T.L. (eds.) GPCE, pp. 211–220. ACM, New York (2006)
31. Czarnecki, K., Eisenecker, U.: Generative Programming: Methods, Tools, and Applications. Addison-Wesley, Reading (2000)

32. Kang, K., Cohen, S., Hess, J., Novak, W., Peterson, A.: Feature-Oriented Domain Analysis (FODA) Feasibility Study. Technical Report CMU/SEI-90-TR-21, Software Engineering Institute, Carnegie Mellon University (1990)
33. Benavides, D., Segura, S., Trinidad, P., Cortés, A.R.: Fama: Tooling a framework for the automated analysis of feature models. In: Pohl, K., Heymans, P., Kang, K.C., Metzger, A., eds.: VaMoS. Volume 2007-01 of Lero Technical Report, pp. 129–134 (2007)
34. Batory, D.: Feature Models, Grammars, and Propositional Formulas. In: Proceedings of the International Software Product Line Conference (SPLC), pp. 7–20 (2005)
35. Lucas, F.J., Molina, F., Álvarez, J.A.T.: A systematic review of uml model consistency management. Information & Software Technology 51(12), 1631–1645 (2009)
36. Usman, M., Nadeem, A., Kim, T.H., Cho, E.S.: A survey of consistency checking techniques for uml models. In: Advanced Software Engineering and Its Applications. ASEA 2008, pp. 57–62 (2008)
37. OMG: Uml infrastructure specification v2.2 (2009)
38. Egyed, A.: Fixing inconsistencies in uml design models. In: ICSE 2007: Proceedings of the 29th International Conference on Software Engineering, Washington, DC, USA, pp. 292–301. IEEE Computer Society, Los Alamitos (2007)
39. Egyed, A., Letier, E., Finkelstein, A.: Generating and evaluating choices for fixing inconsistencies in uml design models. In: ASE, pp. 99–108. IEEE, Los Alamitos (2008)
40. Lopez-Herrejon, R.E., Batory, D.S.: A standard problem for evaluating product-line methodologies. In: Bosch, J. (ed.) GCSE 2001. LNCS, vol. 2186, pp. 10–24. Springer, Heidelberg (2001)
41. Steinberg, D., Budinsky, F., Paternostro, M., Merks, E.: EMF: Eclipse Modeling Framework, 2nd edn. Addison-Wesley Professional, Reading (2008)
42. Biere, A.: Picosat, http://fmv.jku.at/picosat/
43. Jacobson, I., Ng, P.: Aspect-Oriented Software Development with Use Cases. Addison-Wesley, Reading (2004)
44. Lopez-Herrejon, R., Batory, D.: Modeling Features in Aspect-Based Product Lines with Use Case Slices: An Exploratory Case Study. In: Workshops and Symposia at MoDELS (2006)
45. Umapathy, S.: Extension of UML models to Support Feature Modularization of Software Product Lines. Master's thesis, Computing Laboratory, University of Oxford (2007)
46. Kästner, C., Apel, S., Trujillo, S., Kuhlemann, M., Batory, D.S.: Guaranteeing syntactic correctness for all product line variants: A language-independent approach. In: Oriol, M., Meyer, B. (eds.) TOOLS (47). Lecture Notes in Business Information Processing, vol. 33, pp. 175–194. Springer, Heidelberg (2009)
47. Kuhlemann, M., Batory, D.S., Kästner, C.: Safe composition of non-monotonic features. In: Siek, J.G. (ed.) GPCE, pp. 177–186. ACM, New York (2009)

A Model-Based Method for Evaluating Embedded System Performance by Abstraction of Execution Traces

Kouichi Ono[1], Manabu Toyota[2], Ryo Kawahara[1], Yoshifumi Sakamoto[2], Takeo Nakada[1], and Naoaki Fukuoka[3]

[1] IBM Research - Tokyo, 1623-14 Shimotsuruma,
Yamato-shi, Kanagawa, 242-8502 Japan
[2] Component Technology Solution, IBM Japan, Ltd.,
338 Enpukuji-cho, Nakagyou-ku, Kyoto, 604-8175 Japan
{onono,mtoyota,ryokawa,sakay,nakada}@jp.ibm.com
[3] Tokyo R&D Center, KYOCERA MITA Corp., 2-14-9 Tamagawadai,
Setagaya-ku, Tokyo, 158-8610 Japan
naoaki_fukuoka@kyoceramita.co.jp

Abstract. This paper describes a model-based method to evaluate performance of embedded systems. The core technology of this modeling method is reverse modeling based on dynamic analysis of the existing systems. A case study of real MFPs (multifunction peripherals/printers) is presented in this paper to evaluate the modeling method.

1 Introduction

Multi-core architectures have become the focus of boosting our hardware capabilities. However, most of legacy embedded software works on a single-core processor. This makes product development for multi-core architectures using legacy software difficult. In general, it is necessary to decide the system architecture in the early stages of product development to achieve the required performance.

System-level simulations based on models are good solutions for performance estimation in the early stage of product development. UML is widely applied to model a large variety of application software. Nowadays, it is generally recognized that embedded and real-time systems are good target for UML 2.0 and later version (UML 2.x) [1] [2].

This paper proposes an UML 2.x modeling method for performance evaluation of system-level design by reverse modeling of legacy embedded systems. The reverse modeling method in this paper is a reverse engineering for creating abstract behavioral features of models using dynamic analysis of the existing systems. This paper focuses on the architectural design of system components, and the performance optimization of component design is not the scope. Related work is mentioned in Section 2. An overview of our work appears in Section 3. The reverse modeling method is described in Section 4. Section 5 presents a case study applying this method to a real MFP (multifunction peripheral/printer). Section 6 presents an evaluation of this method by comparing the performance estimation results of models with the performance of a real MFP prototype. Finally, Section 7 concludes this paper.

2 Related Work

Reverse engineering is important because most of modeling opportunities target the legacy embedded systems. In general, reverse modeling is a sort of reverse engineering for creating models of the legacy systems. Our method assumes that system development starts from analysis of legacy systems. And, the objective of our method is to decide the system architecture by considering the system performance. Therefore, our method needs to create an abstract model that represents the system architecture.

Riva and Rodriguez proposed a reverse engineering technique for architecture reconstruction by combining static and dynamic information views [3]. They developed a MSC (Message Sequence Charts) visualization tool for the dynamic information view, and two types of abstractions was supported on the tool. Horizontal abstraction lumps instance A and B in a MSC (lifelines in a sequence diagram of UML 2.x) as an instance AB and messages between A and B are suppressed from the view. Vertical abstraction packs a number of messages into a message where those messages are consecutive in chronological order. Our method integrates a number of messages (interactions in a sequence diagram of UML 2.x), however our method differs from the vertical abstraction since our method does not require that the messages are consecutive in chronological order. Our method merges messages with low weights into a message with a high weight, and it is not needed that the merged messages with low weights are consecutive.

3 Modeling Method and Simulation

An overview of our model-based performance evaluation method is shown in Fig. 1. The method starts by capturing the execution traces of the target embedded system's behaviors with a system observation technology [4]. This technology injects small code fragments into the source code which output function IDs and optional data to the system interface. The functions to be injected are specified in a pre-defined list before the target system build. The invocation information of the specified functions will be captured by a dedicated probe, and be recorded with their timestamps and the values of specified parameters. Those code fragments for system observation are low-intrusive since they output small size of data for function IDs basically. It was 0.23% of the total system performance at the case study reported in this paper. Note that the reverse modeling method does not depend on the system observation technology.

The target execution traces are eliminated by the method proposed in this paper. And, sequence diagrams in UML are created by combining dynamic analysis

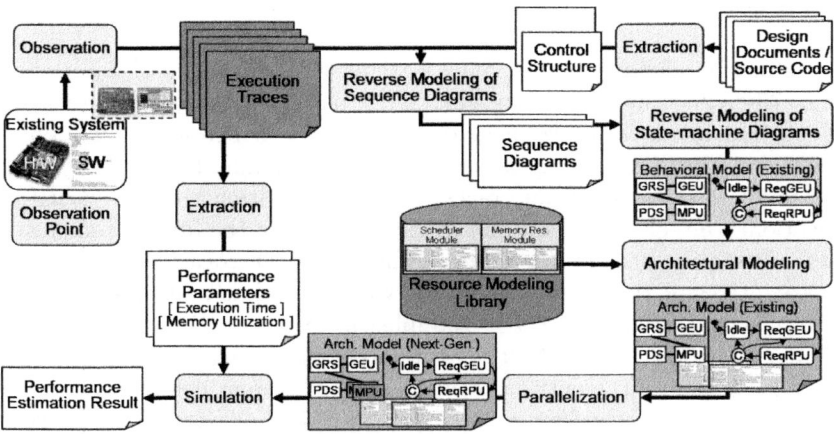

Fig. 1. Overview of Model-based Performance Evaluation

of the eliminated execution traces and static analysis of documents and code. And then state machine diagrams are created from the sequence diagrams. After that, the model is modified to represent the architectural changes that denotes parallelization to improve the system performance for the next-generation products. At the same time, performance information is extracted by analyzing the execution traces to be externalized as files, and used when the model is executed to simulate the system performance. This means that the model simulation is a sort of trace-driven simulation [5].

This paper is focusing on the reverse modeling method, which is the key technology of our work. The reverse modeling method involves the modeling using dynamic analysis, which creates a model from the execution traces captured while observing the behaviors of the legacy embedded system. There are two reasons why the reverse modeling method is defined as a method using dynamic analysis. The first reason is the accuracy of the system behaviors. Static analysis can extract precise information from the source code. However, several aspects of dynamic characteristics make accurate analysis difficult. These include data dependencies, pointers to functions, and others. Dynamic analysis using execution traces can elucidate the performance of software components.

The second reason is abstraction. The complexity of model must be reduced by abstraction of behaviors. To abstract the behaviors, it is crucial to analyze the execution traces from an appropriate viewpoint. Unimportant information for the behaviors as seen from the selected viewpoint should be eliminated in the generated model. Since our method assumes the model is used for the performance estimation by its simulation, our concern is performance. For the dynamic analysis, execution traces can be abstracted when the execution traces include performance information, such as execution times, resource utilization, and so on. However, in the static analysis, source code cannot be abstracted to reveal the performance because performance information is not included in the source code and the performance cannot be predicted without execution.

4 Reverse Modeling of Behavior

The reverse modeling creates behavioral features of a model from execution traces. The execution traces are abstracted based on the performance, so that unimportant invocations are merged to important invocations. The importance of each function invocations is calculated as a weight from the performance information in the execution traces, such as execution time of each function invocation. The selection based on the importance of the function invocations is called *abstraction of execution traces*. The selected invocations are regarded as representatives of the system behavior, which are dominant about the system performance on the behavior. For example, the execution time of each invocation can be used as the weight. And the total execution time of selected invocations is a large portion of the entire execution time of system behavior.

The outlook of *abstraction of execution traces* is shown in Fig. 2. An execution trace includes entries and exits for function invocations, timestamps, and other performance information (such as memory utilization). The performance information is used as weights for the abstraction. The abstraction is based on the premise that objects are identified prior to the abstraction and every function belongs to either one of the identified objects respectively. In Fig. 2, objects V, W, X, Y, and Z have been identified, and functions A and B belong to the object V, functions D and F belong to the object W, functions E, G, L, and M belong to the object X, functions H, N, and O belong to the object Y, and functions I, J, K, and P belong to the object Z. When the execution trace is transformed into a sequence diagram without abstraction, it produces the complicated sequence diagram on the left side of Fig. 2. In the reverse modeling, the execution trace is transformed into an object call tree. Every node denotes a function invocation. With the object call tree, every function invocation is distinguished as an internal interaction within an object or as an interaction between objects. Note that the same function name will appear more than once in the object call tree.

An object call tree T is defined as

$$T = (N, s), \qquad (1)$$

where N is a set of nodes that denote function invocations, and s is a mapping from the node to a sequence of nodes that denotes a list of function invocations called from inside the invocation. The mapping s is defined as a partial function:

$$s : N \longmapsto \mathbf{seq}\, N, \qquad (2)$$

where $\mathbf{seq}\, N$ is a set of sequences of zero of more elements in the set N. The sequence $s(n)$ is a list of sub-nodes of a node n in the object call tree.

Also, a mapping from the function invocation to object o is defined as a total function:

$$o : N \longrightarrow O, \qquad (3)$$

where O is a set of identified objects. The object $o(n)$ is an object where the function invocation n belongs.

A Model-Based Method for Evaluating Embedded System Performance 237

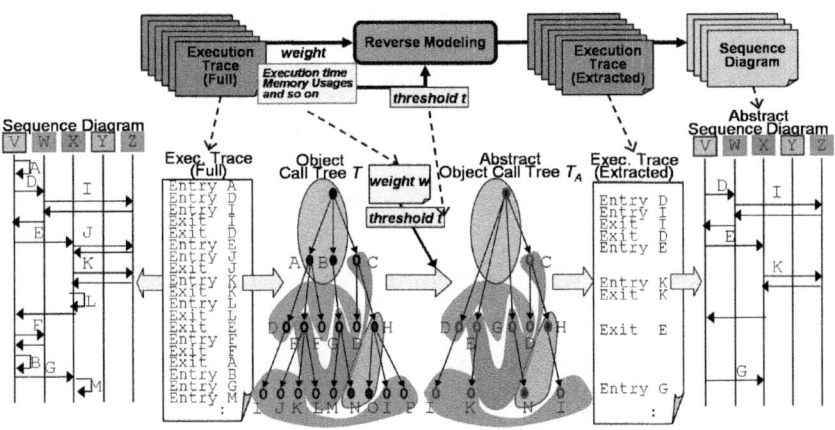

Fig. 2. Abstraction of Execution Traces

Suppose that the weight of the function invocations w is given, which is a mapping from function invocations N to the weight W. The mapping w is defined as a total function as follows.

$$w : N \longrightarrow W \qquad (4)$$

The mapping w must satisfy an invariant such that

$$\forall n \in N \left[w(n) \geq \sum_{i=1}^{\#s(n)} w(s(n)[i]) \right], \qquad (5)$$

where $\#s(n)$ is the length of sequence $s(n)$ and $s(n)[i]$ is an element as position i in the sequence $s(n)$.

The execution time of function invocation satisfies the invariant because the execution time of every function invocation equals the total amount of execution time of the sub-function invocations. Therefore, the execution time can be used as the weight mapping w. Alternatively, the amount of the datagram received from or sent to the network or bus during the function invocation, and the amount of memory allocated during the function invocation can be used as w. The weight mapping w is defined based on performance information considered in the system analysis stage.

An abstract object call tree T_A is defined as

$$T_A = (N_A, s_A), \quad N_A \subseteq N, \quad s_A : N_A \longmapsto \mathbf{seq}\, N_A, \qquad (6)$$

where the node sequence $s_A(n)$ denotes a sequence of node children as function invocations within the function of node n in T_A. In additions, N_A and s_A must satisfy the relationship:

$$\forall n \in N_A,\ \forall i \in \mathbb{N}$$
$$[\ 1 \leq i \leq \#s_A(n) \to r(n, s_A(n)[i], s, o(n), o(s_A(n)[i]))\ ], \qquad (7)$$

where $\mathbb{N}$ is the set of natural numbers. And the reachability predicate $r(m, n, s, o_m, o_n)$ means that it is reachable from the node m to n through the intermediate nodes which belong to o_m or o_n and are calculated by s. The definition of r follows.

$$r(m, n, s, o_m, o_n) \equiv$$
$$o(m) = o_m \wedge [\ m = n \wedge o(n) = o_n \vee m \neq n \wedge rs(m, n, s, o_m, o_n)\ ] \quad (8)$$
$$rs(m, n, s, o_m, o_n) \equiv$$
$$\exists i \in \mathbb{N}, k \in N\ [\quad 1 \leq i \leq \#s(m) \wedge k = s(m)[i]$$
$$\wedge\ (o(k) = o_m \vee o(k) = o_n) \wedge\ r(k, n, s, o(k), o_n)\ ] \quad (9)$$

Suppose that the threshold t is given as a real number in the closed interval $[0, 1]$. And N_A and s_A must satisfy the following relationship to t:

$$\forall n \in N_A \left[\sum_{i=1}^{\#s_A(n)} w(s_A(n)[i]) \geq t * w(n) \right] \quad (10)$$

The object call tree T and the abstract object call tree T_A is shown at the middle in Fig. 2. The difference between T and T_A is the elimination of some nodes whose weights are not dominant to the total amount. The node which is not dominant on performance is eliminated in two ways. The first one is simplification of nodes in an object, which is related to Equation 7. In Fig. 2, the root node invokes the node A and A invokes the node D. Both the root node and A belong to the same object V, and the node D belongs to the object W. In short, the node A is an intermediate node on the interaction between the object V and W, i.e. V interacts with W via the invocation of A. The reverse modeling method suppresses the intermediate nodes by merging them into the ancestor node which is the representative node of the object interactions.

The second one is condensation of leaf nodes, which is related to Equation 10. In Fig. 2, the node E invokes the node J, K and L. The node E and L belong to the same object X, and the node L is simplified and merged to E by the first elimination way described above. The remaining node J and K are leaf nodes and they belong to the object Z which differs from X. It represents that there are object interaction between X and Z. It is supposed that the weight of K invoked from E is high but the weight of J invoked from E is low. The method condenses the leaf nodes with low weights where nodes with high weight exist in the same object of the leaf nodes, by merging them into the ancestor node which is the representative node of the object interactions. Threshold is used for deciding whether the leaf node with low weight to be condensed.

In both node elimination ways, the ancestor node acts over the eliminated nodes. It means that the *abstraction* substitutes the ancestor nodes for the eliminated nodes as the representatives in the system behavior. Note that the node elimination does not remove the eliminated nodes, but merges them to the ancestor nodes for simplifying the behavioral representation.

After the abstract object call tree is created, the execution trace is extracted by filtering with the nodes N_A, then the extracted execution trace is transformed into the abstract sequence diagram shown at the right hand side in Fig. 2. State machine diagrams of the identified objects can be created from the abstract sequence diagram by existing model transformation technologies [6].

5 Case Study - MFP Print Job Processing

A case study about applying this method to a real MFP is presented in this section. And the results of model simulation about performance improvement by parallel processing is also presented. The print job processing component is significant one of MFP components. Fig. 3 is overview of MFP print job processing. A print job is processed with two steps, the former one is the translation of the print job in a PDL (Printer Description Language) into the intermediate primitive commands, the latter one is the rasterization of the intermediate primitive commands to create a logical print page. The intermediate primitive command mechanism is broadly used by the most of printers and MFPs. We have named the intermediate primitive commands as *"Image List (IL)"*, so the former step is IL generation step and the latter step is IL processing step.

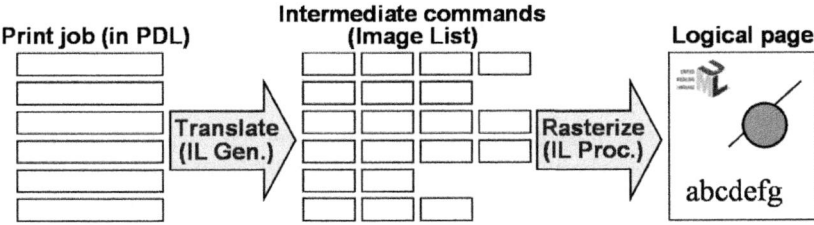

Fig. 3. Overview of MFP Print Job Processing

At first, the behavior of existing product is captured as an execution trace by the observation technology. An execution trace sample is shown at the left side in Fig. 4, which is mainly of IL processing step. The execution trace is converted to the function call tree T_f, and the performance parameters are extracted from the trace shown at the right side in Fig. 4. The nodes in T_f with digits ("14", "15" and "31") and the mark "*" denotes iterative invocations, the digits are the numbers of iterations, and the mark "*" means lots of iterations.

An object call tree T is created from the function call tree T_f by object identification. For the reverse modeling, it is necessary to identify objects by grouping functions or classes of the source code. Since the system-level behavior should be considered as interactions of coarse-grained objects, "modules" specified in the design documents are suitable as the objects at this case.

The object call tree T created from the function call tree T_f is shown at the left side in Fig. 5. The tree T has 15,340 nodes. Since the tree T is large, its sequence diagram must be complicated. Fig. 5 shows the elimination of the tree T by *abstraction* argued in Section 4, in order to create an abstract object

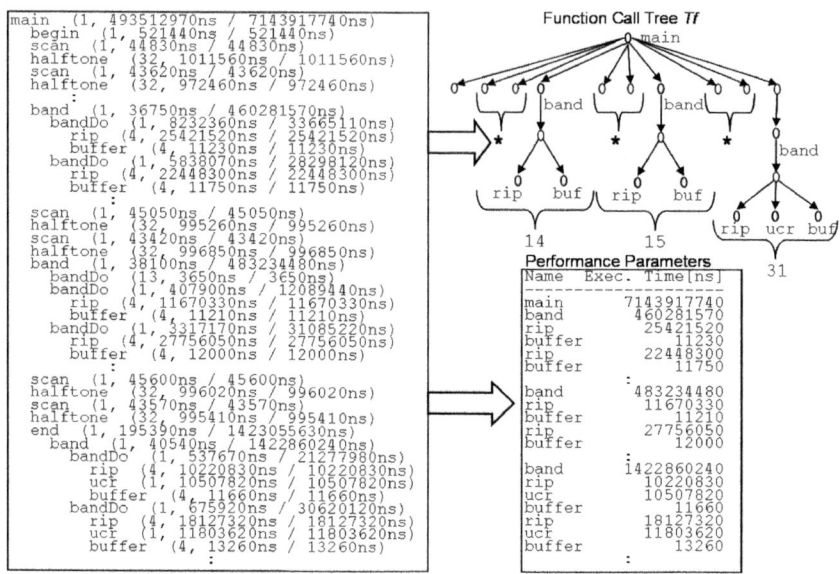

Fig. 4. An Execution Trace of Print Job Processing (as Function Call Tree and Extracted Performance Parameters)

call tree T_A. At the *abstraction* of this case, the execution time of function invocation is used as the weight, and the threshold t given as 0.95 (95%). The nodes with the mark "*" have very short execution times, therefore, the nodes are eliminated although they are numerous. And, the intermediate nodes are merged to the ancestor nodes because they are in the same object of their ancestor. The tree T_A created by the abstraction has 155 nodes. The number of nodes will be reduced considerably by the abstraction method. And the behavioral model created with the abstract tree is appropriately exact because the created abstract tree T_A satisfies that the amount of execution times in T_A must be over 95% (the threshold t) of the total amount of the execution traces.

The threshold t is decided by analyzing the abstraction results of execution traces at all test cases. Fig. 6 shows the rate of execution times at 20 test cases defined as JEITA Printer Benchmark Test Patterns J12 set [7]. It represents that the amount of the selected five functions' execution times (comp, decomp, buf, ucr, rip) is over 95% of the execution times of function "band" at all 20 test cases in J12 set. In P11 case, for example, the summation of execution times about "comp", "buf" and "rip" is over t (=95%) of the execution times of function "band" even if "decomp" and "ucr" are not selected. However, in other cases, it is under t when "decomp" and "ucr" are not selected. Therefore, the five functions are needed to be selected in consideration of all 20 test cases. Besides, if t is raised over 95%, additional functions must be selected because it gets low on the execution time at several test cases (P4, P5 and P8). Since those execution times are relatively short, the number of selected function will increase sharply.

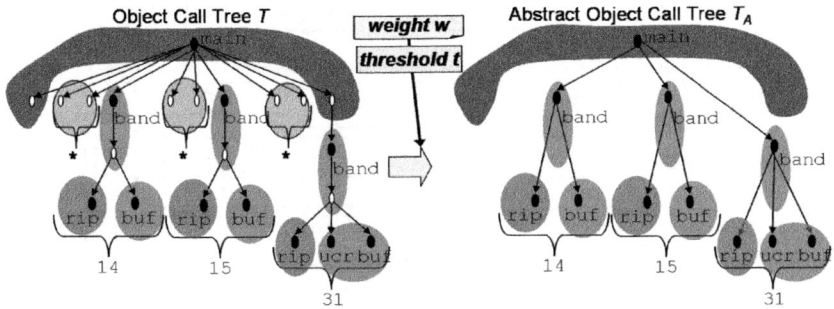

Fig. 5. Abstract Object Call Tree of Print Job Processing

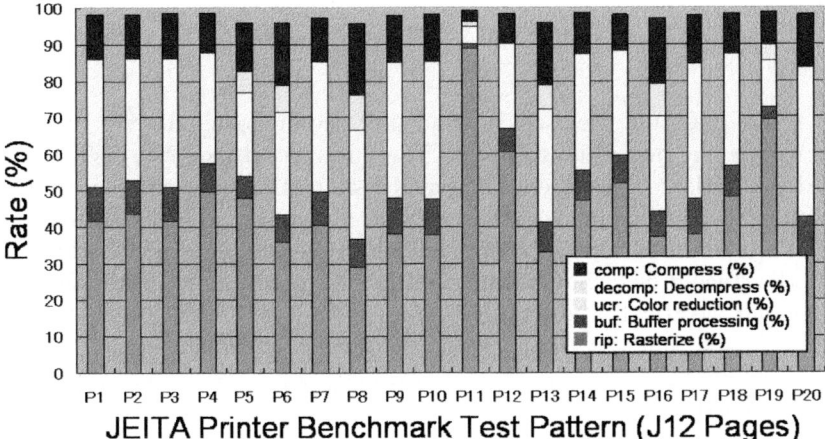

Fig. 6. Rate of Execution Times at JEITA Test Cases

On the other hand, if t is decreased too much, some of those five functions will not be selected. For example, if t is set to 85%, the function "decomp" will not be selected. In this way, it is needed to find an appropriate threshold t in a try-and-select process. The tree T_A shown in Fig. 5 is transformed into the sequence diagram shown in Fig. 7. And the state machine diagram is created from the sequence diagram by existing model transformation technologies [6].

For parallelization of the model, we assumed an AMP (asymmetric multi-processing) architecture, which was the architecture of special-purpose processing units (GEU, RPU, etc.) and a number of general purpose MPUs. Software components are allocated to MPUs. As shown in Fig. 3, major components are IL Generation and IL Processing. And so, we made a decision that IL Processing was allocated to one MPU and IL Generation was allocated to multiple MPUs.

At the same time of the reverse modeling, performance parameters are extracted from the execution traces. The extraction of execution time as performance parameters is shown in Fig. 4. These performance parameters are stored

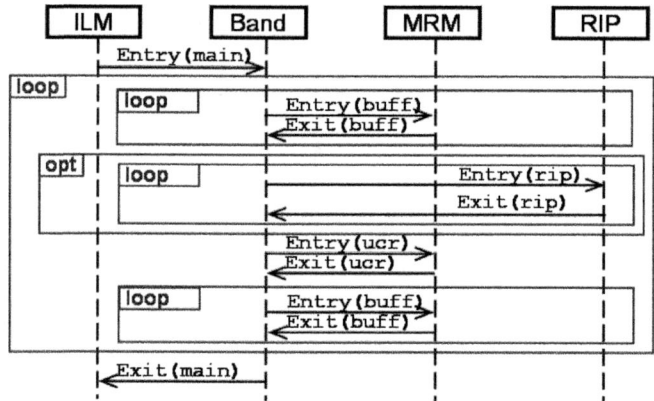

Fig. 7. Abstract Sequence Diagram of Print Job Processing

as external files, and they will be loaded at the model simulation time in order to calculate the performance result. The parallelized model is executed on the timed simulation environment. The model simulation with the performance parameters extracted from execution traces is a sort of trace-driven simulation [5]. Since the system performance of print job processing depends on the print job data, the trace-driven simulation is suitable for performance evaluation of MFP and similar electrical products.

6 Evaluation

As an evaluation of the reverse modeling method, a comparison of system performance data between model simulation and real system is discussed here. As the target real system, we made a MFP product prototype. The MFP prototype was developed on a FPGA board with dual-core PowerPC processors. The source code of existing MFP product was ported to the platform, which was designed for a single processor system. After porting, we re-designed the MFP software for an AMP architecture. The IL Generation component was allocated to one PowerPC processor core, and the IL Processing component was allocated to another PowerPC processor core, and they are working in parallel. As the results of MFP prototype development, we made the prototype for a single processing system and the prototype for an AMP architecture.

The reverse modeling and simulation for performance evaluation were done according to the following procedure. At first, execution traces were captured by observation of the prototype for single processing system. JEITA Printer Benchmark Test Patterns were used for the system observation. And, the model of single processing system was created by the reverse modeling method from these execution traces. At the same time, the performance parameters were extracted from the execution traces. After that, the model of AMP architecture was

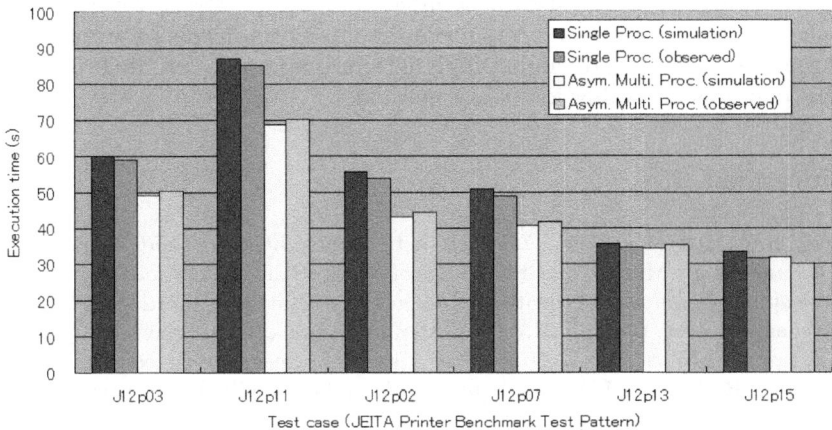

Fig. 8. Evaluation with JEITA Printer Benchmark Test Patterns

created by parallelizing the model of single processing system. And then, performance results were evaluated by simulating the model of AMP architecture with the performance parameters. Finally, the performance evaluation results were compared with the performance data by the system observation of the MFP prototype of AMP architecture.

Fig. 8 shows the comparison of the model simulation results and the MFP prototypes. There are the model of single processing system ("Single Proc. (simulation)"), the prototype for single processing system ("Single Proc. (observed)"), the model of dual-core AMP architecture ("Asym. Multi. Proc. (simulation)"), and the prototype for dual-core AMP architecture ("Asym. Multi. Proc. (observed)"). Six test patterns in J12 set of JEITA Printer Benchmark Test Patterns were used for the comparison. For example, "J12p07" means that the test case uses the page 07 test pattern in J12 set. Each test case consists of the four same pages, and the test case "J12p07" is composed of the four same pages as the page 07 in J12 set. For most print test patterns, the performance evaluation results of the model of dual-core AMP architecture are nearly equal to the results of MFP prototype for dual-core AMP architecture. Note that, for the AMP architecture cases, there are performance overhead about data transfer between processors via the internal bus and memory access. The performance overhead is relatively bigger at the cases of small print test patterns (J12p13 and J12p15) than the cases of large print test patterns (J12p02, J12p03, J12p07 and J12p11).

7 Conclusions

This paper presents a reverse modeling method for performance evaluation using dynamic analysis of legacy embedded systems. The method creates abstract behavioral feature of models by eliminating execution traces of existing products. Abstraction of behavioral feature by eliminating execution traces is the key technology, which is done by considering every function invocation's weight dominant to the total amount how much the function will effect the entire system performance. A case study about applying this method to real MFP is presented in this paper as an evaluation of the method.

References

1. Jeon, S.U., Hong, J.E., Bae, D.H.: Interaction-based behavior modeling of embedded software using UML 2.0. In: Proceedings of Ninth IEEE International Symposium on Object and Component-Oriented Real-Time Distributed Computing (ISORC 2006), Gyeongju, Korea, pp. 351–355. IEEE Computer Society, Los Alamitos (April 2006)
2. Martin, G., Müller, W.: UML for SOC Design. Springer, Dirdrecht (2005)
3. Riva, C., Rodriguez, J.V.: Combining static and dynamic views for architecture reconstruction. In: Proceedings of the Sixth European Conference on Software Maintenance and Reengineering (CSMR 2002), Budapest, Hungary, pp. 47–55. IEEE Computer Society, Los Alamitos (March 2002)
4. Ohba, N., Takano, K.: Hardware debugging method based on signal transitions and transactions. In: Proceedings of the 11th Asia South Pacific Design Automation Conference (ASP-DAC 2006), Yokohama, Japan, January 2006, pp. 454–459 (2006)
5. Prete, C.A., Prina, G., Ricciardi, L.: A trace-driven simulator for performance evaluation of cache-based multiprocessor systems. IEEE Transactions on Parallel and Distributed Systems 6(9), 915–929 (1995)
6. Liang, H., Dingel, J., Diskin, Z.: A comparative survey of scenario-based to state-based model synthesis approaches. In: Proceedings of the 2006 International Workshop on Scenarios and State Machines (SCESM 2006, co-located to ICSE 2006), Shanghai, China, pp. 5–12. IEEE Computer Society / ACM (May 2006)
7. Japan Electronics & Information Technology Industries Association (JEITA): JEITA Printer Benchmark Test Patterns (2003), http://it.jeita.or.jp/document/printer/pattern/J1-J12.pdf

Concordance: A Framework for Managing Model Integrity

Louis M. Rose[1], Dimitrios S. Kolovos[1], Nicholas Drivalos[1,2],
James R. Williams[1], Richard F. Paige[1],
Fiona A.C. Polack[1], and Kiran J. Fernandes[2]

[1] Department of Computer Science, University of York, YO10 5DD, York, UK
{louis,dkolovos,nikos,jw,paige,fiona}@cs.york.ac.uk
[2] The Management School,
University of York, YO10 5DD, York, UK
kf501@york.ac.uk

Abstract. A change to a software development artefact, such as source code or documentation, can affect the integrity of others. Many contemporary software development environments provide tools that automatically manage (detect, report and reconcile) integrity. For instance, incremental background compilation can reconcile object code with changing source code and report calls to a method that are inconsistent with its definition. Although models are increasingly first-class citizens in software development, contemporary development environments are less able to automatically detect, manage and reconcile the integrity of models than the integrity of other types of artefact. In this paper, we discuss the scalability and efficiency problems faced when managing model integrity for two categories of change that occur in MDE. We present a framework to support the incremental management of model integrity, evaluating the efficiency of the proposed approach atop Eclipse and EMF.

1 Introduction

Software development often involves constructing a system by combining numerous types of interdependent artefacts (such as models, source and object code, build scripts and documentation). Some examples of these dependencies include: generating source code and documentation from models, compiling object code from source code, and deploying object code using a build script. When a development artefact is changed, it may affect the integrity of dependent artefacts.

The definition of integrity varies depending on the artefacts being considered. For example, Java object and source code might be considered consistent when the object code contains a .class file for each .java file in the source code. Without automation, detecting, reporting and reconciling integrity problems can arguably become tedious and error-prone. For automatic integrity management, impact analysis is key to efficiency. Incremental compilation, for example, requires impact analysis for identifying the object code artefacts affected by a source code change.

Although models are increasingly first-class citizens in software development, contemporary development environments are less able to automatically manage the integrity of models than the integrity of other types of artefact. In this paper, we propose an efficient framework for managing two categories of model integrity, inter-model and model-metamodel. To demonstrate the soundness of our proposal we have implemented a prototype, named *Concordance*, on top of the widely used Eclipse Modeling Framework (EMF) [1] in the context of the Epsilon GMT component [2].

The rest of the paper is organised as follows. Section 2 discusses inter-model and model-metamodel integrity, highlighting challenges to their automation. Section 3 proposes an integrity management framework that drastically reduces the cost of performing impact analysis for inter-model and model-metamodel integrity checking. Two example uses of the framework are presented in Section 4, while Section 5 evaluates the performance gains delivered through the prototype. Related work and our conclusions are presented in Sections 6 and 7, respectively.

2 Background

Given the overloaded use of the terms *model* and *model element*, we clarify context and relevant abstractions before outlining our proposed approach. Our aim here is not to redefine these terms globally but instead to define a coherent set of abstractions that are both useful for the problem at hand and generic enough so that they can be implemented in a wide range of modelling platforms. Previous work, such as [3], defines similar - but not identical - abstractions which are equally valid and useful for the problems it addresses.

Here, we assume that a model is a collection of model elements, stored in a single file. Each element has a non-volatile identifier that is unique in the context of its containing model. Models are contained in a bounded *workspace* and identified with a unique workspace path (e.g. *models/a.model*). An intra-model reference is captured using only the identity of the target element. As model element identities may not be unique across different models, a cross-model reference captures both the identify of the target element and the workspace path of the target model.

2.1 Cross-Model References

In a non-Model Driven Engineering (MDE) software development process, a model is considered of comparable value to any other documentation artefact, such as a word processor document or a spreadsheet. As a result, the convenience of maintaining self-contained model files which can be easily shared outweighs other desirable attributes, such as modularity. This perception has led to the current situation where single-file models of the order of tens (if not hundreds) of megabytes, containing hundreds of thousands of model elements, are the norm for real-world software projects [4].

In an MDE process, models have a first-class role. Apart from acting as documentation, they are also validated, compared, used to generate other software artefacts, and transformed into models conforming to different modelling languages or representing different levels of abstraction. All of these tasks are performed in automated ways, and often with high frequency. In this setting, as discussed in [4], very large monolithic models are not desirable, because they are generally slow to load and store, and are costly to maintain in memory.

An obvious solution for addressing the problem of large monolithic models is to decompose them into smaller, cross-referencing models. Schematically, model A in Figure 1(a) can be decomposed into models B and C of Figure 1(b), where C contains a cross-reference to B. Contemporary modelling frameworks, such as EMF, natively support cross-model references and lazy loading of cross-referenced models [1, pg408].

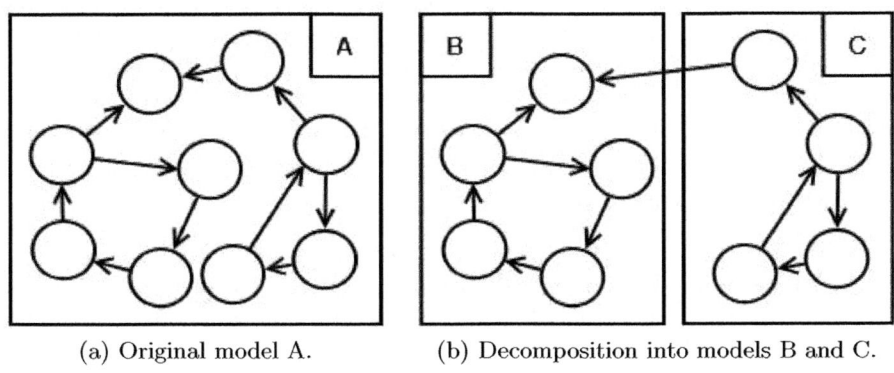

(a) Original model A.   (b) Decomposition into models B and C.

Fig. 1. Model decomposition using cross-references

While decomposing models is technically feasible and beneficial in terms of loading, persistence and memory costs, it also poses a range of new challenges. Since cross-references are uni-directional, identifying all of the incoming cross-references for a particular model without processing all models in the workspace is a challenge. Furthermore, as references are typically stored in the form of relative paths, if a model is renamed, moved or deleted from the workspace, incoming cross-model references are invalidated. Operations that do not affect the path of a model can also affect the integrity of incoming cross-model references: model update operations, for example, (either manual or in the form of an in-place model transformation) can result in the deletion of some model elements. Without an automatic cross-reference maintenance mechanism, problems with the integrity of a model's cross-references will only be identified when a model is loaded by a user or program.

2.2 Model-Metamodel Conformance

A model *conforms to* a metamodel when the metamodel specifies every concept used in the model definition, and the model uses the metamodel concepts according to the rules specified by the metamodel. Metamodel evolution can affect conformance. For example, when a metamodel concept is removed, any models that use the removed concept no longer conform to the metamodel. *Model migration* is a development activity in which instance models are updated in response to metamodel evolution to re-establish conformance.

MDE modelling frameworks implicitly enforce conformance. A model is *bound* to its metamodel, typically by constructing a representation in the underlying programming language (e.g. Java) for each model element and data value. Frequently, binding is strongly-typed: each metamodel type is mapped to a corresponding type in the underlying programming language using mappings defined by the metamodel. Loading a model that does not conform to its metamodel causes an error [5]. In short, MDE modelling frameworks cannot be used to manage any model that does not conform to its metamodel.

In modern MDE development environments, models and metamodels are kept separate. Metamodels are developed and distributed to users. Metamodels are installed, configured and combined to form a customised MDE development environment. Consequently, the instance models of a metamodel can be determined only with an exhaustive search of the metamodel user's development workspace.

2.3 Managing Model Integrity

In an MDE process, models are changed, potentially with high frequency [6]. As discussed above, model changes can originate from diverse sources, such as from a model editor, as the result of a transformation or other model management operation, from other users via a source code management system, and from the configuration of the development environment (e.g. metamodel installation).

Detecting and reacting to model changes is key to managing the integrity of the workspace and its models. Without mechanisms for analysing the impact of model changes, integrity problems are reported only when a model is next loaded. Due to the high frequency of model changes, the brute-force approach of re-examining all models in the workspace whenever one of them changes does not scale (as we demonstrate in Section 5). Without an automated mechanism for managing model integrity, developers must manually maintain and verify the integrity of their workspace, which is arguably a tedious and error-prone task.

3 Proposed Framework

To avoid exhaustively searching the workspace when a model is updated, deleted or moved or when a metamodel is changed, we propose a framework that indexes cross-reference and metamodel usage data. By reacting to create, update, move and delete model events, the data in the index will accurately reflect the current workspace state. The indexed data is exposed to model integrity management clients via methods for visiting models whose inter-model or model-metamodel integrity may have been affected by workspace events.

In this section, we outline the design of our proposed solution in a rigorous manner using UML to capture the structural part and OCL to specify the associated invariants and behavioural semantics of the different components.

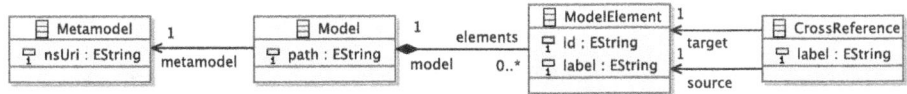

Fig. 2. Persisted data model

3.1 Design

Figure 2 presents an overview of the domain model of the proposed framework. A model element comprises an identifier unique in the context of its containing model, (*id*), a reference to the containing model (*model*) and a short human usable description (*label*) that can prove useful if the actual model element is deleted. Each model is identified by its path in the workspace. Cross-references are represented as a link between two model elements, along with a *label*.

The cross-model nature of cross-references is rigorously specified in the *Inter-Model* OCL invariant of Listing 1. Each *Model* can extract a collection of all of its outgoing references through its *getOutgoingReferences()* method.

```
1   context CrossReference
2      inv InterModel: self.source.model.path <> self.target.model.path
```

Listing 1. Invariants for the Reference class

```
1   context Model::getOutgoingReferences(): Set{CrossReference}
2      post: result->forAll(r:CrossReference|
3         r.source.model.path = self.path
4         and r.target.model.path <> self.path)
```

Listing 2. Post-conditions for the operations of the Model class

Figure 3 presents an overview of the interfaces provided by the proposed framework. Clients implement the ModelChangeListener (MetamodelChangeListener) interface to receive notification of model (metamodel) workspace events. As discussed in Section 2, some of the references in the domain model are uni-directional. The ConcordanceIndex interface exposes methods for navigating those references in the opposite direction. Rather than return a collection of models or cross-references, the methods on ConcordanceIndex use the visitor pattern, which decouples clients from the domain model.

Implementations of the PersistentConcordanceIndex interface respond to model change events, persisting a data model (Figure 2). The visitor methods are implemented by querying the persisted data model. In the following paragraphs, we discuss in detail the way in which each model change operation should be implemented for PersistentConcordanceIndex, presenting semantics in a rigorous manner with OCL post-conditions. For simplicity, we treat the persisted data model as a property of PersistentConcordanceIndex that comprises a set of models and a set of cross-references.

Model Added. The *modelAdded(m:Model)* operation is invoked when a new model (*m*) has been created. The model may or may not be empty upon creation

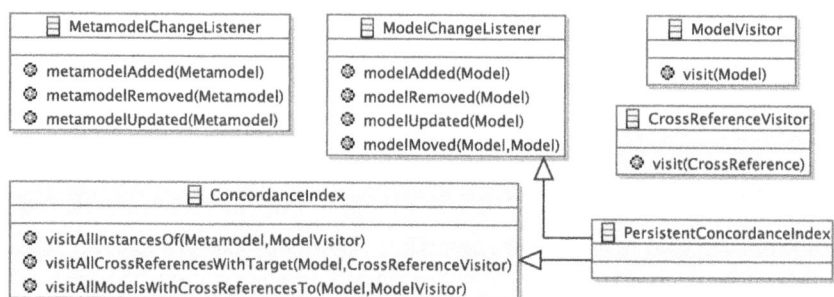

Fig. 3. Interfaces of the proposed framework (shading is irrelevant)

(for example a non-empty model may have been imported to the workspace from an external location). To maintain the index in a consistent state, the operation adds *m* and all of its outgoing references to the database:

```
context PersistentConcordanceIndex::modelAdded(m : Model)
  post AddsModel: self.db.models =
  self.db.models@pre->including(m)

  post AddsNewReferences: self.db.references =
  self.db.references@pre->including(m.getOutgoingReferences())
```

Listing 3. Post conditions for the *createModel(m:Model)* operation

Model Removed. The *modelRemoved(m:Model)* operation is invoked when a model (*m*) has been deleted. The operation deletes *m* and all of its outgoing references from the database:

```
1  context PersistentConcordanceIndex::modelRemoved(m : Model)
2    post DeletesModel: self.db.models =
3    self.db.models@pre->excluding(m)
4
5    post DeletesOutgoingReferences: self.db.references =
6    self.db.references@pre->reject(r|r.source.model.path = m.path)
```

Listing 4. Post-conditions of the *deleteModel()* operation

Model Updated. The *modelUpdated(m:Model)* operation is invoked when the workspace notifies the index manager that an existing model (*m*) has been updated. The operation updates the database by removing the deleted outgoing references of *m* and adding the new outgoing references of *m*.

```
1  context PersistentConcordanceIndex::modelUpdated(m : Model)
2    post UpdatesOutgoingReferences:
3    self.db.references = self.db.references->
4    reject(r|r@pre.source.model.path = m.path)->
5      including(m.getOutgoingReferences())
```

Listing 5. Post-conditions of the *updateModel(m:Model)* operation

Model Moved. The *modelMoved(old:Model, new:Model)* operation is invoked when a model (*m*) has been moved within the workbench. The operation changes the model in the database with path *old* to have path *new*.

```
1  context PersistentConcordanceIndex::moveModel(old:Model, new:Model)
2    post ChangesModelPath:
3      self.db.models->select(m|m.path=old.path)->
4        first.path = new.path
```

Listing 6. Post-conditions of the *moveModel(m:Model)* operation

3.2 Implementation

We have implemented the proposed approach in a prototype (named *Concordance*) on top of Eclipse and EMF, in the context of the Epsilon [2] component of the Eclipse GMT research incubator project. In the prototype, a *ModelChangeReporter* reports model change events to registered *ModelChangeListeners* and is implemented in the form of an Eclipse *builder* that users can enable for selected projects in the Eclipse workspace. Similarly, a *MetamodelChangeReporter* reports metamodel change events to registered *MetamodelChangeListeners*. Unfortunately, the current implementation of EMF does not provide services for receiving notifications of metamodel change events. Instead, we have implemented *MetamodelChangeReporter* as a background task that efficiently polls the EMF metamodel registry, detects changes and reports them as notifications.

Concordance provides an implementation of PersistentConcordanceIndex, H2ConcordanceIndex, that uses a relational database to store and query the workspace state. Alternatively, EMF itself - backed by a relational database using CDO or Teneo [7] for performance reasons - could have been used for this purpose. The visit methods are implemented by querying the database and reconstituting domain model objects.

4 Clients

Using the framework discussed in Section 3, we have implemented two clients for automating the management of model integrity. In this section, we discuss each of these clients in turn.

4.1 Cross-Model Reference Reconciliation

In Section 2, model decomposition using cross-model references was identified as a solution for breaking down large monolithic models. We now recap the key challenges faced when models are decomposed using cross-model references.

Dangling cross-model references can arise when a model is deleted, updated or moved. Manually maintaining and verifying the integrity of cross-model references is arguably a tedious and error-prone task. However, automated reporting and reconciliation of dangling references requires a means for identifying all of the incoming cross-model references for a model and cross-model references can be traversed only from the source model to the target model and are typically stored using relative paths.

The ConcordanceIndex interface, introduced in Section 3, provides methods for identifying incoming cross-model references for a model. The cross-model reference reconciliation client is a ModelChangeListener that uses these methods to identify and report dangling references and to reconcile references when a model is moved.

The cross-model reference reconciliation client detects dangling cross-model references as they occur, rather than when the source model is loaded. When a dangling reference is detected, it is reported using a problem marker on the source model. If the aforementioned reference is reconciled (e.g. a deleted model is restored), then the client identifies that this reference is no longer dangling and removes the corresponding problem marker. Since a model update may add or remove model elements, the cross-model reference reconciliation client treats updates as a model deletion followed by a model addition. Finally, when a model is moved to a different folder, incoming cross-model references to the moved model and outgoing cross-model references from the moved model are reconciled by the client, to use new relative paths. The mechanisms for adding, removing and finding problem markers are specific to the development environment.

Example. Using this prototype, users can now freely move models between different directories/projects of the Eclipse workspace without invalidating cross-model references. Figure 4 presents two simple models *b.model* and *c.model* where an element of *b.model* references an element of *c.model* in line 5 (<*target href="c.model\#_id1"/>*). When *c.model* is moved into folder *d* in Figure 5, the reference - which would otherwise be invalidated - is now updated (<*target href="d\c.model\#_id1"/>*). Also, dangling references produced as a result of deleting or updating models are visualized as errors in the respective workspace files. For example, when *c.model* is deleted from the workspace, an error marker is added to *b.model* and a corresponding message appears in the Problems view.

4.2 Conformance Checking and Model Migration

In Section 2, the way in which metamodel evolution affects instance models was discussed. While manually maintaining and verifying conformance can be tedious and error-prone, automated conformance checking and model migration requires a means for identifying all of the instances of a metamodel; a challenging task as metamodels and models are normally kept separate.

The ConcordanceIndex interface, introduced in Section 3, provides a method for identifying all of the instance models of a metamodel. The conformance managing client is a MetamodelChangeListener that uses this method to report conformance problems and to automatically perform model migration when possible.

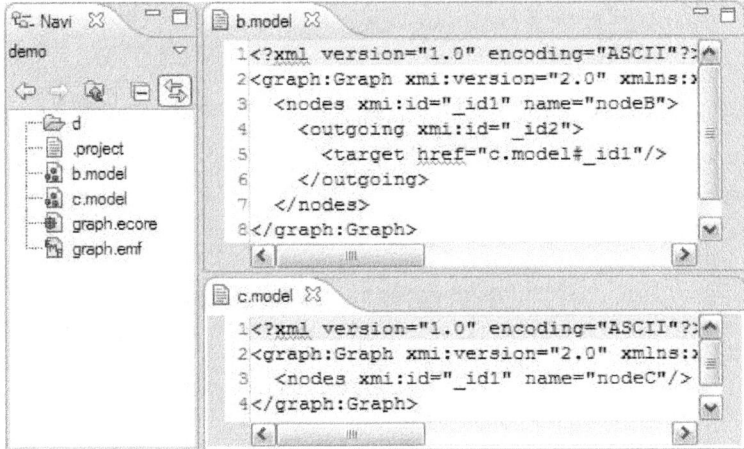

Fig. 4. Contents of models *b.model* and *c.model*

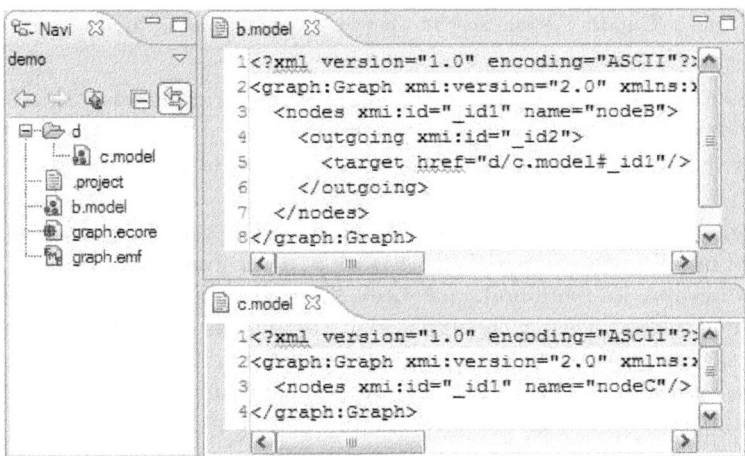

Fig. 5. Modified contents of *b.model* after moving *c.model* to directory *d*

The conformance managing client detects and reports conformance problems when they first occur, rather than when the source model is loaded. When a metamodel changes, the conformance managing client reports conformance problems (like dangling cross-references, conformance problems are marked on the containing model). We have described the conformance checking algorithm previously in [5].

In EMF, metamodels are identified by their namespace URI. Convention dictates that every version of the same metamodel has a different namespace URI. Consequently, when a new version of a metamodel is installed, a metamodel added event is triggered by the framework described in Section 3. The

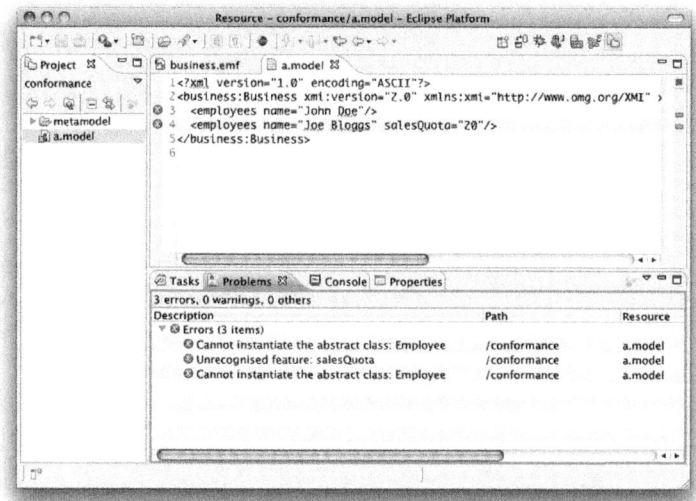

Fig. 6. Visual error markers after a metamodel update

conformance managing client provides an Eclipse extension point that allows metamodel developers to specify a *migration strategy* which can be used to migrate models to conform with the latest version of their metamodel.

Example. Using this prototype, a metamodel update triggers conformance checking on all instance models. In Figure 6, error markers have been added to *a.model* because its metamodel has been changed such that Employee is now an abstract class. By releasing the updated metamodel as a newer version and specifying a migration strategy, the metamodel developer can trigger automatic model migration during metamodel installation in the metamodel user's workspace. For the example shown in Figure 6, the Employees of *a.model* would be migrated to instances of appropriate subclasses as part of the installation of the new version of the metamodel. Consequently, the Problems view at the bottom of Figure 6 would report no conformance errors, and instead display a message stating that a.model conforms to its metamodel.

Implementation. The Java implementation of the conformance managing client is shown in Listing 7. It uses three elements of the infrastructure defined in Figure 3, `MetamodelChangeListener`, `ConcordanceIndex` and `ModelVisistor`. The implementation of `ePackageChanged` (lines 12-14) uses the `visitAllInstancesOf` method on `ConcordanceIndex` from Figure 3 with `ConformanceCheckingVisitor`, an implementation of `ModelVisitor` from Figure 3. `ConformanceCheckingVisitor` (lines 19-24) implements `ModelVisitor#visit` (lines 21-23) by delegating to a service that knows how to check conformance, `XmiConformanceChecker`.

```java
 1  public class ConformanceChecker implements MetamodelChangeListener {
 2
 3      private final ConformanceCheckingVisitor visitor =
 4          new ConformanceCheckingVisitor();
 5
 6      private final ConcordanceIndex index;
 7
 8      public ConformanceChecker(ConcordanceIndex index) {
 9          this.index = index;
10      }
11
12      public void ePackageChanged(EPackage oldEPackage, EPackage newEPackage) {
13          index.visitAllInstancesOf(newEPackage.getNsURI(), visitor);
14      }
15
16      public void ePackageAdded(EPackage ePackage) {}
17      public void ePackageRemoved(EPackage ePackage) {}
18
19      private static class ConformanceCheckingVisitor extends ModelVisitor {
20
21          public void visit(Model model) {
22              new XmiConformanceChecker(model).reportConformance();
23          }
24      }
25  }
```

Listing 7. Java implementation of conformance checking client

5 Evaluation

In this section we use the Concordance prototype presented in Section 3 to compare the performance of the proposed approach with the brute-force approach of examining all models in the workspace to manage integrity.

First, we examined the performance of the proposed framework when used to manage cross-model references. To this end, we set up an experiment where we automatically created 100 different EMF models that conform to the simple graph metamodel of Figure 7. Each model contained 100 nodes and 100 edges. To mimic realistic situations, 20% of the edges were cross-model references (i.e. referenced a target node stored in another model).

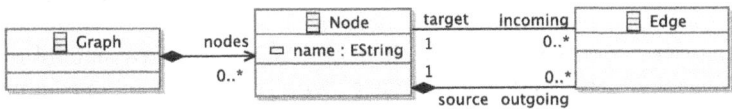

Fig. 7. The Graph Metamodel

Then we indexed all 100 models using Concordance in a one-off step, and subsequently performed 5, 10 and 15 model operations of each kind (move, update, delete) and measured the time needed for each operation to complete. The mean time needed for the one-off indexing was 13.366 sec. After the one-off indexing, the mean times for each operation were 2.484 seconds (Move), 0.056 seconds (Update), 0.008 seconds (Delete). This benchmarking was carried out on a standard departmental machine with two 3GHz cores and 4GB of main memory.

To demonstrate the significant performance gains compared to the brute-force approach, it was not even necessary to implement the brute-force operations in full detail; we only needed to measure the time necessary to load all the models and resolve their external references, since any of the above operations would at least require this. The average result we obtained for this was 8.887 sec per operation.

Brute force operations in our experiment were measured to be - unsurprisingly - significantly slower than incremental operations but did not require the one-off cost of constructing the initial index that incremental operations did. In the next step we aggregated the results to demonstrate that this one-off cost quickly pays off. The total time needed to perform 0, 5, 10, and 15 operations of each type using the brute-force approach[1] and using Concordance appear in Table 1 and graphically in Figure 8.

Table 1. Aggregate time (sec) over different numbers of operations

# of operations	0	5	10	15
Brute force minimum	0	37.395	69.36	120.525
Concordance move	13.366	26.069	40.629	51.576
Concordance update	13.366	13.641	13.815	14.409
Concordance delete	13.366	13.404	13.434	13.52

We devised a similar experiment to evaluate the performance of the proposed approach when used to manage model-metamodel conformance. The graph metamodel shown in Figure 7 was evolved such that Edge was removed, and Node referenced itself directly. We generated a workspace containing 100 different models, 20% graph models conforming to the old metamodel and 80% models conforming to another metamodel. The mean time taken for a brute-force approach – visiting every model in the workspace and determining its metamodel usage data – was 57ms. When Concordance was used, the mean time taken to store the metamodel usage data was 80ms, and 11ms to retrieve the metamodel usage data. Again, by aggregating this data the results demonstrate that using an index quickly pays off. However, because EMF is able to determine metamodel usage data more quickly than it is able to resolve cross-model references, the difference in performance between a brute-force and indexed approach is smaller.

EMF provides mechanisms for tuning the performance of model loading. For example, the DEFER_IDREF_RESOLUTION option forces EMF XMI parser to resolve intra-model references only once the whole model has been parsed, rather than each time an intra-model reference is encountered. Depending on the metamodel, this, and other, EMF options may reduce the time taken to load a model, determine its metamodel usage data and resolve its cross-model

---

[1] For brute-force operations only the loading time has been measured as explained above.

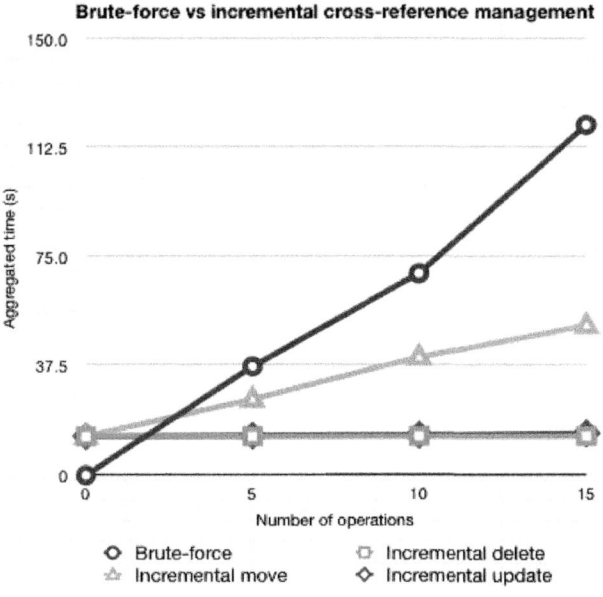

Fig. 8. Plot of the results of Table 1

references. Clearly, reducing the time taken to process a model benefits a brute-force approach for managing integrity. However, the one-off cost of constructing a model index is also reduced when models are processed more quickly.

6 Related Work

When a model evolves, further changes may need to be made to related models to maintain their integrity. This activity is termed *model synchronisation*. In this paper, we focus on two categories of model synchronisation, inter-model and model-metamodel integrity. We now discuss the relationship of our work with other model synchronisation research, and with existing work that makes use of model indexing.

Much of the existing model synchronisation literature focuses on developing a style of model-to-model transformation that can be used to incrementally update models (for example [8,9]). For large monolithic models, transformation execution time has been shown to be significantly reduced by using incremental transformation [8]. Consequently, improving scalability is seen as a primary focus for model synchronisation research. However, we believe that this focus is misplaced, and that enabling the decomposition of large monolithic models provides an alternative means for improving scalability in Model-Driven Engineering.

In [10], we compare and contrast existing approaches for managing model-metamodel consistency. Most such approaches require the user to check conformance and schedule model migration manually. The work presented in this paper provides a framework for automatically detecting, reporting and reconciling model integrity problems, and could theoretically be integrated with all existing model-metamodel consistency management approaches.

CrossX [11] is a component in the Mod4j (Modelling for Java) project, and mediates references between models. The approach used in CrossX is to generate a symbol table model for each model in the workspace. Model cross-references are made via the target's symbol table model, providing a layer of indirection. EMF Index [12] is a proposed project under the Eclipse Modelling Framework Technology Project (EMFT). EMF Index will use the same approach as CrossX, but focuses on model queries and interchangeable persistence mechanisms. As well as reconciling cross-references, CrossX and EMF Index seek to provide support for code completion.

We have focused on providing a framework for detecting model changes that cause a model index (such as CrossX) to become invalid, and reconciling the model index. The EMF Index project proposal recognises the need for such detection and reconciliation: "Whenever it is possible, detect model changes and update the model index automatically."

Research on model synchronisation and cross-references is related to work on model search and model consistency management. Moogle [13] is a model search engine that allows search terms to be entered and checked against a model repository. The search terms encode metamodel information (e.g., metamodel concepts) but do not currently encode richer patterns, such as model subgraphs. Moogle is based on indexes, unlike the EMF Search project[2], which provides an approach for querying EMF models. The EMF Search engine also considers metamodel concepts. Since it is not based on indexes, it is less efficient than Moogle or our approach, as it performs a complete introspection of the EMF model each time a search is carried out. Similar, but not equivalent, functionality is available in IBM's Rational Software Architect (RSA), through its integration with Rational's Asset Manager[3]. The asset manager is a general-purpose application for cataloguing, finding and organising business assets; as such, it is not tailored for models, but can be used to manage entire models, or fragments thereof. The fine-grained indexing and search (e.g., by metamodel concept) that is available with Moogle and EMF Search is not easily accomplished with RSA.

With respect to model consistency management, there is a wealth of research, e.g., on the use of OCL or various logics for specifying consistency rules and establishing or checking that models are consistent; see, for example, [5,14,15], and IBM RSA's consistency analysis support via patterns. Perhaps most relevant to the approach taken in this paper is the xlinkit toolset proposed by Nentwich et al. [16] for consistency of distributed XML documents. xlinkit can be used as a consistency checker (in similar ways to OCL) and to generate links between

---

[2] http://www.eclipse.org/modeling/emft/?project=search#search
[3] http://www-01.ibm.com/software/awdtools/ram/

XML documents. These links can then be stored in a (web-enabled) database that provides indexing and querying facilities. The approach is scalable and has been applied to large XML documents, but is not optimised for models and metamodels.

7 Conclusions and Further Work

We have motivated our work by arguing for the need for MDE environments that automatically detect, manage and reconcile model integrity problems. We have discussed the benefits of model decomposition and automatic model migration, and presented a key challenge for their adoption; detecting, reporting and, where possible, reconciling integrity problems. Feedback is particularly important if integrity is compromised as a result of a user's actions, or as an effect of automated model management operations. We have presented an abstract, but rigorously specified, solution that uses an index to store and manage cross-model references and metamodel usage data. We have demonstrated and evaluated an implementation of our solution on top of the Eclipse Modeling Framework.

Having established this essential infrastructure, we will now implement further clients and refine the framework presented in Section 3. We envisage a client for discovering and visualising end-to-end traceability relationships in the workspace, all the way from requirements models up to detailed design models. Another application is to use the framework to enable incremental model validation and transformation. For example, when a model is modified - and thus needs to be revalidated - the validation engine can easily infer which other models could have been affected by this modification and only validate them - instead of all the models in the workspace.

As further clients are implemented, we expect the framework to become more abstract. In particular, we envisage that the visitor methods and the persisted data model will become more generic. The framework will likely become more flexible, with more of the impact analysis semantics being specified in individual clients. Further extensions to the framework may be required for reacting to coarser- and finer-grained workspace events (for example, changes affecting many models or affecting model elements).

In future iterations of this work we plan to investigate support for non-model artefacts (e.g. plain text, code, documentation), which account for the majority of artefacts managed in the context of a software development process. Our plan is to start with a naive offset/length-based solution and elaborate it using statistical techniques to facilitate references that are more resilient to subsequent text editing actions.

Acknowledgements

The work in this paper was supported by the European Commission via the MODELPLEX project, co-funded by the European Commission under the "Information Society Technologies" Sixth Framework Programme (2006-2009).

References

1. Steinberg, D., Budinsky, F., Paternostro, M., Merks, E.: EMF: Eclipse Modelling Framework, 2nd edn. Addison-Wesley Professional, Reading (2008)
2. Extensible Platform for Specification of Integrated Languages for mOdel maNagement (Epsilon), http://www.eclipse.org/gmt/epsilon
3. Jouault, F., Bezívin, J.: KM3: a DSL for Metamodel Specification. In: Proc. IFIP 2006, Bologna, Italy. LNCS, pp. 171–185 (2006)
4. Kolovos, D.S., Paige, R.F., Polack, F.A.C.: Scalability: The Holy Grail of Model Driven Engineering. In: Proc. Workshop on Challenges in MDE, MoDELS, Toulouse, France, September 2008, pp. 10–14 (2008)
5. Rose, L.M., Kolovos, D.S., Paige, R.F., Polack, F.A.C.: Enhanced automation for managing model and metamodel inconsistency. In: Proc. ASE, pp. 545–549. ACM Press, New York (2009)
6. Mens, T., Demeyer, S.: Software Evolution. Springer, Heidelberg (2007)
7. Eclipse Foundation. Eclipse Modeling Framework Technology (EMFT), http://www.eclipse.org/modeling/emft/
8. Hearnden, D., Lawley, M., Raymond, K.: Incremental Model Transformation for the Evolution of Model-Driven Systems. In: Nierstrasz, O., Whittle, J., Harel, D., Reggio, G. (eds.) MoDELS 2006. LNCS, vol. 4199, pp. 321–335. Springer, Heidelberg (2006)
9. Ráth, I., Bergmann, G., Ökrös, A., Varró, D.: Live model transformations driven by incremental pattern matching. In: Vallecillo, A., Gray, J., Pierantonio, A. (eds.) ICMT 2008. LNCS, vol. 5063, pp. 107–121. Springer, Heidelberg (2008)
10. Rose, L.M., Kolovos, D.S., Paige, R.F., Polack, F.A.C.: An analysis of approaches to model migration. In: Proc. Joint MoDSE-MCCM Workshop, pp. 6–15 (2009)
11. Warmer, J.: Big Models - An Alternative Approach. In: Modeling Symposium, Eclipse Summit Europe, Ludwigsburg, Germany (2008)
12. EMF Index, Project Proposal, http://www.eclipse.org/proposals/emf-index/
13. Lucrédio, D., Fortes, R.P., Whittle, J.: Moogle: A model search engine. In: Czarnecki, K., Ober, I., Bruel, J.-M., Uhl, A., Völter, M. (eds.) MODELS 2008. LNCS, vol. 5301, pp. 296–310. Springer, Heidelberg (2008)
14. Paige, R.F., Brooke, P.J., Ostroff, J.S.: Metamodel-based model conformance and multiview consistency checking. ACM Transactions on Software Engineering and Methodology 16(3) (2007)
15. Egyed, A.: Instant consistency checking for the UML. In: Proc. ICSE 2006, Shanghai, China, pp. 381–390. ACM Press, New York (2006)
16. Nentwich, C., Emmerich, W., Finkelstein, A., Ellmer, E.: Flexible Consistency Checking. ACM Transactions on Software Engineering and Methodology 12(1), 28–63 (2003)

An Integrated Facet-Based Library for Arbitrary Software Components

Matthias Schmidt[1], Jan Polowinski[1],
Jendrik Johannes[1], and Miguel A. Fernández[2]

[1] Technische Universität Dresden, Nöthnitzer Str. 46, 01187 Dresden, Germany
{matthias.schmidt,jan.polowinski,jendrik.johannes}@tu-dresden.de
[2] Department of Broadband Service Platforms, Telefónica R&D, Valladolid, Spain
mafg@tid.es

Abstract. Reuse is an important means of reducing costs and effort during the development of complex software systems. A major challenge is to find suitable components in a large library with reasonable effort. This becomes even harder in today's development practice where a variety of artefacts such as models and documents play an equally important role as source code. Thus, different types of heterogeneous components exist and require consideration in a component search process. One flexible approach to structure (software component) libraries is *faceted classification*. Faceted classifications and in particular *faceted browsing* are nowadays widely used in online systems. This paper takes a fresh approach towards using faceted classification in heterogeneous software component libraries by transferring faceted browsing concepts from the web to software component libraries. It presents an architecture and implementation of such a library. This implementation is used to evaluate the applicability of facets in the context of an industry-driven case study.

1 Introduction

Reusing software components has always been central to software engineering. However, in practice, component reuse is still seldom implemented on a large scale. A reason for this is the lack of generic solutions that fulfill the needs of modern software development, where complex systems are not implemented code-centric and do not only rely on the reuse of source code and binary components. Instead, such systems are realised model-driven and models become equally important reusable components.

In the REUSEWARE[1] [1] project, we developed a generic solution to implement composition systems for model components defined in arbitrary modelling languages. Thus, we provided a technical solution that allows developers to treat all models[2] created during a development process of a complex system as components and store them in a library for reuse.

---
[1] http://reuseware.org
[2] In this paper we refer to all artefacts created in a model-driven process as *models*. This includes documents and source code.

However, a major problem in reuse in general, is locating a desired component in a huge component library. About two decades ago, Príeto-Diaz proposed [2,3] the use of *faceted classification*, a concept from book libraries which was introduced by Ranganathan in the 1930s, for software component libraries. In a faceted classification, not an object as a whole, but different aspects (i.e. facets) of an object are described. For example, well-known facets used in book libraries are author, topic and publisher. Since Ranganathan, attempts were made to realise such classifications for specific component libraries (e.g. [4]), but there has been little interest in this area in the last decade.

Interestingly, concepts of faceted classification can be found today in many online systems, such as e-commerce systems like Ebay or Amazon. These systems make use of a faceted classification to enable *faceted browsing* that, in contrast to traditional web-search, allows for explorative browsing.

The data queried on the web is not very different from the models that make up complex modern software systems. In both cases, different languages and methods are used in combination to specify and compose data. Also, to integrate such heterogeneous data, standards (e.g., issued by the W3C or the OMG) support the creation of common base technologies and tools.

In this paper, we recapitulate Prieto-Díaz's idea of using faceted classification in software reuse by transferring faceted browsing concepts of today's web to software component libraries that meet the demands of model-driven development. For that we take a closer look at component and model libraries as well as facet technologies that are used today in Section 2. We present an architecture and implementation of a facet-based software component library that can handle heterogeneous models defined in arbitrary modelling languages in Section 3. The implementation is based on widely used technologies and standards: The Eclipse Platform [5], the Eclipse Modeling Framework (EMF) [6] and the OMG's MOF standard [7]. We also explore how the greater amount of structure in software components—compared to web data—can reduce the classification effort. To show that the facet-based library can be used to browse and search for different kinds of models, we evaluate it in the context of a case study from the telecommunications domain defined by Telefónica R&D in the European research project MODELPLEX[3] and discuss other applications of it in Section 4. Finally, we conclude in Section 5.

2 Foundations and Related Work

The idea of using a library to maintain a set of components is well known and popular in software engineering. However, component libraries for reuse (called *reuse libraries* in [8]) need to provide additional metadata about their content in order to help users in deciding which component or service does fulfil their needs the best.

As stated by Mili et. al. in their survey of reuse libraries [8], a good reuse solution requires to be efficient, accurate, user-friendly and general. Furthermore,

---

[3] http://www.modelplex.org

the survey classifies the use of facets as a descriptive method and characterises it using a number of criteria. In that way, it identifies the approach as a method of high precision, recall and flexibility and rates the difficulty of use as very low and the method's transparency to the user as very high. As we see these characteristics as crucial for a component library we argue to use faceted component libraries for reuse.

To emphasise that other implementation methods for reuse libraries have drawbacks we visit classic component libraries in Section 2.1, followed by a discussion of libraries for models in Section 2.2. Oriented at the mentioned requirements by Mili et. al., we aim to provide a facet-based library for model components. For that, we transfer well established faceted browsing techniques from online systems and present an implementation based on modelling standards and technologies. The library integrates seamlessly into the widely used software development and modelling environment Eclipse. Nevertheless, the solution is general by being independent of the language a model component is defined in. As a foundation of this solution, we introduce the main ideas of faceted classification in Section 2.3 and analyse early approaches as well as recent applications in Section 2.4.

2.1 Classic Component Libraries

As the main representatives of classic component libraries, we take a closer look at CORBA[4] and UDDI[5]. In principle, they implement different library approaches but have main features in common. They manage a database of components or services while users are able to register new components and search for existing ones. In order to search the database, these systems often implement a naming and/or directory service that give users the possibility to search by name (keyword) or id. As this requires detailed knowledge about the desired component or service there is a need for additional features to support users that do not have this information available. These users would not search by one concrete query but instead browse to get something adequate.

The CORBA middleware manages components as so called objects and offers a naming service to find them. Besides that, trading and property services allow a search based on component attributes [4]. Furthermore, a query service allows reading and manipulating queries on a set of objects using languages such as SQL or OQL. Although a search on the basis of attribute values is possible, CORBA does not provide a method to search on structured metadata due to a missing vocabulary of values. This does not allow for an efficient retrieval of components [9]. As a result, users require detailed knowledge about what they are searching for and might face a situation where effects such as synonyms, antonyms or plural forms complicate the search process.

The directory service UDDI acts as a library for web services in the domain of service oriented architectures (SOA). We see web services as a special case of software components as they provide specific functionality over a well defined

---

[4] http://www.corba.org
[5] http://uddi.xml.org

interface. To describe services, UDDI offers attribute values and enumerated classification [4]. This is implemented by so called White, Yellow and Green Pages which each focus on a specific service aspect. White Pages name attributes of the business that offers the service, Yellow Pages use standard taxonomies such as the North American Industry Classification System (NAICS) to classify business and service while Green Pages include technical details. Hence, to search a web service one can draw upon keywords, attribute values and enumerated classifications. As argued before, we do not see classifications by keywords or attribute values as methods of efficient component retrieval. However, with Yellow Pages UDDI also offers enumerated classification which provides a controlled vocabulary and eliminates effects such as antonyms or plural forms. Nevertheless, we do not think the taxonomies of the Yellow Pages to be adequate for classifying software components, since taxonomies are too large, inflexible and difficult to extend [9]. Although multiple taxonomies are allowed, the user is still required to classify his artefacts in an existing complex schema that might not be designed for his special purposes. Besides, UDDI itself does not support browsing a library and therefore it does not seem appropriate for an exploration by users who do not know in advance what is inside the library. The website seekda![6] adds concepts such as tagging and community evaluation to the UDDI's search engine. That also supports our claim that the UDDI's principles are not sufficient. Note that our work does not aim at providing automatic component selection and binding as UDDI provides for web services. For our work we are interested in the capabilities for manual searching performed by users.

2.2 Component Libraries for Models

In addition to classic component libraries, we shortly analyse the field of component libraries for models. In their *research roadmap* for model-driven development of complex systems [10], France and Rumpe mention the need for reuse of experience, libraries of model operations and full-featured model repositories. However, they do not explicitly request a method for intuitive browsing of model repositories (or libraries). To the best of our knowledge, there is no work aiming at building a *reuse* library (in the sense of Mili et. al.) for models in model-driven development. Surely, libraries specific to modelling languages and models (e.g., model libraries in SysML [11]) or specific to model operations (e.g., libraries of operation in Epsilon [12]) exist. But they are specific to a modelling language and do not integrate concepts for browsing and finding models. Since in model-driven development everything can be treated as a model (e.g., documents, model transformations, model management operations or metamodels) all reuse concerns identified in the mentioned research roadmap can profit from a reuse library for models that is independent of the language a model is defined in.

2.3 Faceted Classification and Faceted Browsing

Faceted classification [13] combines principles from keyword classification and enumerated classification. Keywords (facet values) describing an entity are

---
[6] http://seekda.com

bundled into facets and each of these facets concerns only one single aspect to characterise the entity. Examples are shown in Figure 1 as well as Table 1 and 2. Some facets may be structured and form trees, each representing a single taxonomy, others may be flat [14,15]. All facets as one create a multi-dimensional classification.

Faceted Browsing is a user interface paradigm based on flexible classification and has the following principles [16,17]: The process of faceted browsing interactively constructs a query on the data while the user performs multiple simple refinement steps. At the beginning a complete set of items is presented, which is then reduced to a subset by making restrictions to the values of one or multiple facets (*zoom-in* navigation step). The subset can again be extended by taking back restrictions (*zoom-out* navigation step). Zoom-in and zoom-out navigation steps may be performed for all facets in any order. Note that this enables the user to choose his own navigation path—this is a main difference to fixed taxonomies which imply that the user follows the way the taxonomy was once constructed by its author. Another important feature of a faceted browser is the exclusion of empty result sets by construction. For this purpose only facet values that are available in the current result set are suggested as filtering options to the user.

As the system presents facets and facet values in the user interface, the user gets an impression of which options are on-hand. This way he learns about options he could not have named correctly in a textual query either because he has only partial knowledge of the domain or simply because the options did not come to his mind. Especially in this context, offering a description of the meaning of facets and facet values can further add to the guidance of the user.

2.4 Facets in Use

Many application examples show that facets define an intuitive classification schema. It is not only used in classic media libraries but was applied to software component libraries two decades ago. [2,4] describe experiences made with component libraries that make use of faceted classifications. Although these examples characterise faceted classification as a promising approach, they can not directly be applied to todays' model-driven software development. At that time, software components were defined as programmatic functionality for reuse. Today, heterogeneous artefacts such as models, documents or binary components implemented in various languages need to be taken into account to support the whole model-driven development process. Furthermore, the Internet has changed the way components are delivered and today work is more and more shifted to a community rather than to single persons. These new aspects of component reuse require a new evaluation of faceted classification.

Since the first approaches for facet-based software component libraries were introduced, other fields of application made use of faceted classifications. Hence, today there are many websites and desktop applications using this approach to browse huge amounts of data. Here, it is not always obvious that facets are used because the terms *category* and *filter* are often used as synonyms. This seems to

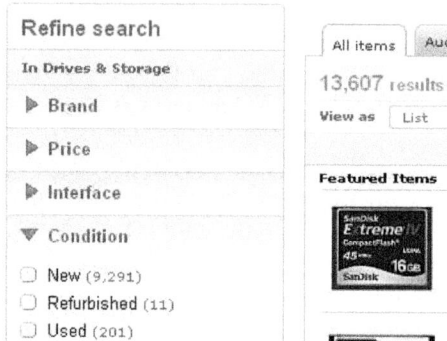

Fig. 1. Ebay uses facets to browse auctions

be appropriate as they emphasise the structuring character and explain the way faceted browsing is performed.

[16] analyses a number of websites, web technologies and desktop programs that use faceted browsing. Applications such as iTunes[7] and foobar2000[8] or generic browsers such as Flamenco[9], Exhibit[10] and Longwell[11] show that the faceted browsing paradigm can be used in various fields of applications. In addition, websites such as Amazon[12], Google Base[13] or Ebay[14] use faceted browsing to give the user access to their dataset. Figure 1 shows Ebay as an example. Here auctions of flash memory drives are presented which can be browsed using facets such as *Brand*, *Price*, *Interface* or *Condition*. Depending on the auction's type other facets are shown which makes facets such as *Megapixel* or *Optical Zoom* available for Digital Cameras. To sum up, all these examples show that faceted browsing offers a flexible method of exploring arbitrary data.

3 A Facet-Based Component Library

We see faceted classifications and faceted browsing, which has shown its applicability in various online systems, as efficient and user-friendly methods to search libraries of model components. To apply this in practice, a facet-based library system is needed that is integrated into the user's software development and modelling environment.

This section introduces an architecture for such a system and a concrete implementation that is based on the Eclipse Modeling Framework (EMF) [6] and

---

[7] http://www.apple.com/itunes
[8] http://foobar2000.audiohq.de/foo_facets
[9] http://flamenco.berkeley.edu/
[10] http://simile.mit.edu/wiki/Exhibit
[11] http://simile.mit.edu/wiki/Longwell
[12] http://www.amazon.com
[13] http://base.google.com/
[14] http://www.ebay.com

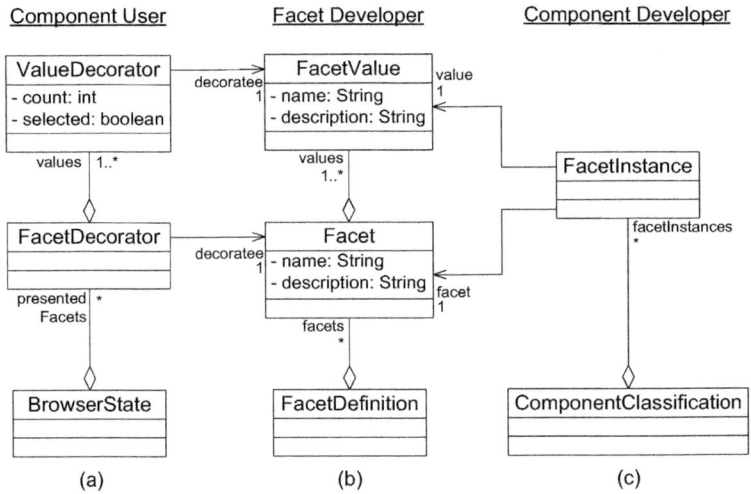

Fig. 2. Metamodel for faceted classification

integrated into the Eclipse Platform. We chose these technologies over generic browsers mentioned in Section 2.4, because Eclipse provides a popular platform for software development and modelling. Thus, the library integrates seamlessly into the development and modelling environment, which turned out to be an important usability factor (cf. Section 4.1).

The architecture is oriented towards the principle of faceted classification and the user interface paradigm of faceted browsing discussed in Section 2.3. First, a domain expert—the *facet developer*—defines facets (Section 3.1) that can be used by *component developers* to classify components in a second step (Section 3.2). Third, *component users* browse the component repository by specifying faceted queries via zoom-in and zoom-out (Section 3.3). We captured the concepts of faceted definition, component classification and component browsing in a metamodel shown in Figure 2.

3.1 Facet Definition

We first discuss the concepts for *facet definition* that are shown in Figure 2 (b). The facet developer has to perform a domain analysis in order to specify terms and concepts of the domain in focus [18]. This leads to a number of Facets which are grouped in a FacetDefinition. A Facet consists of a name and a description that gives component developers an idea of the facet's semantics. Besides that, Facets own a set of FacetValues that have a name and description as well. These three concepts allow the facet developer to define and maintain facets and their vocabulary. FacetDefinitions are later available to component developers to create ComponentClassifications (cf. Section 3.2).

Based on the metamodel we defined graphical user interface tooling that can be used by the facet developer. The tooling is integrated into Eclipse and parts

Table 1. General facets to classify components

Facet	Description	Examples
Composition Role	The role the components plays when composed with other components	Port, Sender, Client
Information Hiding	The degree of encapsulation provided by a component	Whitebox, Greybox, Blackbox
Language	The language the component is modelled in	UML, SysML, AADL Java
License	The legal agreement the component is published under	GNU GPL, Mozilla Eclipse Public License
Maturity	The status of development or usability the component is in	Alpha, Beta, Released
System Layer	The system architecture's level where the component is to be used	GUI, Persistence, Core, Transport

of it are directly generated from the metamodel using EMF. The tooling includes an editor that allows for creation of new facet definitions by instantiating the metamodel. It furthermore supports the facet developer in deleting specifications, removing, adding or editing facets as well as deploying specifications to component developers. Usually, facets have to be defined once for a specific component type (e.g., for one modelling language) to capture domain concepts of that component type. However, to capture the right domain concepts in Facets and FacetValues, experimenting with classifying concrete components is often required. Thus, having the facet definition tooling integrated in the same tool that is used for component development (which is Eclipse in our case) is helpful.

Standard Facet Catalog. In contrast to domain-specific facets, there are facets to describe model components independently of their application domain. They are inspired by facet sets mentioned in [3,4] and target syntax, semantics, composition interfaces and other implementation aspects of components. Table 1 shows an excerpt of these facets, which we provide as a standard catalog. They can be used by component developers directly for general faceted classification of software components. This standard catalog of facets is not closed or complete. It is rather expected that there are additional facets sufficiently adequate to classify model components independent of language and application domain.

3.2 Component Classification

Once facets are defined and deployed, components can be classified by component developers. A ComponentClassification (Figure 2 (c)) classifies one component and consists of a list of FacetInstances. A FacetInstance represents the usage

An Integrated Facet-Based Library for Arbitrary Software Components   269

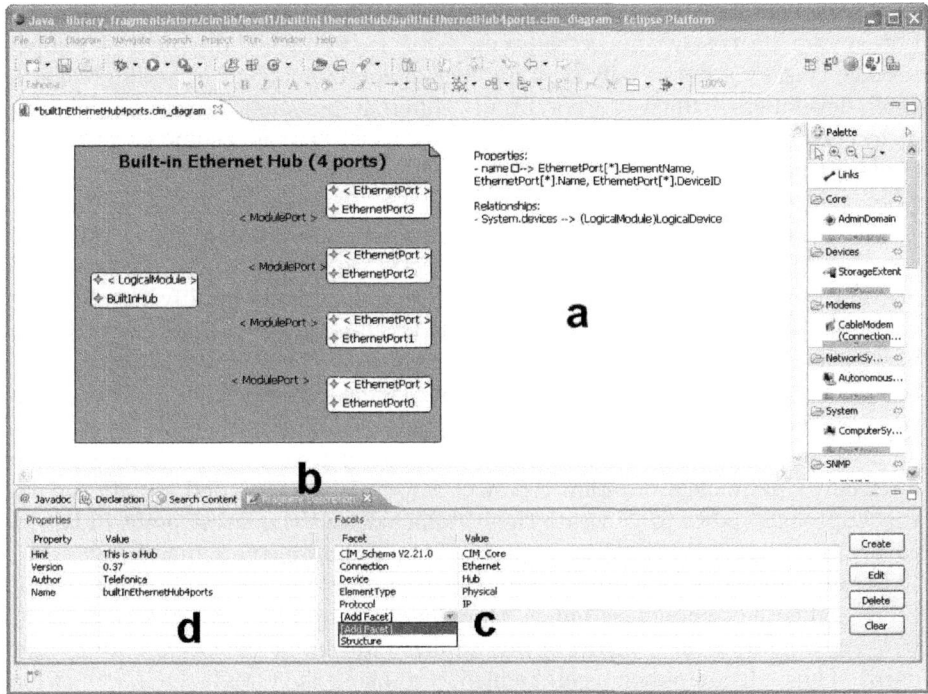

Fig. 3. The library's component classification

of one facet to classify a component and encapsulates the Facet itself and one FacetValue that describes the component best. Note that only facet values that were assigned to the facet by the facet developer can be selected, thus ensuring that the vocabulary is controlled. This is inline with the definition of faceted classification in [4] which is not enforced by all faceted browsers.

For component developers, Eclipse-integrated graphical tooling is provided for component classification. Eclipse, which provides a wide range of editors to create and modify all kinds of models, acts as component development environment. Thus, a component developer can develop and classify model components in the same integrated environment. Figure 3 shows a typical component classification example. Here, a CIM model component (CIM is a domain-specific modelling language that we will introduce in Section 4.1) is created in the CIM editor integrated in Eclipse (a). Our tooling provides a special view (b) that is used to classify the component in the currently active editor. This view offers the opportunity to select available facets and choose one given value for each (c) to create a ComponentClassification. The available facets were specified in a facet definition and loaded into the library beforehand. (In this example we use domain-specific facets that are described in Section 4.1.) Additionally, some attributes can be defined to add more information about the component (d).

Automated Classification. The manual classification process in a facet-based library can be costly and error-prone. This is because component developers need to classify a potentially high number of components with facets defined by facet developers (which are potentially different persons). Errors in the usage of facets might occur if the semantics of a facet were not sufficiently defined. Besides that, manually created component classifications might become invalid when the component evolves.

These issues can be addressed by a rule-based automation of the classification process. This approach uses information retrieval to generate a faceted classification from the component itself. Software components qualify for this technique because they are very low on free text [2] and have an inner structure—in particular models that conform to a metamodel. This approach can relieve a component developer from classifying components. Furthermore, the facet developer that creates the facet, gains control over how it is used. That means no deep knowledge of the facet is needed by the component developer since the facet developer makes sure that the facet is used in the intended way. In the end, this approach allows to generate the classification at the latest point in time to ensure that it reflects the current state of the software component.

In our implementation, all components are represented as EMF models within Eclipse. The metamodels—that is, the languages in which the components are written—are all defined in Ecore (an implementation of the OMG's MOF standard). Thus, all components can be inspected using the OMG's OCL [19] (which is aligned with MOF) as a query language. We allow facet developers to define automated classification rules in the form of OCL queries for arbitrary component types. Consequently, this approach is directly usable by facet developers who are familiar with the MOF and the OCL standards.

3.3 Component Browsing

After a faceted classification has been done and the components have been registered in the library, the component user can perform faceted browsing. The state of the browsing is captured in a `BrowserState` (Figure 2 (a)). A `BrowserState` holds a set of `FacetDecorators` where each refers to one of the facets that is currently explored by the component user. `ValueDecorators` represent the `FacetValues` the component user specifies to narrow down his search. Furthermore, `ValueDecorator` consists of a counter that indicates how many components will remain in the result if the user selects the `FacetValue` and a flag to represent the selection.

Following Figure 2 (a), we implemented a faceted browser that provides different facilities for the zoom-based exploration process (cf. Section 2.3) and supports different ways to present browsing results, following the works [16,17]. The features range from special widgets to present facets, over a free-text search to features such as grouping and sorting. Figure 4 shows our faceted component browser with important parts marked. These parts include the main functionality of a faceted browser, which are the result view (A), a grouping and sorting facility for the result view's entries (B) as well as six widgets to present available

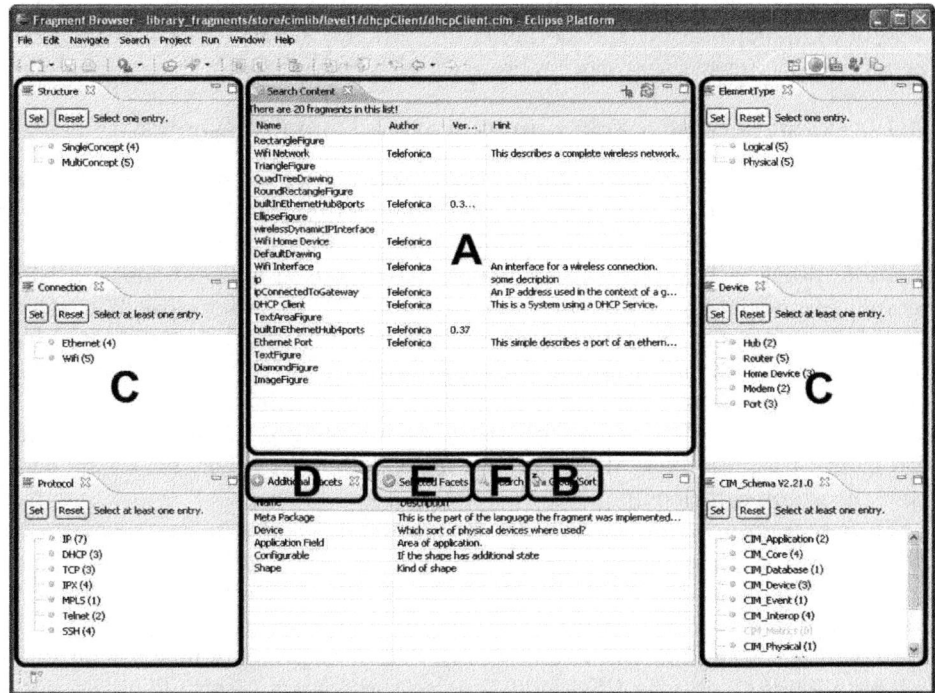

Fig. 4. The library's faceted component browser

facets and their values (C). As there might be more than six facets available, a separate view lists the others not presented (D). While the user selects facets and values to perform zoom-in and zoom-out steps with (C) and (D), the current search query is shown in another view (E). Finally, a search view gives the opportunity to perform a free-text search over available facets and classifications (F) [15]. These features define a faceted browser that can be used to search arbitrary model components classified in the way shown in Section 3.2.

After the component user has found a suitable component, he can directly open other views or editors to inspect or to reuse the component. In our evaluation, we used the browser together with REUSEWARE, which is also integrated into Eclipse and provides a graphical composition editor. The component user can directly drag&drop components from the result view (A) into REUSEWARE's composition editor. Thus, the browser integrates tightly with the component users development environment.

4 Evaluation

To show the applicability of our facet-based library, we tested it with different models defined in different modelling languages. In Section 4.1, we describe an evaluation we performed with a domain-specific modelling language, where we collected feedback from the domain experts on the usability of our approach and our implementation. Furthermore, in Section 4.2, we discuss other types of models and artefacts that can be browsed with our approach.

4.1 Evaluation with Telecommunication Domain Experts

We performed an evaluation of our facet-based library in the context of a case study defined by Telefónica R&D in the European project MODELPLEX [20]. In the case study, Telefónica uses an EMF implementation of the Common Information Model (CIM) [21] and an Eclipse-integrated graphical editor to define graphical models of telecommunication networks [22]. In earlier work [23], we created a composition environment with REUSEWARE that is also integrated into Eclipse. This environment can be used to define reusable CIM model components and compose them to larger network models. In this evaluation, we provided the domain experts at Telefónica with the library tooling presented in this paper. To gain a first feedback, their task was to classify 20 CIM model components and then browse for components using the faceted browser.

In preparation for the evaluation, we created a set of domain-specific facets for the CIM language. For that we performed, in collaboration with the domain experts, a domain analysis and found a set of six facets (cf. Table 2). In addition to the general facets (cf. Table 1), they allow a classification specific for the telecommunication domain. A telecommunication expert can now use our integrated tooling to classify CIM models using the domain facets. Thus, he works in the terminology of his domain and does not need any knowledge about, for example, source code components or their classification. Other telecommunication experts can then use these domain-specific facets with our faceted browser to browse a library of CIM model components.

The remainder of this section consists of three parts, where we summarise the feedback we got from interviewing the domain experts concerning domain facet definition, component classification and component browsing respectively.

Domain Facet Definition. The experts recognised facets as a useful approach for classifying CIM components in general. However, they see a potential weakness of the approach in the fact that facet developers bear a huge responsibility. First, these developers restrict facets and facet values that are the base for all later classifications and browsings. Second, they need to clarify the meaning of facets and values and should take the component developers' perspective into account. These aspects indicate that it is crucial for both, classification and browsing to have well defined facets available.

Component Classification. Faceted classification with its restrictive character[15] appears to be an adequate method for structuring a component library for the domain experts. If the facets are well defined they can support even a large number of component developers to classify their work without creating anomalies such as synonyms, antonyms or plural-forms. In addition to that, the

---

[15] Restrictive with respect to the controlled vocabulary.

Table 2. Telecommunication specific facets

Facet	Description	Examples
CIM-Schema	Uses CIM specific terms to classify the component	CIM-Core, CIM-User CIM-Interop
Connection	Names the main connection used by the component	Ethernet, Wifi, Bluetooth
Device	Describes which sort of device is used by the component	Hub, Router, Modem
Element Type	Distinguishes between conceptual and real life components	Logical, Physical
Protocol	Names the main protocol used by the component	IP, DHCP, IPX, SSH Telnet
Structure	Gives a hint about the component's inner structure	SingleConcept, MultiConcept

experts pointed out, that providing domain knowledge as facets and facet values can simplify work especially in a huge domain such as telecommunication. This is because component developers and users do not have to remember all domain concepts on their own.

The automated classification appears to be a very useful approach for practical use. Rather than classifying huge sets of components by hand, the domain experts, in the roles of component developers, want to use as much automation as possible. Therefore, rules must be specified that cover important aspects of the domain. We identified many opportunities for CIM model components to specify such rules for automation (e.g., for the facets CIM-Schema or Structure).

Together with the domain experts, we identified one particular application of automation rules as an interesting alternative to using the specific classification tool. In the case of CIM components, adding notes to a graphical component diagram was a common method used by the domain experts. These notes contained information that could be extracted and translated into facet values. This was seen as a useful feature by the domain experts since it gives them the opportunity to define facet values directly in their models. This supports our argument that a tight integration of development environment and library system is crucial. All in all, the automated classification support was seen as a critical feature for broad industrial acceptance of faceted classification by the domain experts.

Component Browsing. Faceted browsing was received by the domain experts as an intuitive and user-friendly method to search in a huge repository of components. They acknowledged that step-wise searching in a faceted browser supports component users that think in the problem space rather than in the solution space. As transferring ideas between both worlds is a major challenge in finding the right component for reuse, presenting facets and values can help.

The domain experts, who used the composition environment for CIM without the facet-based library beforehand, stressed the importance of integrating the library system into the composition environment. For them it was very important that a discovered component was directly reusable from the search result view of the component browser.

Nevertheless, the experts missed some features while testing the browser. The browser always constructs a query using logical AND concatenation of all selected facet values. The domain experts encountered cases, where there was a need to express that a facet value should NOT be set or where OR concatenations would be desirable. They suggested that the browser could be improved in the way that the component user selects a facet value that should not be met by the desired components or other configuration facilities, in order to influence the construction of the actual queries based on the selected facet values. Ultimately, the domain experts also suggested that for complex searches a SQL-like query language over the facet data would be helpful for experienced users. Nevertheless, the faceted browsing process has shown to be intuitive as it supports the user in various ways.

The overall results of the evaluation are positive. In particular, the following points were stressed:

- Faceted classification and browsing are promising methods to structure and explore libraries of domain-specific model components.
- Automatic rule-based classification appears to be important for usability and acceptance of the library system.
- The integration of the library system with component development and composition environment is important to support the reuse process.

4.2 Evaluation Using Other Model Component Types

The previous section showed the applicability of our approach to one kind of domain-specific model components. To support our claim that faceted classification and browsing can be used for arbitrary types of model components and that this is supported by our implementation, we tested our approach and implementation with different models, documents and code defined in different languages.

We experimented with languages and components used in the demonstrator system we realised in [24]. There, we performed a component-based and model-driven development of a system using different kind of components including OpenOffice documents, UML models, models defined in graphical and textual domain-specific languages and Java source code.

For all these component types, EMF metamodels and Eclipse-integrated tooling exists. As our implementation was created on the same platform we were able to classify components in their development environment. One interesting point to mention is, that we were able to define facets that were specific to the development process but not to a specific modelling or implementation language. For instance, it was possible to relate each component to one use case in the system. Thus, we defined a facet *UseCase* and classification rules that identified which component was related to which use case. We were then able to use the browser to identify all components related to a specific use case.

5 Conclusion

This paper presented a new approach to facet-based software reuse libraries that takes the requirements of model-driven software development practice into account. The novelties of our approach, compared to earlier facet-based library approaches, are the integration of modern faceted browsing concepts from online systems and the support for software components of arbitrary languages, which is in particular important for model-driven development where models defined in different languages are the components.

We presented an implementation that is integrated into the widely used Eclipse development and modelling environment. Since a variety of languages and tooling for Eclipse and the EMF does already exist, many developers can directly use our implementation in an integrated manner without adaptation effort. This was also vital to transfer our research results into practice.

Our evaluation with the Telefónica domain experts showed that the approach is applicable in practice to browse libraries of domain-specific model components. The results stress the importance of having the library system tightly integrated into the development and composition environment. This improves the usability, since the users have all tools needed available in a single environment. In our case, these tools are Eclipse editors and the REUSEWARE composition tooling.

The first evaluation and experiments we performed can only indicate the potential of an integrated, generic facet-based software component library system. Thus, in the future, we plan to optimize our implementation with regards to performance and to conduct further evaluations on larger component collections.

Acknowledgments

This research has been co-funded by the European Commission in the 6th Framework Programme project MODELPLEX contract no. 034081 (cf. www.modelplex.org) and the European Social Fond / Free State of Saxony, contract no. 80937064.

References

1. Heidenreich, F., Henriksson, J., Johannes, J., Zschaler, S.: On Language-Independent Model Modularisation. In: Katz, S., Ossher, H., France, R., Jézéquel, J.-M. (eds.) Transactions on Aspect-Oriented Software Development VI. LNCS, vol. 5560, pp. 39–82. Springer, Heidelberg (2009)
2. Prieto-Díaz, R.: Implementing faceted classification for software reuse. Communications of the ACM 34(5), 88–97 (1991)
3. Prieto-Díaz, R., Freeman, P.: Classifying Software for Reusability. IEEE Software 4(1), 6–16 (1987)

4. Poulin, J.S., Yglesias, K.P.: Experiences with a Faceted Classification Scheme in a Large Reusable Software Library (RSL). In: Proc. of COMPSAC 1993, pp. 90–99. IEEE, Los Alamitos (November 1993)
5. Eclipse Foundation: Eclipse platform technical overview (April 2006)
6. Steinberg, D., Budinsky, F., Paternostro, M., Merks, E.: Eclipse Modeling Framework, 2nd edn. Pearson Education, London (2009)
7. Object Management Group: MOF 2.0 Core Specification (January 2006), http://www.omg.org/spec/MOF/2.0
8. Mili, A., Mili, R., Mittermeir, R.T.: A survey of software reuse libraries. In: Annals of Software Engineering, January 1998, vol. 5, pp. 349–414. Springer, Heidelberg (January 1998)
9. Rao, C.G., Niranjan, P.: An integrated classification scheme for efficient retrieval of components. Journal of Computer Science 4(10), 821–825 (2008)
10. France, R., Rumpe, B.: Model-driven Development of Complex Software: A Research Roadmap. In: FOSE 2007: 2007 Future of Software Engineering, May 2007, pp. 37–54. IEEE Computer Society, Los Alamitos (May 2007)
11. Object Management Group: SysML 1.0 Specification (September 2007), http://www.omgsysml.org
12. Kolovos, D.S., Paige, R.F., Polack, F.: The Epsilon Object Language. In: Rensink, A., Warmer, J. (eds.) ECMDA-FA 2006. LNCS, vol. 4066, pp. 128–142. Springer, Heidelberg (2006)
13. Priss, U.: Faceted Knowledge Representation. Electronic Transactions on Artificial Intelligence 4, 21–33 (2000)
14. Allen, R.B.: Retrieval from facet spaces. Electronic Publishing 8(2&3), 247–257 (1995)
15. Hearst, M.: Design Recommendations for Hierarchical Faceted Search Interfaces. In: ACM SIGIR Workshop on Faceted Search (August 2006)
16. Polowinski, J.: Widgets for Faceted Browsing. In: Proc. of HCI 2009. LNCS, vol. 5617, pp. 601–610. Springer, Heidelberg (2009)
17. Sacco, G.M., Tzitzikas, Y.: Dynamic Taxonomies and Faceted Search: Theory, Practice, and Experience. Springer, Heidelberg (August 2009)
18. Prieto-Díaz, R.: A Faceted Approach to Building Ontologies. In: Proc. of IRI 2003, pp. 458–465. IEEE, Los Alamitos (October 2003)
19. Object Management Group: Object Constraint Language 2.0 (May 2006), http://www.omg.org/spec/OCL/2.0
20. MODELPLEX Project: Deliverable D1.1.a (v3): Case Study Scenario Definitions (March 2008), http://www.modelplex.org
21. Distributed Management Task Force Inc. (DMTF): Common Information Model Standards (January 2010), http://www.dmtf.org/standards/cim
22. Evans, A., Fernández, M.A., Mohagheghi, P.: Experiences of Developing a Network Modeling Tool Using the Eclipse Environment. In: Paige, R.F., Hartman, A., Rensink, A. (eds.) ECMDA-FA 2009. LNCS, vol. 5562, pp. 301–312. Springer, Heidelberg (2009)
23. Johannes, J., Fernández, M.A.: Adding Abstraction and Reuse to a Network Modelling Tool using the Reuseware Composition Framework. In: Proc. of ECMFA 2010. LNCS, Springer, Heidelberg (June 2010)
24. Johannes, J.: Controlling Model-Driven Software Development through Composition Systems. In: Proc. of NW-MODE 2009 (August 2009)

Precise Specification of Design Pattern Structure and Behaviour

Ashley Sterritt, Siobhán Clarke, and Vinny Cahill

Lero@TCD,
Distributed Systems Group,
Trinity College Dublin
{firstname.lastname}@scss.tcd.ie

Abstract. Applying design patterns while developing a software system can improve its non-functional properties, such as extensibility and loose coupling. Precise specification of structure and behaviour communicates the invariants imposed by a pattern on a conforming implementation and enables formal software verification. Many existing design-pattern specification languages (DPSLs) focus on class structure alone, while those that do address behaviour suffer from a lack of expressiveness and/or imprecise semantics. In particular, in a review of existing work, three invariant categories were found to be inexpressible in state-of-the-art DPSLs: dependency, object state and data-structure. This paper presents Alas: a precise specification language that supports design-pattern descriptions including these invariant categories. The language is based on UML Class and Sequence diagrams with modified syntax and semantics. In this paper, the meaning of the presented invariants is formalized and relevant ambiguities in the UML Standard are clarified. We have evaluated Alas by specifying the widely-used Gang of Four pattern catalog and identified patterns that benefitted from the added expressiveness and semantics of Alas.

1 Introduction

Object-oriented design patterns 'capture design experience in a form that people can use effectively' [1] to develop software with improved non-functional properties such as re-usability, extensibility and loose coupling. Design patterns (later referred to as patterns) dictate certain relationships between classes and objects such as inheritance, object composition, delegation and information hiding. In a pattern implementation, the actor that performs an action is important, in contrast to an algorithm, which may be implemented by any combination of actors. Thus, patterns define object-oriented protocols that must be followed in an implementation. Pattern specifications define a number of roles, most of which are mutually exclusive, to be filled by actors (classes, objects or methods) in the implementation. Precise specification of pattern structure and behaviour communicates the invariants imposed by a pattern on a conforming implementation and enables accurate formal software verification, by, for example, avoiding false positives due to specifications that are too generic.

We performed an analysis of the widely-used Gang of Four (GoF)[1] pattern catalog from which we identified five invariant categories that were used to classify existing work in the area. These categories are cardinality, dependency, control flow, object state and data structure.

Design patterns place constraints on multiple entities (objects, classes and inheritance hierarchies) and are also more generic than concrete software architectures as they describe interactions between entities, whose number and type are unknown. Patterns thus present a subtly different specification challenge. Patterns such as the Abstract Factory and Visitor patterns place constraints on the relation between the number of entities (classes and methods) occuring in separate inheritance hierarchies. For example, in the Visitor pattern, each ConcreteVisitor should have a `visit` method for each ConcreteElement in the Element hierarchy. We refer such invariants as *cardinality* invariants.

The key invariant of numerous GoF patterns, for example the Façade and Abstract Factory patterns, can be expressed informally as "Class A should not be directly associated with Class B" or "Class A shouldn't be hard-coded to use a particular subclass of Class B". The first of these informal statements refer to the static type of variables and has been termed *interface dependency*, while the second refers to the creation of instances of one class by another and is termed *implementation dependency*.

Object state invariants concern the runtime values of objects and their attributes such as whether they have been initialized or not, the equality of attributes and object identity. The Memento pattern's intent is 'to capture and externalize an object's state so that the object can be restored to this state later.[1]' Thus, an invariant on a Memento implementation is that a subset of the state of the Memento is in some relation (e.g., equality) to the state of another object (the Originator), at a particular point in the execution (Memento creation). Also, the state of the objects should remain in this relation until some other execution point (some undo operation). This particular invariant sub-category is called *inter-object state dependency*. *Control flow* invariants are defined as invariants that place constraints on the control-flow in a pattern. Relevant control flows are sequencing, method calls, conditionals and loops.

A number of GoF design patterns describe the use of or are often applied to user-defined recursive *data structures* that are required to demonstrate properties such as being cycle free or not containing elements that are shared (i.e., have two distinct objects that hold references to it). The Composite pattern, for example, "composes objects into tree structures to represent part-whole hierarchies"[1]. In most realizations of the Composite pattern, sharing of sub-trees or leaves is prohibited as this complicates traversal or violates the tree's semantics. In the Decorator pattern, adding a new Decorator to the Decorator chain should not make the Decoratee object unreachable.

Three of these five categories were found to be insufficiently addressed (i.e., inexpressible or ambiguously defined) by the state-of-the-art DPSLs. The three insufficiently addressed categories are (implementation) dependency, object state and data structure. This paper presents Alas (Another Language for pAttern

Specification): a precise specification language that supports design-pattern descriptions including the three invariant categories discussed above. The language is based on UML Class and Sequence diagrams with modified and extended syntax and semantics. UML is the de facto standard for object-oriented software modelling, and UML Sequence diagrams provide a suitable level of granularity at which to describe the inter-object protocols imposed by design patterns. Nevertheless, a number of syntax extensions and clarifications of existing concepts are required for UML to be suitable for precise specification of design patterns enabling formal software verification. In the current version of Alas, there is no concurrency: it can describe only sequential programs. This choice was made to simplify the initial design and the planned supporting verification tool. We plan to add support for concurrency in a future version.

While we chose UML as a basis for Alas, UML in its current form was considered unsuitable for precise design-pattern specification for a number of reasons. Le Guennec et al. [2] notes that UML, despite its templates and parameterized binding, is not suited to expressing cardinality invariants. This is due to a lack of control over the number of bindings that can be made between classes and roles. In addition, patterns require logical statements to be made about software structure, making it necessary to use the Object Constraint Language (OCL) [3] at the meta-model level to define non-standard, pattern-specific entities. Many constructs (such as the CombinedFragments newly introduced in UML 2.0) are described too informally to be the basis for software verification, where precise semantics are required. Also, as design patterns are generic solutions that can be applied in many different contexts, their specifications need to mirror this genericity in some ways that are not supported in UML. One example occurs when one object's value should be some function of another objects, but this function is not common to all pattern variants. The 'reflects' keyword, introduced in Contracts [4] can be used to express this abstract state dependency.

When placing invariants on the state of interacting objects, it is necessary to distinguish between aliases (two names that refer to the same object) and copies (two objects with identical values). As discussed in Section 3, UML and OCL are vague with regard to this distinction. Alas defines binary object predicates isAlias and isCopy to resolve this ambiguity. As OCL lacks an operation to express transitive closure, expressing these data-structure 'shape' invariants in OCL would be verbose and error-prone. For example, the user must be careful to write constraints that do not go into infinite cycles and are undefined. Alas contains basic transitive operations on recursive data structures and uses these to define shape properties such as heap-sharing (two distinct objects holding references pointing to the same object), the existence of cycles and reachability.

In UML Sequence diagrams, a Lifeline represents one and only one object: "While Parts and StructuralFeatures may have multiplicity greater than 1, Lifelines represent only one interacting entity... If the referenced ConnectableElement is multivalued... then the Lifeline may have an expression (the selector') that specifies which particular part is represented by this Lifeline. [5]" This prevents the user from specifying the common case of a method being invoked on each element of an unbound collection in turn. We formalize an existing idiom for expressing this case, by relaxing the binding semantics under particular conditions, allowing them to represent different objects at different times.

The structure of the remainder of this paper is as follows: Section 2 discusses related work. Section 3 introduces Alas through examples relating to the invariant categories described in this paper. Section 4 defines a precise meaning for each of the non-standard extensions and clarifications provided in Alas. Section 5 evaluates the expressiveness of Alas compared to the state-of-the-art DPSLs with respect to the GoF catalog. Finally, Section 6 concludes and considers some directions for future work.

2 Related Work

Numerous DPSLs choose to focus on a pattern's 'essence' or 'leitmotif', specifying design pattern structure that is thought to be common to all pattern variants. These approaches are typically also capable of expressing cardinality invariants. LePUS [6] defines a graphical notation for expressing sets of classes in an inheritance hierarchy and sets of associated methods, along with relationships between them such as invocation and creation. This allows cardinality constraints to be specified simply, graphically and precisely, as it is based on higher-order logic. Le Guennec et al. [2] and Mak et al. [7] handle cardinality invariants using a UML Profile that introduces multiplicities in UML Collaborations at the meta-model level. Lauder and Kent [8] introduce a fourth compartment into the UML Class syntax that utilizes their constraint diagrams, which are also based on set semantics. However, each of these DPSLs, by focusing on structure only, completely ignore the behaviour required to satisfy a pattern's intent.

In RSL [9], a renaming map is used to associate entities in patterns to their corresponding implementation entities, supporting cardinality as well as implementation dependency invariants. The specifications in RSL, however, are verbose and implementation-oriented, making the intent of the pattern hard to understand without significant effort. Lano et al. [10] formally specify patterns in detail, including behaviour such as method calls and object creation, and define a refinement relationship between a software program before and after applying a pattern. The refinement proof must be performed manually though, and this is challenging, given the mathematical basis of the language. BPSL [11] supports the specification of the structure and behaviour of patterns, using first-order logic and the Temporal Logic of Actions (TLA), respectively. The structural part has a similar expressiveness to UML Class diagrams while the behavioural part describes some object state properties such as value equality of variables at a particular execution state. As only one pattern specification is presented, it is difficult to assess the applicability of the language to patterns in general. Dong et al. [12] also utilize TLA for pattern behaviour specification with some precise implementation conformance rules, but with less expressiveness overall.

RBML [13] and FUJABA [14] use UML 2.0 Class and Sequence diagrams to specify pattern structure and behaviour, such as method calls, conditionals and loops. RBML also provides role realization multiplicities to describe cardinality invariants, and is thus one of the most expressive DPSLs overall. It does not address object state or data structure invariants, however, and makes no effort to define a precise semantics for the language. In summary, of the five invariant categories we identified, cardinality and control-flow are well supported in the literature, dependency has had some attention while there are significant gaps in the support for object-state and data-structure invariants.

3 Pattern Specification in Alas

In Alas, pattern specifications are made up of structural diagrams and behavioural diagrams. Alas structural diagrams are UML Class diagrams augmented with first-order logic, ranging over structural entities (classes and methods), to support the specification of cardinality invariants. Interface dependency invariants are supported using binary class operators such as hasRef and calls, along with logical conjunction, disjunction and negation. Implementation dependency invariants are discussed in the following section.

Behavioural diagrams in Alas are based on UML 2.0 Sequence diagrams, currently making use of only the alt, opt and loop CombinedFragments to express control-flow invariants. Object-state invariants are placed in constraint boxes that are connected to particular points in the control flow. These boxes can contain standard OCL collection operators such as set intersection and union. Non-standard extensions allow the expression of, for example, inter-object state dependency and data structure invariants.

3.1 Implementation Dependency Invariants

The dependency invariants in some patterns, including AbstractFactory, Prototype, Bridge and State, are more subtle than simply forbidding variables of a particular type in class definitions. A summary of their common intent might be that "a client holds a reference to an object, but is not hard-coded to a particular implementation (subclass)." The Abstract Factory pattern "provide[s] an interface for creating families of... objects without specifying their concrete class." Thus, a client should never contain the code: Maze aMaze = new Maze() or BombedMaze bMaze = ... as the first performs the initialization itself, and the second commits to a particular subclass. Instead, creation of the object is delegated to a factory object. This is described in the Alas invariant below:

Client hasRef Product AND NOT (Client hasRef ConcreteProduct) AND
    NOT (Client isInitializer ConcreteProduct) .

where ConcreteProduct inherits from Product. isInitializer is a binary operator that states that the subject (first) operand, which may be a class or method, calls the second operand's constructor directly. The first two clauses state that the Client has a reference to the superclass (`Product`), but not to a particular set of subclasses of `Product`: those that inherit from `ConcreteProduct`. The third predicate states that the Client does not initialize any object that is a subclass of Product. Note that dependency predicates apply to a class and all its subclasses, unless over-ridden by other predicates, as shown above.

3.2 Object-State Invariants

The role of a Factory Method is to return a newly created instance of a Product class. Thus, a key invariant of the Factory Method pattern is that a new object is returned, i.e., the object created by the Product constructor is the same object that is returned by the Factory Method. A related creational pattern is the Prototype pattern, which avoids creating a new instance by copying a prototypical one. One invariant of the Prototype pattern is that the object returned by the Prototype's `clone()` method is *not* the same object as the prototype, but should have identical values for some subset of its state. Thus, to specify the Factory Method and Prototype patterns precisely, it is necessary to be able to express the concepts of object identity and value equality.

The OCL Standard ([3] Appendix A: Semantics, Section 2.2) suggests that the meaning of the equality operator, when applied to two object operands, is defined as value equality: "The equality of values of the same type can be checked with the operation $=_t$" (defined for all types) and indeed the implementation of Dresden-OCL's [15] equality operator calls the Java `equals()` method. Collection operators, which one might expect to be defined in terms of object identity, also seem to be value-based. Set subtraction, for example, is defined as "S - <v>: produces a Sequence equal to S, but with all elements equal to v removed." This potentially removes many objects with equal values, rather than a single object uniquely identified by v.

Object identity is discussed briefly in Appendix A, Section 1.2.1: "Objects are referred to by unique object identifiers" [3]. The set `oid(c)` is also defined as the set of object identifiers for a class. This set is not used in the definition of any of the relevant OCL operators, adding to the evidence that objects are compared by value. The UML Standard also makes little reference to object identity. A DataType is described as being "similar to a Class. It differs from a Class in that instances of DataType are identified only by their value." However, the meta-class Class has no attributes or associations that could be used to store identity and both Class and DataType occur at the same level of the UML meta-inheritance hierarchy, inheriting directly from Classifier, and nothing else.

Object identity and value equality are distinguished explicitly in Alas using the `isAlias` and `isCopy` binary operators respectively. These are defined precisely in terms of object identifiers and values in Section 4. The key invariant of the Factory Method pattern uses `isAlias`, and is shown in Figure 1. Note that in Alas conditions are connected at any branching or joining of control-flow. The connection position of the invariant in Figure 1 is equivalent to a postcondition in OCL. Conditions do not need to span multiple lifelines as there

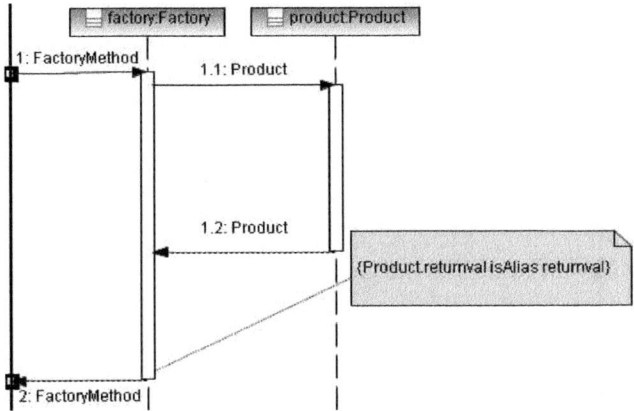

Fig. 1. Use of the `isAlias` predicate to specify object identity in the Factory Method specification

is no concurrency. The `clone()` method of the Prototype pattern also has an attached postcondition, specified as: `returnval isCopy prototype.this`. This condition identifies the `prototype` object and the newly-created and returned object as copies.

It is possible that two lifelines in the same diagram become bound to the same object in the implementation. If a lifeline is intended to identify one unique interacting entity, as suggested by the UML standard, then this binding is a violation of the pattern specification. Roles in the specification are thus always mutually exclusive. We have found that this creates a difficulty in specifying the Chain of Responsibility (CoR) pattern in the case that there is no default Handler for requests. The role of the object that creates the request and the object that handles the request could be the same object, though it is necessary to represent the two roles in two separate lifelines. For this reason, we have defined a n-ary operator `notMutEx` that specifies that two lifelines in a sequence diagram (or two classes in a structural diagram) are not required to be bound to different entities.

3.3 Control-Flow Invariants

In the Observer pattern, when an update occurs to the Subject's state, it calls its `notify` method. `Notify` iterates over the Subject's list of Observers, calling `Update` on each of them in turn. The specification of this behaviour is given in Figure 2, where the names of the loop variable and lifeline selector match. While this is an existing idiom used for describing interactions with entities that have an unbounded number of elements, it is non-standard for two reasons: it requires a redefinition of the immutable lifeline/object binding and the only valid loop operands defined in the standard are `maxint` and `minint` or a boolean expression.

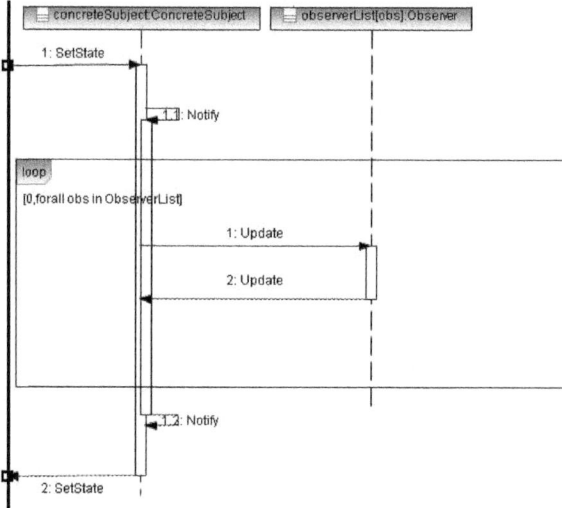

Fig. 2. Specification of the Subject's *Notify* method that involves iteratively calling each object in an unbounded structure

3.4 Data-Structure Invariants

To specify data-structure shape invariants, the specification language must be capable of expressing relations between the position of objects in a recursive structure. There is no primitive operator in OCL for expressing transitive closure directly and it is not discussed in the latest OCL Standard [3]. To obtain the transitive closure of a relation, the user may write a recursive function similar to:

```
allPredecessors = self.predecessor
    → union (self.predecessor.allPredecessors) .
```

This statement, however, may not have the desired effect, as it may go into an infinite loop if the data structure has cycles and would then evaluate to an undefined value. Some tools supporting OCL, such as Eclipse, provide a safe closure operation, by building a collection using an iterative fixpoint algorithm [16]. Also, in OCL queries and constraints, it is possible only to refer to objects that are navigable from the contextual object via associations. In a singly-linked list, for example, this corresponds to all the objects occuring later in the list than the contextual object. When defining data-structure properties, however, it is often more convenient to refer to an object's predecessors: whether heap-sharing occurs can be expressed succinctly by evaluating if the object has two or more immediate predecessors (see section 4). In OCL, it would be necessary to begin from the root of the structure and attempt to identify two (potentially very long) paths to the object.

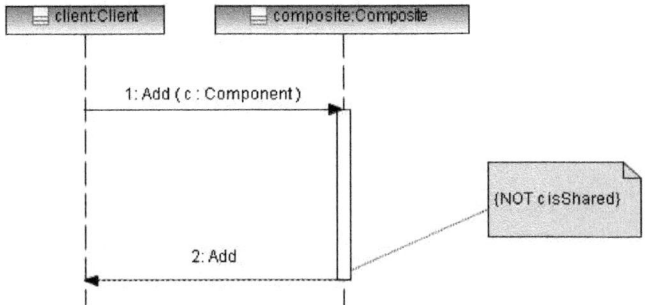

Fig. 3. Specification of a *Composite*'s *Add* method where sharing of nodes is forbidden

Alas data-structure predicates are defined in terms of transitive and non-transitive (one step) versions of the primitives `isPredecessor` and `isSuccessor`. This simplifies the definition of transitive closure relations when compared to OCL and allows for safer and more concise specification. The invariant of the Composite pattern is specified in Figure 3. Note that this invariant is sufficient to ensure the Composite tree is cycle-free, as long as c is the only Component added to the tree in the `add()` method and the `add()` method is the only method that adds to the tree. The first node in a cycle must have two predecessors, i.e. applying the `isShared` predicate to it would evaluate to true.

The CoR pattern decouples the sender and receiver of a request by creating a chain of objects, each of which has the option to handle the request or pass it on. A desirable property of the CoR pattern is that every request eventually gets handled by some Handler. This is often ensured by providing a root Handler that is the end of every chain of Handlers, which can provide some default response. This is specified in Alas using predicates as 'There exists a handler that is capable of providing a response to this request type and this handler is reachable from every other handler" (see Figure 4). The constraint box contains a first-order logic statement quantifying over each object in the Handler chain. The @ sign is an ASCII substitute for the first-order logic 'it holds that' from Z notation. The specification states that the role `default`'s `HandleRequest` method will always call its `ServeRequest` method, i.e., it will never forward the message without handling it. Note that Alas's default semantics is that a diagram specifies required and not optional behaviour (i.e., universally quantified paths). In this way, it is equivalent to a Sequence diagram placed entirely within an `assert` fragment. Diagrams with existential path quantifiers are outside the scope of this paper. Note, the definition of the `chain` data structure is omitted here, but currently data-structure definitions are done textually. These examples show that Alas data structure predicates allow sophisticated statements to be made about the recursive data structures in programs concisely that were previously inexpressible in the context of DPSLs.

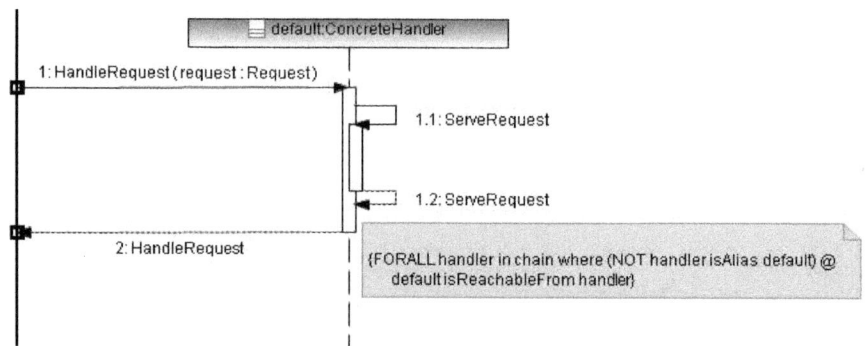

Fig. 4. Specification of the CoR pattern, where a *default* handler is the final node in a chain

4 Semantics

With limited space, this section provides definitions of only some of the more important syntactic elements introduced in the previous section. The meaning of dependency syntax elements is straight-forward and has been sufficiently described in the previous section for an intuitive understanding. Control-flow invariants make use of the `alt` and `opt` CombinedFragments. These are only informally described in the UML Standard and could be interpreted as either mandatory or potential choice. In Alas they are interpreted as mandatory choice, following Lund and Stølen [17]. This means that an `opt` CombinedFragment, for example, in an Alas behavioural diagram indicates that a conditional statement should occur in the implementation. Potential choice (where a conditional in the specification indicates that the implementor can choose whether or not to implement the behaviour) is useful in pattern variant specification. A `variant` CombinedFragment, which has one or many compartments, each indicating an implementation option, is also being defined.

4.1 Object State

To define object state invariant syntax, the state of a program is represented as a transition system. In each state ($s \in S$), there is a set of objects (O) that can grow and shrink between states as objects are created and destroyed, but represent a fixed set in any one state. Each object has a unique identity, which can be accessed using the function $id(o)$. Each object has a set of attributes (A), each element of which is accessed using the notation $obj.a$, and also a subset of attributes CA (i.e., $CA \subset A$) that is considered when deciding if an object is a copy of another. CA is problem-specific and is defined by the user. The value of attributes in each state can be obtained using the function $Val(a)$. Each object is bound to a set of role names (N), and the function $obj(n)$ maps a role name to its object.

We can now define the Alas operators `isAlias` and `isCopy`:

`name isAlias otherName` $\rightarrow_{def} obj(name) = obj(otherName)$.
`name isCopy otherName`
$\rightarrow_{def} \forall ca : CA \bullet Val(obj(name).ca) = Val(obj(otherName).ca)$.

For two objects to be copies of one another, they must be the same kind, but not the same type. Both operators are commutative and transitive. Each role in Alas behavioural diagrams is by default mutually exclusive, so given two role names *name* and *otherName* of the same kind, it holds that:

$$\neg \exists name, otherName \bullet obj(name) = obj(otherName).$$

This can be over-ridden in Alas using `isAlias`, or the `notMutEx` n-ary operator, which has been used in the specification of the CoR pattern variant where there is no default handler.

4.2 Control Flow

The UML Standard implies that there is an immutable binding between a lifeline name in a specification and an object in a candidate implementation. A selector may identify an object in a fixed position in a structure and the absence of a selector leads to an arbitrary object being bound, but these bindings are still to single objects and immutable. It also limits the valid operands that may be used in loop fragments to `maxint` and `minint` or a boolean expression. This prevents the user from specifying interactions with structures of an a priori unknown (or mutable) size. More formally, for a transition system covering the part of the program referred to by the specification with initial state *is* and final accepting state *fs* and ordering relation $\geq$ ('happens before or simultaneous'), the standard interpretation is defined as:

$$\forall s1, s2 : S | (is \geq s1 \geq fs) \wedge (is \geq s2 \geq fs) \bullet obj(n, s1) = obj(n, s2).$$

where $obj(name, state)$ is an extended version of the function defined in the previous section that maps a name in a particular state to an object. In Alas, when a selector is specified that is identical to the loop variable, this requirement is relaxed to allow rebindings to occur each time the object's lifeline returns the flow of control. For a specified call event transition *ctA* and its accompanying return event transition *rtA*, *ctA* and *rtA* can replace *is* and *fs* in the above constraint. After the object returns the flow of control, it releases its binding. After the loop variable is incremented, the lifeline is then free to be rebound to the new value of the variable (one greater than the previous value). The formalization of this idiom, and the corresponding extension of the allowed operands of the loop CombinedFragment enables the precise specification of interactions with unbounded data structures.

4.3 Data Structure

A recursive data structure is defined as a directed graph, where the nodes are objects (with unique identities) that may occur more than once in the structure and the edges are references labelled by their variable name. Null is a valid value for a node. The extent of the data structure stretches from some root node until all paths from the root encounter a null node. We define hasSuccessor* as a transitive binary operator taking two object operands that evaluates to true if it is possible to navigate along the direction of the references from the first operand to the second operand. hasPredecessor* is a similar operator, though it navigates in the opposite direction to the references (this operator distinguishes Alas from OCL in this context). Both operators have a non-starred counterpart, that indicates navigation is only performed for one step. Thus, o hasSuccessor p is true iff one of o's immediate successors is p. Data-structure properties can be defined using these operators and first-order logic. Here, the definition of isCycleFree, isReachableFrom and isShared is shown:

$$ds\ isCycleFree \Leftrightarrow$$
$$\forall x, y : ds\ |\ x\ hasSuccessor* y \bullet \neg x\ hasPredecessor* y.$$
$$x\ isReachableFrom\ y \Leftrightarrow x\ isSuccessor* y.$$
$$x\ isShared \Leftrightarrow$$
$$\exists y, z : ds \bullet x\ hasPredecessor\ y \wedge x\ hasPredecessor\ z.$$

where ds represents some data structure, and x and y are two objects. These invariants are challenging to verify, and are the focus of an active area of research in software verification [18][19].

5 GoF Evaluation

We used Alas to specify the GoF pattern catalog (omitting the Interpreter pattern as a domain-specific special case of the Composite pattern). Table 1 shows the invariant categories common to Alas and other DPSLs. Class diagrams with directed and aggregation associations and generalizations are ubiquitous, and are omitted for the sake of brevity. Over-riding is required in numerous GoF patterns and can be specified in the usual way in UML: by including the method or attribute in the over-riding subclass definition. Class identity involves comparing two class names for equality (names are unique) and is done using the notation objectRole.class, similarly to the OCL objectRole.oclIsTypeOf(class). In both tables (Table 1 and 2), patterns with no relevant invariant categories are omitted, though they have been specified.

Table 2 outlines pattern invariants belonging to novel invariant categories in Alas, as well as the non-standard and clarified UML elements required for each pattern specification. It can be seen that 11 patterns can be described in more detail using the novel invariant categories, with seven benefitting from either flexible role-actor binding, inter-object state dependency or data structure.

Table 1. Pattern invariants common to Alas and state-of-the-art DPSLs in GoF design pattern catalog specifications

Design pattern	Invariant type
Abstract Factory	Cardinality
Factory Method	Control-flow
Singleton	Control-flow (conditional), object state (null)
Adapter	Control-flow
Bridge	Control-flow
Composite	Object-state (Set operations)
Decorator	Interface dependency, control-flow
Façade	Interface dependency, control-flow
Flyweight	Control-flow (conditional), object state (null)
Proxy	Interface dependency, control-flow (conditional)
CoR	Control-flow (conditional)
Command	Control-flow
Iterator	Object state (Sequence operations)
Mediator	Class identity, interface dependency, control-flow
State	Class identity, control-flow
Strategy	Interface dependency, control-flow
Visitor	Cardinality, control-flow

Table 2. Novel invariant categories in Alas and non-standard UML syntax and semantics in GoF design pattern catalog specifications

Design pattern	Invariant type	Non-standard UML
Abstract Factory	Implementation dependency	Object identity
Builder	Implementation dependency	Method set
Factory Method	-	Object identity
Prototype	-	Value equality
Singleton	-	Control-flow (conditional)
Composite	Data-structure	Flexible role-actor binding
Decorator	Data-structure	-
Flyweight	-	Control-flow (cond.), object identity
Proxy	-	Control-flow (conditional)
CoR	Data-structure	Control-flow (cond.), object identity
Command	Implementation dependency	-
Iterator	Implementation dependency	Object identity
Memento	Inter-object state dependency	-
Observer	Inter-object state dependency	Flexible role-actor binding
Strategy	Implementation dependency	
Template Method	-	(Ordered) method set

Eleven GoF pattern specifications make use of non-standard UML syntax and semantics, with object identity or value equality concepts being used in six patterns, some of which were creational, structural or behavioural. Four patterns have conditional control-flow, method sets are used to specify two patterns while flexible object role-actor bindings are used in two patterns: Observer and Composite. (Ordered) method sets are beyond the scope of this paper.

The distinction between interface and implementation dependency and datastructure invariants occur in five and three patterns respectively. Inter-object state dependency invariants occur in only two GoF patterns, but this is also an ongoing software verification challenge, with implications for modular reasoning and non-functional properties such as extensibility and maintainability [20], so they have already been shown to have widespread application outside the GoF pattern catalog. While the flexible object role-actor binding occurs only in the specification of the Observer pattern, it is useful wherever an operation is applied to every element in an unbounded (growable) collection. Finally, method sets occur in only two patterns, and ordered methods only in relation to the Template Method pattern. It is conceivable that ordered sets of methods occur frequently in software frameworks, but future work will include searching for more situations where this concept is applicable.

6 Summary, Conclusions and Future Work

In this paper, we present Alas, a design pattern specification language capable of expressing a number of invariant categories not addressed by state-of-the-art DPSLs. Each of these categories is motivated by examples from the GoF design pattern catalog and an example of an Alas specification of each category is presented. While UML is the de facto standard in object-oriented software modelling, patterns provide a different modelling challenge, as illustrated by the large body of literature on DPSLs. Also, formal software verification requires specifications with precise semantics. For this reason, non-standard UML syntax and semantics is introduced and defined. The specifications of all but one of the GoF patterns using Alas are classified according to the invariant categories they require, and the increased expressiveness of Alas with respect to the state-of-the-art is found to provide a benefit for just under half of the catalog.

In a short paper, it has not been possible to describe all the features of the language and their precise meaning. Some of the features omitted or only mentioned in this paper are Alas structural diagrams (UML Class diagrams with some modifications), cardinality invariants, pattern variant specfication, legal interleavings of pattern and non-pattern behaviour and temporal operators, including path operators (similar to LSC [21] hot and cold charts).

Planned future work includes specifying patterns outside the GoF catalog to evaluate the general applicability of Alas. Currently, the semantic definition of Alas is also incomplete. A verification tool capable of demonstrating a refinement relation between a pattern specification and a design is currently under development. Finally, as patterns impose invariants on all the members of an inheritance hierarchy, the concept of behavioural subtyping is relevant. More work is required to understand the obligations of Alas behavioural invariants on all subclasses of a specified class role.

Acknowledgements. The authors would like to thank Mélanie Bouroche and Serena Fritsch for reading drafts and providing feedback. This work was supported, in part, by Science Foundation Ireland grant 03/CE2/I303_1 to Lero - The Irish Software Engineering Research Centre (www.lero.ie).

References

1. Gamma, E., Helm, R., Johnson, R., Vlissides, J.: Design Patterns: Elements of Reusable Object-Oriented Software. Addison-Wesley, Reading (1995)
2. Le Guennec, A., Sunyé, G., Jézéquel, J.: Precise Modeling of Design Patterns. In: Evans, A., Kent, S., Selic, B. (eds.) UML 2000. LNCS, vol. 1939, pp. 482–496. Springer, Heidelberg (2000)
3. OMG: Object Constraint Language, Version 2.0 (2006), http://www.omg.org/cgi-bin/doc?formal/2006-05-01
4. Helm, R., Holland, I.M., Gangopadhyay, D.: Contracts: Specifying Behavioral Compositions in Object-Oriented Systems. SIGPLAN Not. 25(10), 169–180 (1990)
5. OMG: Unified Modeling Language: Superstructure (2009), http://www.omg.org/docs/formal/09-02-02.pdf
6. Eden, A.H.: Formal Specification of Object-Oriented Design. In: Proceedings of the International Conference on Multidisciplinary Design in Engineering (2001)
7. Mak, J.K.H., Choy, C.S.T., Lun, D.P.K.: Precise Modeling of Design Patterns in UML. In: ICSE 2004, Washington, DC, USA, pp. 252–261. IEEE Computer Society, Los Alamitos (2004)
8. Lauder, A., Kent, S.: Precise Visual Specification of Design Patterns. In: ECOOP 1998: Proceedings of the 12th European Conference on Object-Oriented Programming, London, UK, pp. 114–134. Springer, Heidelberg (1998)
9. Flores, A., Cechich, A., Aranda, G.: A Generic Model of Object-Oriented Patterns Specified in RSL, pp. 44–72. IGI Publishing (2007)
10. Lano, K., Bicarregui, J., Goldsack, S.: Formalising Design Patterns. In: RBCS-FACS Northern Formal Methods Workshop (1996)
11. Taibi, T., Ngo, D.C.L.: Formal Specification of Design Patterns - A Balanced Approach. Journal of Object Technology 2(4), 127–140 (2003)
12. Dong, J., Alencar, P., Cowan, D.: Formal Specification and Verification of Design Patterns, pp. 94–108. IGI Publishing (2007)
13. France, R.B., Kim, D.K., Ghosh, S., Song, E.: A UML-Based Pattern Specification Technique. IEEE Transactions on Software Engineering 30(3), 193–206 (2004)
14. Wendehals, L., Orso, A.: Recognizing Behavioral Patterns at Runtime using Finite Automata. In: WODA 2006: Proceedings of the 2006 international workshop on Dynamic systems analysis, pp. 33–40. ACM, New York (2006)
15. Demuth, B., Wilke, C.: Model and Object Verification by Using Dresden OCL. In: Proceedings of the Russian-German Workshop Innovation Information Technologies: theory and practice, Ufa, Russia, July 25-31 (2009)
16. Dwyer, M., Hatcliff, J., Howell, R.: Lecture 14: Advanced OCL Expressions, Kansas State University (2001)

17. Lund, M.S., Stølen, K.: A Fully General Operational Semantics for UML 2.0 Sequence Diagrams with Potential and Mandatory Choice. In: Misra, J., Nipkow, T., Sekerinski, E. (eds.) FM 2006. LNCS, vol. 4085. Springer, Heidelberg (2006)
18. Sagiv, M., Reps, T., Wilhelm, R.: Parametric Shape Analysis via 3-Valued Logic. ACM Transactions on Programming Languages and Systems 24(3), 217–298 (2002)
19. Berdine, J., Calcagno, C., Cook, B., Distefano, D., OHearn, P.W., Wies, T., Yang, H.: Shape Analysis for Composite Data Structures. In: Computer Aided Verification (2007)
20. Clarke, D.G., Potter, J.M., Noble, J.: Ownership Types for Flexible Alias Protection. SIGPLAN Not. 33(10), 48–64 (1998)
21. Damm, W., Harel, D.: LSCs: Breathing Life into Message Sequence Charts. In: Formal Methods in System Design, pp. 293–312. Kluwer Academic Publishers, Dordrecht (1998)

Coping with Variability in Model-Based Systems Engineering: An Experience in Green Energy

Salvador Trujillo[1], Jose Miguel Garate[2], Roberto Erick Lopez-Herrejon[3],
Xabier Mendialdua[1], Albert Rosado[2], Alexander Egyed[3],
Charles W. Krueger[4], and Josune de Sosa[1]

[1] IKERLAN Research Centre, Mondragon, Spain
{strujillo,xmendialdua,jdesosa}@ikerlan.es
[2] Alstom Wind Power, Barcelona, Spain
{jose-miguel.garate,albert.rosado}@power.alstom.com
[3] Johannes Kepler University, Linz, Austria
{roberto.lopez,alexander.egyed}@jku.at
[4] BigLever Software, Austin, TX, USA
ckrueger@biglever.com

Abstract. Model-Based Systems Engineering (MBSE) is an emerging engineering discipline whose driving motivation is to provide support throughout the entire system life cycle. MBSE not only addresses the engineering of software systems but also their interplay with physical systems. Quite frequently, successful systems need to be customized to cater for the concrete and specific needs of customers, end-users, and other stakeholders. To effectively meet this demand, it is vital to have in place mechanisms to cope with the variability, the capacity to change, that such customization requires. In this paper we describe our experience in modeling variability using SysML, a leading MBSE language, for developing a product line of wind turbine systems used for the generation of electricity.

1 Introduction

In many domains, software engineering is but one discipline that contributes to the success of software systems. Indeed, software systems rarely stand alone but must be integrated into larger systems comprising specialized hardware and merging the expertise of a wide range of technologies – mechatronics, electrical engineering, aeronautics, etc. *Software-intensive systems* characterize such systems where software interacts with other software, systems, devices, sensors, and with people [1].

For software engineering, the development of software-intensive systems poses new challenges – from people who do not have the same technological background (which hampers their communication), to historical boundaries (development roles and responsibilities that have existed for a long time). In particular, in those domains where software has not been a vital part of a system but is increasingly becoming one, the introduction of software engineering has become a source of confusion – as roles and responsibilities must shift but the various disciplines are not able to individually decide how to best do that. The role of software engineering is then often one of a "back-end" engineering discipline that is no longer able to make or affect important design decisions.

Model-Based Systems Engineering (MBSE) recognizes the new unifying role that modeling ought to take for the engineering of software-intensive systems, namely, providing a "common language" for communication among the multiple disciplines involved in the development of this type of systems. It should be noted though that this effort is by no means an attempt to replace the rich and expressive modeling concepts that exist and have proven invaluable in each of the distinct disciplines. On the contrary, the aim is to foster the understanding and exchange of information among all stakeholders. SysML is an example of a modeling language conceived to play that unifying role [2].

There is however one crucial need that has not been addressed in modeling languages such as SysML. Quite often, software-intensive systems need to be customized to fit the concrete and particular needs of different clients, users, developers, etc. The capacity of change that software artifacts must have to meet all the customization needs is collectively referred to as *variability* [3], and thus it must be readily expressed in modeling languages that aim to capture system customization demands.

In this paper, we present an approach to support variability in SysML and how it has been applied to an ongoing project on wind turbine systems for the generation of electricity. We summarize the lessons learned during the modeling and development of a family of wind turbine systems and what we believe are new venues of experimentation and research.

2 Systems Engineering

Systems Engineering has as its function to guide the engineering of complex systems [4]. It differs from traditional engineering in that it focuses on a system as a whole, that is, as a set of diverse and interrelated components that have complex relations amongst them. Next we provide the basic background on MBSE followed by a short description of the key characteristics of SysML used in our work.

2.1 Model-Based Systems Engineering

Model-Based Systems Engineering (MBSE) is defined by the International Council on Systems Engineering (INCOSE), as the formalized application of modeling to support system requirements, design, analysis, verification and validation activities beginning in the conceptual design phase and continuing throughout development and later life cycle phases [5]. This emerging discipline has evolved as a result of the increasing reliance on *Model-Driven Engineering (MDE)* technologies over the last decade [6]. Following the MDE philosophy, MBSE models not only serve as documentation but can also be executed for simulations to further assist with the verification and validation of design decisions.

There has been an extensive research effort and applications of MBSE lead by INCOSE, OMG, and several other organizations. Many different methodologies have been proposed. A survey by Estefan describes the salient characteristics of some of them [7]. This survey highlights the importance that using systems engineering modeling standards brings for tool vendors and users.

Similarly, there are several modeling languages and environments that have been developed and adopted for different types of application domains and user communities. An example of a proprietary environment for Model-Based design for dynamic and embedded systems is Simulink [8]. Another example is Dymola, used primarily in the automotive, aerospace, and robotics industries [9].

2.2 Systems Modeling Language Overview

The System Modeling Language (SysML) is a general-purpose modeling language for systems engineering applications [2]. SysML is an extension of a subset of the U*nified Modeling Language (UML)* [10]. SysML shares with standard UML the following behavior diagrams: sequence, state machines, and use case. In structure diagrams, SysML shares package diagrams and extends UML's activity, block definition, and internal block diagrams. SysML also adds two new types of diagrams: requirement, and parametric (an extension to internal blocks).

The basic structural units in SysML are *blocks*. They can represent hardware, software, mechanical parts, or other sorts of element that can constitute a system. There are two types of blocks: block definition diagrams describe the system hierarchy and system/component classifications, and internal block diagrams model the internal structure of a system in terms of its parts, ports, and connectors.

The requirements diagram describes the requirements hierarchies and their derivation. This diagram provides the means to relate a requirement to its corresponding model element(s). The parametric diagram captures constraints on system property values (e.g. physical constraints like weight) to help the integration of design models with engineering models.

Multi-View Modeling (MVM) is a common modeling practice that advocates that multiple, different and yet related models are required to represent the perspectives and information needs of diverse system stakeholders throughout the development process [11,12]. SysML is an example of MVM because of its distinct diagram types. A crucial issue in MVM is the expression and maintenance of the semantic relationships that exist amongst the elements in the distinct views.

3 Wind Turbine Systems and MBSE

The consumption of energy has dramatically increased in the last century, with the negative effect of incrementing pollution and CO2 emissions. Nowadays, there is evidence that this prolonged consumption has caused significant impact on the environment. Most notably, the planet is facing a steadily complex problem derived from the global climate change known as Global Warning [13]. There are currently worldwide efforts to produce renewable energy with reduced impact on the environment. Wind energy is a major player in this market accounting for a significant rate of the renewable production. In some western European countries it has reached 20% market penetration with the aid of government subsidies [14].

The production of wind power is typically achieved by an array of wind turbines put together in a location called wind farm. The locations where wind farms are installed can vary significantly, for example in the sea, deserts, mountains, etc. Wind turbines are complex engineering systems that are composed of several mechanical elements and subsystems such as blades, pitch, rotor, generator, and current inverter. In charge of the turbines there is a control system that actually manages the entire power production process of a wind turbine system. The economical and ecological importance of wind power combined with the technological and engineering challenges of the wind turbine systems presents an ideal opportunity to exploit the substantial benefits of employing MBSE.

3.1 Why Use SysML?

Wind turbine systems, as any complex system, have a large number of functional, performance, physical and interface requirements which have to be satisfied during the development process. This implies the need for a comprehensive requirements engineering and management during the project. The number of requirements in our systems are counted by the hundreds. The capacity of SysML to deal with large systems and the mature tool support available were deciding factors in our selection.

Structurally, wind turbine systems consist of various elements, such as tower, nacelle, rotor, blades, blade pitches, sensors, actuators, generator, inverter, refrigeration subsystems, and so on. The control system alone consists of several main subsystems. These subsystems offer all kinds of information and interfaces. Their management alone is challenging because it typically involves teams from multidisciplinary backgrounds such as aeronautical (wind) engineers, electrical engineers, and software engineers. Additionally, our project involved geographically distributed project teams which demanded a common modeling representation and understanding. In this working environment, the ability to represent the system structurally, the modeling language expressiveness for all the participating engineering disciplines, availability of extensive documentation, and an increasing community of users were all crucial factors in favor of SysML.

Wind turbine systems, like many complex systems, must promptly adapt to changing environment conditions; in our case, conditions such as wind speed, direction, or temperature. This rapid adaption makes behavioral expressiveness a stringent requirement of a modeling language for this domain. The most remarkable challenge is the real-time demands imposed to effectively control the conversion of wind energy into AC electricity and its transfer to the electric grid. SysML can meet these domain needs.

The ability to adapt the system design to respond to the needs of a customer with a reduced time-to-market is especially challenging in this sector due to the rapid pace of change in the wind power industry. Next we present the sources that originate the variability in our wind turbine systems to subsequently describe how they are addressed.

3.2 Sources of Variability

Wind turbine systems often need to be customized to meet the needs of different clients and locations worldwide. A one-size-fits-all system is inappropriate because of the large variability involved. In general, the sources of the variability in this domain can be categorized as follows:

- Different power generation requirements. For instance, typical requirements range from 850 KW to 3 MW. As expected, to meet the demands on such a wide range, different topologies, technologies and consequently different system elements are needed.
- Different controlled elements. As an example, consider the alternatives for cooling parts of a system: refrigerated air, refrigerated water, or a combination of both. The existence of alternatives like these implies that the elements involved most likely differ.
- Different controlling strategies. For example, a system could be deployed in geographical locations with extreme weather conditions of cool, heat, humidity, etc. Consequently, the control behavior of the system elements may vary according to the deployment site.
- Different locations. In this case, countries or regions may have specific legal or environmental regulations that must be fulfilled.

All these sources of variabilities can describe the whole range of wind turbine systems available in the market. Nonetheless, like most product line systems, it is unfeasible to attempt at tackling all of them in a single product line. Thus

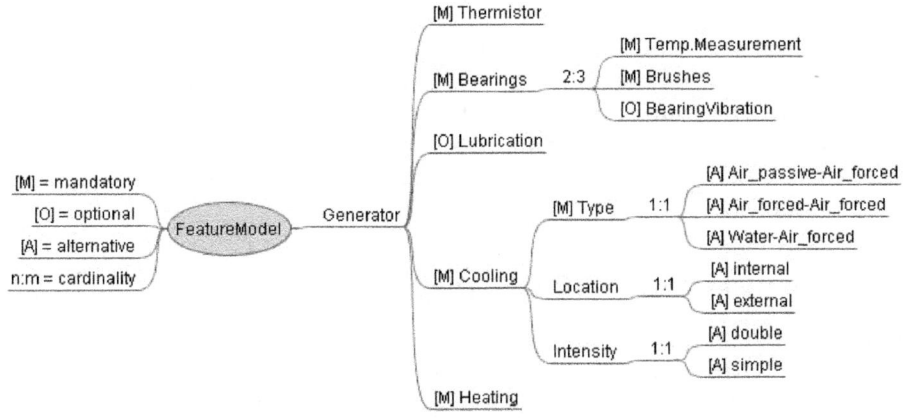

Fig. 1. Feature model - Partial subsystem

a careful scoping (selection of which features to include in a product line) is required.

Figure 1 shows a feature model, rendered as a mind map for simplicity, of our scoped product line. The focus in this paper is on the generator subsystem of the wind turbine. For example, in this figure, `Cooling` denotes a mandatory feature as all generators do require a refrigeration system. The generators we considered can have three cooling alternatives denoted with the features: `Air_passive-Air_forced`, `Air_forced-Air_Forced`, and `Water-Air_forced`. A generator has only one of these alternatives installed, denoted with cardinality 1:1 in the figure. Next we present how these sources of variability were handled using variability management for our wind turbine systems.

4 Variability Management with SysML

A *Software Product Line (SPL)* is a set of software-intensive systems that share a common, managed set of features satisfying the specific needs of a particular market segment or mission and that are developed from a common set of core assets in a prescribed way [15]. The significant benefits of applying SPL practices have been extensively documented and corroborated both in academia and industry [15,16,17]. Amongst them, the reduced time-to-market and the increased reuse of assets throughout the entire development cycle.

SPL approaches can be broadly categorized in two main groups depending on how they express variability in software artifacts. In *compositional* approaches, also known as with *positive variability* [18], the variable parts are encapsulated in modular units which are put together according to the features selected for building a system [19,20]. In *integrative* approaches, also known as with *negative variability*, the artifacts contain both the common and variable parts. Building a system means keeping the variable parts of the desired features in the artifacts while removing those parts belonging to unselected features [21,22].

Generally speaking, *variation points* are the places in the artifacts where variation can occur [23]. More concisely, a variation point is the representation of a variability subject within domain artifacts enriched by contextual information [17]. The context mentioned in this definition refers to the instantiation logic or mechanism to realize an actual artifact variant. In the case of integrative variability, the variation points and their instantiation logic are commonly denoted explicitly in the artifacts. An example of this are the *#ifdefs* macros of preprocessors.

4.1 Variation Points in SysML Diagrams

Variability is handled by using the notion of variation point of the BigLever Gears tool. System modeling is done by using IBM Rational Rhapsody. We handle variability in the diagrams by using the IBM Rational Rhapsody/Gears Bridge [24,25]. In short, these bridge tool provides support in three forms:

- Representation of variation points into model elements.
- Mappings among those variation-point-elements and features. These mappings are referred to as *feature logic*, and express the impact of features in model elements.
- Derivation of specific models according to feature selections, a process called *actuation*.

Engineering a system using SysML involves representing different diagrams, each providing a different perspective on the model such as structure or behavior. For example, Figure 2 shows a simplified block definition diagram for the generator subsystem of the wind turbine system. The upper side of this figure depicts the *blocks* Generator, Bearings, Refrigeration, and Electrical subsystem. These blocks corresponds to the major constituent elements of the generator subsystem. Some of these blocks are as well subdivided into further elements.

As highlighted before, our wind turbine systems form a family of products and as such they ought to be modeled. Consequently, variability must be reflected in the modeling diagrams. An example of this variability is the different refrigerating strategies; in our case, a system may be cooled using air or water.

Variability is expressed in SysML using stereotypes that represent the variation points of the different elements in the diagram. Figure 2 shows in block Refrigeration an «AttributeVariationPoint» to capture the variability of refrigeration strategies.

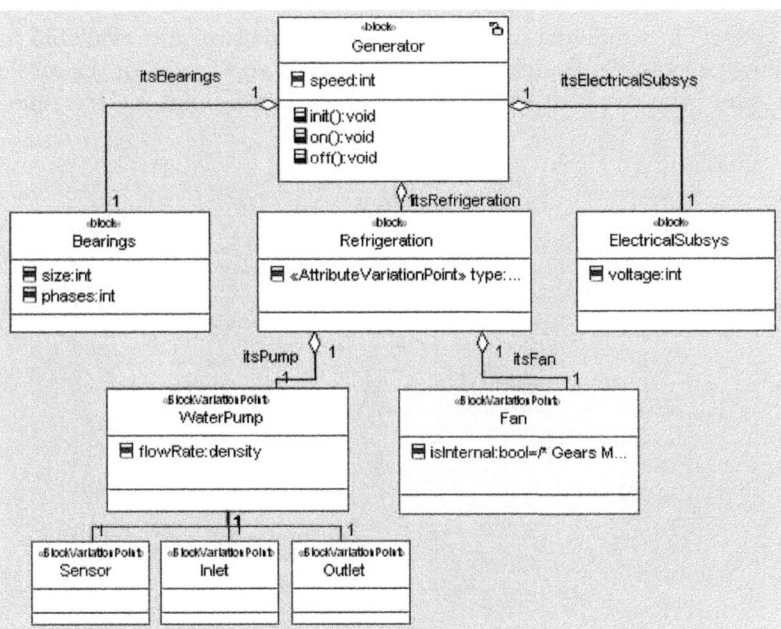

Fig. 2. Block Definition Diagram with variation points

The WaterPump block models the water refrigeration strategy (in Figure 1 is feature Water-Air_forced), and the block Fan models the air strategy (feature Air_forced-Air_forced in Figure 1). In both cases, the entire block element is variable which is denoted with «BlockVariationPoint».

Next we describe how actuation works. As a first step, the features desired for a particular member of the product line are selected. All common model elements, those without variation point stereotypes, will be part of the resulting diagram. The conditions associated to each element with a variation point (feature logic) are evaluated, if the conditions hold the respective element will be part of the resulting diagram. For instance, consider a wind turbine system that is refrigerated with water. For this option, feature Water-Air_forced is selected. The feature logic of the variation point of attribute type in Refrigeration block sets the initial value according to the selection. The feature logic of WaterPump, Sensor, Inlet, and Outlet causes these blocks to be included. In contrast, the logic of Fan will exclude this block when selecting Water-Air_forced.

Modeling variability at the family level, as opposed to each single system, fosters the reuse of system diagrams. But most importantly, it empowers the system designer with an enriched and new global perspective of all the design decisions and trade-offs involved. This perspective should not only address the needs of software engineers, but also those from the multiple disciplines usually involved in the conception and design of complex systems.

4.2 Variation Points in Multiple Views

Since SysML has different views, variation points are also available for their elements. For example, Figure 3 shows a simplified statechart for the refrigeration subsystem of the wind turbine system. The variation point mechanisms are the

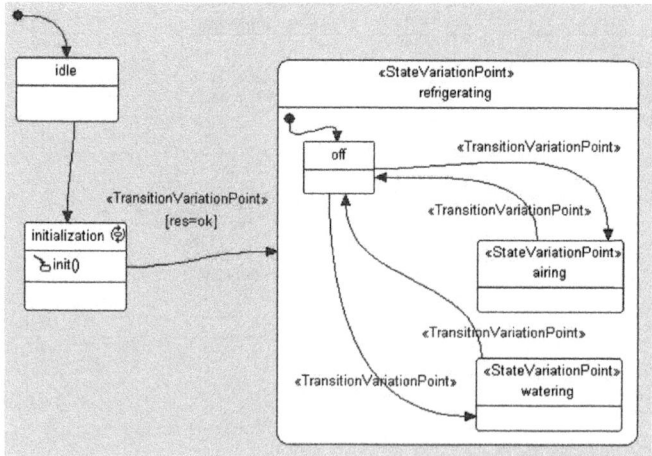

Fig. 3. Statechart diagram with variation points

Table 1. Elements supported in SysML

Diagram	Element	Stereotype
Block Definition	Block	BlockVariationPoint
Internal Block	Part	ObjectVariationPoint
	Attribute	AttributeVariationPoint
	Operation	PrimitiveOperationVariationPoint
	Port	PortVariationPoint
Statechart	State	StateVariationPoint
Activity	Transition	TransitionVariationPoint
	Action	ActionVariationPoint

same as to those described for block diagrams. Besides statecharts and block definition diagrams, variability support is also available for internal block and activity diagrams. Table 1 summarizes the diagrams, their elements and the stereotypes to represent a variation point.

Note that Figure 3 specifies the behavior of the Refrigeration block in Figure 2. Notice here that the operations used within actions or transitions of a statechart should be defined in a block model. Such kind of dependencies among different views are common and make possible the communication among the distinct engineering disciplines. Hence the need of checking consistency of the different diagrams.

4.3 Perspective and Lessons Learned

The development of systems involve the combination of skills from different disciplines. Wind turbine systems are not an exception. Our team involves over two dozen engineers from software, embedded systems, mechanical and aeronautical backgrounds. This is an ongoing project that started two years ago. At present our focus is code generation from some models targeted to parts of the software architecture. Our preliminary results indicate an encouraging improvement in coping with the inherent system complexity. One of the reasons is that systems are now specified in terms closer to the problem domain, which gives engineers the ability to detect and resolve problems at that level while separating them from the software implementation details.

We summarize the lessons learned as follows:

- *Design as a continuum.* System design is a continuous process where each discipline focuses on certain design parts most frequently develop in parallel disciplinary teams. Introducing variability further accelerates this continuous process because changes may have a broader impact on the entire development process. Having a common approach to handle variability across engineering disciplines plays thus a pivotal role.
- *Living with inconsistencies.* In this paper we assumed that the different system views should at anytime be consistent. However, there may be intermediate stages during the development in which certain inconsistencies may be allowed temporarily until some parts are completed by different teams.

- *Clearly defined system-software boundaries.* Recognizing the significance of separating systems from software engineering seems trivial. However, when considering the close relationships among different elements, it is far from obvious. This realization was a turning point in our project, and marked a first-step towards engineering our family of wind turbine systems. Our initial conception of variability shifted from a software-centric to a broader system perspective.
- *Software design driven by system design.* The ability to delay or lately modify design decisions is relevant in our case since the software have to fit the system elements it is controlling. Frequent situations of last-minute modifications in the system are now mitigated by the variability handling.

5 Related Work

There exist an increasing body of literature at the intersection of product lines and MBSE. In this section we present those pieces of work that most closely related to our approach and research experience.

Dauenhauer et al. describe an approach to model variability for testbed automation systems [26]. Contrary to our work, they use a positive variability approach whereby a models is constructed from a set of models through model transformations. Additionally, they define their own metamodel to represent and implement variability.

Beuche et al. present an approach for modeling binding-times using Simulink [27]. They define a metamodel for representing variation points in models of this language. In that sense, it follows a similar approach to ours because they also represent variability in terms of variation points that are made explicit in the models.

Favaro and Mazzini extend *FeatuRSEB*, a method for domain modeling, with SysML constructs [28]. This approach leverages SysML specific diagrams as follows: block diagrams to represent its so called context models and higher level architecture, requirements diagrams for its domain requirement models, and parametric diagrams to document its business decisions. One of the key differences with our work is that this extension to FeatureRSEB does make variation points explicit in SysML diagram elements.

6 Conclusions and Future Work

This paper described an approach to cope with variability in SysML modeling. We reported our experience in applying this approach as part of an ongoing project on wind turbine systems for electricity generation. This application has proven successful because it treats system variability in an uniform way; in our case, this uniform treatment has improved of the overall development process.

Our work has also highlighted the need of mechanisms to ensure the consistency among the different SysML diagrams. We plan to leverage our experience and tool support in incremental consistency of UML models to address this pressing need [29,30].

Acknowledgments. This work was co-supported by the Spanish Ministry of Science & Innovation under contract TIN2008-06507-C02-02. This work is partially funded by the Austrian FWF under agreement P21321-N15. We would like to express our gratitude to Glenn Meter and Marty Bakal for their promptly support with the Gears/Rhapsody bridge. We would like to thank also to Oskar Berreteaga, David Gonzalez and Antonio Perez for their early advise.

References

1. Wirsing, M., Banâtre, J.P., Hölzl, M.M., Rauschmayer, A. (eds.): Soft-Ware Intensive Systems. LNCS, vol. 5380. Springer, Heidelberg (2008)
2. Object Management Group (OMG), Sysml http://www.omgsysml.org
3. Svahnberg, M., van Gurp, J., Bosch, J.: A taxonomy of variability realization techniques. Softw., Pract. Exper. 35(8), 705–754 (2005)
4. Kossiakoff, A., Sweet, W.: Systems Engineering. Principles and Practice. Addison-Wesley, Reading (2003)
5. International Council on Systems Engineering (INCOSE): Systems Engineering Vision 2020. Technical Report INCOSE-TP-2004-004-02 (September 2007)
6. Bézivin, J.: On the unification power of models. Software and System Modeling 4(2), 171–188 (2005)
7. Estefan, J.A.: Survey of Model-Based Systems Engineering (MBSE) Methodologies. Technical report (September 2007)
8. MathWorks: Simulink, http://www.mathworks.com/
9. Modelica: Dymola, http://www.3ds.com/products/catia/portfolio/dymola
10. Object Management Group (OMG): Unified Modeling Language (UML), http://www.uml.org
11. Finkelstein, A., Gabbay, D.M., Hunter, A., Kramer, J., Nuseibeh, B.: Inconsistency handling in multperspective specifications. IEEE Trans. Software Eng. 20(8), 569–578 (1994)
12. Nuseibeh, B., Kramer, J., Finkelstein, A.: A framework for expressing the relationships between multiple views in requirements specification. IEEE Trans. Software Eng. 20(10), 760–773 (1994)
13. Intergovernmental Panel on Climate Change (IPCC): IPCC Assessment Reports, http://www.ipcc.ch/
14. World Watch Institute: Wind Power Increase in 2008 Exceeds 10-year Average Growth Rate (May 2009), http://www.worldwatch.org/
15. Clements, P., Northrop, L.: Software Product Lines - Practices and Patterns. Addison-Wesley, Reading (2001)
16. van der Linden, F., Schmidt, K., Rommes, E. (eds.): Software Product Lines in Action. Springer, Heidelberg (2007)
17. Pohl, K., Bockle, G., van der Linden, F.: Software Product Line Engineering - Foundations, Principles and Techniques. Springer, Heidelberg (2006)
18. Groher, I., Völter, M.: Using aspects to model product line variability. In: SPLC (2) (2008)
19. Mezini, M., Ostermann, K.: Variability management with feature-oriented programming and aspects. In: Taylor, R.N., Dwyer, M.B. (eds.) SIGSOFT FSE, pp. 127–136, ACM, Newyork (2004)
20. Batory, D.S., Sarvela, J.N., Rauschmayer, A.: Scaling step-wise refinement. IEEE Trans. Software Eng. 30(6), 355–371 (2004)

21. Gomaa, H., Olimpiew, E.M.: Managing variability in reusable requirement models for software product lines. In: Mei, H. (ed.) ICSR 2008. LNCS, vol. 5030, pp. 182–185. Springer, Heidelberg (2008)
22. Zhang, H., Jarzabek, S.: XVCL: a mechanism for handling variants in software product lines. Sci. Comput. Program. 53(3), 381–407 (2004)
23. Jacobson, I., Griss, M., Jonsson, P.: Software Reuse: Architecture, Process and Organization for Business Success. Addison-Wesley Professional, Reading (1997)
24. Krueger, C.W.: Leveraging integrated model-driven development and software product line development technologies. In: OOPSLA 2007: Companion to the 22nd ACM SIGPLAN conference on Object-oriented programming systems and applications companion, pp. 836–837. ACM, New York (2007)
25. Krueger, C., Bakal, M.: Systems and software product line engineering with sysml, uml and the ibm rational rhapsody biglever gears bridge. IBM White paper (2009)
26. Dauenhauer, G., Aschauer, T., Pree, W.: Variability in automation system models. In: [31], pp. 116–125.
27. Beuche, D., Weiland, J.: Managing flexibility: Modeling binding-times in simulink. In: Paige, R.F., Hartman, A., Rensink, A. (eds.) ECMDA-FA 2009. LNCS, vol. 5562, pp. 289–300. Springer, Heidelberg (2009)
28. Favaro, J.M., Mazzini, S.: Extending FeatuRSEB with Concepts from Systems Engineering. In: [31], pp. 41–50
29. Egyed, A.: Instant consistency checking for the uml. In: Osterweil, L.J., Rombach, H.D., Soffa, M.L. (eds.) ICSE, pp. 381–390. ACM, NewYork (2006)
30. Egyed, A.: Fixing inconsistencies in uml design models. In: ICSE '07: Proceedings of the 29th International Conference on Software Engineering, Washington, DC, USA, pp. 292–301. IEEE Computer Society, Los Alamitos (2007)
31. Edwards, S.H., Kulczycki, G. (eds.): ICSR 2009. LNCS, vol. 5791. Springer, Heidelberg (2009)

On the Combination of Domain Specific Modeling Languages

Antonio Vallecillo

GISUM/Atenea Research Group, Universidad de Málaga, Spain
av@lcc.uma.es

Abstract. Domain Specific Modeling Languages (DSMLs) are essential elements in Model-based Engineering. Each DSML allows capturing certain properties of the system, while abstracting other properties away. Nowadays DSMLs are mostly used in silos to solve specific problems. However, there are many occasions when multiple DSMLs need to be combined to design systems in a modular way. In this paper we discuss some scenarios of use and several mechanisms for DSML combination. We propose a general framework for combining DSMLs that subsumes them, based on the concept of viewpoint unification, and its realization using model-driven techniques.

1 Introduction

Complexity is one of the major drawbacks that UML [1] currently faces. Its metamodel of hundreds of classes and relationships between them represents a challenge for all its stakeholders. Users have serious problems for understanding its intricate structure and tend to use just the bit they know and feel comfortable with (around 20% according to the latest surveys). Formalists have problems for specifying its formal semantics and continually uncover subtle problems and ambiguities. Tool vendors find it very difficult to implement all its features (e.g., how many tools you know that can draw multiple clients or suppliers in a UML dependency?).

And even if UML provides a large number of concepts, they are still insufficient to capture some of the specific aspects required for modeling particular kinds of systems. To address this issue, UML counts on extension mechanisms for defining new modeling languages. For example, SysML [2] extends UML to define a general-purpose modeling language for systems engineering applications. The UML Profile for MARTE [3] provides another extension of UML for modeling real-time and embedded systems. The problem, again, is the size and complexity of these extensions, which does not help making them more understandable, manageable, usable or analyzable—specially when their accidental complexity is added to the intrinsic complexity of the systems being modeled. And then we may need to combine several of these extensions, something whose results are neither clearly defined nor predictable...

The problem, as we see it, is not so much with UML itself (although it still has some issues that can be resolved, UML is a very powerful and widely used modeling notation with many supporting tools), but with its complexity—which hinders its full usability by average system modelers.

When looking for solutions, many people are starting to use Domain Specific Modeling Languages (DSMLs). These small and focused languages are becoming commonplace for specifying systems at a high-level of abstraction, using a notation very close to the problem domain and quite intuitive for the domain expert. A DSML provides a language to describe a *view* of the system, concentrating on the elements which are relevant to that particular view. However, the use of small DSMLs becomes a real problem when we need to compose them to specify a complete system. How to combine DSMLs? Which mechanisms are available for composing them? How to prove the correctness and consistency of the composition?

There is a growing number of works on DSML composition, which address the problem from different perspectives and using different combination operations: metamodel merging [1,4,5], metamodel extension [6], template instantiation [7], language embedding [8,9], different flavors of model inheritance [10], model and metamodel weaving [11,12,13] (also referred to as metamodel interfacing [7]), even product-line configuration techniques [14]. However, not all of them provide solutions to all cases, and most of them are quite limited.

In this paper we discuss different scenarios of use, and different mechanisms for DSML combination; the advantages they introduce, as well as their limitations. We propose a general framework for combining DSMLs that subsumes them, based on the concept of viewpoint unification [15] and its realization using model-driven techniques.

2 A Brief Introduction to DSMLs

When working on a large system it is unrealistic to capture all the necessary information, constraints and decisions in a single flat specification, or even in a straightforward hierarchical specification based on successive refinements [16]. Structuring the specification into viewpoints gives much more flexibility. A *view* is a representation of the whole system from the perspective of a viewpoint. Each view focuses on the elements relevant to that particular viewpoint, abstracting away all irrelevant details. The view elements represent the system elements, as seen from the corresponding viewpoint.

Each viewpoint has a *viewpoint language* (i.e., a DSML) for describing the corresponding views. Each view then is a *model* that conforms to the corresponding DSML metamodel. Because the different viewpoints stress different aspects of the design, and use different techniques for doing so, each designer (or stakeholder) will be most comfortable with their own style of language and notation. For example, people writing processes and algorithms will probably think better in *imperative* terms (and use xUML, BPMN or Java), while business rule experts will find more suitable a *declarative* language (such as SVBR or OCL). Moreover, the models describing the separate views are independently expressed: they are each formed from a separate set of interrelated concepts, but no model element makes direct reference to terms in any other view model.

The goal of DSMLs is to allow domain experts to specify and reason about their systems using intuitive notations, closer to the language of the problem domain, and at the right level of abstraction. These are *specific* because they restrict themselves to one particular problem domain, supporting higher-level abstractions than general-purpose modeling languages and sacrificing generality to gain in specificity and concreteness.

This makes them easy to learn and to use (by the domain experts), manageable, usable and analyzable. Furthermore, the rules of the domain are included into the language as constraints, disallowing the specification of illegal or incorrect models of the views.

Finally, we should recall that defining a DSML involves at least three aspects: the domain concepts and rules (abstract syntax); the notation used to represent these concepts—let it be textual or graphical (concrete syntax); and the semantics of the language. The *abstract syntax* of a DSML is normally defined by a metamodel, which describes the concepts of the language, the relationships between them, and the structuring rules that constrain the model elements and their combinations in order to respect the domain rules. The *concrete syntax* of a DSML provides a realization of the abstract syntax of a metamodel as a mapping between the metamodel concepts and their textual or graphical representation. A language can have several concrete syntaxes. Finally, a DSML may have different kinds of *semantics*, depending on the aspects we want to emphasize. Thus, we can have structural semantics (describing what correct models produced with this DSML actually mean), behavioral semantics (how they behave along some time model), etc. [17]

3 Mechanisms for Combining DSMLs

The fact that each view provides only a partial specification for the system, requires mechanisms for combining DSMLs (and also their corresponding models) to be put in place. It is essential to observe that the combination of DSMLs should yield another Modeling Language (although not "Domain Specific" any more!), able to represent a metamodel for the "unified" models that provide a reconciled, integrated and virtual representations of the separate views of a system specification.

The following questions need to be answered: How can such a combined Modeling Language be built? How does it relate back to the individual DSMLs (and associated tools)? How to construct its metamodel? And its concrete syntax? How to define its semantics? These are the questions that we will try to answer here.

Note that such a combined Modeling Language (and its associated metamodel) can become too complex to be usable by modelers, and will not normally be presented to any user. Same as it happens with the output of a program compiler, which produces an executable model by combining information about the program itself, the execution platform, the hardware architecture, etc. The resulting model, which is in binary form, is not for human consumption; users only deal with specific views of it: the functionality, the configuration files, the information about the dynamic libraries, the deployment information, etc. Compiler and associated tools make the appropriate connections. Other tools, such as symbolic debuggers, can use parts of these models to provide the user with *new* views of the system at a high level, for instance during program execution.

The final goal is that tools can construct part or all of such a unified model where they need to manipulate information from more than one viewpoint, or to extract information from it. In this way, the user will normally work with the individual DSMLs, and leave the combining tools to build the unified models as needed.

For the combination of two or more DSMLs (and their associated metamodels and models) we need to address three main issues: (1) how to describe the correspondences between the concepts of the languages (i.e., at the metamodel level) and between the elements in each view (i.e., at model level); (2) how to "integrate" the models that represent the views into a global workable model (using the views and their correspondences); and (3) how to relate the unified model with the original views, so that the original views can be extracted from the unified model. The first problem deals with **Relating** the individual views; the second one with their **Synthesis**; and the last one with the **Analysis** of the unified model.

3.1 Relating Models: Correspondences

Dividing a system specification into a set of views provides a powerful mechanism for achieving the required level of abstraction, simplicity and modularity. However, the specifications must be a *coherent* description of a single target system. It is therefore essential that the views be linked, and this is done by establishing a set of **correspondences** between them. Correspondences do not form part of any one of the DSMLs, but provide statements that relate the various different views—expressing their semantic relationships [16]. Hence, a proper system specification consists of a set of viewpoint specifications, each one expressed in a viewpoint DSML, together with a set of correspondences between them.

The majority of the existing proposals for viewpoint modeling do not consider correspondences between viewpoints, or assume they are trivially based on name equality between correspondent elements, and implicitly defined. In fact, most proposals and tools for merging models (including UML 2) take a simplistic approach to matching based on names: if the same name appears in two views, they are assumed to represent two aspects of the same object. However, if the models are to be developed by separate teams, it is not safe to assume they share a single namespace, or that name assignments are unique. It is also often the case that the correspondences are not simply one-to-one; the relationships between elements will generally be more complex.

Several authors have proposed different approaches to express correspondences, specially when views are expressed as UML models, using different alternatives: from OCL constraints to UML abstraction dependencies (see [18] for a discussion about some of these approaches). Other proposals use model weaving techniques for relating the elements of different views, defining ad-hoc correspondence metamodels [19], general-purpose model weaving notations and tools [12,13] or even bi-directional model transformation languages such as QVT.

Correspondences need normally be specified at two levels, depending on whether they relate metamodel or model elements. In the first case, correspondences determine the relationships that should exist between concepts of the two DSMLs to be combined. For example, if we are combining class diagrams with statecharts, a correspondence between the two language metamodels can specify that every UML class should be related to one or more statecharts (the ones that define the behavior of the instances of that class). But then, instances of such correspondences (called *correspondence links*) should be specified at the model level, identifying which are the individual statecharts that should be related to a particular class. Making an analogy with programming languages, you need to define first how the grammars of the two languages can be related, and then how two individual programs are related using such relations.

There are also situations where establishing correspondences becomes a difficult task, and cannot be automated. For example, a complex structure in one model can express a concept that is expressed by another complex structure in another model, but there is no obvious mapping for the individual elements even though the structures as a whole are similar. Correspondences between non-structural elements (e.g., constraints or pieces of behavior) are not trivial, either. A very illustrative introduction to the nature of correspondences and their associated problems and limitations can be found in [16].

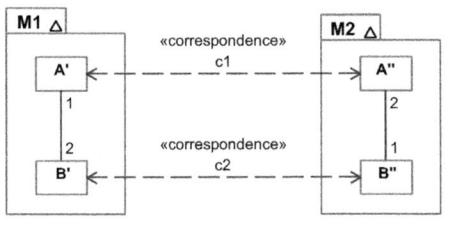

It is also worth noting that, given two models, there are many different ways of relating their elements. An example of the correspondence between two models (that may represent different viewpoints, or different views) is depicted in Fig. 1. Depending on the constraints defined by the individual correspondences, the specifications can be "consistent" or not. The key question here is the meaning of *consistency*. We will come back to this later in Sect. 4. So far we would only like the reader to consider if the system specification shown in Fig. 1 is consistent w.r.t. the two defined correspondences (c1 and c2) or not.

Fig. 1. Correspondences between two models

3.2 Viewpoint Synthesis

Some authors have proposed a number of techniques for combining (meta)models. They can be basically grouped in three categories, which are discussed in this section.
Metamodel Extension. One possible approach to DSML combination consists of extending one language (the pivot) with the concepts of the other (the extension). These new elements were not originally present, but some of them may make references to existing ones. There are several situations where such an extensibility mechanism is useful and essential, e.g., in the case of hierarchies of metamodels or to modularly endow a language with features not originally present.

An *extensionOf* relation between the two language metamodels was formally introduced in [6]. It subsumes previous proposals for implementing different flavors of *model inheritance* [10] or *template instantiation* [7].

Given two metamodels[1] M_i and M_e that conform to the same reference model (or metametamodel) $\mathcal{M}$ and that represent the initial metamodel and the extension (M_e), and given a correspondence mapping $\epsilon : M_i \rightarrow M_i \cup M_e$ that defines how elements in the initial metamodel are mapped to elements in the union model (the one that contains all elements of both metamodels), the authors in [6] show how to compute the **synthesized** metamodel $M_i \oplus_\epsilon M_e$ with the "duplicate-free union" of the two metamodels being combined.

Here, the relationship between the metamodels is accomplished by a user-defined specification ϵ of the correspondences between the elements that should be "unified".

This approach to DSML composition is effective when we want to re-use an existing DSML and complement it with another (that can be reused, too), and the relation

---
[1] Metamodels are models too, so most of the definitions of this paper apply equally to models.

between the two is *complementary* (the extending language *complements* the other) and *conservative* (the extensions are compatible with the pivot language's concepts and do not break its semantics). Aspect-oriented modeling approaches could fit into this category, since they allow extending models with new properties. Other languages provide extension mechanisms for facilitating this task (e.g., UML Profiles allow extending the UML metamodel to incorporate new features).

Another benefit of this approach is that the concrete syntax of the resulting DSML can be easily defined (see, e.g., [20]), and the combined semantics can be defined as well (at least in theory), because the extensions have to be conservative [4].

One disadvantage of this approach is its limited use, only for conservative extensions of a language and not for combining DSMLs in general. In addition, combining separate extensions is not a trivial task: although each one can be conservative w.r.t. the pivot language, the consistency of the extensions compositions is not guaranteed (two extensions may impose contradictory conditions on the global combined model).

Metamodel Merge. Model merge is a more powerful composition operation that does not assume an unbalanced combination, but tries to combine *peer* languages. For example, UML 2 defines an operation, package merge, that takes the contents of two packages (models or metamodels) and produces a new package that combines their contents [1]. Package merge was partially inspired by two specification combination mechanisms offered in Catalysis: "and" and "join" [4]. However, both differ substantially from package merge: The "and" operation is for use with subtyping, while the "join" operation allows a specification to impose additional preconditions to those defined in another view [21]. The problem, as it stands today, is that the current definition of this UML operation is neither precise nor sound, and it does not consider possible conflicts between the structural constraints of the metamodels that are merged. As a result, it may break the well-formed rules of any of the languages it combines [4]. Besides, the solution adopted in UML 2 is too simplistic: elements are merged based on name matching and the resulting extended elements have all the properties of the elements they merge (we shall see that this becomes a problem, too).

MetaGME [7] enables Metamodel Merge through the use of three types of class inheritance and a special Class Equivalence operator, used to show a full union between two classes. The unioned classes cease to exist as distinct metamodel elements, instead fusing into a single class. The union process is very similar to merging classes through Package Merge, except that the operation takes place at the class level instead of the package (or metamodel) level, and the two merged classes do not need to have the same name because of the use of the Class Equivalence operator.

Pottinger and Bernstein proposed in [5] a more general approach to model merging, using user-defined correspondences between the views. They presented an algorithm that, given the two models and a set of user-defined correspondences between them, provides a merged model which is the duplicate-free union of the two models with respect to the set of correspondences. The authors identify different kinds of possible conflicts, some of which may be resolvable, others are not in general. Their approach subsumes previous works from the database and semantic web communities on generic model merging, database view integration and ontology merging, by generalizing these approaches and providing a unified algorithm.

Although trying to compute the duplicate-free union of two metamodels by merging them could a priori be an excellent solution for DSML combination, it does not work in all cases. Merges have to be meaningful from an architectural (and methodological) point of view: not always the metamodels of two languages are amenable to merging because their underlying semantics are different and incompatible. Think for instance of two languages for describing behavior, one based on synchronous interactions and the other on asynchronous interactions. You can relatively easily relate their metamodels using correspondences, but you cannot easily merge them into a single unified metamodel. A similar situation happens if you try to merge a Class and E/R notations into one single unified language. Or think of combining Java and COBOL programs into the same language. Or programs written in my two favorite DSLs: LaTeX and Excel...

Furthermore, merging models usually implies carrying forward all the properties of all merged model elements. In other words, model merge only allows injection relationships between the models being merged and the resulting model. For example, in UML an element resulting from the merge must not be any less capable than it was prior to the merge. This means, among other things, that the resulting navigability, multiplicity, visibility, etc. of a receiving model element will not be reduced as a result of a package merge [1]. Then, if you consider again the models in Fig. 1, merging the classes according to the correspondences leads to inconsistent cardinality constraints. Does this mean that these two models cannot represent views of the same system? Probably they can (see, e.g., Fig. 3, whose orthographic views M1 and M2 have the same constraints), but the problem is that package (or model) merge is not the right combination operator for integrating them.

Language Embedding. An alternative approach to building a DSML from scratch is to inherit the infrastructure of some other language, tailoring it in special ways to the domain of interest. This is called language embedding [8,9]. In this way, the embedded language can reuse the syntax of the host language, its module system, existing libraries, associated tools, etc. The embedding is normally defined in terms of a mapping function that describes how the guest language concepts are encoded in terms of the host language concepts. Furthermore, in case of host languages with precise semantics, the embedding mapping can serve to provide translational semantics to the guest language (i.e., the semantics of the guest language concepts is defined in terms of the interpretation of the translated concepts in the host language).

In other words, if MM_g and MM_h are the language metamodels of the guest and host languages, the embedding is a mapping $\varepsilon : MM_g \rightarrow MM_h$. Normally, such a mapping is not explicitly defined anywhere, and there is no explicit trace between the two languages—losing therefore the connection with the concrete syntax and tools associated to the original DSML.

Of course, the host language should be expressive (and malleable) enough to represent the concepts of the guest. Usually, functional languages such as Haskell or Scala, or formal-based languages such as Maude have proved to be good hosts.

UML has been used as the host language for a wide range of DSMLs. UML is very expressive, well-know and it counts on tool support—well, mainly model editors. In fact, UML was originally created to combine (by hosting) the original Booch, OMT and OOSE methods and notations, incorporating slightly modified versions of languages such as Harel's Statechart notation [22], or ITU-T's Message Sequence Charts (MSC) [23]. Thus, UML defines a global metamodel with all the original notations it combines (for use cases, class diagrams, state charts, sequence charts, etc.).

From a theoretical perspective, the use of the host language metamodel can help maintaining the coherence and conceptual integration among the viewpoints elements. However, this approach presents some problems from a practical point of view. Firstly, in many occasions it means re-defining the original languages to integrate them into the host language metamodel, something which normally hampers the use of existing editors and analysis tools for the original languages (e.g., the tools available for Harel's Statecharts or for ITU-T's Message Sequence Charts are not easily accessible from UML). Secondly, some of the adaptations have respected the original semantics of the languages, but others had to suffer some modifications or severe cuts (e.g., Statecharts in UML 1). Thirdly, the relationship between the elements of the different languages is not obvious in general, and gets usually blurred—mainly because of the intricate nature of the global metamodel, and because in many cases it is built without mechanisms for expressing the correspondences between the viewpoints. Finally, language embedding may force to ask users to stop using their domain specific notations, small and concise languages and specific tools, and to start using a (probably more) complex language (at least, far more expressive).

In general, a common Modeling Language that accommodates all DSMLs is feasible if the number of viewpoints is small and semantically consistent, and if as user you are happy to forget about the individual DSMLs and their associated tools. But it is rather artificial if the DSMLs are loosely coupled or describe the system at very different levels of abstraction/granularity.

Embedding and extensions. In many occasions, host languages also count on extension mechanisms for facilitating the embeddings[2]. For example, UML counts on Profiles to help defining/hosting new languages. UML Profiles also allow users to define the embedding function explicitly, indicating which UML metaclasses are extended.

Another example is WebDSL [24], a textual DSML for developing dynamic Web Applications that incorporates different languages for expressing the concerns involved in any Web system. WebDSL is is extensible, so new languages can be added as plugins to cope with new concerns. No explicit embedding mappings ε between the guests and host language are defined, though.

Embedding languages in this way is not free from problems, either. Let us mention the most significant issues that we have found when working with UML profiles, although they are generic to this kind of approaches. First, well-defined UML profiles cannot break the semantics of UML (at least, in theory); however, they can easily introduce semantic inconsistencies between each other when two or more, independently defined, are applied together (e.g., see the problems of combining SysML and MARTE profiles in [25]). Second, the use of UML as a modeling notation introduces some restrictions and limitations, which may force design choices sometimes unnatural when modeling certain domain concepts; for example, SysML models *Requirements* by

---

[2] In these cases, extending a language can also be seen as a form of embedding. The difference is usually a matter of degree, and from where we look at it: from the host side (that gets extended) or from the guest side (that gets embedded).

extending UML classifiers, a decision which can be considered (at least) arguable. Finally, the complexity of the UML metamodel does not help when looking for elements that can represent the domain concepts. In our previous experience with UML profiles to model languages such as WebML [26] or the RM-ODP viewpoint languages [19], we found that some times we had too many choices (e.g., it was difficult to decide whether some concepts had to be represented by UML classes or by UML components, because their differences are quite subtle), while in other occasions we could not find any UML element to represent what we wanted (e.g., expressing ODP policies was not a trivial task). There is also the issue of the concrete syntax: adopting UML graphical notation is a suitable choice when the embedded language does not have its own concrete syntax (such as UML4ODP or SysML) because many people are familiarized with UML boxes and lines, and the learning curve is small; but the results obtained when trying to mimic other concrete syntaxes are not good, basically due to the reduced facilities of UML Profiles for adopting new graphical notations [26]. Worse than that, what we have found is a recurrent undesirable situation when modelers embed DSMLs into UML. Since the frontier between the embedded and the host language disappears, users start making use of many UML concepts that were not part of their original DSMLs, producing models that are correct w.r.t. the UML metamodel, but incorrect w.r.t. their original languages.

The key question, as we mentioned at the beginning, is whether users should know about this combined Modeling Language at all, or should the tools be responsible for converting the models written in the original DSMLs, back and forth to the integrated model written in the global language. In this way, the user will normally work with the individual DSMLs, and leave the combining tools to build the unified models as needed. Probably in this scenario is where the full potential of UML could be better exploited.

3.3 Analysis of the Integrated Models

Independently from how the synthesized model has been built, there should be a way to extract the views from the integrated model. Although not so much discussed in the MDE community, this is a well known problem in databases, a part of the *data integration* problem [27]. This is the problem of combining data residing at different sources, and providing the user with a unified view of the data. In this approach, the user queries over the global schema have to be reformulated in terms of a set of queries over the sources.

One of the current limitations of language embedding is that there is no trace back to the original language that has been embedded. Basically, more than "combining" the languages, they are re-defined from scratch using the metamodel of the host language, and with no explicit backward connections to the original DSMLs. This is for instance the case of UML with statecharts or MSCs. The situation is not better with languages defined using UML Profiles: although the embedding mapping ε is explicitly defined, the reverse projection is not.

Furthermore, what happens with the tools (editors, analyzers, etc.) of the individual views? It is important to have access to the tools available for individual DSMLs from the combined DSML environment. It is not clear how this can be achieved using language embedding mechanisms. This is another reason for being the tools, and not the users, the ones that should combine their models into an integrated Modeling Language.

4 Viewpoint Unification

Our proposal for DSML combination builds on the idea of viewpoint unification, originally proposed by Boiten, Derrick, Bowman and Steen for studying the consistency between viewpoint-based specifications [15]. In that work, a set of viewpoints is considered to be *consistent* if there exists at least one "implementation" that satisfies all the views. This is equivalent to check that the views do not impose contradictory requirements on the system. A detailed study of the formal basis for viewpoint unification mechanisms can be found in [15]. Here we extend that notion in order to deal as well with the correspondences between the viewpoints, and with the explicit representation of the relations between the unified model and the views.

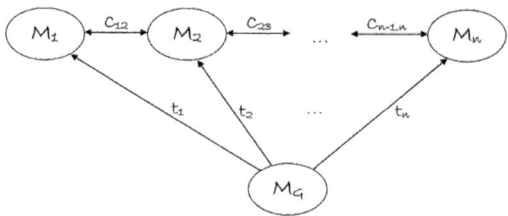

Fig. 2. A unified model

The idea consists in considering that the DSMLs to combine provide a set of *viewpoint languages* to describe one system, and hence the models written according to these DSMLs represent the system *views* (as proposed in RM-ODP [28] or in [29]). Because all viewpoints correspond to the same system, and will eventually be realized by one implementation, there must be a way to combine them. Intuitively, the way to combine the languages is by providing a *new language* and a set of *mappings* between the new language and the viewpoint languages (Fig. 2), with the additional property that the mappings respect the constraints imposed by the correspondences.

The more general process to create the metamodel of the new language M_G and the mappings $t_1, \ldots, t_n$ is based on the **unification** of the viewpoint languages metamodels. The mappings capture the relations between the unified metamodel and the individual viewpoints metamodels, acting as **projections** of M_G [29]. The consistency of the specification is guaranteed by the fact that the mappings should respect the correspondences between the viewpoints: two projections of the same system over two different viewpoints must be related by the correspondences in a consistent way.

Definition 1 (Model Unification). *Given a set of models $M_1, M_2, \ldots, M_n$, and a set of correspondences between them $c_{ij} = C(M_i, M_j) \subseteq \mathbb{P}(M_i) \times \mathbb{P}(M_j)$, a unification is a new model M_G and a set of functions $t_i : M_G \to M_i$ (projections) that respect the set correspondences, i.e., $C(t_i(M_G), t_j(M_G))) \subseteq C(M_i, M_j)$.*

In case of combining DSMLs by unification, models $M_1, M_2, \ldots, M_n$ are the metamodels of the languages to combine, and M_G is the metamodel of the unified language.

The form of unification depends on the DSMLs to be combined, the correspondences defined between them, and the different relations that can be defined between the unification and the views. For example, the metamodel M_G of the unified language could be defined by applying model extension or model merge operations on the metamodels of the viewpoint languages (in those cases where this makes sense). Or we could use the metamodel of an existing language as global metamodel M_G (this is language embedding). Alternatively, unification offers further options such as defining an ad-hoc metamodel (neither the duplicate-free union nor an existing language metamodel) for combining particular DSMLs, as we shall see below.

We can also identify different kinds of mappings, depending on the sort of relationship between the unified metamodel and each viewpoint metamodel—we should allow to relate them in different ways. In some proposals, the mappings are defined between the viewpoint languages and the unified model, and they are called *development relations* [15]. They represent the inverse mappings of our projections. For instance we can have *refinement* relations, *abstractions*, *equivalences* and relations which can broadly be classified as *implementations*. These different kinds of relations are best distinguished by their basic properties. Refinements are reflexive and transitive (i.e., a preorder); abstractions are the dual of refinements; equivalences are reflexive, symmetric and transitive; and implementation relations only need to be reflexive [15]. Transitivity is a very expensive property, but crucial for enabling incremental development of specifications towards realizations. Implementation relations are the most common relations, they just establish correspondences between the unified metamodel and the viewpoint metamodels. For example, consider a requirements specification of the system written using OMG's Business Motivation Model (BMM) notation and a functional specification using LOTOS (ISO/IEC 880). A unified model may be expressed in a completely different notation, and related to the former by a logical satisfaction relation, and to the latter by a behavioral conformance relation.

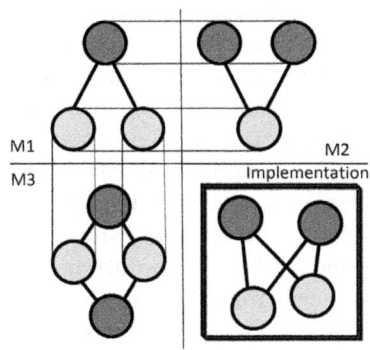

Fig. 3. Orthographic views of a 3D object

Our approach to DSML combination subsumes previous approaches (see Sect. 5), and allows a wider range of possible combinations. For example, consider again the models in Fig. 1. Merging them was not possible because the merge operator finds inconsistencies between the cardinality constraints of the classes to merge. However, consider the orthographic representation of a 3D object shown in Fig. 3, whose views M1 and M2 present similar correspondences to the classes in Fig. 1, but for which a combined model is possible (shown as the Implementation).

In fact, the two models shown in Fig. 1 admit one unification, given by a model MG with two classes A and B related by an association whose cardinality is 2 in both ends, plus two projections T1 and T2—see Fig. 4.

The first projection T1 transforms each pair of A instances of MG related to a pair of B instances into one single A' instance, and transforms B instances into B' without modifying them. The second projection T2 does the analogous transformation with B" and A" instances, respectively. This represents, for instance, a system in which both A and B elements are replicated. View M1 abstracts away the replication of A elements, while View M2 does the same for B elements.

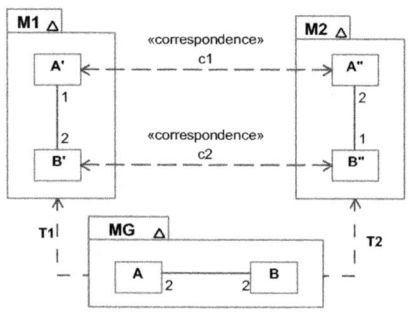

Fig. 4. The Unified Model for Fig. 1

Of course, the unification is only possible if correspondences c1 and c2 are one-to-many and many-to-one, respectively. Otherwise the unification is not possible: suppose that correspondence c1 was one-to-one, i.e., it imposed that every A' instance should be related to exactly one A" instance. In this case, there is no implementation possible for the system and therefore the multi-viewpoint specification becomes *inconsistent*.

5 Discussion

Relationship with previous approaches. Our proposed unification can be seen as a generalization of previous approaches to DSML combination, discussed in Sect. 3. In model extension and model merge, the unified metamodel M_G is nothing but the duplicate-free union of the viewpoint metamodels. The *development* relations in these cases coincide with injection mappings defined by these two approaches (e.g., ϵ in case of model extension), and the projections t_i are just the inverse of these injections. One of the benefits of our approach is that we request that the projection mappings are explicitly defined. One of the benefits of the model extension and model merge approaches is that they provide mechanisms and algorithms for building the unified model (in those situations in which they can be applied), because the unified model coincides with the combined model they construct—sometimes called the *least developed unification* [15].

Language embedding is also a particular case of our approach, in which the metamodel M_G is an existing one. Users normally define the development mappings that describe how the DSMLs concepts are encoded as M_G elements. In our case, we explicitly ask to specify the inverse projections t_i too, to be able to trace back to the original languages and to automatically obtain the views from the unified model.

We are of course conscious that the synthesis process cannot always be fully automated, as we have tried to illustrate with the simplistic example shown in 4. There are, however, other occasions in which such a combined model can be synthesized from the views, as it happens when model extension or model merge approaches are possible. But in these cases the projections are easy to define, because they are nothing but the inverse of the development mappings.

Realizing the Mappings. The advent of MDE has provided a set of appropriate mechanisms and tools for specifying and implementing both the viewpoint correspondences and the t_i projections. For instance, model weaving [12] is a technology that can be very useful to implement model extension and model merging, as described in [11,13]. More importantly, model transformations can play a key role for realizing the mappings so that they can be automated. In the best case we will be able to define bidirectional model transformations that allow the mappings to work in both directions.

In a typical application scenario, a user will be confronted with two DSMLs that have to be combined. The first step is to define the correspondences between their metamodels using model weaving techniques. Then the user should investigate whether model extension or model merge can produce a satisfactory and consistent unified metamodel (in case the projections of the duplicated-free union of the two languages metamodels respect the correspondences constraints). If so, implementing the algorithms described in [6] or in [5] using model transformations is the solution. Once defined, the projections from the unified metamodel to the views should be defined in terms of model transformations, to be able to perform automatic analysis (these projections are basically the inverse of the development mappings defined by the algorithms).

Alternatively, the user may consider embedding the languages into an existing language, if none of the issues we have identified in Sect. 3.2 represent a serious problem for her. In this case the development relations are just the embedding mappings, which can be implemented in terms of model transformations, too (see, e.g., [30,31,32,33]). Apart from the intrinsic problems of defining the mappings and the projections (which are not normally difficult from a conceptual point of view but rather cumbersome from a technical perspective), special care should be taken for making sure that the correspondences constraints are respected by the projections.

Finally, in case none of the previous approaches offers a neat solution, the user might consider specifying an ad-hoc language for hosting the combination. As major benefits, the relationships between the combined DSMLs and the unified language can be of different types, and implemented as model transformations (in both directions: development and projections) that will fit the particular requirements of the individual languages. The main problem is the complexity involved in defining the unified language so that it represents the consistent "least development unification" of the DSMLs to combine. The good news is that this new language has to be defined only once for every combination of languages.

What happens with the concrete syntax? In our proposal, users do not need to use the combined language and thus there is no need to provide a concrete syntax for it. In case of model extension, some authors have proposed a way to combine the concrete syntax as well [20]. But in general this is a difficult issue because of the semantic implications of symbols: usually every symbol conveys an associated meaning. For instance, a box is associated to a classifier in UML; a stick figure is an actor, etc. There is no major problem when the concepts of the combined languages are kept separated, or just extended, but not mixed. But when the concepts are mingled in the combined language the situation becomes more complex, and trying to use the icons of one or the other language may introduce semantic problems to the reader of the combined diagrams. And if we try to choose a different notation for the combined language, the users might get completely confused with the new notation.

In language embedding we get the opposite problem because users tend to focus more on the host language notation—the embedded language symbols usually become (inconized) annotations to the host language symbols. But the look-and-feel of the resulting diagrams resembles too much the host language notation, and thus the benefits of working with *domain specific* languages melt away. However, this might not be a problem but an advantage when the embedded language does not have any associated concrete syntax, as we explained before.

What happens with the semantics? There have been different proposals for the compositional definition of the semantics of DSMLs using diverse formalisms, see, e.g., Refs. [34,35,36,37]. These works are usually valid when the relation between the viewpoints and the unified metamodel are basically injections. But in general combining the semantics of the languages is not a trivial task and deserves its own line of research—specially when we allow different kinds of relations between the unified metamodel and each viewpoint metamodel. In an unification context, the semantics of the individual DSMLs and the unified language are preserved. Model transformations provide here the *semantic brigdes* that allow mapping ones into the others. Furthermore, model transformations can serve to define the (translational) semantics of those languages that do not count on an explicit definition of their semantics, as mentioned in Sect. 3.2.

6 Conclusions and Future Work

In this paper we have discussed and analyzed the most common techniques for DSML combination, and classified them in three main categories according to the operations they use: model extension, model merge and language embedding. These techniques are useful in some circumstances, but rather limited in others. Then we have proposed a more general framework for combining DSMLs that subsumes them, based on the concept of viewpoint unification, and its realization using model-driven techniques. The framework has allowed us to put these combination techniques in context, and formulate them in similar terms. In fact, they all represent different ways to find a global metamodel that can host the languages to combine. But these approaches have similar problems, too. Firstly, none of them specifies in an explicit way the traces back to the original notations that permit making use of the tools available for these languages. Secondly, they allow only one kind of relationship between the languages to combine and the global metamodel (basically, injection). The first problem is solved in our proposal by requesting the explicit specification of the mappings from the global metamodel to the languages metamodels. The second problem is the one that imposes stronger limitations on existing approaches for combining DSMLs because it forces the global metamodel elements to incorporate all the capabilities of the individual views, and to respect the constraints defined by both the viewpoints and the correspondences. We have introduced a simple example that shows that such limitation is too restrictive, and normally unrealistic for composing rich DSMLs. Our approach overcomes this limitation by allowing different kinds of relations between the viewpoint languages and the global metamodel (abstractions, refinements, implementations, etc.) and also by checking the consistency of the specifications using the projections of the global metamodel.

We are currently working on the unification of the viewpoint languages defined by some multi-view proposals, such as UWE [38] and the RM-ODP [28]. This is the context in which the work presented here has been developed, based on our experiences and findings when combining these languages. Although there are still many issues to resolve, we have tried to show how the MDE technologies can significantly help in combining DSMLs by formulating the problem in terms models and relations (transformations) between them.

Acknowledgements. We would like to thank José E. Rivera, Francisco Durán and Jordi Cabot for their comments on a previous version of this paper, and to the anonymous referees for their insightful comments and suggestions. This work has been partially supported by Spanish Research Projects TIN2008-03107 and P07-TIC-03184.

References

1. OMG: Unified Modeling Language 2.1.1 Superstructure Specification. OMG, Needham (MA), USA, OMG doc. formal/07-02-05 (2007)
2. OMG: Systems Modeling Language. OMG, Needham (MA), USA (2008)
3. OMG: UML Profile for MARTE: Modeling and Analysis of Real-Time and Embedded systems. OMG, Needham (MA), USA (2009)
4. Zito, A., Diskin, Z., Dingel, J.: Package merge in UML 2: Practice vs. theory? In: Nierstrasz, O., Whittle, J., Harel, D., Reggio, G. (eds.) MoDELS 2006. LNCS, vol. 4199, pp. 185–199. Springer, Heidelberg (2006)
5. Bernstein, P.A., Pottinger, R.A.: Merging models based on given correspondences. In: VLDB 2003, Berlin, Germany pp. 862–873 (2003)
6. Barbero, M., Jouault, F., Gray, J., Bézivin, J.: A practical approach to model extension. In: Akehurst, D.H., Vogel, R., Paige, R.F. (eds.) ECMDA-FA. LNCS, vol. 4530, pp. 32–42. Springer, Heidelberg (2007)
7. Emerson, M., Sztipanovits, J.: Techniques for metamodel composition. In: Proc. of the 6th Workshop on Domain Specific Modeling at OOPSLA 2006, pp. 123–139 (2006)
8. Hudak, P.: Building domain-specific embedded languages. ACM Comput. Surv. 28(4) (1996)
9. Hofer, C., Ostermann, K., Rendel, T., Moors, A.: Polymorphic embedding of DSLs. In: Proc. of GPCE 2008, Nashville, TN, pp. 137–148. ACM, New York (2008)
10. Ledeczi, A., Nordstrom, G., Karsai, G., Volgyesi, P., Maroti, M.: On metamodel composition. In: Proc. of CCA 2001, pp. 756–760 (2001)
11. Estublier, J., Vega, G., Ionita, A.D.: Composing domain-specific languages for wide-scope software engineering applications. In: Briand, L.C., Williams, C. (eds.) MoDELS 2005. LNCS, vol. 3713, pp. 69–83. Springer, Heidelberg (2005)
12. Didonet Del Fabro, M., Jouault, F.: Model transformation and weaving in the AMMA platform. In: GTTSE 2005. LNCS, vol. 4143, pp. 71–77. Springer, Heidelberg (2005)
13. Bézivin, J., Bouzitouna, S., Didonet Del Fabro, M., Gervais, M.P., Jouault, F., Kolovos, D., Kurtev, I., Paige, R.F.: A canonical scheme for model composition. In: Rensink, A., Warmer, J. (eds.) ECMDA-FA 2006. LNCS, vol. 4066, pp. 346–360. Springer, Heidelberg (2006)
14. White, J., et al.: Improving domain-specific language reuse with software product line techniques. IEEE Software 26(4), 47–53 (2009)
15. Bowman, H., Steen, M., Boiten, E.A., Derrick, J.: A formal framework for viewpoint consistency. Formal Methods in System Design 21(2), 111–166 (2002)
16. Linington, P.: Black Cats and Coloured Birds What do Viewpoint Correspondences Do? In: Proc. of WODPEC 2007, Maryland, USA (2007)
17. Clark, T., Sammut, P., Willans, J.: Applied Metamodelling, 2nd edn., Ceteva (2004)

18. Romero, J.R., Jaén, J.I., Vallecillo, A.: Realizing correspondences in multi-viewpoint specifications. In: Proc. of EDOC 2009, Auckland, NZ, pp. 163–172. IEEE Computer Society, Los Alamitos (2009)
19. ISO/IEC: Information technology – Open distributed processing – Use of UML for ODP system specifications. ISO and ITU-T, ISO/IEC IS 19793, ITU-T X.906 (2008)
20. Pedro, L., Risoldi, M., Buchs, D., Barroca, B., Amaral, V.: Composing visual syntax for domain specific languages. In: Proc. of HCI 2009, San Diego, CA. LNCS, vol. 5611, pp. 889–898. Springer, Heidelberg (2009)
21. D'Souza, D.F., Wills, A.C.: Objects, Components, and Frameworks with UML. In: The Catalysis Approach, Addison-Wesley, Reading (1999)
22. Harel, D.: Statecharts: a visual formalism for complex systems. Science of Computer Programming 8, 231–274 (1987)
23. ITU-T Recommendation Z.120: Message Sequence Charts (1994)
24. Groenewegen, D.M., Hemel, Z., Kats, L.C.L., Visser, E.: WebDSL: A Domain-Specific Language for Dynamic Web Applications. In: Mielke, N., Zimmermann, O. (eds.) Companion to OOPSLA 2008, pp. 779–780. ACM, New York (2008), http://webdsl.org
25. Espinoza, H., Cancila, D., Selic, B., Gérard, S.: A practical approach to model extension. In: Paige, R.F., Hartman, A., Rensink, A. (eds.) ECMDA-FA 2009. LNCS, vol. 5562, pp. 98–113. Springer, Heidelberg (2009)
26. Moreno, N., Fraternali, P., Vallecillo, A.: WebML Modelling in UML. IET Software 1(3), 67–80 (2007)
27. Lenzerini, M.: Data integration: A theoretical perspective. In: Proc. of PODS 2002, pp. 233–246 (2002)
28. ISO/IEC: RM-ODP. Reference Model for Open Distributed Processing. ISO and ITU-T, Geneva, Switzerland, ISO/IEC 10746, ITU-T Rec. X.901-X.904 (1997)
29. Atkinson, C., Stoll, D.: Orthographic modeling environment. In: Fiadeiro, J.L., Inverardi, P. (eds.) FASE 2008. LNCS, vol. 4961, pp. 93–96. Springer, Heidelberg (2008)
30. Abouzahra, A., Bézivin, J., Didonet Del Fabro, M., Jouault, F.: A practical approach to bridging domain specific languages with UML profiles. In: Best Practices for Model Driven Software Development Workshop at OOPSLA (2005)
31. Bézivin, J., Hillairet, G., Jouault, F., Kurtev, I., Piers, W.: Bridging the MS/DSL tools and the Eclipse modeling framework. In: Proc. of the International Workshop on Software Factories at OOPSLA (2005)
32. Wimmer, M., Schauerhuber, A., Strommer, M., Schwinger, W., Kappel, G.: A semi-automatic approach for bridging DSLs with UML. In: Proc. of 7th Workshop on Domain-Specific Modeling at OOPSLA (2007)
33. Brambilla, M., Fraternali, P., Tisi, M.: A transformation framework to bridge Domain Specific Languages to MDA. In: Chaudron, M.R.V. (ed.) Models in Software Engineering. LNCS, vol. 5421, pp. 167–180. Springer, Heidelberg (2009)
34. Chen, K.: et al.: Semantic anchoring with model transformations. In: Hartman, A., Kreische, D. (eds.) ECMDA-FA 2005. LNCS, vol. 3748, pp. 115–129. Springer, Heidelberg (2005)
35. Ruscio, D.D., Jouault, F., Kurtev, I., Bézivin, J., Pierantonio, A.: Extending AMMA for supporting dynamic semantics specifications of DSLs. Technical Report 06.02, Laboratoire d'Informatique de Nantes-Atlantique (LINA), Nantes, France (2006)
36. Doh, K.G., Mosses, P.D.: Composing programming languages by combining action-semantics modules. Sci. Comput. Program. 47(1), 3–36 (2003)
37. Pedro, L., Amaral, V., Buchs, D.: Foundations for a Domain Specific Modeling Language prototyping environment: A compositional approach. In: Proc. of the DSM workshop at OOPSLA 2008, Nashville, TN, pp. 26–33 (2008)
38. Koch, N., Knapp, A., Zhang, G., Baumeister, H.: UML-Based Web Engineering: An Approach Based on Standards. In: Web Engineering: Modelling and Implementing Web Applications. Human-Computer Interaction Series, vol. 12, pp. 157–191. Springer, Heidelberg (2008)

Joint Language and Domain Engineering

Tobias Walter[1,2], Fernando Silva Parreiras[1], Steffen Staab[1], and Jürgen Ebert[2]

[1] Institute for Web Science and Technology, University of Koblenz-Landau
Universitätsstrasse 1, Koblenz 56070, Germany
{walter,parreiras,staab}@uni-koblenz.de
[2] Institute for Software Technology, University of Koblenz-Landau
Universitätsstrasse 1, Koblenz 56070, Germany
ebert@uni-koblenz.de

Abstract. In domain-specific development model-driven development environments play an important role. Most of these environments only provide support for language engineering, but do not consider the second dimension which is concerned with domain engineering. In this paper, we join the concerns of language engineering and domain engineering towards a new comprehensive approach of domain-specific development. It allows domain designers to build domain models containing both, types and instances, and it allows language designers for defining language metamodels. Furthermore, based on the integrated description logics the environment provides services for productive modeling in domain and language engineering.

1 Introduction

Today, domain-specific development is based on model-driven development (MDD) [1]. In [2] we have presented an environment called *OntoDSL* which allows for developing and using description logic-based domain-specific languages. The environment supports both language designers and language users. A *language designer* provides domain-specific languages (DSL) to language users by defining an abstract syntax in the form of a metamodel, a concrete syntax (e.g. of a textual or visual kind) and semantics. All three steps are related to *language engineering*. The *language user* makes use of the DSL and builds *domain models* by creating instances of elements like classes and associations of the metamodel.

In *OntoDSL*, we consider metamodel hierarchies to describe the specification and the use of DSLs. At the *M3 layer*, a metametamodel is defined. At the *M2 layer*, the language is specified by defining a metamodel. Its elements are instances of elements in the metametamodel. At the *M1 layer*, the specified language can be used by creating a domain model, which is a linguistic instance of the DSL metamodel. For example, a class Device at the M2 layer allows for creating linguistic instances like cisco at the M1 layer.

In contrast to language engineering, which is based on hierarchies related by linguistic instantiation, another important dimension of model-driven development is the engineering of the domain, where hierarchical layers are related by ontological instantiation. [3].

In *domain engineering* the role of a *domain designer* is involved. A domain designer has the task to formally describe an existing or new domain. The result of domain engineering is a domain model which consists of both *domain instances* and *domain types* which classify the instances. Since a domain designer can create both instances and types in one domain model and can assign types to instances by a *hasType*-relationship, domain engineering requires ontological instantiation. For example, the domain designer wants to explicitly define that the domain instance cisco7603 has the domain type Cisco.

Our work is based on the work of Atkinson and Kühne [3,4]. They claim, that metamodeling is an essential foundation for model-driven development but does not meet all the technical requirements for MDD environments. However, it can be extended to provide the full support for language engineering with an *instanceOf*-relation and domain engineering with a *hasType*-relation.

The MOF (Meta Object Facility) language [5] and its derivatives mainly provides linguistic instantiation where some parts of language engineering are supported. The ontological *hasType*-relation may be defined, but it would be just a simple UML association. Its meaning would remain implicit and would not be recognized and supported by the tools. Furthermore, the use of DSLs, where a language user builds domain models containing linguistic instances of concepts in the DSL metamodel, is separated from domain engineering, where a domain designer creates domain models, which consist of domain type and instance definitions.

1.1 Challenges

To accomplish the definition of a *hasType*-relation with explicit semantics and a joint design of domain models, using a DSL together with the facilities of domain engineering, we have to deal with the following challenges:

1. **Explicit modeling ontological and linguistic instantiation relationship:** One challenge in today's model-driven development environments is that they should allow for explicitly modeling both, ontological and linguistic, instantiation relationship to support both, domain and language engineering [3]. To create elements in a domain model domain designers and language users require a (domain-specific) language represented by a metamodel. This language should prescribe the design of domain models and provide a linguistic instantiation mechanism for designing types and instances in domain models. In addition domain designers require explicit modeling of an ontological instantiation relationship. It allows for assigning a domain type to domain instances in the domain model.
2. **Combination of Language Engineering and Domain Engineering:** A second challenge is related to the joint use of linguistic and ontological instantiation. The problem in using pure DSLs which only allow for creating linguistic instances of elements in the metamodel is a lack of flexibility in dynamically extending the set of domain types in domain models [3]. Domain designers might identify domain types and instances, where language designers formalize them by creating a DSL for language users to create models describing e.g. products or components for

software systems [6]. Domain designers call for the capability iteratively to define or extend the set of domain types for modeling domain instances. This requires the simultaneous definition of types and instances in one domain model. Here the need of an appropriate language metamodel is needed which provides concepts to allow for defining both, types and instances. On the other side, since pure domain engineering allows to create arbitrary domain types, different domain models of the same domain could have different types which do not fit together. Here some prescribing language for domain models can be necessary to make them comparable and capable of being integrated.

3. **Services and Constraints:** The validity of domain models is an important challenge. If models are invalid, domain designers and language users want to debug their domain models to find errors inside them and to get an explanation how to correct the model. They want to have information about consequences of applying given domain constructs. The MDD environment should be able to provide suggestions to language users and domain designers. In the case of building domain models, language users normally start the modeling with general and abstract concepts, since they have not the complete knowledge of all constructs provided by the DSL or they want to keep variability in extending the model [7]. Hence they want to classify conforming model elements according to concept descriptions in the language metamodel. In the case of domain engineering, domain designers want to classify existing domain instances. Since often domain instances exist without any domain type, domain designers want to get suggestions of possible types automatically. To define the validity an appropriate constraint language is needed. Language designers have to define constraints to restrict the use of concepts in the metamodel. Domain designers have to define constraints to refine the domain description. Furthermore, constraints for domain designers must cover both, instance and type layer.

This paper is structured as follows: In section 2, we sketch the application context and show the differences between linguistic and ontological instantiation. We present a running example for joint language and domain engineering illustrating the three challenges. After some foundations of description logics and its need in software engineering in section 3, we present the architecture of an environment which provides both, language engineering with linguistic instantiation and domain engineering with ontological instantiation in section 4. At the end of this paper, we compare our approach with the challenges (section 5) and with related work (section 6).

2 Running Example

In this section, we first start with an introduction of the application context which gives an idea of the different dimensions of metamodeling. Afterwards we present a simple running example where we show a domain-specific language and its domain model which allows for defining an ontological instantiation relation.

2.1 Application Context

Generally, *language designers* using MDD environments require the facility to define the abstract syntax, at least one concrete syntax and the semantics of the language to be designed [3]. The abstract syntax can be defined by a metamodel. The concrete syntax can be specified by textual or visual notations. Semantics may be defined by a natural language specification or may be captured (partially) by logics (e.g. description logics [8,9]).

From the language engineering perspective and with regard to figure 1(a) linguistic instantiation supplies a linear metamodeling hierarchy [4]. The metametamodel is instantiated by the language designer to define the metamodel. The metamodel itself is instantiated by a language user to build domain models. For example, the metatype elements and the metainstance elements in the metamodel are linguistic instances of the metametamodel element class. type elements and instance elements in the domain model are linguistic instances of the metatype element and metainstance element at the M2 layer. In figure 1(b) the elements in figure 1(a) are exemplified by concrete model elements from the domain of network devices (cf. section 2.2). Here, Device is a metatype and a possible linguistic instance of Device is Cisco. On the right side of figure 1(b), we have DeviceInstance as a metainstance. A linguistic instance of DeviceInstance is cisco7603 at the M1 layer.

At the M1 layer, a domain designer is able to define at least two ontological layers (*O2* and *O1*) within his domain model. He is able to define type elements (at *O2*), corresponding instance elements (at *O1*) and connecting them by an ontological *hasType*-relation. The relation itself is defined in the metamodel which strongly prescribes the design of domain models (e.g. types cannot be connected to other types via hasType). The M0 layer represents the real world objects, e.g. concrete devices and its categories. With regard to figure 1(b) Cisco is a domain type which has a domain instance called Cisco7603 via an ontological hasType relation. The hasType relation between a Device and a DeviceInstance is defined at the M2 layer. Furthermore, a domain designer can specialize domain types by creating *subclass*-relationships, or vice versa subsume given domain types by one super type. For example, domain type Cisco in figure 1(b) could have the specialization CiscoWAN or CiscoLAN.

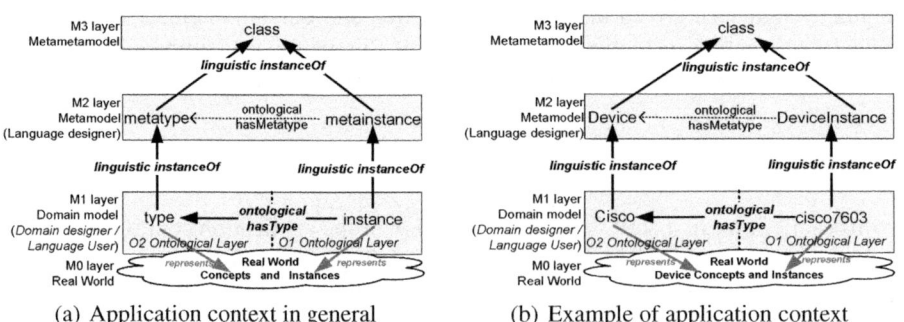

(a) Application context in general (b) Example of application context

Fig. 1. Linguistic and ontological metamodeling

While metamodels of DSLs on the one side are used to prescribe the design of domain models, on the other side, initial domain models are used to extract the metamodel of a language. At first, a domain designer would create types and instances in his domain model. A language designer considers the domain model and extracts relevant concepts for the metamodel [10].

In the following, we are going to present an example which is provided by one of the industrial partners of the MOST project[1]. This example exemplifies all *challenges (1)* to *(3)* introduced in section 1. With regard to figure 1 the following example depicts how the elements **metatype, metainstance, type** and **instance** are concretely defined in a metamodel and a domain model and how the instantiation relations are modeled.

2.2 Example

Comarch[2], a polish IT company specialized in software for telecommunication providers, uses different model-driven methods for software development where different kinds of domain-specific languages (DSLs) are deployed during the modeling process. Some of the tools that Comarch develops for telecommunication providers are dealing with modeling physical network devices. This is a domain-specific task, since different configurations of network devices have to be modeled. The following language metamodel (figure 2) and domain model (figure 3) are designed by using a textual concrete syntax which is based on an extended KM3-syntax [11].

1. Explicit modeling ontological and linguistic instantiation relationship: The domain of physical network devices can be described by a simple DSL, which provides the core metatypes like **Device, Slot** and **Card**. Comarch language designers want to provide the facilities of domain engineering to language users and domain designers to create domain models at the M1 layer. Thus, they have to provide a language which allows for creating domain types and instances in domain models. Furthermore, the ontological instantiation relation must be explicitly defined. Metatypes together with the connecting **metareferences** describe the general structure of a network device and are defined in an M2 metamodel which is depicted in figure 2. In the same metamodel the Comarch language designer defines metainstances using the **metainstance**-keyword. Here the ontological instantiation relation is defined by the **hasMetatype**-keyword.

A domain model is depicted in figure 3 and consists of linguistic instances of model elements in the metamodel. Here both domain types and instances are defined using the **type**- and **instance**-keyword. Using the **instanceOf**-keyword each domain type and domain instance can be defined as a linguistic instance of a corresponding metatype and metainstance. For example, domain type **Cisco** is a linguistic instance of **Device**, while **supervisor720** is a linguistic instance of **CardInstance**.

A mandatory task in creating domain models is the definition of an explicit hasType-relation between instances and domain types. In the example in figure 3, a domain designer wants to use the **hasType**-keyword to define that the ontological instance **supervisor720** has the named type **CiscoCard**. References like **hasSlot** in the type

---

[1] http://www.most-project.eu
[2] http://www.comarch.com

```
1  metatype Device {
2      metareference hasSlot [1−*]: Slot;
3  }
4  metatype Slot {
5      metareference hasCard [0−*]: Card;
6  }
7  metatype Card { }
8
9  metainstance DeviceInstance hasMetatype Device, equivalentWith restrictionOn
       hasSlot with some restrictionOn hasCard with some Card {
10     metalink hasSlot [1−*]: SlotInstance;
11 }
12 metainstance SlotInstance hasMetatype Slot {
13     metalink hasCard [0−*]: CardInstance;
14 }
15 metainstance CardInstance hasMetatype Card { }
```

Fig. 2. M2 metamodel of the core DSL

definitions on the one side represent links which are linguistic instances of corresponding references in the metamodel, on the other side, they define new references for links between ontological instances.

Furthermore, constraints based on description logics [9] should be defined in the metamodel. For example, in figure 2 an equivalentWith-axiom is used to define that each device instance must be linked with at least some card via some slot, which cannot be defined by cardinalities, because slots optionally could be empty.

2. Combination of Language Engineering and Domain Engineering: To ensure the correctness of domain models Comarch wants to prescribe the design of each domain model. The core domain should be described by a DSL which is used by domain designers und language users to build domain models. So far, the DSLs designed by Comarch do not allow for creating both types and instances in the domain model. To accomplish the prescription of the design of domain models, a Comarch language designer wants to describe DSLs in a way like it is done in figure 2. Here the metamodel of a DSL is depicted which allows for describing the core domain of physical network devices, but as well distinguishes between domain types and instances.

Language users and domain designers get this metamodel and can create linguistic instances, which build the domain model depicted in figure 3. Thus every domain model can consist of domain types (using the type-keyword) and corresponding instances (using the instance-keyword). Furthermore, each complete device has to follow the given structure of the order *device-slot-card*, and has to contain at least one card, which is prescribed by the DSL. Without a DSL that prescribes the design of domain models a second domain designer would be able to create domain models which describe devices containing elements in the order *device-card*. Such models of the same domain would not be comparable with other domain models and capable of being integrated.

3. Services and Constraints: Language designer and domain designer at Comarch want to define constraints in their language metamodels and domain models. Using a metamodeling language (like KM3 [11]) and in addition some constraint language (like OCL) as yet, maybe would not help Comarch, since the designers want to define constraints that cover at least two layers - one type layer and one instance layer.

```
1  type Cisco instanceOf Device equivalentWith restrictionOn hasSlot with some
      restrictionOn hasCard with some Supervisor {
2     reference hasSlot [1−∗]: CiscoSlot;
3  }
4  type CiscoSlot instanceOf Slot {
5     reference hasCard [0−∗]: CiscoCard;
6  }
7  type CiscoCard instanceOf Card { }
8  type HotSwappableOSM instanceOf Card, extends CiscoCard { }
9  type Supervisor instanceOf Card, equivalentWith oneOf( supervisor720, supervisor360
      ) { }
10
11 instance cicso7603 instanceOf DeviceInstance{
12    hasSlot slot1;
13 }
14 instance cisco7604 instanceOf DeviceInstance, hasType restrictionOn hasSlot with
      some restrictionOn hasCard with some Supervisor {
15 }
16 instance slot1 instanceOf SlotInstance, hasType CiscoSlot {
17    hasCard supervisor360;
18 }
19 instance supervisor720 instanceOf CardInstance, hasType CiscoCard { }
20 instance supervisor360 instanceOf CardInstance, hasType CiscoCard { }
```

Fig. 3. M1 domain model containing types and instances

For example, a domain designer restricts the domain type Cisco by defining that it must be connected within the domain model in figure 3 with at least one Supervisor-card via a slot. The type Supervisor is equivalent to a set of two domain instances, namely supervisor360 and supervisor720. Here a constraint is used, which covers both layers for types and instances. In figure 3, below the definition of domain types, the definition of domain instances occurs. Here the instance cicso7604 has an anonymous type which restricts that it must be connected with some instance of Supervisor.

Language users want to have services for validating domain models with regard to the metamodel. Domain designers also want to validate their domain models and check the consistency of domain instances with regard to the domain types. Furthermore, they require classification of domain instances with suggestions of suitable types to be assigned to instances in the domain model. So far, Comarchs MDD environments do not support validation and classification services cannot be realized based on the current domain models.

The domain instance cisco7604 leads to an inconsistency. As an explanation, an MDD environment should return a debugging relevant fact which gives the information that a link to a supervisor card is missing. Since not every instance in the domain model is assigned to a domain type, domain designers require suggestions of suitable types. For example, they want to have Cisco as possible domain type of cisco7603 (because it is connected via a slot with some supervisor card).

3 Description Logics-Based Metamodeling

Description logics[9] are a family of logics for concept definitions that allows for separate as well as for joint sound and complete reasoning at the model and at the instance level given the definition of domain concepts.

OWL2, the web ontology language, is a W3C recommendation with a very comprehensive set of constructs for concept definitions [12] and represents a concrete implementation of a description logic.

In this paper, we use OWL for specifying classes, properties and individuals of a domain, instead of OCL, the Object Constraint Languages [13], which is an expression language to specify constraints for UML diagrams.

3.1 Description Logics for Language and Domain Engineering

The domain-specific language engineering process can be divided into different phases [14]: *analysis*, *design* and *implementation*. In this paper, we mainly concentrate on the *design phase* of DSLs. Here a metamodel of the language is specified, together with concrete syntax and semantics. MOF-like metametamodels usually describe the metamodels. The semantics of MOF-based metamodels is limited in comparison to the ones of description logics, and the latter one provides a better support for reasoning than MOF-based languages [15]. Description logics-based approaches lead to formal domain-specific metamodels that may be exploited for a variety of services, from consistency checking to semi-automatic engineering and to explanations [2].

As described in [16] the process of domain engineering can be divided into three main parts: *domain analysis*, *infrastructure specification* and *infrastructure implementation*. The domain analysis phase considers the identification and analysis of domain knowledge to be reused in software engineering. The result of domain analysis is a formal *domain model* of the problem domain. In this paper, we consider the task of creating domain models. As described in [16], ontologies can help in the language specification by capturing the problem domain, conceptualizing it, and later constraining the interpretation by further formal axioms.

3.2 Example

In the following, we consider the running example again and define the domain model presented in figure 3 as a knowledge base using description logics in figure 4.

The axioms (1) to (4) define the description logics TBox. The TBox is used to specify concepts (corresponding to classes in UML) which denote sets of individuals and roles (corresponding to associations in UML) which define binary relations between individuals. At first the concept Cisco is defined as an anonymous class which demands that each individual of Cisco is connected with some individual of type Supervisor via the hasSlot- and hasCard-role (1). In (2) the concepts CiscoSlot and CiscoCard are defined as a subclass of *top* ($\top$). The *top*-concept is the common super type of all defined concepts in the knowledge base and captures all individuals in the domain. In (3) the HotSwappableCard is defined as a subclass of CiscoCard. In (4) the Supervisor concept is defined as an enumeration of the individuals supervisor720 and supervisor360.

The axioms (5) to (10) define the description logics ABox. Here the concrete knowledge is asserted defining individuals of concepts and linking them using the roles defined in the TBox. In (5) the individual cisco7603 is defined but has no direct type. In (6) the individual cisco7604 is defined, which has an anonymous type. It defines, that the individual must be connected by the hasSlot and hasCard-role with some individual of type Supervisor. Furthermore, all necessary individuals for slots and cards are defined (7, 8). Using role assertions all the individuals are linked and represent a concrete configuration of a *Cisco7603* device (9, 10).

$$Cisco \equiv \exists hasSlot.(\exists hasCard.Supervisor) \quad (1)$$
$$CiscoSlot, CiscoCard \sqsubseteq \top \quad (2)$$
$$HotSwappaleOSM \sqsubseteq CiscoCard \quad (3)$$
$$Supervisor \equiv \{supervisor720, supervisor360\} \quad (4)$$
$$cisco7603 \in \top \quad (5)$$
$$cisco7604 \in \exists hasSlot.(\exists hasCard.Supervisor) \quad (6)$$
$$slot1 \in Slot \quad (7)$$
$$supervisor720, supervisor360 \in Card \quad (8)$$
$$(cisco7603, slot1) \in hasSlot \quad (9)$$
$$(slot1, supervisor360) \in hasCard \quad (10)$$

Fig. 4. Description logics knowledge base representing the domain model from figure 3

3.3 Open and Closed World Assumption

While the underlying semantics of MOF-based class modeling adopts the closed world assumption (CWA), description logics adopt the open world assumption (OWA) by default. Traditional design of domain models is based on the closed-world assumption where the elements in the model are known and unchanging. The open world assumption assumes incomplete information as default and allows for validating incomplete domain models which are still in the design phase. However, research in the field of combining description logics and logic programming [17] provides solutions to support description logics-based reasoning with the closed world assumption as well [18]. Thus we are able to switch between reasoning with OWA and CWA.

Since description logics are useful in domain engineering for joint reasoning at the type layer and instance layer, for handling incomplete domain models and in language engineering for validating domain models with regard to its metamodel, we propose to develop language metamodels (cf. figure 2) and domain models (cf. figure 3) with embedded description logics-based constraints in an integrated manner. Our intention is to allow domain and language designers to create domain models and metamodels with the language they are familiar with as much as they can and selectively annotate elements with simple description logics-based constraints.

4 Metamodeling with Linguistic and Ontological Instantiation

In this section, we will present the approach and architecture which provide linguistic and ontological metamodeling. In section 4.1, first we present the overall approach and the architecture. In section 4.2 we present an excerpt of the integrated metametamodel, and give an idea how it relates to a concrete syntax. In section 4.3 we present the different kinds of services which are provided by the environment.

4.1 Overall Approach

Figure 5 presents a multi-layered architecture depicting the *OntoDSL*-environment usable for language engineering and extended with new functionalities for domain engineering.

Core of the environment is the *Ontology-based MetaModeling Language (OntoM2L)* at the M3 layer, whose abstract syntax is described by an integrated metametamodel. It consists of an (extended) *KM3 metametamodel* [11] integrated with an *OWL2 metamodel* [12], which implements a description logic. An excerpt of the metametamodel is depicted in figure 6. Linguistic instances of the integrated metametamodel lie at the M2 layer. Here the environment provides the facility for language engineering and allows for building DSL metamodels. These metamodels can contain the definition of domain metatypes and metainstances. The DSL defined at the M2 layer is used to describe the core of a domain and can be used by a domain designer and language user to built domain models at the M1 layer. Because the metamodel allows for creating domain types (using the M2 concept **metatype**) and domain instances (using the M2 concept **metainstance**), domain designers and language users are able to model two ontological layers O2 and O1. Layer O2 consists of domain types and layer O1 consists of domain instances. Both ontological layers are connected by the explicit ontological *hasType*-relation between domain types and instances.

The OWL2 part of *OntoM2L* can be used to define axioms and restrictions in the metamodel and domain model. To reason on the additional semantics, especially the one of the explicit hasType- and instanceOf-relations, the domain model at the M1 layer with its types and instances is transformed to a description logics TBox and ABox, represented by the **DE Ontology**. Its TBox describes the terminology of the domain and represents the domain types together with its constraints, while the ABox contains concrete assertions about domain instances. In the case of language engineering the metamodel together with its metatypes and metainstances is transformed into the TBox contained by the **LE Ontology**. Each linguistic instances of the metamodel are transformed into the ABox. The two knowledge bases, which are implemented by an OWL2 ontology, are used by an inference engine, which provides additional services. These services for validating and explaining the metamodel can be used by the different users of the environment.

4.2 Implementation

In the following, we present some technical details of the environment and give an idea, how it is implemented.

Abstract syntax. Figure 6 depicts an excerpt of the integrated metametamodel, which is part of OntoM2L and consists of two main parts: the *KM3+instance metametamodel* and the *OWL2 metamodel*.

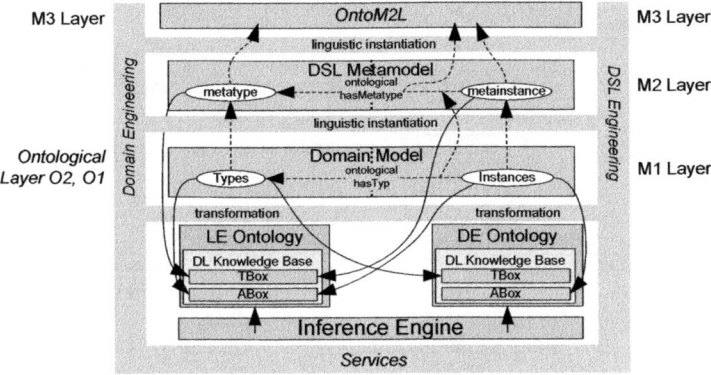

Fig. 5. Architectural overview of the environment

The *KM3+instance metametamodel* provides all the concepts for modeling (meta-) types and (meta-)instances and adopts the *OWL2 metamodel*. For example, the class KM3Class is a specialization of OWLClass, thus it is possible to restrict classes by several class axioms provided by the OWL2 metamodel. KM3Instance is a specialization of OWLIndividual and Instantiation is a specialization of ClassAssertion. In OWL class assertions are used to define the class expressions as type of an individual. The *KM3+instance metametamodel* differentiates between elements of M2 layer and M1 layer. M2 elements, for example, are Metatype and Metainstance. Both can be connected by a MetaHasType relation. M1 elements, for example, are Type and Instance which optionally can be connected by a HasType relation.

The metametamodel allows for defining the linguistic instanceOf-relationship between M2 and M1 elements using the InstanceOf-class. Each linguistic instance must have exactly one metatype or metainstance. We must mention that several constraints for a restricted use of the metametamodel are not depicted in figure 6. They allow for defining, that Type only can be linguistic instance of Metatype, Instance only can be linguistic instance of Metainstance and HasType only can be linguistic instance of MetaHasType.

All classes in the M3 metametamodel which are specialization of M2Element are also specialization of KM3Class which is specialization of OWLClass. Hence their instances, which are represented at the M2 layer, are transformed to a TBox in the description logics knowledgebase (cf. figure 5). In the case of reasoning services for language engineering all instances of M1Element, which lie at the M1 layer, are transformed into a description logics ABox. Hence M1Element is specialization of KM3Instance in the metametamodel, because the ABox consists of instance definitions.

In the case of services for domain engineering we differ between elements for types and instances at the M1 layer. All instances of Type are transformed into a description logics TBox, hence Type is a specialization of KM3Class in the metametamodel. All instances of Instance are transformed into a description logics ABox. Hence Instance is a specialization of KM3Instance in the metametamodel.

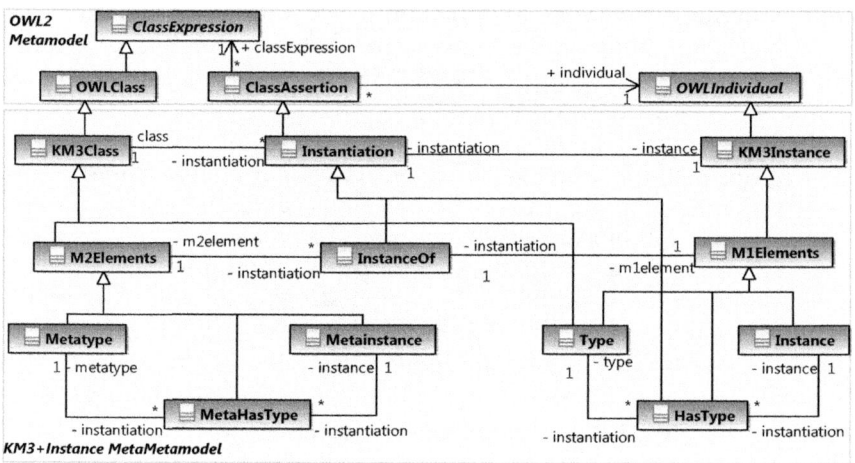

Fig. 6. M3 metametamodel providing modeling of ontological- and linguistic instantiation

Concrete syntax. In figure 2 an example of a DSL metamodel is depicted, in figure 3 we see a conforming domain model. In both figures, a textual concrete syntax was used by the designer to implement the models.

The syntax in the examples was built by combining different existing concrete syntaxes. We took the KM3 syntax[11] and extended it to allow designers to model instances. The motivation is that designers should use the extended Java-like KM3 syntax as much as they can. To take benefit from OWL as an implementation of a description logic, they should be able to annotate elements of their models in a textual and integrated manner. Hence, we extended the grammar of the KM3 concrete syntax by new non-terminals which are defined in grammars of a textual OWL2 concrete syntax.

For each model element residing in an M2 metamodel or M1 domain model the concrete syntax provides specific keywords. The metatype- and metainstance-keywords allow for creating new linguistic instances of class Metatype- and Metainstance of the integrated metametamodel in an M2 metamodel. The type- and instance-keywords allow for creating new linguistic instances of class Type- and Instance of the integrated metametamodel in an M1 domain model.

The instanceOf-keyword is used to set up the linguistic instanceOf-relation between M1 and M2 layer which is represented in the metametamodel by the InstanceOf-class. The hasType-keyword is used to assign a domain type to a domain instance, which is in the metametamodel defined by using the HasType-class.

4.3 Services

In this section, we want to expose the services of the MDD environment for domain and language engineering. All services base on standard reasoning services and are provided to designers and users without any effort. This means that users and designers do not have to be familiar with using and reasoning of description logics knowledge bases.

Services for language engineering. Based on the knowledge base **LE Ontology** representing the language metamodel and the domain model, the environment provides several services to both language user and language designer. Language users mainly rely on services for validating their domain models and suggesting model elements to be used. Suggestion services can be realized by dynamic classification. It allows for determining the classes which one instance belongs to, based on all descriptions in the domain model and metamodel. The correctness of the domain-specific language under development is important for languages designers. Thus, they want to check the consistency of the developed language, or they might exploit information about concept satisfiability, checking if it is possible for a concept in the metamodel to have any instances. If language users want to verify whether all restrictions and constraints imposed by the metamodel hold, they can use a reasoning service to check the consistency of the domain model. An important feature of the environment is, if the model or metamodel are inconsistent or contain unsatisfiable concepts, the users and designers get additional explanations which lead to debug relevant facts and help in correcting the models [19].

Services for domain engineering. The services for domain designers rely on the extracted description logics knowledge base **DE Ontology**. With regard to the example in figure 3 they want to check, if all instances are consistent with regard to the domain types. Furthermore, they want to check if it is possible to create instances of a given type, in other words if types are satisfiable. Since at the beginning of describing the domain often instances exist in the model without any domain type, domain designers automatically want to classify them to get its possible types.

5 Discussion of the Approach

In this section, we establish the viability of our approach by a proof of concept discussion. We analyze the approach with respect to the challenges of section 1.1.

To address the modeling of ontological and linguistic instantiation relationship (challenge 1) we built a metametamodel, which allows for defining metatypes and metainstances within a language metamodel at the M2 layer. This metamodel allows for creating types and instances in one domain model. Furthermore, the metametamodel allows for explicitly designing a linguistic-instanceOf relationship, which relates elements of two different modeling layers, and an ontological hasType-relationship which allows for relating domain types with corresponding domain instances at the M1 layer.

To consider the combination of language engineering and domain engineering, we created a metametamodel that joins both concerns (challenge 2). Language designers using the metametamodel can design DSL metamodels at the M2 layer which is related to language engineering. Domain designers and language users are able to create domain models containing both, domain types and instances. Domain models lie at the M1 layer and must conform to DSL metamodels via the linguistic instanceOf-relationship.

To have a language that allows for defining constraints (challenge 3) we considered the extended KM3 metamodel and integrated it with the existing OWL2 metamodel at the M3 layer. Designers are able to define several constraints for types and instances and in addition constraints and axiom that cross type and instance level.

The defined metamodels are transformed into a pure description logics knowledge base. Thus we use model-theoretic semantics, which is taken into account by the environment for providing different services. These services are used by designers and users to validate models. If the model is not valid, they get several explanations and debugging relevant facts (challenge 3).

6 Related Work

In the following, we want to compare our approach with related work. In the first part of this section, we will depict related work on foundations of model-driven development environments. In the second part, we give some related work which is dealing with ontological metamodeling. The third part of this section discusses related approaches enriching the expressiveness of modeling languages.

Already in 2003, Atkinson et. al defined requirements of model-driven development infrastructures. Besides requirements for defining abstract syntax, concrete syntax and semantics within the infrastructure, they suggest to consider the dimensions of language engineering and domain engineering [3]. As proposed in [3] we provide the facility to built types and instances at the same model layer and thus allow for dynamically extending the set of domain types available for modeling.

In [20] a metamodeling language is presented which allows for building ontological theories as a base for modeling languages from the philosophical point of view. The M3 metamodel consists of elements for individuals and universals (types) and in addition provides a textual concrete syntax. In addition to this approach, we already provide formal semantics in particular for the *hasType*-relation, at least if the developed models are transformed into a description logics TBox and ABox. In [21] an ontological metamodel extension for generative architectures (OMEGA) is described as an extension to the MOF 1.4 metamodel that allows for ontological metamodeling. The core addition to the original MOF model is the introduction of concepts for MetaElement and Instance, which form the basis for all instantiations. In fact, the *hasType*-relation between Instance and MetaElement is implemented by a simple UML association which does not provide any semantics to further tools.

There are many model-based development environments for DSLs available in the market like, for example, MetaEdit+ [22] or ATLAS Model Management Architecture (AMMA) [23]. These environments are aligned with the OMG four-layer metamodel architecture. Some of them provide support for specifying queries and constraints, e.g. with OCL-like languages. Here checking constraints and executing queries takes place on one single layer. Instead, our description logics-based approach allows for defining constraints that cover model and instance layer and provides querying and reasoning simultaneously on both of them. Several approaches describe transformations of MOF-based models to knowledge representation languages where reasoning and querying are adopted. For example, [24] presents transformations from MOF-based models to Alloy, [25] presents an approach to describe the semantics of MOF-based models with F-Logic. Instead of these approaches, where the expressiveness available for designers is limited to MOF (plus OCL), we provide integrated modeling. Thus the designer benefits from the expressiveness of OWL additionally to the one of MOF.

7 Conclusion

We have shown how a combination of an extended KM3 metametamodel and the OWL2 metamodel supports language and domain engineering. Description logics can support modeling and give constraints and semantics covering both, the instances and types defined in a model. We have presented an integrated approach where the modelers are able to use a simple, Java-like syntax but in addition can benefit from a language which provides much expressiveness and services for productive modeling. Furthermore, we presented an approach of joint domain- and language engineering. The result of language engineering is a new DSL, which defines the core of a domain and prescribes the design of domain models. Domain engineering, which results in a domain model, provides the facility to define new domain types during modeling, which is in general not possible using pure language engineering approaches. Currently rely on two ontological layers, since they can be covered by one OWL ontology, the work in the future may consist of generalizing the approach to allow modeling an arbitrary number of ontological layers.

Acknowledgement. We like to thank Krzysztof Miksa from Comarch for providing the use cases. This work is supported by EU STReP-216691 MOST.

References

1. Kelly, S., Tolvanen, J.P.: Domain-specific modeling: enabling full code generation. Wiley-IEEE Computer Society Pr. (2008)
2. Walter, T., Silva Parreiras, F., Staab, S.: OntoDSL: An Ontology-Based Framework for Domain-Specific Languages. In: Schürr, A., Selic, B. (eds.) MODELS 2009. LNCS, vol. 5795, pp. 408–422. Springer, Heidelberg (2009)
3. Atkinson, C., Kühne, T.: Model-driven development: A Metamodeling Foundation. IEEE Software 20(5), 36–41 (2003)
4. Mernik, M., Sloane, A.: When and how to develop domain-specific languages, vol. 37, pp. 316–344. ACM, New York (2005)
5. OMG: Meta Object Facility (MOF) Core Specification (January 2006), http://www.omg.org/spec/MOF/2.0/
6. Weiss, D., Lai, C.: Software product-line engineering. Addison-Wesley, Reading (1999)
7. Tairas, R., Mernik, M., Gray, J.: Using ontologies in the domain analysis of domain-specific languages. In: Models in Software Engineering. LNCS, vol. 5421, pp. 332–342. Springer, Heidelberg (2009)
8. Berardi, D., Calvanese, D., De Giacomo, G.: Reasoning on UML Class Diagrams. Artificial Intelligence 168(1-2), 70–118 (2005)
9. Baader, F., Calvanese, D., McGuinness, D., Nardi, D., Patel-Schneider, P.: The description logic handbook. Cambridge University Press, New York (2007)
10. Guizzardi, G., Pires, L., Van Sinderen, M.: On the role of domain ontologies in the design of domain-specific visual modeling languages. In: Proceedings of the 2nd Workshop on Domain-Specific Visual Languages, 17th ACM Conference on Object-Oriented Programming, Systems, Languages and Applications, OOPSLA 2002 (2002)
11. Jouault, F., Bezivin, J.: KM3: a DSL for Metamodel Specification. In: Gorrieri, R., Wehrheim, H. (eds.) FMOODS 2006. LNCS, vol. 4037, pp. 171–185. Springer, Heidelberg (2006)

12. Motik, B., Patel-Schneider, P.F., Horrocks, I.: OWL 2 Web Ontology Language: Structural Specification and Functional-Style Syntax (October 2009), http://www.w3.org/TR/owl2-syntax/
13. OMG: Object Constraint Language Specification, version 2.0. Object Management Group (June 2005)
14. Mernik, M., Sloane, A.: When and how to develop domain-specific languages. ACM Computing Surveys (CSUR) 37(4), 316–344 (2005)
15. Happel, H.J., Seedorf, S.: Applications of ontologies in software engineering. In: Workshop on Sematic Web Enabled Software Engineering, SWESE 2006, pp. 5–9 (2006)
16. de Almeida Falbo, R., Guizzardi, G., Duarte, K.: An ontological approach to domain engineering. In: International Conference on Software Engineering and Knowledge Engineering, SEKE 2002. International Conference Proceedings, vol. 27, pp. 351–358. ACM Press, New York (2002)
17. Motik, B., Horrocks, I., Rosati, R., Sattler, U.: Can OWL and logic programming live together happily ever after? In: Cruz, I., Decker, S., Allemang, D., Preist, C., Schwabe, D., Mika, P., Uschold, M., Aroyo, L.M. (eds.) ISWC 2006. LNCS, vol. 4273, pp. 501–514. Springer, Heidelberg (2006)
18. Parsia, B., Sirin, E.: Pellet: An OWL DL Reasoner. In: International Workshop on Description Logics, DL 2004. CEUR Workshop Proceedings, vol. 104 (2004)
19. Parsia, B., Sirin, E., Kalyanpur, A.: Debugging OWL ontologies. In: International Conference on World Wide Web, WWW 2005, pp. 633–640. ACM, New York (2005)
20. Laarman, A., Kurtev, I.: Ontological Metamodeling with Explicit Instantiation. In: Conference on Software Languages Engineering, SLE 2009. LNCS, Springer, Heidelberg (2009)
21. Gitzel, R., Ott, I., Schader, M.: Ontological Extension to the MOF Metamodel as a Basis for Code Generation, vol. 50, pp. 93–115. Oxford University Press, Oxford (2007)
22. Kelly, S., Lyytinen, K., Rossi, M.: MetaEdit+: A Fully Configurable Multi-User and Multi-Tool CASE and CAME Environment, pp. 1–21. Springer, Heidelberg (1996)
23. Kurtev, I., Bézivin, J., Jouault, F., Valduriez, P.: Model-Based DSL Frameworks. In: Companion to the 21st ACM SIGPLAN symposium on Object-oriented programming systems, languages, and applications, pp. 22–26. ACM, New York (2006)
24. Anastasakis, K., Bordbar, B., Georg, G., Ray, I.: UML2Alloy: A challenging model transformation. In: Engels, G., Opdyke, B., Schmidt, D.C., Weil, F. (eds.) MODELS 2007. LNCS, vol. 4735, p. 436. Springer, Heidelberg (2007)
25. Gerber, A., Lawley, M., Raymond, K., Steel, J., Wood, A.: Transformation: The missing link of MDA. In: Corradini, A., Ehrig, H., Kreowski, H.-J., Rozenberg, G. (eds.) ICGT 2002. LNCS, vol. 2505, pp. 90–105. Springer, Heidelberg (2002)

An Automated Approach to Transform Use Cases into Activity Diagrams

Tao Yue[1,2], Lionel C. Briand[2], and Yvan Labiche[1]

[1] Carleton University, Software Quality Engineering Lab,
1125 Colonel By Drive
Ottawa, ON K1S 5B6, Canada
labiche@sce.carleton.ca
[2] Simula Research Laboratory & University of Oslo,
P.O. Box 134, Lysaker, Norway
{tao,briand}@simula.no

Abstract. Use cases are commonly used to structure and document requirements while UML activity diagrams are often used to visualize and formalize use cases, for example to support automated test case generation. Therefore the automated support for the transition from use cases to activity diagrams would provide significant, practical help. Additionally, traceability could be established through automated transformation, which could then be used for instance to relate requirements to design decisions and test cases. In this paper, we propose an approach to automatically generate activity diagrams from use cases while establishing traceability links. Data flow information can also be generated and added to these activity diagrams. Our approach is implemented in a tool, which we used to perform five case studies. The results show that high quality activity diagrams can be generated. Our analysis also shows that our approach outperforms existing academic approaches and commercial tools.

Keywords: Use Case; Use Case Modeling; UML; Activity Diagram; Transformation; Traceability; Automation; Natural Language Processing.

1 Introduction

Use case modeling, through use case diagrams and use case textual specifications, is commonly applied to structure and document requirements (e.g., [15]). In this context, UML Activity diagrams are often used to: 1) Visualize use case scenarios in a graphical form to better understand and analyze them (e.g., [20]), which becomes paramount when use cases are large and complex; 2) Model work flows and data flows, which information is embedded in use case descriptions (e.g., [5]); 3) Complement analysis models by providing an additional, complementary view to class and interaction diagrams (e.g., [9]), and 4) Generate test cases complying with use cases (e.g., [17]). Automated support to transform a use case description into an (initial) activity diagram is therefore important. Though activity diagrams do not add information to a use case model, they are more amenable to supporting various analyses and can be a starting point for developing more detailed behavioral models. In other words, a use case model is used to document requirements to facilitate communication among stakeholders whereas activity diagrams provide a more detailed, interpretable representation used to facilitate automated analysis, for example for the purpose of test case generation.

Additionally, automated transformation would enable automated traceability from requirements to activity diagrams. Traceability is important during software development since it allows engineers to understand the connections between various artifacts of a software system. Traceability is also mandated by numerous standards (e.g., IEEE Std. 830-1998 [1]) to support, for example, safety verification [18].

We conducted a systematic literature review [26] on transformations of textual requirements into analysis models, including class, sequence and activity diagrams. We also reviewed more recent publications that were not included in our initial systematic review, as well as existing commercial tools. Existing approaches were compared with our tool according to a set of criteria (Section 6). Results show that some approaches are not fully automated, that the automated ones are not necessarily practical and complete, and that most of them do not provide support for traceability.

The basis of our approach is a use case modeling approach RUCM [24], which relies on a use case template and a set of restriction rules for textual Use Case Specifications (UCSs) to reduce the imprecision and incompleteness inherent to UCSs. We have conducted a controlled experiment to evaluate RUCM and results indicate that RUCM, though it enforces a template and restriction rules, has enough expressive power, is easy to use, and helps improve the understandability of use cases and the quality of derived analysis models [24].

The current work is part of the aToucan approach and tool [25], which aims to transform a Use Case Model (UCMod) produced with RUCM into a UML analysis model that includes class, sequence and activity diagrams. aToucan involves three steps. First, requirements engineers manually define use cases by following RUCM [24]. Second, aToucan reads these textual UCSs to identify Part-Of-Speech (POS) and grammatical relation dependencies of sentences, and then records that information into an instance of the metamodel UCMeta (our intermediate model) (Section 2.2). The third step is to transform the instance of UCMeta into an analysis model as an instance of the UML 2.0 metamodel. During these transformations, aToucan establishes traceability links between the UCMod and the generated UML diagrams.

In this paper, we focus on the RUCM to activity diagrams transformation of aToucan. Specifically, aToucan can automatically generate two types of activity diagrams for each use case: A *detailed activity diagram* shows the main use case flow as well as all alternative flows in one activity diagram; An *overview activity diagram*, on the other hand, only details the main use case flow while the alternative flows are detailed in parts of the sequence diagram aToucan generates for the use case. The activity diagram of the main flow refers to parts of the sequence diagram thanks to the UML 2.0 notions of `CallBehaviorAction` and `Interaction`. Overview activity diagrams therefore help to handle complexity in use case descriptions (complex flows, numerous flows). Our approach can also automatically attach data flow information to generated (overview or detailed) activity diagrams. This is useful to measure complexity or facilitate data flow-based testing for instance [23]; however these topics are out of the scope here and will be investigated in the future.

Five case studies have been performed to evaluate activity diagrams generated by aToucan. Results show that complete and correct (against UCSs) activity diagrams can be generated and traceability links can also be correctly established. Our study also indicates that aToucan outperforms three commercial tools.

The rest of the paper is organized as follows. Section 2 discusses RUCM and UCMeta. Section 3 discusses our transformation approach. Tool support is briefly discussed in Section 4. Case studies are discussed in Section 5. Section 6 discusses related work. Section 6 concludes the paper.

2 Background

We briefly review the use case modeling approach RUCM (Section 2.1) and the intermediate model (UCMeta) of our transformations (Section 2.2) [24].

2.1 RUCM

RUCM encompasses a use case template and 26 well-defined restriction rules [24]. Rules are classified into two groups: restrictions on the use of Natural Language (NL), and rules enforcing the use of specific keywords for specifying control structures. The goal of RUCM is to reduce ambiguity and facilitate automated analysis. A controlled experiment evaluated RUCM in terms of its ease of application and the quality of the analysis models derived by trained individuals [24]. Results showed that RUCM is overall easy to apply and that it results in significant improvements over the use of a standard use case template (without restrictions to the use of NL), in terms of the correctness of derived class diagrams and the understandability of UCSs. Below we discuss the features of RUCM that are particularly helpful to generate activity diagrams. An example of UCS documented with RUCM is presented in Table 1.

A use case description has one basic flow and can have one or more alternative flows (first column in Table 1). An alternative flow always depends on a condition occurring in a specific step in a flow of reference, referred to as *reference flow*, which is either the basic flow or an alternative flow itself. We classify alternative flows into three types: A *specific alternative flow* refers to a specific step in the reference flow; A *bounded alternative flow* refers to more than one step in the reference flow–consecutive steps or not; A *global alternative flow* (called *general alternative flow* in [3]) refers to any step in the reference flow.

Distinguishing different types of alternative flows makes interactions between the reference flow and its alternative flows much clearer. For specific and bounded alternative flows, a RFS (Reference Flow Step) section specifies one or more (reference flow) step numbers. Whether and where the flow merges back to the reference flow or terminates the use case must be specified as the last step of the alternative flow. Branching condition, merging and termination are specified by following restriction rules that impose the use of specific keywords (see below). By doing so, we can avoid potential ambiguity in UCSs caused by unclear specification of interactions between the basic flow and its alternative flows, and facilitate automated generation of activity diagrams.

RUCM defines a set of keywords to specify conditional logic sentences (IF-THEN-ELSE-ELSEIF-ENDIF), concurrency sentences (MEANWHILE), condition checking sentences (VALIDATES THAT), and iteration sentences (DO-UNTIL). These

Table 1. Use case Withdraw Fund (originally from [11], and written here by applying RUCM)

Use Case Name	Withdraw Fund		
Brief Description	ATM customer withdraws a specific amount of funds from a valid bank account.		
Precondition	The system is idle. The system is displaying a Welcome message.		
Primary Actor	ATM customer	Secondary Actors	None
Dependency	INCLUDE USE CASE Validate PIN.	Generalization	None
Basic flow steps	1) INCLUDE USE CASE Validate PIN. 2) ATM customer selects Withdrawal. 3) ATM customer enters the withdrawal amount. 4) ATM customer selects the account number. 5) The system VALIDATES THAT the account number is valid. 6) The system VALIDATES THAT ATM customer has enough funds in the account. 7) The system VALIDATES THAT the withdrawal amount does not exceed the daily limit of the account. 8) The system VALIDATES THAT the ATM has enough funds. 9) The system dispenses the cash amount. 10) The system prints a receipt showing transaction number, transaction type, amount withdrawn, and account balance. 11) The system ejects the ATM card. 12) The system displays Welcome message. **Postcondition**: ATM customer funds have been withdrawn.		
Specific Alt. Flow (RFS Basic flow 8)	1) The system displays an apology message MEANWHILE the system ejects the ATM card. 2) The system shuts down. 3) ABORT. **Postcondition**: ATM customer funds have not been withdrawn. The system is shut down.		
Bounded Alt. Flow (RFS Basic flow 5-7)	1) The system displays an apology message MEANWHILE the system ejects the ATM card. 2) ABORT. **Postcondition**: ATM customer funds have not been withdrawn. The system is idle. The system is displaying a Welcome message.		
Global Alt. Flow	IF ATM customer enters Cancel THEN 1) The system cancels the transaction MEANWHILE the system ejects the ATM card. 2) ABORT. ENDIF **Postcondition**: ATM customer funds have not been withdrawn. The system is idle. The system is displaying a Welcome message.		

keywords greatly facilitate the automated generation of activity diagrams as they clearly indicate when alternative flows start and which kind of alternative flow starts, for which there exist a direct mapping to some UML activity diagram notation. For example, concurrency sentences with keyword MEANWHILE can be accurately transformed into a fork node, a join node, and a number of actions between the fork and join nodes corresponding to the parallel sentences connected by keyword MEANWHILE. Keywords ABORT and RESUME STEP are used to describe an exceptional exit action and where an alternative flow merges back in its reference flow, respectively. An alternative flow ends either with ABORT or RESUME STEP, which means that the last step of the alternative flow should clearly specify whether the flow returns back to the reference flow and where (using keywords RESUME STEP followed by a returning step number) or terminates (using keyword ABORT).

2.2 UCMeta

UCMeta is the intermediate model in aToucan [25], used to bridge the gap between a textual UCMod and a UML analysis model (class, sequence and activity diagrams). As a result, we have two transformations: from the textual UCMod to the intermediate model, and from the intermediate model to the analysis model. Metamodel UCMeta also complies with the restrictions and use case template of RUCM. The current version of UCMeta is composed of 108 metaclasses and is expected to evolve over time. The detailed description of UCMeta is given in [25].

UCMeta is hierarchical and contains five packages: UML::UseCases, UCSTemplate, SentencePatterns, SentenceSemantics, and SentenceStructure. UML::UseCases is a package of UML 2 superstructure [19], which defines the key concepts used for modeling use cases such as actors and use cases. Package UCSTemplate models the concepts of the use case template of RUCM: those concepts model the structure that one can observe in Table 1. SentencePatterns is a package describing different types of sentence patterns, which uniquely specify the grammatical structure of simple sentences, e.g., SVDO (subject-verb-direct object) (Table 1, Basic flow, step 2). SentenceSemantics is a package modeling the classification of sentences from the aspect of their semantic functions in a UCMod. Each sentence in a UCS can either be a ConditionSentence or an ActionSentence. Package SentenceStructure takes care of NL concepts in sentences such as subject or Noun Phrase (NP). Package UCSTemplate is mostly related to the activity diagram generation and therefore it is the only package discussed below due to space limitation.

Package UCSTemplate not only models the concepts of the use case template but also specifies three kinds of sentences: SimpleSentences, ComplexSentences, and SpecialSentences. In linguistics, a SimpleSentence has one independent clause and no dependent clauses [4]: one Subject and one Predicate. UCMeta has four types of ComplexSentences: ConditionCheckSentence, ConditionalSentence, IterativeSentence, and ParallelSentence, which correspond to four keywords that are specified in RUCM (Section 2.1) to model validations (VALIDATES THAT), conditions (IF-THEN-ELSE-ELSEIF-THEN-ENDIF), iterations (DO-UNTIL), and concurrency (MEANWHILE) in UCS sentences. UCMeta also has four types of special sentences to specify how flows in a use case or between use cases relate to one another. They correspond to the keywords RESUME STEP, ABORT, INCLUDE USE CASE, EXTENDED BY USE CASE, and RFS (Reference Flow Step).

3 Approach

Recall that our objective is to automatically transform a textual UCMod expressed using RUCM into UML activity diagrams while establishing traceability links. We present an overview of our approach in Section 3.1 and then detail transformation rules (Section 3.2) and traceability (Section 3.3). More details are available in [27].

3.1 Overview

In this section, we use Fig. 1 as a running example. It shows a piece of the use case description of Table 1: Fig. 1 (a). First, a textual UCMod (Fig. 1 (a)) is automatically transformed into an instance of UCMeta (Fig. 1 (b)) through a set of transformation rules. For example, basic flow step 8 of Fig. 1 (a) is transformed into an instance of ConditioncheckSentence (Fig. 1 (b)). Notice in Fig. 1 (b) that this ConditioncheckSentence instance is linked to a BasicFlow instance (step 8 is part of the basic flow in Table 1) of the UseCaseSpecification of UseCase Withdraw Fund. Fig. 1 (b) does not show how the sentence of step 8 is further transformed into instances of UCMeta (e.g., verb, subject). Second, the UCMeta instance is automatically transformed into a UML analysis model through another set of transformation rules. The (UML 2.0) analysis model contains a class diagram, and a sequence and an activity diagram for each use case. Generating class and sequence diagrams is discussed in [25]. In this paper, we particularly focus on the transformation to activity diagrams.

As mentioned earlier, two types of activity diagrams can be generated for a use case, i.e., from an instance of UCMeta. A *detailed activity diagram* shows the main use case flow as well as all alternative flows in one activity diagram: Fig. 1 (d); whereas an *overview activity diagram* only details the main use case flow while the alternative flows are detailed in parts of the sequence diagram generated for the use case (instances of Interaction): Fig. 1 (c). To illustrate the difference, first note that the parts of Fig. 1 (c) and (d) highlighted with rectangles detail the main flow of the use case in the same way: one can recognize step 8 ("The system VALIDATES THAT ...") followed by a decision node (the validation may be successful or not). In the detailed activity diagram (Fig. 1 (d)) the alternative flow (i.e., when the validation fails) is specified in its entirety (circled set of nodes). Instead, in the overview activity diagram (Fig. 1 (c)), the alternative flow leads to a node labeled ref INTERACTION ..., specifying that the alternative flow can be obtained from an interaction, specifically from a part of the sequence diagram aToucan generated for the use case. The complete activity diagrams generated for use case *Withdraw Fund* is provided in [27].

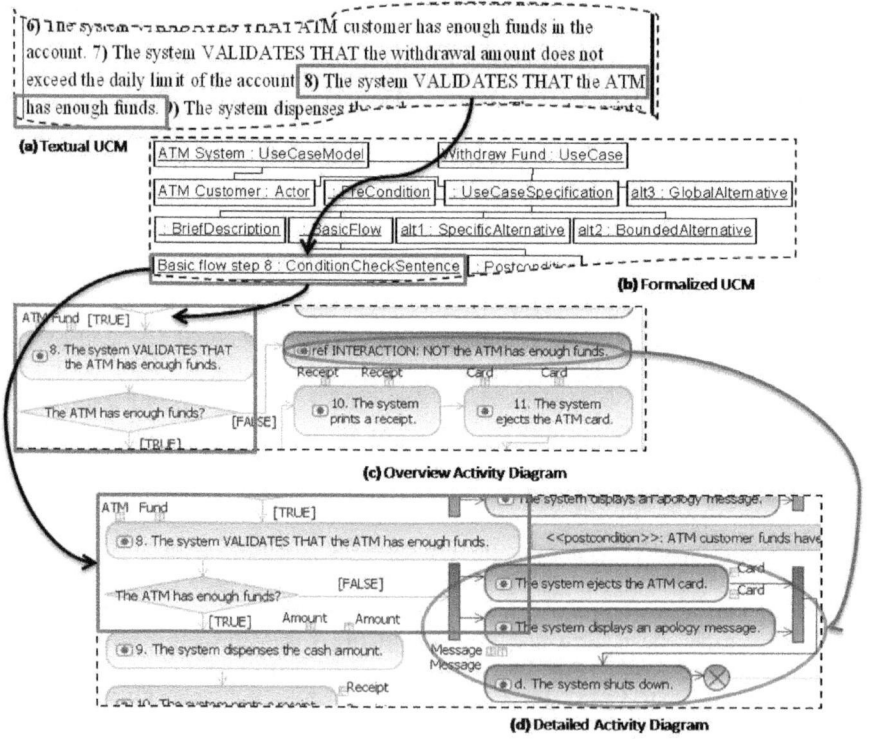

Fig. 1. Running example

Overview activity diagrams are similar to UML Interaction Overview Diagrams [19] in the sense that both use `CallBehaviorAction` referring to instances of `Interactions` of sequence diagrams. However, UML Interaction Overview Diagrams only "focus on the overview of the flow of control where the nodes are `Interactions` or `InteractionUses`" [19] while our Overview Activity Diagram can contain other activity nodes such as instances of `CallOperationAction`.

During the transformations, two sets of traceability links are established: between the elements in the textual UCMod and the elements of the instance of UCMeta, and between these instances and the model elements of the UML analysis model. For instance, step 8 of the use case specification of Table 1 is linked to the `ConditionCheckSentence` instance highlighted in Fig. 1 (b), which is itself linked to the activity nodes labeled 8 (The System ...) in Fig. 1 (c) and (d). Notice that when necessary, direct traceability links between the textual UCMod and the analysis model can be easily derived from the transitive closure of these two sets of traceability links.

3.2 Transformation Rules

The transformation from an instance of UCMeta to activity diagrams involves 19 rules, summarized in Table 2. Subscripts on rule numbers (Column 1, Table 2) indicate the type of the rule: "c" and "a" denote composite and atomic rules, respectively; a composite rule is decomposed into other composite or atomic rules whereas an atomic rule is not.

Rule 1 invokes rules 1.1-1.4 to generate an activity diagram for each use case. Rules 1.1-1.3 process three types of sentences: `SimpleSentence`, `ComplexSentence`, and `SpecialSentence`. Rule 1.4 processes the `GlobalAlternativeFlows` of a use case. Rules 1.5 and 1.6 transform the precondition and the postcondition of a use case into instances of `Constraint` (a metaclass of the UML 2.0 metamodel) attached to the generated activity (precondition) and corresponding `FlowFinalNode` (postcondition). Atomic rules 1.2.1-1.2.4 are invoked by composite rule 1.2 to process four different types of complex sentences that lead to different control flows in the activity diagram (e.g., decision node in rule 1.2.1). Atomic rules 1.3.1-1.3.4 are invoked by rule 1.3 to process four different types of special sentences: to specify include and extend relations between use cases, to specify abort and resume. Rule 1.4 transforms a global alternative flow. Recall that a global alternative flow refers to any step in the reference flow (Section 2.1). For example, the global alternative flow of use case *Withdraw Fund* (Table 1) refers to every step of the basic flow; the ATM customer can cancel the transaction at any time of the execution of the use case. To model this in an activity diagram, we transform the flow into an instance of `AcceptEventAction`, `InterruptibleActivityRegion` and a set of actions corresponding to the steps of that flow. `AcceptEventAction` "is an action that waits for the occurrence of an event meeting a specified condition" [19] and `InterruptibleActivityRegion` (e.g., the basic flow of use case *Withdraw Fund*) is used to abort all flows in the region when an `AcceptEventAction` (e.g., ATM customer enters Cancel—the condition of the global alternative flow) occurs. Thanks to this modeling feature of UML 2.0, we can easily model global alternative flows. Swimlanes are automatically determined for a sentence according to subject types: either "the system" or an actor.

Note that rules 1.2.1, 1.2.2, and 1.4 generate different sets of model elements for detailed and overview activity diagrams. For example, if an overview activity diagram is generated, composite rule 1.2.1 generates an instance of CallBehaviorAction to refer to the Interaction corresponding to the alternative flow of a condition check sentence; otherwise rule 1.2.1 invokes rules 1.1-1.3 to process the sentences of the alternative flow to generated actions, edges, etc, and create a detailed activity diagram.

Table 2. Summary of transformation rules

Rule #	Description
1$_c$	Generate an activity diagram for a use case.
1.1$_a$	Generate an instance of CallOperationAction for each simple sentence.
1.2$_c$	Invoke rules 1.2.1-1.2.4 to process each complex sentence.
1.2.1$_c$	ConditionCheckSentence: Generate a CallOperationAction and a DecisionNode. Invoke rules 1.1-1.3 to handle the sentences contained in the alternative flow corresponding to the sentence (detailed activity diagram) or refer to the Interaction corresponding to the alternative flow (overview activity diagram).
1.2.2$_c$	ConditionalSentence: Generate a DecisionNode. Invoke rules 1.1-1.3 to process sentences contained in the sentence and its alternative flow (detailed activity diagram) or refer to the Interaction corresponding to the alternative flow (overview activity diagram) if such an alternative flow exists.
1.2.3$_c$	ParallelSentence: Generate a ForkNode and a JoinNode. Invoke rules 1.1-1.3 to process the concurrent sentences contained the parallel sentence.
1.2.4$_c$	IterativeSentence: Generate a DecisionNode. Invoke rules 1.1-1.3 to process sentences contained in the iterative sentence.
1.3$_c$	Invoke rules 1.3.1-1.3.4 to process each special sentence.
1.3.1$_a$	IncludeSentence: Generate a CallBehaviorAction that refers to the Interaction corresponding to the included use case.
1.3.2$_a$	ExcludeSentence: Generate a CallBehaviorAction that refers to the Interaction corresponding to the extending use case.
1.3.3$_a$	AbortSentence: Generate a FlowFinalNode.
1.3.4$_a$	ResumeStepSentence: Generate a ControlFlow edge back to the node corresponding to the step specified in the ResumeStepSentence.
1.4$_c$	GlobalAlternativeFlow: Generate an AcceptEventAction and InterruptibleActivityRegion. Invoke rules 1.1-1.3 to process the sentences of the alternative flow (detailed activity diagram) or refer to the Interaction corresponding to the alternative flow (overview activity diagram).
1.5$_a$	Precondition: Generate a Constraint as the precondition of the activity. The content of the constraint is the precondition of the use case.
1.6$_a$	PostCondition: Generate a Constraint for each flow final node as its postcondition. The content of each constraint corresponds to the postcondition of each flow of events of the UCMod.
2$_c$	Attach data flow information to an activity diagram.
2.1$_a$	SimpleSentence with transaction type Initiation, ResponseToPrimaryActor or ResponseToSecondaryActor: Generate an OutputPin for the CallOperationAction generated for the NPs of the sentence.
2.2$_a$	SimpleSentence with transaction type InternalTransaction: Generate an InputPin and an OutputPin for the CallOperationAction generated for the sentence (excluding "the system" and actors).
2.3$_a$	ConditionCheckSentence: Generate an InputPin for the CallOperationAction generated for the NPs of the sentence (excluding "the system" and actors).

Rule 2 invokes rules 2.1-2.3 to attach data flow information to an already generated activity diagram. These rules generate instances of either InputPin or OutputPin for each call operation action. These input and output pins correspond to entity classes that have been generated from the NPs contained in use case sentences when the class diagram of the system was generated [25]. For example, the basic flow step 8 of use case *Withdraw Fund* (Table 1) is a condition check sentence (Fig. 1 (a)). It is transformed into an action and a decision node by rule 1.2.1: (Fig. 1 (c) and (d)). Because the NP "enough funds"—i.e., the object of the condition (simple sentence) of the condition check sentence at step 8—has been transformed into class Fund when the class diagram was generated, we attach an instance of InputPin (pin) to the action corresponding to step 8 and type the pin with class Fund: pin.type = Fund, as show in Fig. 1 (c) and (d).

The rationale for adding data flow to an activity diagram is the following. Steps of a UCS can be one of the following five types: 1) Initiation: the primary actor sends a request and data to the system; 2) Validation: the system validates a request and data; 3) InternalTransaction: the system alters its internal state (e.g., recording or modifying something); 4) ResponseToPrimaryActor: the system replies to the primary actor with a result; 5) ResponseToSecondaryActor: the system sends requests to a secondary actor. We generate data flow through input and output pins according to these definitions as follows: We generate output pins for actions in the activity diagram that correspond to use case steps of type Initiation, ResponseToPrimaryActor, and ResponseToSecondaryActor since these sentences either output data (Initiation) or send a result to actors (ResponseToPrimaryActor or ResponseToSecondaryActor); Since use case steps of type InternalTransaction specify that the system records or modifies data, we generate input and output pins for the actions corresponding to these sentences; Since condition check sentences are all of type Validation and they validate a request and data, input pins should be generated for the corresponding actions in the activity diagram. As suggested earlier, the pins are typed by the entity classes that compose the domain model (class diagram) automatically created from use case descriptions by aToucan [25], which are identified by analyzing sentences (e.g., subjects).

Notice that each rule is further specified by a precondition, although these preconditions are not shown in Table 2. As a simple example, the precondition of rule 1.2.3 specifies that the sentence being transformed into model elements is a parallel sentence (Section 2.1) and that an activity has been generated for the use case and is available to contain the elements being generated by the rule.

3.3 Traceability

We establish two sets of traceability links during the transformation from a textual UCMod to activity diagrams: from the UCMod to the instance of UCMeta and from the UCMeta instance to the automatically generated activity diagrams. If necessary, direct traceability links from the textual UCMod to the activity diagrams can be derived from these two sets.

Traceability links from UCMod to UCMeta link the fields of the use case template used to document textual UCSs to instances of the corresponding metaclasses in UCMeta. For example, field *Brief Description* of the use case template is linked to an instance of metaclass BriefDescription of UCMeta. A sentence in the brief description is then linked to an instance of metaclass Sentence of UCMeta. For example, as shown in Fig. 1 (a) and (b), the basic flow step 8 of use case *Withdraw Fund* is transformed into `Basic flow step 8 : ConditionCheckSentence` of the intermediate model while a traceability link is established between these two elements. We believe that it is not cost effective to establish links at a finer granularity (e.g., between elements of sentences and UCMeta metaclass instances).

Regarding the second set of traceability links, UCMeta metaclass instances are linked to corresponding model elements in the UML activity metamodel based on our transformation rules. For example, we establish two traceability links between a condition check sentence (e.g., `Basic flow step 8 : ConditionCheckSentence` of the UCMeta instance as shown in Fig. 1 (b)) and its corresponding action (an instance of `CallOperationAction`, e.g., `action 8. The system VALIDATES THAT the ATM has enough fund` as shown in Fig. 1 (c)) and decision node (e.g., `The ATM has enough fund` as shown in Fig. 1 (c)) generated during the transformation when rule 1.2.1 is invoked, respectively.

4 Automation

Our approach has been implemented as part of aToucan [25]. aToucan aims to automatically transform requirements given as a UCMod in RUCM into a UML analysis model including a class diagram, and a set of sequence and activity diagrams. It relies on a number of existing technologies. aToucan is built as an Eclipse plug-in, using the Eclipse development platform. UCMeta is implemented as an Ecore model, using Eclipse EMF [8], which generates code as Eclipse plug-ins. The Stanford Parser [21] is used as a NL parser in aToucan. It is written in Java and generates a syntactic parse tree for a sentence and the sentence's grammatical dependencies (e.g., *subject*, *direct object*). The generation of the UML analysis model relies on Kermeta [14]. It is a metamodeling language, also built on top of the Eclipse platform and EMF. The target UML analysis model is instantiated using the Eclipse UML2 project, which is an EMF-Based implementation of the UML 2 standard.

The architecture of aToucan is easy to extend and can accommodate certain types of changes. Transformation rules for generating different types of diagrams are structured into different packages to facilitate their modifications and extensions. Thanks to the generation of an Eclipse UML2 analysis model, generated UML models can be imported and visualized by many open source and commercial tools. Similarly, though UCSs are currently provided as text files, a specific package to import UCSs will allow integration with open source and commercial requirement management tools. More details on the design of aToucan can be found in [25].

We adapted the traceability model proposed in the traceability component (fr.irisa.triskell.traceability.model) of Kermeta [14] to establish traceability links. Details of the traceability model is discussed in [25].

5 Case Studies

In this section, we discuss how we validated our approach (Section 5.1) and also compare our approach with three commercial tools (Section 5.2).

5.1 Validation Procedure and Summary of Results

We used five different software system descriptions (18 use cases altogether) to assess our approach. They are from different sources: three are from textbooks and two were created by Masters students. Since the UCSs of these systems come from different sources, they were re-written by applying RUCM.

The goal of our validation was two-fold: (1) To assess whether our transformation rules are complete: does it accommodate all UCSs in our case studies? (2) To determine whether our transformation rules lead to activity diagrams that are syntactically and semantically correct. Syntactic correctness means that a generated activity diagram conforms to the UML 2.0 activity diagram notation. Semantic correctness means that a generated activity diagram correctly represents its UCS; all the steps described in the flows of events of the UCS are correctly transformed by following the transformation rules and no redundant model elements are generated. In order to check correctness and completeness, the validation procedure is as follows. 1) Given a UCMod in RUMC as input, aToucan automatically generates an activity diagram for each UCS of the UCMod. 2) For each UCS, we check whether each step of the flows of events and the precondition and postconditions have been properly transformed. 3) We check whether each generated activity diagram is syntactically and semantically correct. 4) We check whether the data flow information (input and output pins) attached to each activity diagram is properly generated.

Following the above procedure, for all 18 use cases, we achieved 100% completeness and correctness with aToucan, and 100% of the traceability links were also correctly established. Regarding the completeness and correctness of data flow information attached to each activity diagram, aToucan was not able to generate input and output pins for some actions. First, transformation rules 2.1-2.3 (used to generate data flow information) rely on package SentenceStructure of UCMeta. Recall that a NL parser is used in our approach to parse each textual sentence and the parsing result is transformed into instances of model elements (e.g., Object) of package SentenceStructure (Section 2.2). The NL parser has limitations and cannot always produce a correct result. Therefore the instances of the model elements of package SentenceStructure do not always correctly correspond to their textual sentences. Second, each generated pin is typed to a class of the class diagram; however the automatically generated class diagram is not 100% correct and complete (see [25] for details), again partly because of limitations of the NL parser. As a result, it is possible that there is no matching class found for an element of a sentence (such as an object—recall rule 2 in Section 3.2) and therefore no pin is generated. Besides, whether data flow information can be deemed correct also depends on what it is used for. For example, if it is used to automatically generate test cases, manual refinement of the automatically generated data flow information is absolutely required. Therefore, here, we don't evaluate the correctness of generated data flow information but its completeness, measured by the ratio of occurrences of missing pins over the total number of instances of CallOperationAction in an activity diagram. Results show that the average completeness of data flow information across all the five case study systems is 85%. Due to space constraints, detailed data is provided in [27].

5.2 Comparison with Three Commercial Tools

Visual Paradigm [22], Ravenflow [20], and CaseComplete [6] are commercial tools that can automatically transform requirements into UML activity diagrams. We tested them by using the use case of Table 1 since it contains three different types of alternative flows, concurrency sentences, and validation sentences. Various features of UCSs are therefore considered and this use case can be considered complete in terms of UCS and generated activity diagram features. The UCS was rewritten according to the format requirements of each tool. The details of the re-written UCSs and automatically generated activity diagrams are presented in [27]. In the rest of the section, we summarize their main differences.

1. Visual Paradigm and CaseComplete can transform the flows of events of a use case into an activity diagram. Each flow of events needs to be structured using a simple use case template (basic flow and its extensions). Ravenflow does not require a use case template, but a set of writing guidelines are proposed (not enforced by the tool though) to guide users to write sentences that can be correctly parsed by the tool. For example, "if...then.... Otherwise,..." is suggested to write a conditional sentence. A "!' at the end of a sentence indicates the termination of a flow. Since Ravenflow does not require UCSs be structured, alternative flows may be very hard to describe in unstructured sentences. aToucan is based on RUCM (a use case template and a set of restriction rules), which have been experimentally evaluated to be easy to apply [24]. The benefits of using RUCM to facilitate the automated generation of activity diagrams was discussed in Section 2.1.
2. None of the three commercial tools can generate forks and joins because concurrency sentences are not recognized. Our approach is based on RUCM, which specifies the keyword MEANWHILE (Section 2.1) to help users specify concurrency sentences. Therefore, aToucan can generate a fork, a join, and a set of parallel sentences between the fork and the join (Section 3.2) for each concurrency sentence. Visual Paradigm and CaseComplete do not support swimlanes. Both our approach and Ravenflow support swimlanes—one swimlane per actor and one swimlane for the system—but have different mechanisms to identify actors. Ravenflow relies on Natural Language Processing (NLP) techniques to identify possible actors to generate corresponding swimlanes, which means that the tool might falsely identify actors. Recall that Ravenflow does not have a use case template to structure use case steps. However, our tool is based on RUCM, and primary and secondary actors of each use case are clearly specified in each UCS. Also thanks to RUCM, aToucan can also automatically transform global alternative flows (Section 3.2). It is very hard to find an alternative way to specify global alternative flows in the requirements format required/enforced by the three commercial tools.
3. None of the three commercial tools can support include and extend use case relationships because they can only transform a single use case instead of a use case model (UCMod). aToucan takes a UCMod as input and use case relationships are naturally supported.
4. Visual Paradigm and CaseComplete cannot generate any data flow information since they do not use any NLP technique. Ravenflow can generate data flow information but to a quite limited extent: it generates data flow only when the data

is manipulated by two swimlanes, as indicated in the writing guidelines provided along with the tool. This means that Ravenflow cannot derive data flow information from sentences with transaction types InternalTransaction and Validation. aToucan does not have such a limitation.

6 Related Work and Comparison

We conducted a systematic literature review [26] on transformations of textual requirements into analysis models, including class, sequence, and activity diagrams. The review identified 20 primary studies (16 approaches) based on a carefully designed paper selection procedure in scientific journals and conferences from 1996 to 2008 and Software Engineering textbooks. The method proposed here is based on the results of this review, with a particular focus on automatically deriving activity diagrams from UCMods. There also exists several literature works recently published that were therefore not included in our systematic literature review. In this section, we evaluate our approach by comparing it with these existing literature works and also three existing commercial tools: Visual Paradigm for UML [22], Ravenflow [20], and CaseComplete [6]. We define a set of evaluation criteria for comparison, which are in part from the system review we conducted [26]:

1) **Requirements:** We need to know the requirements format (e.g., formalized use cases) required by a specific approach so that we can assess how difficult it is to document requirements.
2) **NLP:** We need to be aware of whether or not any NLP techniques are applied. We can then assess whether or not certain features (e.g., automatically derive swimlanes) can be supported by the approach.
3) **Automation:** This criterion evaluates whether a transformation is automated, automatable, semi-automated, or manual. An approach is automated if it has been fully implemented. If a transformation algorithm is proposed in a paper, then we assess whether we deem the description to be sufficient to implement it, and if this is the case, the transformation approach is deemed automatable. In some cases, a transformation is semi-automated because user interventions are required. Last, some approaches are entirely manual.
4) **Traceability:** We check whether traceability links between requirements and analysis model elements are established when a transformation is performed.
5) **Objective:** The original objective of each approach can help us understand their limitations and motivate our work.
6) **Activity diagram:** We evaluate the activity diagrams that each approach is able to derive from requirements with respect to the following four aspects: 1) their types (standard, extended, or non-standard notation), 2) important model elements that are expected to be generated (e.g., swimlanes), 3) whether include and extend relationships of use cases are supported, and 4) whether data flow information can be generated. Activity diagrams conforming to the UML specification [19] are standard activity diagrams; extended activity diagrams are those based on a profile of the UML specification; non-standard activity diagrams do not conform to the UML specification.

The evaluation results are summarized in Table 3 and Table 4. The first columns of these two tables show the approaches we evaluated. The first four rows are the approaches proposed in existing research works; the following three rows are the selected commercial tools; the last row is our approach: aToucan. The rest of the columns are arranged according to the evaluation criteria.

As shown in Column 2, Table 3, one approach [12] formalizes use cases as instances of a metamodel, similarly to aToucan. However, the metamodel instance has to be manually provided by the user directly, instead of being transformed automatically from another (more simple) representation (RUCM), thereby leading to substantial user effort. Two approaches ([13] and [9]) take unstructured requirements (plain text) as inputs to derive activity diagrams. Both are not fully automated. An approach is proposed in [16] to manually transform exceptional use cases into extended activity diagrams. Special stereotypes (e.g., <<failure>> and <<handler>>) are introduced to specify exceptional handling concepts. Visual Paradigm [22] and CaseComplete [6] can automatically transform flows of events of a use case into an activity diagram. Both tools require a similar and simple use case template to structure flows of events. Ravenflow [20] can automatically visualize a set of sequential and textual steps into an activity diagram and no structured format (e.g., template) is needed to document these steps. Ravenflow however suggests users follow a set of writing principles, some of which are very similar to the restriction rules of RUCM used in aToucan. Because Ravenflow does not rely on a use case template, it becomes very difficult to specify alternative flows in a use case and their interactions with the basic flow.

Table 3. Evaluation summary (part I)

Approach	Requirements	NLP	Automation	Traceability	Objective
[12]	Formalized UCs	No	Automated	No	Visualize use cases and facilitate test generation
[13]	Unstructured requirements	Yes	Automatable	No	Complement analysis models
[9]	Unstructured requirements	Yes	Semi-automated	No	Complement analysis models
[16]	Exceptional UCs	--	Manually	No	Formalize UCs to reduce ambiguities
[22]	Flows of events of UCs	No	Automated	Yes	Visualize flows of events of UCs
[20]	Restricted sequential steps	Yes	Automated	Yes	Visualize textual sequential steps
[6]	Flows of events of UCs	No	Automated	No	Visualize flows of events of UCs
aToucan	RUCM models	Yes	Automated	Yes	All of the above

Table 4. Evaluation summary (part II)

Approach	Activity Diagram						
	Type	Swimlane	Fork and join	Decision node	Global alternative flows	Include or extend	Data flow
[12]	Standard	Yes	No	Yes	No	No	No
[13]	Extended	No	No	Yes	No	--	No
[9]	Standard	No	Yes	No	No	--	No
[16]	Extended	--	--	--	--	--	--
[22]	Standard	No	No	Yes	No	No	No
[20]	Standard	Yes	No	Yes	No	--	Yes
[6]	Non-standard	No	No	No	No	No	No
aToucan	Standard	Yes	Yes	Yes	Yes	Yes	Yes

As shown in Column 3, Table 3, except for one manual approach, three existing approaches rely on NLP techniques. The approach proposed in [12] does not apply any NLP techniques because it requires formalized use cases as its inputs. Visual Paradigm [22] does not rely on any NLP technique; therefore it cannot automatically generate swimlanes, forks and joins. Four existing approaches are automated (Column 4) and only two commercial tools have traceability capability (Column 5).

The objectives of the existing approaches are different, as shown in Column 6, Table 3. The approach proposed in [12] aims to visualize use cases and therefore automated test generation can be facilitated. Visualizing use cases or their scenarios for the purpose of better understanding and analyzing them is a common practice [2, 10] and the idea of activity diagram-based test generation is also promoted in [7, 17]. Both the approaches proposed in [13] and [9] can generate analysis models including class and activity diagrams. Generated activity diagrams, as part of the generated analysis models, model dynamic behavior of a system. The approach proposed in [16] however simply uses activity diagrams as a means to formalize textual use cases. All three commercial tools visualize either flows of events of use cases (i.e., [6, 22]) or sequential textual steps (i.e., [20]) in activity diagrams for the purpose of helping users to construct and understand requirements. Our approach however applies to any of these objectives.

The approaches proposed in [13, 16] cannot generate standard UML activity diagrams (Column 2, Table 4). Mustafiz et al. [16] propose an approach to manually transform exceptional use cases (with elements that allow the modeling of system behavior in exceptional situations) into activity diagrams extended by specific stereotypes. Ilieva and Ormandjieva [13] propose an automatable approach to transform requirements into extended activity diagrams—activity diagrams integrated with the concepts of actors, business rules, and messages. As shown in Columns 3-6, except for the manual approach, swimlanes are only supported by two approaches: one of them [12] requires formalized use cases as input and the other [20] relies on NLP techniques to automatically identify swimlanes (similarly to aToucan); only one approach [9] supports forks and joins but it is semi-automated; decision nodes are supported by most of the non-manual approaches; Global alternative flows are not supported by any of the existing approaches. The approaches that are not manual and take use cases as inputs, do not support include and extend relationships of use cases. Ravenflow is the only existing approach that can generate data flow information (similarly to aToucan), and we have discussed differences in Section 5.2.

To compare with these existing approaches, our approach can automatically transform each use case of a UCMod into two types of standard UML 2.0 activity diagrams while fully supporting traceability. Additionally, as part of the functionality of aToucan, automatically generated activity diagrams are naturally consistent with other UML analysis model diagrams such as sequence diagrams and horizontal traceability (across different diagrams) can then be supported. Swimlanes, decision nodes, forks and joins, include and extend relationships, and data flow information are all supported by our approach. Besides, thanks to RUCM, our approach can also transform global alternative flows.

7 Conclusion

Providing automated support to derive UML analysis models, including class, sequence and activity diagrams from use case requirements is an important step of model-driven development. Even if such models end up being incomplete and an initial step towards analyzable models, the potential benefits are substantial. However this step has not received enough attention in large part because requirements (e.g., Use Case Specifications—UCSs) are essentially textual documents and tend to be unstructured. Therefore their automated analysis is difficult to achieve.

In this paper, we propose an approach, supported by the aToucan tool [25], to automatically generate activity diagrams from a Use Case Model (UCM) documented using a novel approach (Restricted UCM or RUCM) and specifically designed to facilitate this automated transition. In our previous work, RUCM has also been shown to facilitate the understanding of system requirements and therefore its advantages do not come at the expense of system comprehension. Additionally, traceability links can be generated between requirements and activity diagrams while transformations are performed. This is important since traceability links allow engineers to understand the connections between artifacts and is also mandated by numerous standards (e.g., IEEE Std. 830-1998 [1]) to support, for example, safety verification [18].

Automatically generated activity diagrams could be used, for example, to visualize use cases in a graphical form, to analyze them to support the behavioral modeling of the system, or to facilitate test case generation based on techniques using activity diagrams in input. Though such activity diagrams do not add information to the use case models, they are more amenable to various forms of analysis and can be seen as a starting point for developing more complete, detailed activity diagrams. In other words, RUCM is used to document system requirements whereas activity diagrams are developed to facilitate various types of automated analyses.

Five case studies have been performed using the aToucan tool. As expected, results show that our approach can generate higher quality activity diagrams than alternative approaches (including three commercial tools) based on a number of evaluation criteria. These criteria relate to automation, traceability, the completeness of activity diagrams, and the ease of writing requirements.

Acknowledgement

The work of Lionel Briand and Tao Yue was supported by a grant from Det Norske Veritas, Norway, in the context of the ModelME! project.

References

1. IEEE Std. 830-1998, IEEE Standard for Software Requirement Specification (1998)
2. Berenbach, B., Inc, S.C.R., Princeton, N.J.: The evaluation of large, complex UML analysis and design models. ICSE (2004)
3. Bittner, K., Spence, I.: Use Case Modeling. Addison-Wesley, Boston (2002)
4. Brown, E.K., Miller, J.E.: Syntax: a linguistic introduction to sentence structure. Routledge (1992)

5. Bruegge, B., Dutoit, A.H.: Object-Oriented Software Engineering Using UML, Patterns, and Java. Prentice-Hall, Englewood Cliffs (2009)
6. CaseComplete: http://www.casecomplete.com/
7. Chen, T.Y., Tang, S.F., Poon, P.L., Tse, T.H.: Identification of categories and choices in activity diagrams. In: QSIC 2005, Citeseer, pp. 55-63 (2005)
8. Eclipse Foundation: Eclipse Modeling Framework
9. Fliedl, G., Kop, C., Mayr, H.C., Salbrechter, A., Vöhringer, J., Weber, G., Winkler, C.: Deriving static and dynamic concepts from software requirements using sophisticated tagging. Data Knowl. Eng. 61, 433–448 (2007)
10. Fowler, M.: UML distilled: a brief guide to the standard object modeling language. Addison-Wesley, Reading (2003)
11. Gomaa, H.: Designing Concurrent, Distributed, and Real-Time Applications with UML. Addison-Wesley, Reading (2000)
12. Gutiérrez, J.J., Clémentine, N., Escalona, M.J., Mejías, M., Ramos, I.M.: Visualization of Use Cases through Automatically Generated Activity Diagrams. In: Czarnecki, K., Ober, I., Bruel, J.-M., Uhl, A., Völter, M. (eds.) MODELS 2008. LNCS, vol. 5301, pp. 83–96. Springer, Heidelberg (2008)
13. Ilieva, M.G., Ormandjieva, O.: Models Derived from Automatically Analyzed Textual User Requirements. Soft. Eng. Research, Management and Applications (2006)
14. Kermeta: Kermeta metaprogramming environment. Triskell team
15. Kruchten, P.: The Rational Unified Process: An Introduction. Addison-Wesley, Reading (2003)
16. Mustafiz, S., Kienzle, J., Vangheluwe, H.: Model transformation of dependability-focused requirements models. In: ICSE Workshop on Modeling in Software Engineering (2009)
17. Nebut, C., Fleurey, F., Le Traon, Y., Jezequel, J.M.: Automatic test generation: A use case driven approach. IEEE TSE 32, 140–155 (2006)
18. Olsen, G.K., Oldevik, J.: Scenarios of traceability in model to text transformations. ECMDA-FA. Haifa, Israel (2007)
19. OMG: UML 2.2 Superstructure Specification
20. RAVENFLOW: http://www.ravenflow.com/
21. The Stanford Natural Language Processing Group. The Stanford Parser version 1.6
22. Visual Paradigm for UML: http://www.visual-paradigm.com/product/vpuml/
23. Waheed, T., Iqbal, M.Z.Z., Malik, Z.I.: Data Flow Analysis of UML Action Semantics for Executable Models. ECMDA-FA (2008)
24. Yue, T., Briand, L.C., Labiche, Y.: A Use Case Modeling Approach to Facilitate the Transition Towards Analysis Models: Concepts and Empirical Evaluation. In: Schürr, A., Selic, B. (eds.) MODELS 2009. LNCS, vol. 5795, pp. 484–498. Springer, Heidelberg (2009)
25. Yue, T., Briand, L.C., Labiche, Y.: Automatically Deriving a UML Analysis Model from a Use Case Model. Carleton University (2009)
26. Yue, T., Briand, L.C., Labiche, Y.: A Systematic Review of Transformation Methodologies between User Requirements and Analysis Models. Carleton University (2009)
27. Yue, T., Briand, L.C., Labiche, Y.: An Automated Approach to Transform Use Cases into Activity Diagrams. Carleton University, Technical report SCE-10-01 (2010)

Author Index

Acher, Mathieu 3
Albert, Patrick 173
Al-Hilank, Samir 116
Atkinson, Colin 1

Balderas-Contreras, Tomás 20
Bézivin, Jean 32
Bouchoucha, Arbi 156
Boukadoum, Mounir 156
Briand, Lionel C. 337
Brunelière, Hugo 32

Cabot, Jordi 32
Cahill, Vinny 277
Champeau, Joël 189
Charfi, Anis 48
Clarke, Siobhán 277
Clasen, Cauê 32
Clowes, Darren 62
Collet, Philippe 3
Colombo, Pietro 74
Combemale, Benoit 90
Corcoran, Diarmuid 2
Crégut, Xavier 90
Cumplido, René 20

Dawson, Ray 62
de Sosa, Josune 293
Didonet Del Fabro, Marcos 173
Drexler, Johannes 116
Drivalos, Nicholas 245

Ebert, Jürgen 321
Egyed, Alexander 217, 293
Eichberg, Michael 104
Ellner, Ralf 116
Engels, Gregor 201

Faudoux, Raphaël 90
Fernandes, Kiran J. 245
Fernández, Miguel A. 132, 261
France, Robert 3
Fukuoka, Naoaki 233

Garate, Jose Miguel 293
Gerth, Christian 201

Holmes, Chris 62

Johannes, Jendrik 132, 261
Johnson, Julian 62
Jouault, Frédéric 32
Jung, Martin 116

Kakade, Rupesh 144
Kawahara, Ryo 233
Kessentini, Marouane 156
Khendek, Ferhat 74
Kips, Detlef 116
Kleiner, Mathias 173
Kloppenburg, Sven 104
Kolovos, Dimitrios S. 245
Kolovos, Dimitris 62
Koudri, Ali 189
Krueger, Charles W. 293
Küster, Jochen Malte 201

Labiche, Yvan 337
Lahire, Philippe 3
Lavazza, Luigi 74
Leilde, Vincent 189
Le Lann, Jean-Christophe 189
Lopez-Herrejon, Roberto Erick 217, 293

Mendialdua, Xabier 293
Mezini, Mira 48, 104
Monperrus, Martin 104
Müller, Heiko 48
Murugesan, Mohan 144

Nair, Mohanan 144
Nakada, Takeo 233

Ono, Kouichi 233

Paige, Richard F. 62, 245
Pantel, Marc 90
Pavei, Jonatas 90
Perugu, Bhupal 144

Author Index

Philippsen, Michael   116
Polack, Fiona A.C.   245
Polowinski, Jan   261
Probets, Steve   62

Rodriguez-Gomez, Gustavo   20
Rosado, Albert   293
Rose, Louis M.   62, 245

Sahraoui, Houari   156
Sakamoto, Yoshifumi   233
Schmidt, Matthias   261
Silva Parreiras, Fernando   321

Staab, Steffen   321
Sterritt, Ashley   277

Toyota, Manabu   233
Trujillo, Salvador   293

Vallecillo, Antonio   305

Walter, Tobias   321
Williams, James R.   245

Yue, Tao   337

GPSR Compliance

The European Union's (EU) General Product Safety Regulation (GPSR) is a set of rules that requires consumer products to be safe and our obligations to ensure this.

If you have any concerns about our products, you can contact us on ProductSafety@springernature.com

In case Publisher is established outside the EU, the EU authorized representative is:

Springer Nature Customer Service Center GmbH
Europaplatz 3
69115 Heidelberg, Germany

Batch number: 09478804

Printed by Printforce, the Netherlands